JAVA FOR COBOL PROGRAMMERS

JAVA FOR COBOL PROGRAMMERS

John C. Byrne

Charles River Media, Inc.
Rockland, Massachusetts

Publisher: David F. Pallai
Production: PageMasters & Company
Cover Design: The Printed Image
Printer: InterCity Press, Rockland, MA.

CHARLES RIVER MEDIA, INC.
P.O. Box 417
403 VFW Drive
Rockland, Massachusetts 02370
781-871-4184
781-871-4376 (FAX)
chrivmedia@aol.com

This book is printed on acid-free paper.

John C. Byrne. *JAVA for COBOL Programmers*
ISBN: 1-886801-84-3

Printed in the United States of America
00 01 5 4 3 2 First Edition

DEDICATION

Many thanks to the friends, colleagues, and family members who supported (or at least put up with) my efforts as I completed this book. Special thanks to Mike Sapozhnikov, and his careful attention to so many details.

Table of Contents

INTRODUCTION iii

PART 1—INTRODUCING JAVA 1

CHAPTER 1—OBJECTS AND CLASSES 3

THE COBOL SUBROUTINE 3
CALLING A SUBROUTINE 4
TERMS TO REVIEW—SUBROUTINES 10
OBJECTS AND JAVA 11
TERMS TO REVIEW—OBJECTS 13
RUNTIME INTERPRETATION AND JAVA BYTE CODES 19

CHAPTER 2—INTRODUCING THE JAVA DEVELOPMENT ENVIRONMENT 19

RUNTIME INTERPRETATION AND JAVA BYTE CODES 19
APPLICATIONS VS. APPLETS VS. SERVELETS 22
GETTING STARTED WITH JAVA 2'S JDK 24
APPLETS WITH JDK 27
GETTING STARTED WITH J++ 30
APPLETS WITH J++ 34
REVIEWING OUR SAMPLES 38

CHAPTER 3—MESSAGES AND METHODS 43

MESSAGES IN JAVA 46
MULTIPLE MESSAGES 47
METHOD OVERLOADING IN COBOL 50
TERMS TO REVIEW 55
EXERCISES: CLASSES, OBJECTS, AND METHODS 55
REVIEWING OUR SAMPLES 75
HELLOWORLD—THE APPLICATION 80
HELLOWORLD—THE APPLET 82
ERRORMSG—THE CLASS 83

CHAPTER 4—CLASS MEMBERS 85

JAVA MESSAGES 89
CLASSES, OBJECTS, AND MEMBERS REVIEW 91
OBJECTS AND COBOL 92
USING OBJECTS IN JAVA 97
JAVA DATA MEMBERS 98
LOCAL VARIABLES 101
PRIMITIVE DATA TYPES 102
METHOD MEMBERS 104
CONSTRUCTORS 106
EXERCISES: CLASS MEMBERS 108
REVIEWING OUR SAMPLES 126

CHAPTER 5—INHERITANCE, INTERFACES, AND POLYMORPHISM 129

INHERITANCE AND OBJECT-ORIENTED DESIGN 129
INHERITANCE AND OBJECTS 131
INHERITING METHODS 131
REDEFINING A METHOD 133

EXTENDING A METHOD 134
WHY INHERITANCE? 136
INHERITANCE, DESIGN PATTERNS, AND COBOL 138
MORE COBOL DESIGN PATTERNS 140
INHERITANCE AND JAVA 149
SHARING VARIABLES AND METHODS 156
HIDING VARIABLES AND METHODS 156
THIS 157
INTERFACE INHERITANCE 158
USING INTERFACES 160
HIDING METHODS AND MEMBERS 161
THROWS AND NOT THROWS 161
POLYMORPHISM 162
EXERCISES 163
EXPERIMENT A BIT 191
REVIEWING OUR SAMPLES 192

PART II—JAVA'S SYNTAX 195

CHAPTER 6—JAVA SYNTAX 197

COBOL VS. JAVA SYNTAX 197
JAVA COMMENTS 200
JAVA OPERATORS 203
BINARY ARITHMETIC OPERATIONS 203
UNDERSTANDING REFERENCE VARIABLES WITH COBOL 209

CHAPTER 7—FLOW CONTROL 211

CODE BLOCK 211
IF 212
WHILE 216
DO .. WHILE 218
FOR 219
SWITCH 220
BREAK, CONTINUE 221
EXERCISES: JAVA'S SYNTAX 225
REVIEWING OUR EXERCISES 251

CHAPTER 8—STRINGS, STRINGBUFFERS, NUMBERS, AND BIGNUMBERS 253

STRINGS 253
COMPARING STRINGS 254
WORKING WITH STRINGS 256
NUMERIC WRAPPER CLASSES 259
STRING BUFFERS 262
BIGNUMBERS 264
EXERCISES: STRINGS, STRINGBUFFERS, NUMBERS, AND BIGNUMBERS 269
REVIEWING OUR EXERCISES 289

CHAPTER 9—ARRAYS, VECTORS, AND OTHER COLLECTIONS 291

ARRAYS 291
ARRAYS AS PARAMETERS 295
VECTORS 295
COLLECTIONS 299

EXERCISES: ARRAYS, VECTORS, AND OTHER COLLECTIONS 313
REVIEWING OUR EXERCISES 326

CHAPTER 10—EXCEPTIONS, THREADS, AND GARBAGE COLLECTORS 329

EXCEPTION CLASS HIERARCHY 331
CREATING EXCEPTIONS 332
USING EXCEPTIONS 334
EXCEPTION PROCESSING SUGGESTIONS 338
EXCEPTION PROCESSING SUMMARY 339
THREADS 339
INHERITING FROM THREAD 340
IMPLEMENTING RUNNABLE 341
SYNCHRONIZATION 342
BENEFITS AND CAUTIONS 344
GARBAGE COLLECTION 345

PART III—MORE JAVA 347

CHAPTER 11—MANAGING YOUR JAVA SOFTWARE 349

CLASSES AND FILENAMES 349
CLASSPATH 351
CODEBASE 352
PACKAGES 352
INSIDE A PACKAGE 354
NAME COLLISIONS 355
PACKAGES AND FILENAMES 356
COMPRESSED PACKAGES 357

CHAPTER 12—INDUSTRY INITIATIVES 361

IDE'S 361
AWT, JFC/SWING, AND AFC/WFC 365
JDBC 367
ENTERPRISE JAVA BEANS 368
JAVA APPLICATION SERVERS 370
JAVA CLONES 371
IBM'S SAN FRANCISCO PROJECT 371
UNIFIED MODELING LANGUAGE 372
COBOL/JAVA INTEGRATION TOOLS 375

CHAPTER 13—INTRODUCTION TO XML 377

THE BASICS 377
XML VS. HTML 378
DTDS 380
DTD COMPONENTS 381
DOCUMENT TYPE DECLARATION 384
A COMPLETE XML DOCUMENT 385
AUTHORING XML DOCUMENTS 386
XML AND JAVA 386
XML AND HTML 386
WHERE TO USE XML 387
EDI 388
XML AND OAG 389
ONLINE XML 397
OTHER OPPORTUNITIES 398

APPENDIX A—ABOUT THE CD 401

APPENDIX B—JAVA INFORMATION AVAILABLE ELSEWHERE 403

JAVA RESOURCES 403
JAVA MAGAZINES 404
JAVA TOOLS 404
COBOL INFORMATION 404
MISCELLANEOUS REVIEWS 405
ACTIVE SERVER PAGES (ASP) 407

APPENDIX C—BUZZWORDS 407

Introduction

When it comes to ideas that demand the attention of those in the MIS industry, few examples compare to the excitement, notice, and hype generated by the idea called Java. The promise of this new, cross-platform, object-oriented language (with its simplified syntax) has garnered the support of developers, tools vendors, industry pendants, and, of course, the occasional consultant. It is virtually impossible to pick up a computer magazine that does not contain a Java article.

While all this excitement is going on, the more day-to-day responsibilities of an MIS shop continue. Applications need to be rolled out, existing systems supported (has anyone heard of a Y2K problem lately?), and an occasional enhancement delivered. Most of these systems are fundamental to the business but use other tools (insert the word *legacy* here). The people that support these systems are valuable repositories of business processes information and how computers are used (and sometimes how computers are *not* being used) to meet those business processes requirements.

Your average Cobol programmer is very busy and in demand right now, contrary to reports. This joke was popular a few years ago:

Question: What did the Cobol programmer say to the C++ programmer at McDonalds?

Answer: Would you like fries with that order?

If the pundits are correct this time, many systems, including core business systems, will be rewritten or replaced with new ones written in Java. Most could probably use a rewrite in any case, and the allure of using new technology, including a new language, will likely overwhelm more than one VP of MIS. Who better to build these new systems than the people who understand how the business works? Does it make sense to assign these projects to the person who is writing his or her first business system?

Some of Java's development efficiencies are available in any language, including Cobol. For example, coding styles that make use of subroutines implement important OO design principals. In fact, if a system were to aggressively define coding styles and subroutine (or copy member) usage models, then such a system could be described as an OO-based system. Any large, well-designed Cobol application development environment necessarily defines and supports most good OO design techniques in the form of subroutines, copy members, and coding standards.

However, in procedural language environments such as Cobol, the OO developer is not directly supported by the compiler or the runtime system. A case could be made that OO development environments *primarily make the compile and runtime tools aware of good, efficient coding techniques that have been in use for some time in traditional languages.*

A natural language is the tool people use to communicate ideas to each other. Languages have a syntax and a vocabulary of terms that provide structure and organization to ideas. If one person adheres to the rules and provides a linguistic shape and organization to his or her ideas, it is possible to communicate with another person.

Computer languages perform very much the same role. Computer languages define a vocabulary and syntax structure that is suitable for a computer to understand. Programmers learn these rules and convert ideas into code. A programmer's effectiveness is largely determined by how well he or she can communicate with the computer. (Of course, there is the testing, training, documentation, and support parts of the job, but programmers would be better off reading Dr. Spock rather than Dr. Chomsky to gain insights here!)

When people learn a new natural language, they often compare the new terms and syntax with what is already familiar to them. Language learning materials will often have glossaries or translations of terms. The new syntax is defined, in part, by comparing it to the student's "native" syntax. In fact, most people who learn a new language think in their native language, and mentally translate into the other. Only when they are very comfortable with the new language, will they finally think in the new language.

Instead of describing the Java object concepts and syntax in the abstract, or based on references using C or C++ programming languages, we will review various object concepts first in a Cobol context, and then the Java syntax that supports this concept. In Chapters 6 & 7, after you are familiar with the underlying concepts, we will review the complete Java syntax.

If you're a Cobol programmer and you've written a subroutine— a subroutine that was used by someone else—then you already understand the most important Java concepts—or the important concepts of any OO language, for that matter. Sure, the syntax is different and more powerful, but the principle that one person writes code so it can be used by others without having to understand all of its details is the core principal behind many of the OO design objectives.

You still need to understand the user's needs, and specs are still required. You may even be able to adjust end-user requirements based on technical issues, since it is expected that existing components will be reused. In theory, most development projects in an OO environment will consist of collecting and shaping end-user requirements and then "assembling" solutions, using as many exiting building blocks as possible.

Once you've decided to learn Java, the secret to success is to use the same process as when learning any new thing. Break down the information into manageable pieces, leverage what you already know, pick a good learning environment, and plunge ahead. You already know the hard part (i.e., how to translate business requirements into a computer language). Now you just need to learn a few new design principles, a new syntax, and some state-of-the-art integrated development environment. This book will help you get started.

PART I

Introducing Java

CHAPTER

1

Objects and Classes

Java's popularity is due to a number of factors. One of the biggest reasons is that it is a true object-oriented language. This sounds impressive, but what exactly *is* an object-oriented language? In fact, what is an *object*?

Simply put, an object is a collection of code organized to perform a function or to simply retain some information on behalf of another program. Objects are created and then used by other programs to perform these functions on behalf of the other programs.

Object-oriented languages, and the object-oriented design approach, contain many ideas already familiar to you. Chapters 1 through 5 will start by describing these concepts, based on the Cobol language. We will then compare Java's definition of objects, and the syntax that supports it, to these concepts. This should help you acquire a good understanding of the basic object-oriented concepts.

THE COBOL SUBROUTINE

We'll start with the Cobol subroutine. A Cobol subroutine is a source file that contains Cobol code and implements a logical function. It is organized so that other programs can prepare the appropriate information, call the subroutine, and perform the function. Subroutine parameters are described in the

LINKAGE SECTION of the subroutine. The subroutine is able to evaluate or modify passed parameters as part of its algorithm.

The calling program uses a subroutine when it defines and prepares the parameter items for the subroutine, and then calls it. The parameters are passed to the subroutine, using the CALL SUBROUTINE USING statement. After the subroutine completes its function, the calling program can examine the parameter items to see the information returned by the subroutine.

CALLING A SUBROUTINE

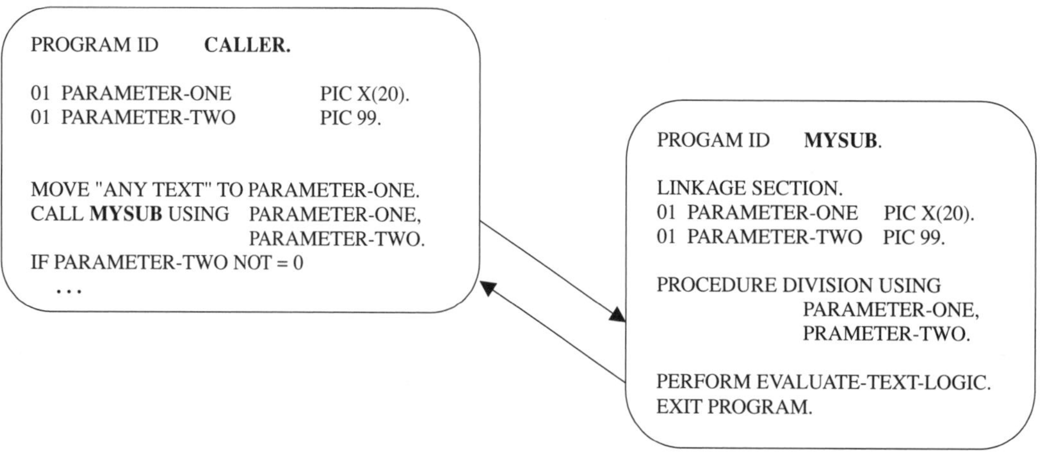

FIGURE 1.1. Calling a subroutine.

In Figure 1.1 the calling program (CALLER) prepares a text item as a parameter. It then calls the subroutine (MYSUB), passing this parameter, and another parameter.

The subroutine accepts both of these parameters. Its algorithm is roughly defined as follows: Evaluate the first parameter and set the second, based on some predefined criteria. The details of the evaluation function (that is, the heart of the subroutine's algorithm) are embedded in the subroutine.

The calling program can now evaluate the return parameter, in effect using the evaluation logic of the subroutine. The calling program only needs to know how to call the subroutine and how to evaluate the result of that call. It does not need to know any other details of the subroutine's internal logic.

Objects behave in much the same manner. An *object* is a collection of code that accepts parameters, implements a function, and returns information to the calling program. Objects, however, differ from a standard Cobol subroutine in a number of ways. One important difference is the fact that objects are created dynamically (at runtime) by a program. They are always associated with, or "tied to," the program that created them. Furthermore, a program can create many objects of the same type, or class. Thus:

An object can be understood as a subroutine called with a particular set of linkage items.

Suppose you've defined a subroutine as follows:

MYSUB COBOL

```
IDENTIFICATION DIVISION.
PROGRAM-ID. MYSUB.

***********************************************************************
* This routine accepts a text item as a parameter and evaluates the    *
* text. If the text is all spaces, MSG-SIZE will be set to 0. Else,    *
* MSG-SIZE will be set to 1.                                           *
* The text item will also be stored in the passed control structure in *
* MSG-TEXT.                                                            *
***********************************************************************

DATA DIVISION.
WORKING-STORAGE SECTION.
```

*   These are the subroutine parameter definitions.

```
LINKAGE SECTION.
01 MYSUB-CONTROL.
     03      MSG-TEXT      PIC X(20).
     03      MSG-SIZE      PIC 9(8).

01 TEXT-STRING                  PIC X(20).
```

```
*     This is the interface definition for the subroutine.

PROCEDURE DIVISION USING MYSUB-CONTROL, TEXT-STRING.

MYSUB-INITIAL SECTION.
MYSUB-INITIAL-S.

*     Perform the subroutine's function. Test the passed string for spaces
*     and set MSG-SIZE accordingly.

     IF TEXT-STRING = SPACES
          MOVE 0 TO MSG-SIZE
     ELSE
          MOVE 1 TO MSG-SIZE.
     MOVE TEXT-STRING TO MSG-TEXT.
EXIT-PROGRAM.
     EXIT PROGRAM.
```

Now, suppose you've written a calling program that uses this subroutine:

CALLER COBOL

```
IDENTIFICATION DIVISION.
PROGRAM-ID. CALLER.
DATA DIVISION.
WORKING-STORAGE SECTION.

*     Create the parameter definitions.

01 MYSUB-CONTROL.
     03      MSG-TEXT      PIC X(20).
     03      MSG-SIZE      PIC 9(8).
01 TEXT-STRING                  PIC X(20).

PROCEDURE DIVISION.

START-PROGRAM SECTION.
START-PROGRAM-S.

*     Prepare the parameters.

     MOVE "ANYTEXT" TO TEXT-STRING.
```

```
*       Call the subroutine.

        CALL "MYSUB" USING MYSUB-CONTROL, TEXT-STRING.

*       Evaluate the result.

        IF MSG-SIZE OF MYSUB-CONTROL = 0
           DISPLAY "MSG SIZE equals 0"
        ELSE
           DISPLAY "MSG SIZE equals," MSG-SIZE.

 EXIT-PROGRAM.
        EXIT PROGRAM.
        STOP RUN.
```

Let's examine these two programs from an object-oriented perspective, using the terminology of the object-oriented design methodology.

You can consider the subroutine MYSUB a *class*. That is, every time MYSUB is called—even if it is called from different programs—it will behave the same way. Any features, or logic, that MYSUB has will be available to all calling programs. At the same time, some parts of MYSUB are not available to the outside world. For example, any variables in MYSUB's WORKING STORAGE are *private* to MYSUB. And the details of MYSUB's logic are not known to any calling programs; only its *interface* (or LINKAGE SECTION) is published.

You can consider any *instance* of the parameter item MYSUB-CONTROL in a calling program as an *object* after MYSUB has been called. That is, after MYSUB has performed its logic (at the request of a calling program), the result of that logic is available in MYSUB-CONTROL.

A calling program can examine or modify the contents of items in MYSUB-CONTROL (MSG-TEXT or MSG-SIZE) and perform some logic based on those contents. These items are called *class data members* in OO terminology.

Another program can call MYSUB, with its own MYSUB-CONTROL (parameter), and evaluate the result. In this case, CALLER #1's copy of MYSUB-CONTROL will, of course, not be affected by CALLER #2. Each instance of a MYSUB-CONTROL area will now contain unique information. In this case, the unique MYSUB-CONTROL areas are *objects*. In fact, a single calling program can manage two separate MYSUB-CONTROL(s) as long as they have unique names:

CALLER COBOL

```
IDENTIFICATION DIVISION.
PROGRAM-ID. CALLER.
DATA DIVISION.
WORKING-STORAGE SECTION.
```

*   Create one set of parameter definitions.

```
01 MYSUB1-CONTROL.
     03     MSG-TEXT      PIC X(20).
     03     MSG-SIZE      PIC 9(8).
```

*   Create a second set of parameter definitions.

```
01 MYSUB2-CONTROL.
     03     MSG-TEXT      PIC X(20).
     03     MSG-SIZE      PIC 9(8).

01 DISPLAY-MESSAGE        PIC X(20).
01 TEXT-STRING            PIC X(20).

PROCEDURE DIVISION.

PROGRAM-START SECTION.
PROGRAM-START-S.
```

*   Prepare the first set of parameters, and call MYSUB.

```
     MOVE "ANYTEXT" TO TEXT-STRING.
     CALL "MYSUB" USING MYSUB1-CONTROL, TEXT-STRING.
```

*   Prepare the second set and call MYSUB.

```
     MOVE SPACES TO TEXT-STRING.
     CALL "MYSUB" USING MYSUB2-CONTROL, TEXT-STRING.
```

*   Evaluate the data associated with the first set and then the second
*   set.

```
     IF MSG-SIZE OF MYSUB1-CONTROL > 0
          MOVE MSG-TEXT OF MYSUB1-CONTROL TO DISPLAY-MESSAGE
     ELSE IF MSG-SIZE OF MYSUB2-CONTROL > 0
          MOVE MSG-TEXT OF MYSUB2-CONTROL TO DISPLAY-MESSAGE.

     DISPLAY "DISPLAY-MESSAGE: ", DISPLAY-MESSAGE.
```

```
EXIT-PROGRAM.
    EXIT PROGRAM.
    STOP RUN.
```

You can consider each *instance* of MYSUB-CONTROL (after MYSUB has been called) as *class instances*, or *objects*. In our example, MYSUB1-CONTROL is one object, and MYSUB2-CONTROL is a second. It is up to the calling program (the consumer of MYSUB) to manage these objects (i.e., the two instances of MYSUBx-CONTROL) as part of the application logic.

For example, if one MYSUBx-CONTROL contains an error message from the database system, and the other MYSUBx-CONTROL contains an error message from the communications system it is up to the calling application to decide which one to display at the correct time.

```
*   Prepare the database message parameters, and call MYSUB.

    MOVE "Unable to connect to the DataBase." TO TEXT-STRING.
    CALL "MYSUB" USING MYSUB1-CONTROL, TEXT-STRING.

*   Prepare the communications message parameters, and call MYSUB.

    MOVE "Invalid connection request." TO TEXT-STRING.
    CALL "MYSUB" USING MYSUB2-CONTROL, TEXT-STRING.

*   Prepare the generic message parameters, and call MYSUB.

    MOVE "An unknown error has occurred." TO TEXT-STRING.
    CALL "MYSUB" USING MYSUB3-CONTROL, TEXT-STRING.

    . . .
```

Later on in this program:

```
*   An error has occurred. The type of error has been recorded in
*   DISPLAY-MSG-TYPE-SW.
*   Evaluate which type of error occurred, and display the correct error
*   message text item.

    IF DISPLAY-MSG-TYPE-SW = "D"
        MOVE MSG-TEXT OF MYSUB1-CONTROL TO DISPLAY-MESSAGE
    ELSE IF DISPLAY-MSG-TYPE-SW = "C"
        MOVE MSG-TEXT OF MYSUB2-CONTROL TO DISPLAY-MESSAGE
    ELSE
        MOVE MSG-TEXT OF MYSUB3-CONTROL TO DISPLAY-MESSAGE.
    PERFORM DISPLAY-ERROR-MESSAGE.
```

The previous code fragments are examples of how a Cobol program might use three objects. Each of these objects is based on the class MYSUB.

TERMS TO REVIEW—SUBROUTINES

Here are some of the concepts we've discussed and how to understand them from a Cobol perspective.

Class: A subroutine is similar to a class. It can perform certain functions when called. These functions are defined by the subroutine developer. Many calling programs can use this subroutine in order to perform those functions.

Interface: The signature, or parameter specification, for a particular subroutine (or class, in OO terms). In Cobol, a subroutine's signature is the list of items in the subroutine's LINKAGE SECTION. Some items in an interface may be input parameters, and some may be result parameters, or both.

Object: An instance of a class, similar to an instance of our Cobol subroutine's CONTROL area, after the subroutine has been called. You can think of an object as the result of initializing the subroutine or calling it for the first time. This result is stored in the subroutine's CONTROL area.

Class Data Members: The data items that are associated with the subroutine (or class). Class data members include both the data elements in the subroutine's LINKAGE SECTION and the data elements in the subroutine's WORKING STORAGE.

Private: Any data elements (or members) that *belong* to the class but are not available outside the class. In Cobol, the items in a subroutine's WORKING STORAGE area are private. (This Cobol allegory is not precise; we will clarify it as we go.)

Public: Any data elements (or members) that *belong* to the class but are available outside the class. They are similar to items in a Cobol subroutine's LINKAGE SECTION.

The elementary items in MYSUB-CONTROL (e.g., MSG-TEXT and MSG-SIZE) can be considered *class data members* for the following reasons:

- **They are data elements that belong to the *class definition*.** This means that they are only useful as part of the parameter definition for MYSUB. The items in MYSUB-CONTROL will behave correctly (i.e., MSG-SIZE will be set to 0 or 1) only after MYSUB is called.
- **They are unique to each *instance* of the class.** More than one instance of MYSUB-CONTROL can be defined and passed as a parameter to MYSUB. The items in any instance of MYSUB-CONTROL will contain information based on the last time MYSUB was called with that instance of MYSUB-CONTROL.
- **They can be evaluated and/or set by both the calling program and the subroutine.** The data items in the MYSUB-CONTROL define the interface to MYSUB. This means that a calling program can communicate with MYSUB by using the data items defined in MYSUB-CONTROL.

OBJECTS AND JAVA

Let's examine what we've discussed using Java's syntax. This is the outline of a Java class definition:

ERRORMSG CLASS

```
public class ErrorMsg {
     public String msgText;
     public int  msgSize;
          ...
 // Some logic
          ...
}
```

The first line defines the class.

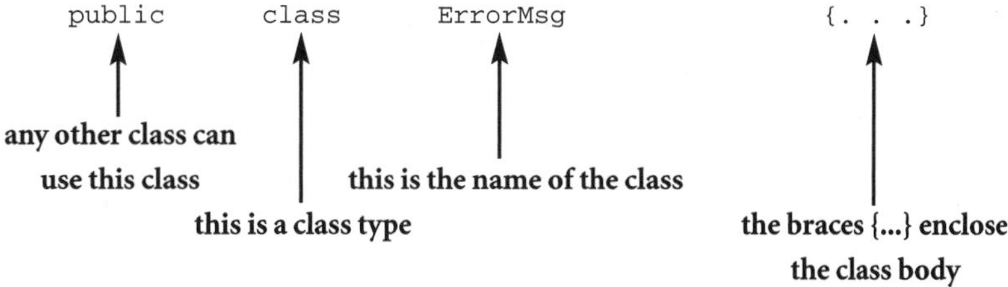

These next two lines declare the class instance data members. These are associated with each instance of this class and can be of any valid type. In many ways they are analogous to the data items in MYSUB-CONTROL.

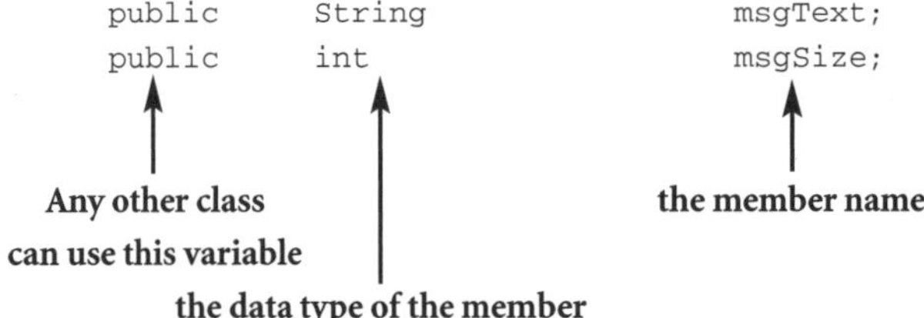

These two statements define the public data members for the class ErrorMsg.

The statements could be read this way: "The first data member is a **public** data member, it's type is **String**, and it's name is **msgText**." "The second data member is a **public** data member, it's type is **int**, and it's name is **msgSize**."

In order to use (or to call) this class, the consumer of this class (i.e., the caller) creates a new instance of the class with the *new* operation. This is very similar in concept to our Cobol example where we defined several unique MYSUBx-CONTROL areas in our calling Cobol program.

CALLER CLASS

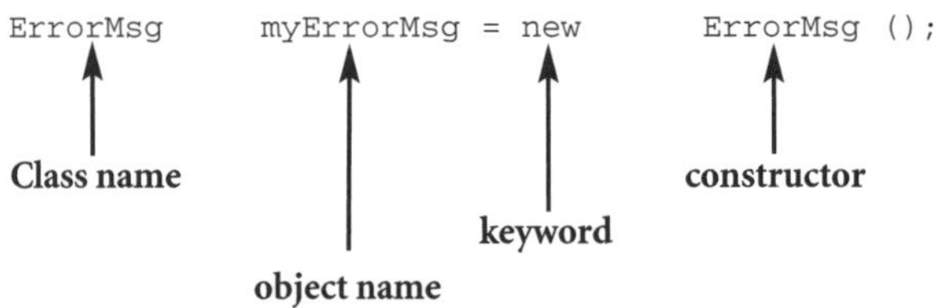

This statement could be read as follows:

"Create a **new** object of class **ErrorMsg**, and give it the name **myErrorMsg**."

This statement allocates memory for the new object, calls its *constructor* (more on this later), and returns a *reference variable* (a kind of pointer) to this new object. In our example, the pointer to our new class is stored in the object reference variable **myErrorMsg**. This reference variable is managed by the calling program in a manner very similar to the way MYSUBx-CONTROL areas are managed in our Cobol program. Note that the class name and the constructor name are the same, and that the constructor is called with an empty parameter list, indicating the default constructor.

Later, the program that contains this statement can use the reference variable name **myErrorMsg** to refer to any class data members that belong to this object. The "." operator is used to access members of an object. The member name is used to specify which member is being accessed.

For example, statement (1) will assign a String containing "Some Text" to the member variable **msgText.** The object that is modified is "pointed to" by the reference variable **myErrorMsg.**

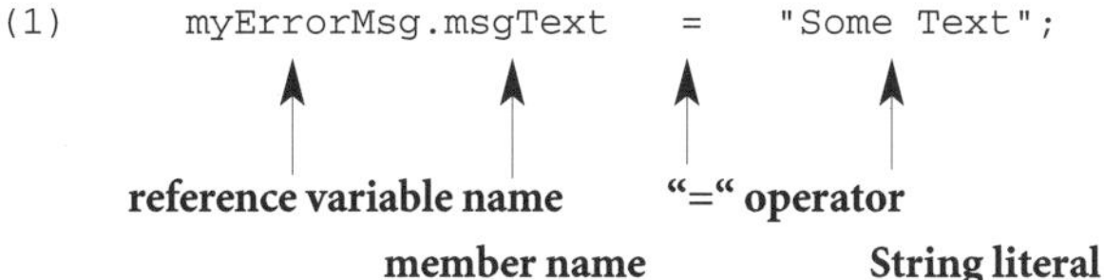

Statement 2 is another example of how **myErrorMsg.msgText** can be used:

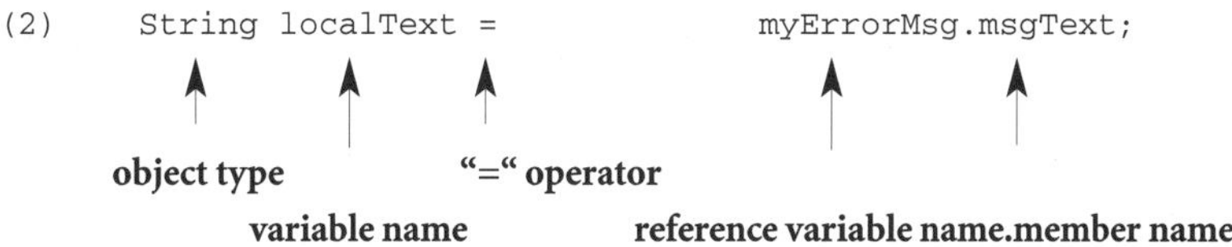

Statement (1) assigns the String "Some Text" to the data member msgText. The object who's data member is being set is, of course, **myErrorMsg.** This object is an object of type **ErrorMsg.** That is, it is an instance of the class **ErrorMsg.** Statement (2) assigns the current String in the data member **msgText** to a local String variable called **localText.**

TERMS TO REVIEW—OBJECTS

Here are some object-oriented concepts and how to understand them from a Java perspective.

Class: "A Java class is a collection of related data and the methods that operate on that data."[1] In concept, a Java class is similar to a Cobol subroutine; it contains some data elements, it can perform functions when requested, and the subroutine developer defines these functions. Many calling programs can use this class to perform available functions and can manage the data that belong to the class.

---

1. *Java in a Nutshell*, Flanagan (O'Reilly)

Object: An instance of a class. This is similar to an instance of a Cobol subroutine and a unique set of LINKAGE AREA items. You can think of an object as the result of initializing the class or calling it for the first time. However, unlike a Cobol subroutine, many instances of a class can be easily created and managed by the same calling program.

Reference Variable: A variable that contains a pointer to an object. After an object is created, the reference variable *points* to it. A reference variable is used by the calling program to access the data members and functions (that is, the *methods*) that belong to the object. This is similar to an instance of CALLER's MYSUBx-CONTROL area after the subroutine has been called.

New: The Java operation that creates an instance of the class, (i.e., the object). It returns a *reference variable* that points to the new object.

Constructor: A special type of method that is part of every class. This method is called when the class is first created.

Class Data Members: The data items that are associated with the class. They include all of the data elements that are defined in the class. These variables are created at the same time each instance of a class is created. They normally belong to each instance of a class and are not shared by unique class instances.

Private: Any data elements (or members) that *belong* to the class but are not available outside the class. Private data elements are identified with the keyword *private*. They are similar in this respect to items in a Cobol subroutine's WORKING STORAGE area, since a calling program cannot directly access these items.

Public: Any data elements (or members) that *belong* to the class but are available outside the class. Public data elements are identified with the access keyword *public*. Similar in this respect to items in a Cobol subroutine's LINKAGE SECTION.

Now let's explore another object-oriented design principal and how it relates to some Cobol concepts.

A calling program contains its objects.

Try to visualize for a moment what happens when a Cobol main program calls a subroutine. At runtime, and after the subroutine has been called, both the main program and the subroutine exist in memory. The executing program environment (the Cobol run unit) contains both the main program and the subroutine, as depicted in Figure 1.2

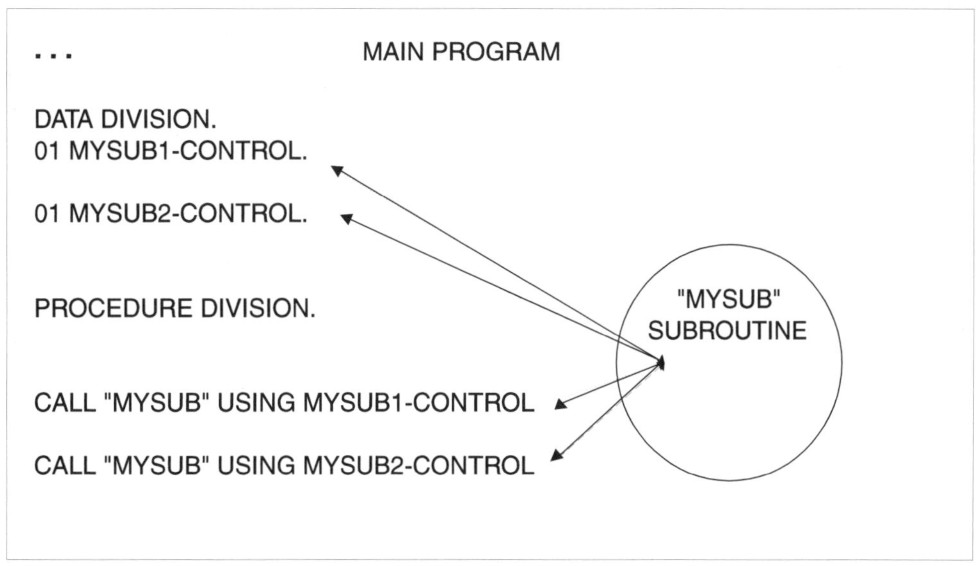

FIGURE 1.2. A Cobol run unit.

The items passed in the USING clause are the parameters to the subroutine. The subroutine can access any of the items that have been passed to it and can access items in its own working storage area. The MYSUBx-CONTROL areas contain the results of the most recent call to MYSUB.

Note that while the main program can access items in the passed parameters, it cannot access any items in the subroutine's WORKING STORAGE area. Further, Figure 1.2 shows two separate instances of MYSUBx-CONTROL data items but only one instance of the MYSUB subroutine. This means that all of the items in MYSUB's WORKING-STORAGE AREA will be shared, regardless of whether MYSUB1-CONTROL or MYSUB2-CONTROL is passed. Because of this limitation, our Cobol program does not behave exactly like an object.

In much the same way, a Java program contains any instances of the classes that it creates. The major difference between a Cobol subroutine and a Java class is that a Java program can contain many instances of its classes. These are called objects. (See Figure 1.3)

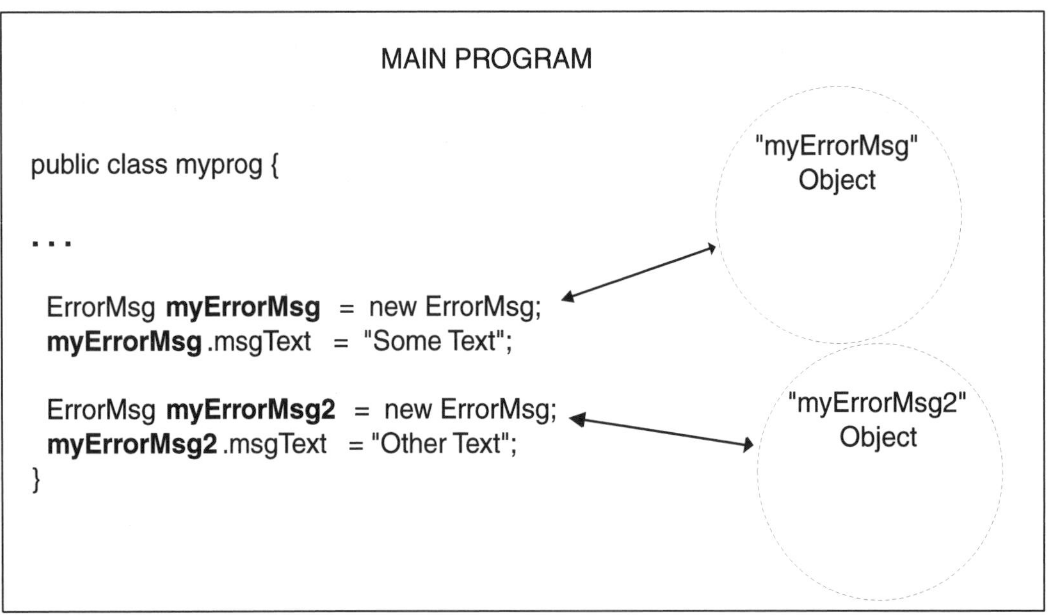

FIGURE 1.3. A Java run unit.

The *new* operation creates a completely new instance of the class in memory, including any private data members (WORKING STORAGE items) and then loads the class code into memory, if it has not been loaded already. All of the data members defined for that class are created. A reference variable is returned from the new operation, and this reference variable, or handle, points to the new class instance. These class instances are called objects.

Like items in a Cobol routine's LINKAGE SECTION, public data members defined by the class can be accessed by either the main (calling) program or by the object itself. Unlike the Cobol subroutine's WORKING STORAGE AREA, internal data members are not shared between instances of these two classes.

An object reference variable (for example, myErrorMsg) points to each unique instance of the class. The Java main program uses the reference variable to refer to the data members of a particular class instance in much the same way that

Cobol's OF operator works (for example, MSG-TEXT **OF** MYSUB1-CONTROL). Therefore, the statement

```
myErrorMsg.msgText      = "Some Text";
```

could be compared to the Cobol statement

```
MOVE "Some Text" TO MSG-TEXT OF MY-ERROR-MSG.
```

It's time to interrupt from our object-oriented presentation and write some code. Before we write our first program, however, let's take to a moment to examine how Java programs are compiled and executed.

CHAPTER

2

Introducing the Java Development Environment

RUNTIME INTERPRETATION AND JAVA BYTE CODES

Java's designers had a number of primary design objectives. As we have seen, object orientation is one of them. Another is the premise that a program can be compiled on any machine and the output of the compiler simply moved to another machine, where it will execute without changes. This concept is captured in the Java mantra "Write once, run anywhere."

In an Internet environment, the movement to the execution machine (an end user's PC, for example) is automatically performed by the browser without any special commands by the user. The net result is simplified administration of the applications and immediate access to any Java application for the end user.

To accomplish this, the Java compiler does not create *executable* code—meaning a program that runs natively on a given system. Instead, the Java compiler creates an *intermediate representation* of your program. This representation is somewhere between source code and native machine code. It is called *Java byte codes*. These byte codes are the content that is moved to a computer system at runtime to be executed on that system.

Since the byte codes are not in a format that is native to any system, they can't be executed directly on any system. Instead, a native program interprets the byte codes and performs the application functions expressed in the byte codes. This interpreter is called a *Java virtual machine*, since it creates a virtual system environment in which Java byte codes can execute.

This concept is not new. Interpreted languages such as Lisp and SmallTalk have worked this way for years. Some cross-platform Cobol compilers (notably from MicroFocus and AcuCorp) also provide this same type of "instantaneous portability" feature, using a byte code or intermediate version of compiled Cobol programs.

Figure 2.1 shows the compile and execution procedure for a simple Java application.

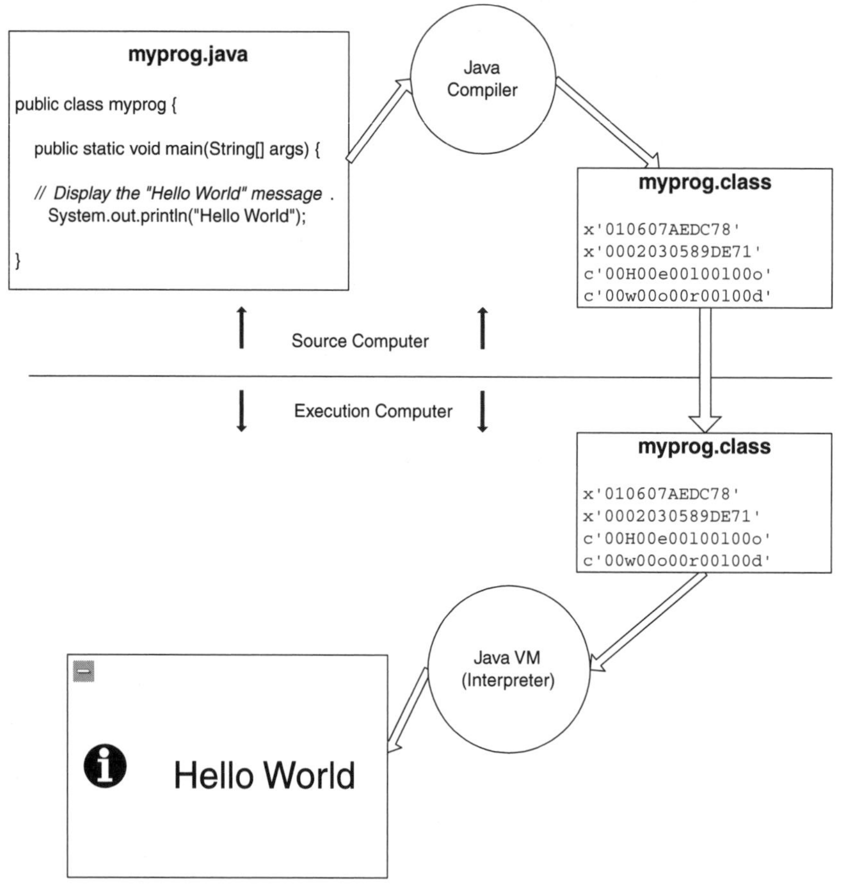

FIGURE 2.1. The Java Compile/Execution process.

In theory, the only prerequisite to running a Java program on a system is the requirement that a appropriate Java virtual machine (VM) be available on that system. As you might suspect, the reality is somewhat different.

Sun has attempted to define a standard definition for the Java VM, but as with any design document, certain details tend to crop up during the implementation phase. Naturally, as a vendor creates a Java VM, problems will be solved in the manner best suited to the vendor. As a result, minor differences in the various virtual machines can create subtle variations on how a Java program behaves.

To complicate matters, there is no *technical* reason why vendors can't extend the VM or provide a proprietary class library (a class library is a set of reusable programs) in order to deliver some features unique to their personal version of the Java language. Naturally, these extensions will not be available in other VMs, limiting the freedom of the end user to select different virtual machines or operating systems.

Finally, some operating system functions and some details of the way an application interacts with the operating system are not exactly the same across all operating systems. Java does a credible job of defining standards that shield most applications from these differences, but it does not cover *all* cases. As a result, some low-level application functions are not defined by Java, or are left to the individual VM implementation to deliver.

A good example of all three of these issues is the curious fact that Java doesn't define a reliable (or "pure Java") notion of a standard output display device. The System.out.println statement in Figure 2.1 is not technically 100% pure Java, even though it appears in almost every Java reference manual! It is left up to the VM's implementation of the System.out object to decide what to do with System.out.println.

To really complicate matters further, Java VMs are often delivered as part of a browser application (such as Netscape's Communicator or Microsoft's Internet Explorer). Java applications that are imbedded in an Internet document (called Java applets) execute as part of the browser interface. The browser actually controls some of the details of how the application looks (such as the default font to use).

The result of all these variables is the insider's rueful observation about the true nature of Java's cross-platform portability: "Write once, debug everywhere." The implication is that a software provider should test a product on several different combinations of operating systems/browsers/VMs, to make sure the application works correctly in all of the target execution environments. This has certainly been the case with many interactive Java applications.

Don't despair, however. For one, you probably won't use `System.out.println` in a real program. There are a number of class libraries available that define powerful mechanisms to build graphical user interfaces (GUIs). Sun provides their AWT and the new JFC/Swing class graphical libraries, which run on all platforms. Microsoft provides their WFC class libraries, which are available on Windows platforms. Any of these class libraries provide excellent mechanisms to build first-rate GUIs.

Another point to consider is that server-based Java applications are likely to be less susceptible to these variations, and most business logic will be server-based. The majority of the differences between Java runtime environments arise from to user interface issues. Since server applications don't have their own user interface, they are, by and large, unaffected by most of the runtime environment differences. Server applications will experience some variations in runtime environments, but these variations are fairly technical in nature (such as the mechanism to use for access to the native system), and normally they are easy to isolate.

APPLICATIONS VS. APPLETS VS. SERVELETS

Java programs run in one of three contexts: as an applet, as an application, or as a servelet.

As the name suggests, an *applet* is an application fragment. It is not a complete application but rather more an extension of another application. Most often, the application extended is a browser, either Netscape's Navigator or Microsoft's Internet Explorer. In fact, any application can be extended with Java applets. The only requirement is that the application to be extended must provide a Java runtime environment.

Conversely, a Java *application* is a complete application. It can run stand-alone or independent of any other application. A Java application still needs a runtime interpreter, but this interpreter is a stand-alone program whose only responsibility is to execute and support Java applications.

A stand-alone interpreter is often a native program, suitable for executing on the host platform. For example, Sun's stand-alone interpreter is named java.exe, and it is executed like any other application. Sun provides a version of the java.exe program for both Windows and the Solaris operating system. The only job of the stand-alone interpreter is to execute the Java byte codes and to perform the functions requested by the application.

Like an applet, a *servelet* is also an application fragment. Instead of extending a browser, a servelet extends some application environment or system on the server. Servelet-extensible databases are becoming quite popular, for example. Servelets do not directly create user interfaces, and they are often used to code business logic. Many Cobol programs will likely be translated into servelets.

Enough with the concepts. It's time to write some code. It's a good idea to mix reading about concepts with working on those concepts.

In order to write programs in Java, you will need a few tools. At a minimum, you will need a Java compiler and a Java virtual machine to interpret and execute your code. If you are lucky (and smart), you will use an integrated development environment (IDE) from a Java tool vendor. IDEs combine compilers, VMs, a nice editor, and some type of project management tool into an integrated system. Symantec, Microsoft, Sun, and Imprise (formerly Borland) all sell excellent Java development environments.

Often the tools take full advantage of a graphical operating system such as Windows. These products take most of the grunt work out of the development experience, and they allow you to focus more time on your programming problem and less on tedious chores like managing files.

A popular toolset is Sun's Java Development Kit (JDK), which is part of their Java 2 platform solution. The JDK includes a free Java compiler and runtime environment and is available from Sun at www.java.sun.com. It is also included on the CD. You can just download this to your PC and use it. Of course, it doesn't have a graphical editor, and is not a visual integrated development environment, but you can't beat the price.

Microsoft's Java development environment is Visual J++™. This is part of their Visual Studio development tool suite, and it shares many features with Visual C++™ and VB™. It is a very rich, graphical development tool, one well suited for both the beginner and the expert.

On the downside, Microsoft's tools are very Windows-centric; it is very difficult to tell if the Java code you've written in J++ will work on any other platform. In fact, there are certain things that you can do in J++ that will definitely prevent your code from working on another platform.

Learning how to use a new development environment can be a difficult step in transitioning from a Cobol developer to a Java developer. These initial exercises are geared toward helping you become familiar with a new environment more than reviewing the concepts already discussed. After you've mastered (or at least come to terms with) the development environment, we'll use these exercises to review the concepts presented. Therefore, we'll begin by concentrating on learning the development environment, instead of understanding the code samples. (The code samples will be explained and reviewed later.) To help you get started, step-by-step introductions to both the JDK for the Java™ 2 platform (formerly code-named JDK™ 1.2) and Visual J++™ are presented.

Note: Commands that you are expected to execute (either with a mouse or by typing the command) are identified with the arrowhead marker at the beginning of the command.

GETTING STARTED WITH JAVA 2'S JDK

Sun's product has good introductory documentation available for it. An excellent one is on Sun's Java Web site. These following steps will guide you through the process of creating your first Sun-flavored Java application and applet.

First, install the JDK development environment. You can download it from the CD included with this book or from Sun's Web site. Follow the instructions on the installation Web page to install the software properly.

You may need to add the directory that contains the JDK executables to your PATH environment variable. This variable controls how Windows finds programs to execute. In Windows 95 and 98, you can use the sysedit function (menu path Start → Run → Sysedit) to edit the autoexec.bat file. Assuming you have installed the JDK to the default directory (c:\jdk1.2), add a line to the end of the autoexec.bat file that reads: SET PATH=%PATH%; C:\JDK1.2\bin

Changing the autoexec.bat file requires that you reboot your PC.

On Windows NT, use the System icon on the control panel to modify the environment variable directly. Add the JDK path ('C:\JDK1.2\bin') to the end of this variable. After it has been properly installed on your PC, the JDK utilities must be used from a MS-DOS command window. You can start up a MS-DOS window by using this menu path, beginning with the Windows task bar: Start → Programs → MS-DOS Prompt.

In the command window, you can execute the Java compiler (javac.exe), the Java runtime (java.exe), and the applet viewer (appletviewer.exe). All of these programs take parameters, such as the name of the Java file to be compiled. You should also install the DosKey program (type doskey in the command window). This program remembers your DOS commands, which you can recall and edit using the cursor keys.

The source can be modified with any text editor, including, for example, Wordpad. Java source files are standard text files, including line ending sequences (CR, LF on PCs). Wordpad is very popular for this task, since you can save and compile the Java source without closing down Wordpad. Just make sure you save the Wordpad files as "text" files, rather than as "document" files. Freeware and shareware text editors are available at these Web sites: www.mctamata.com and www.freeware32.com

Now, its time to get started.

1. Make a directory to contain your Java files. From the DOS window, you can create a directory on the C: drive by typing

➢ cd C:\

➢ mkdir java4cobol

2. Change the current directory in your command window to the directory you just created:

➢ cd c:\java4cobol

3. Using a text file editor, enter this Java source.

```
public class HelloWorld {

     public static void main(String[] args) {
          System.out.println ("Hello World!");

     }
}
```

4. Save the source to a file named c:\Java4cobol\HelloWorld.java.
5. Compile your Java source with the JDK compiler (javac.exe) in the DOS command window:

➢ javac HelloWorld.java

6. Your HelloWorld Java program should compile successfully. If it doesn't, there are three possible problems:

- **Cannot find the javac program.** Check your PATH environment variable by using the "set" command in the DOS window. It should contain the directory where the program javac.exe is (normally c:\JDK1.2\bin).
- **Cannot find HelloWorld.java.** Check the spelling, and make sure you used the correct case. Are you in the directory where the source file was saved (C:\java4cobol)?

- **The compile reported some errors.** Check your source file. It should be exactly as presented here.
- Check the Sun Web site for additional suggestions.

7. Now run your program, using the Java runtime that comes with the JDK:

➢ java HelloWorld

If you've done everything correctly, then your MS-DOS window should look like Figure 2.2.

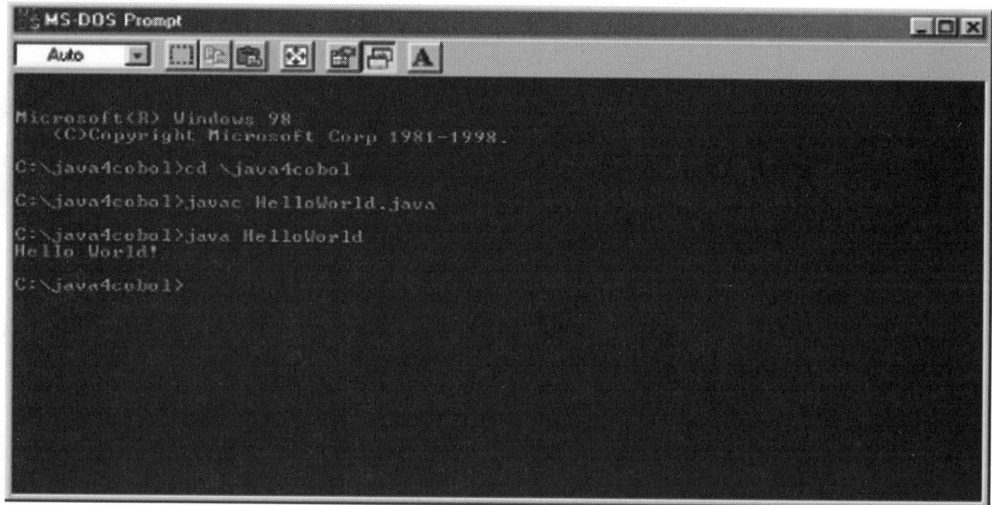

FIGURE 2.2. "Hello World!" the program.

Congratulations! You should be proud of your first JDK program. It is full of potential.

Experiment with the program a little bit in this environment. You can make the changes in the text editor you have chosen. Compile it by typing "javac HelloWorld.java" in the command window. After your program is compiled, you can execute it from the MS-DOS command window by typing "java HelloWorld."

- Change the message from “Hello World!” to “Watson come here!”
- What happens if you add a second System.out.println statement to your program?

APPLETS WITH JDK

Now we’ll write our first Java applet in this environment and run it in the Applet viewer.

1. Using either the Windows Explorer or a DOS command, create a new directory (or folder, in Explorer terminology) called “applet” in the java4cobol directory. Your applet files will be stored in this directory.
2. Using a text editor, create a Java source file named HelloWorld.java in this directory. The source file should contain these statements:

```
import java.applet.Applet;
import java.awt.Graphics;
public class HelloWorld extends Applet {
     public void paint(Graphics g)
     {
          g.drawString("Hello Applet World!", 5, 25);
     }

}
```

3. In the DOS command window, change the current directory to your applet directory:

➢ cd c:\java4cobol\applet

4. Compile your applet, using the javac compiler:

➢ javac HelloWorld.java

Again, your applet should compile successfully at this point. If it doesn’t, review the previous suggestions.

Applets are meant to be executed in a hosting environment, often a web browser. Web browsers display information in HTML documents and are instructed to execute applets by special commands in the HTML document. The HTML command to execute an applet is the <applet> tag. This tag instructs the browser to run the applet specified in the applet tag.

You do not need to be an HTML expert for this step, but you will need to create a simple HTML document.

5. Using a text editor, create an HTML document named HelloWorld.html in your applet directory. The file should contain these statements:

```
<html>
<head>
<title>HelloWorld</title>
</head>
<body>
<hr>
<applet
code=HelloWorld
width=200
height=200>

</applet>
<hr>
</body>
</html>
```

Remember to save this file under the name HelloWorld.html, and to save it as a text file, not as a document.

6. In the DOS command window, execute the appletviewer program to display your applet. Make sure you are in the applet directory.

➢ appletviewer HelloWorld.html

7. If you've done everything correctly, then your MS-DOS window and your applet viewer window should look like Figure 2.3

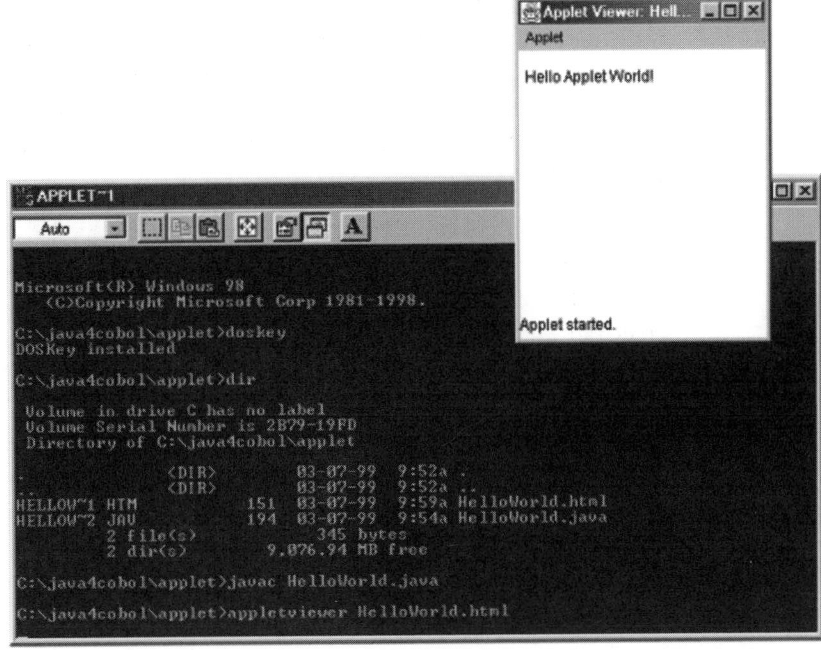

FIGURE 2.3. "Hello World!" in the applet viewer.

Experiment with this applet as well. You can make the changes in the text editor and recompile and execute the program in the DOS command window. You will need to exit the applet viewer every time you run your program by clicking the X widget at the top right of the applet viewer window. Or, you can use the reload function in the applet menu.

- Change the message from "Hello World!" to "Watson come here!"
- What happens if you add a second "g.drawString" statement to your program?
- Why do you think only one message showed up? (Hint: drawString is a graphically oriented function, whereas println is a line-oriented function.)
- What do you think the numbers 5, 25 control on the page?
- What happens if you change the 5 to a 6?
- What happens if you change the 25 to a 35?

GETTING STARTED WITH J++

Microsoft's product comes with a good introductory manual, but here are some basic introductory steps anyway.

1. Start the J++ design environment. After it has been properly installed on your PC, it is likely available by following this menu path, beginning with the Windows task bar:

➢ Start → Programs → Microsoft Visual J++

2. Create a new project, using this menu path in the J++ tool:

➢ File → New

- Select the Project dialog tab, and choose the 'Java Project' type from the list of available projects.
- Type in the name of your project (java4cobol).
- Leave the other defaults as is, and click OK

3. Add a new class to your project using this menu path: Insert → New Class.

- Type in the name of this class "HelloWorld" (case sensitive).
- No need to specify a super class in the Extend text field.
- Choose the Public modifier.
- Click OK.

4. Type in this Java code inside the HelloWorld skeleton that J++ has created:

```
public static void main(String[] args) {
        System.out.println ("Hello World!");

    }
```

At this time, your class definition source code should look like this:

```
//
//
// HelloWorld
//
//
public class HelloWorld
{

    public static void main(String[] args) {
        System.out.println ("Hello World!");

    }
}
```

We'll discuss each line of code and what it means in a minute, but right now we're focused on mastering the development environment.

5. Compile the program, using this menu path:

➢ Build → Build java4cobol

6. If everything is okay so far, then you should get a message in your output window (at the bottom of the screen) that says something like "java4cobol - 0 error(s), 0 warning(s)." If you have gotten any warnings or errors, your development environment is not set up properly, or perhaps you've not typed the code in properly. The only useful suggestions are to get some help or to reinstall it if possible. One tip: It may be necessary to point your class path directory list to the location of your classes.zip file.

7. Now it is time to run the program. Use this menu path:

➢ Build → Execute HelloWorld

- An information dialog should appear. It is asking you how to run your project. Enter the class file name "HelloWorld" (case sensitive).
- There are two radio button choices: "Run project under browser" and "Run project under stand-alone interpreter." Click the stand-alone choice for now; we'll explain the difference later.

8. An MS-DOS-type window should briefly appear. If you look quickly, and if your PC is slow, you will see the message "Hello World!" in the DOS window. It may not seem like much, but you've just written your first Java program!
9. You can stop the window by using the debugger:

- Position the cursor to the brace (}) that terminates the main class. This is the second to last line in your source file.
- Use this menu path to run the program in debug mode until this line is reached:

➢ Build → Start Debug → Run to Cursor

- An MS-DOS window should appear with your message. You can toggle to it by pressing ALT-TAB or by using the task bar at the bottom of your screen.

The Java runtime used by J++ in this case (jview.exe) is the stand-alone Java runtime that Microsoft provides. This runtime is not normally used with production Java applications. More often, the Java runtime is built into the browser, or a back-end application server contains the runtime used in production Java environments. jview.exe is a simple stand-alone interpreter. Its primary use is in debugging Java applications. This runtime interpreter is essentially a non-Windows program. It is actually better to execute this runtime from a DOS command window. This may sound shocking in this day and age, but it is true of the Sun runtime as well, so it's not a bad idea to get used to it.

To run the program with the stand-alone interpreter, open a DOS command window and run the program jview, with your class as its parameter:

10. Starting from the Windows task bar, follow this menu path:

➢ Start → Programs → MS-DOS Prompt.

11. Go to the directory where your class file (the output of the compile step above) was created. It is likely the same directory as your source file.

➢ Cd myjavadirectory

(By default it will be C:\Program Files\DevStudio\MyProjects\java4cobol, or you can use its eight character alias name of C:\Progra~1\DevStu~1MyProj~1\java4C~1.)

12. Execute the Java runtime and have it interpret your class:

➢ jview HelloWorld

If everything went okay, you should see a window that appears similar to the one in Figure 2.4.

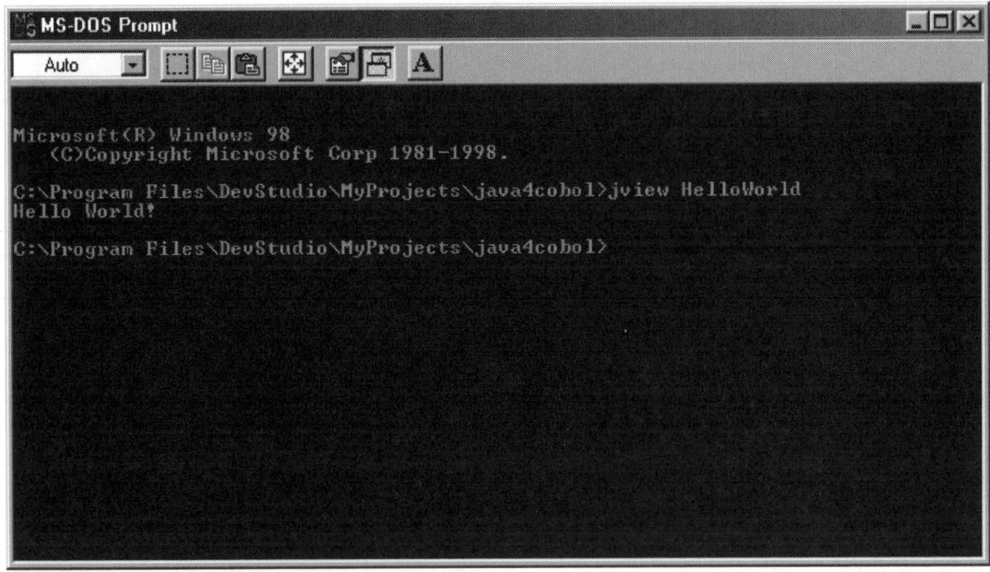

FIGURE 2.4. "Hello World!" the program.

Experiment with the program a little bit. You can make the changes in the development environment and recompile the program using the Build → Build java4cobol menu path. After it is compiled, you can execute the changed program either within the development environment (menu path Build → Execute HelloWorld) or from the MS-DOS command window (jview HelloWorld).

- Change the message from "Hello World!" to "Watson come here!"
- What happens if you add a second "System.out.println" statement to your program?

APPLETS WITH J++

Now, we'll write our first Java applet, and run it in the browser.

1. Create a new project, using this menu path in the J++ tool:

➢ File → New

- Select the Project dialog tab, and choose the Java Project type from the list.
- Type in the name of your applet project (HelloWorldapp).
- Leave the other defaults as is, and click OK.

2. Add a new class to your project, using this menu path: Insert → New Class.

- Type in the name of this class: HelloWorld (case sensitive).
- Type "Applet" in the text field labeled Extend.
- Choose the Public modifier.
- Click OK.

Your source text should contain the skeleton code generated by J++ and look something like this:

```
import java.applet.Applet;

//
//
// HelloWorld
//
//
public class HelloWorld extends Applet
{


}
```

3. Add this line after the first line:

```
import java.awt.Graphics;
```

4. Add these lines in the body of the class:

```
    public void paint(Graphics g)
    {
        g.drawString("Hello Applet World!", 5, 25);
    }
```

Your source code should now look like this:

```
import java.applet.Applet;
import java.awt.Graphics;
//
//
// HelloWorld
//
//
public class HelloWorld extends Applet
{

    public void paint(Graphics g)
    {
        g.drawString("Hello Applet World!", 5, 25);
    }

}
```

5. Compile the program using this menu path:

➢ Build → Build HelloWorldapp

6. If everything is okay so far, then you should get a message in your output window (at the bottom of the screen) that says something like "HelloWorldapp - 0 error(s), 0 warning(s)." If you have gotten any warnings or errors, your development environment is not set up properly, or perhaps you've typed something incorrectly. The only useful suggestions are to review your work, get some help or to reinstall it if possible. It may be necessary to point your class path directories to the location of your classes.zip file.

7. Now it is time to run the program. Use this menu path:

➢ Build → Execute.

- An information dialog should appear. It is asking you how to run your project. Enter the class file name HelloWorld (case sensitive).
- There are two radio button choices "Run project under browser" and "Run project under stand-alone interpreter." Click the Browser choice.
- Make sure the Browser text field points to a working Java-enabled browser. The default for the Microsoft browser is C:\ProgramFiles\InternetExplorer\Explore.exe.
- Click OK.

8. A Browser Window should appear, and your text "Hello Applet World!" should be on a text area in the window. Congratulations on writing your first applet! Your window should look something like Figure 2.5.

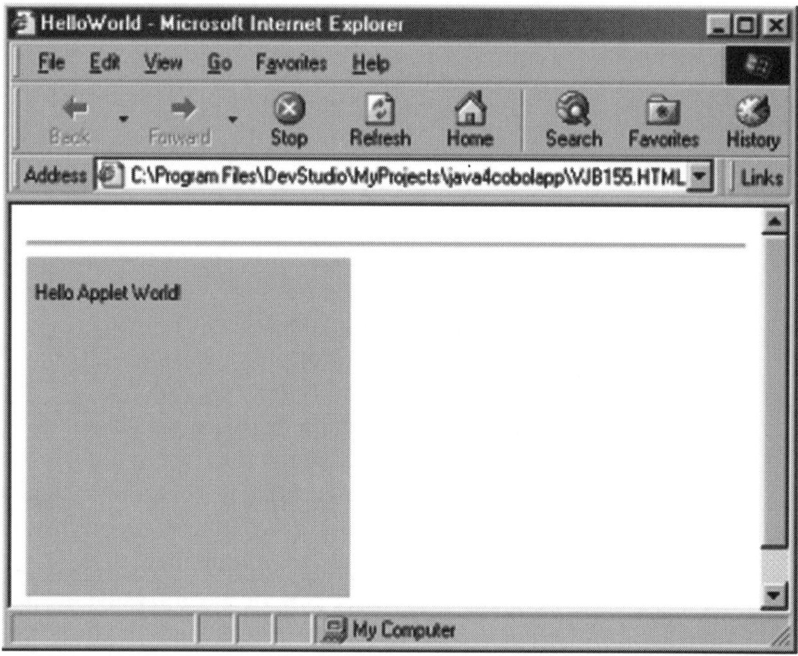

FIGURE 2.5. "Hello World!" the applet.

Experiment with this applet as well. You can make the changes in the development environment and recompile the program using the Build → Build HelloWorldapp menu path. After it is compiled, you can execute the changed program either within the development environment (menu path Build → Execute HelloWorld), or from the MS-DOS command window ("jview /a HelloWorld"). Notice how the Execute menu choice has changed; it now knows the name of the class to run. Refer to Figure 2.5 to make sure you've done the right thing.

- Change the message from "Hello World!" to "Watson come here!"
- What happens if you add a second g.drawString statement to your program?
- Why do you think only one message showed up? (Hint: drawString is a graphically oriented function, whereas println is a line-oriented function.)
- What do you think the numbers 5, 25 control on the page?
- What happens if you change the 5 to a 6?
- What happens if you change the 25 to a 35?

You can run this applet from the MS-DOS command window as well. Start a command window, and change directory to the directory that contains your class. It is likely the same directory as your source file.

➢ cd myjavadirectory

(By default it will be C:\Program Files\DevStudio\MyProjects\HelloWorldapp, or, you can use its eight character alias name of C:\Progra~1\DecStu~1\MyProj~1\Hellow~1.)

- Execute the stand-alone Java runtime, and have it interpret your class. This time, you will need to use the /a option for jview. This option creates an applet viewer to host your applet.

➢ jview /a HelloWorld

If everything went okay, you should see a window named "Microsoft Applet Viewer" that appears similar to the one in Figure 2.6

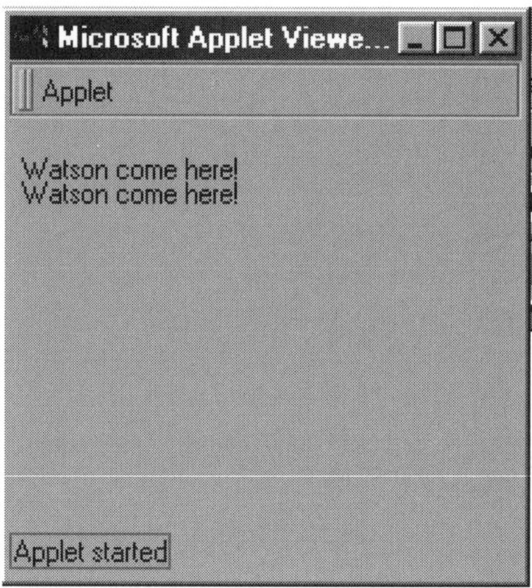

FIGURE 2.6. "Watson come here!" in the applet viewer.

TECHNICAL NOTE: Notice that the class name of the Applet is the same as our original Java application (\java4cobol\HelloWorld). The runtime environment takes the directory path into consideration when loading and executing Java code, so this is an important fact to remember! Many times the wrong class will be loaded and executed, or the runtime environment will not find your class due to directory naming issues. You are well advised to understand how this works. We will discuss the particulars of class path management later.

REVIEWING OUR SAMPLES

We kind of rushed through some of the code and the changes made to the code in our efforts to explain the development environment issues, so let's take a minute to review, starting with the first application.

- Our first program was a stand-alone *application*. That is, it only needed a runtime interpreter to execute. For JDK this was java.exe, and for J++ this was jview.exe.

- The main program (the class that gets the ball rolling)) in a Java application must have a specific interface. It must have a public method with this interface definition:

  ```
  public static void main(String[] args)
  ```

- This method accepts a single parameter (named args in our example). This parameter must be defined as an array of Strings (String[]). The String array represents the runtime arguments to the program (as in "jview HelloWorld argument1 argument2").
- The class that contains this interface (HelloWorld, in our example), does not need to be any particular name, but it may need to be public, depending on the requirements of the runtime environment. It also must be a *static* class, meaning only one instance of the class can exit at a time.
- The internal name of the class (in the source program HelloWorld.java) and the external name of the class (the HelloWorld.class file built by the compiler) must be the same.
- A Java application run in this manner does not expect to have a graphical user interface environment available to it. It does expect to be able to write to a logical file known as *standard out*, and read from *standard in*. These files are more or less the equivalent of the ACCEPT and DISPLAY verbs that interact with the CRT in Cobol programs.
- For most Windows-based Java interpreters, standard out and standard in are directed towards an MS-DOS command window. Java applications run this way are not graphical applications.
- The statement `System.out.println ("Hello World!");` writes to standard out. It performs the println() method in a built-in object named `System.out`. This method accepts a String input parameter and writes it to 'standard out'. Think of it as analogous to this Cobol statement:

  ```
  DISPLAY "Hello World!".
  ```

- Subsequent calls to println write a new line of text to standard out.

The next program we wrote was a Java *applet*.

- An applet expects to be supported by some type of graphical hosting environment
- Most often, the graphical hosting environment is a browser.
- Some stand-alone Java runtime environments also provide a built-in graphical hosting environment, or *applet viewer*. For J++, this was jview.exe, with an applet viewer option, and for the JDK, this was appletviewer.exe. The applet viewer is an excellent tool for testing your applets.
- The main program (the program that gets the ball rolling) with a Java applet is the hosting environment (the browser or the applet viewer). It calls the paint() function in your class so that you can display information to the screen. The paint() function must have a specific interface. It must have a public method with this interface definition:

  ```
  public void paint(Graphics g)
  ```

- This method accepts a single parameter. It is a Graphics object (named g in our example).
- The class that contains this interface (HelloWorld, in our example) does not need to be any particular name, but it does need to be public. This class must be of the sort that *extends*, or inherits, from a class named Applet. (We will discuss *inheritance* later, but a sobering note: it does not mean Daddy Warbucks is going to give you lots of money.)
- The statement `import java.applet.Applet;` at the beginning of the class tells the Java compiler where to find the Applet class.
- The internal name of the class (in the source program) and the external name of the class (the HelloWorld.class file built by the compiler) must be the same.
- A Java program run in this manner expects to have a graphical user interface environment available to it. It also does expect to be able to write to a logical file known as standard out, and read from standard in.
- Standard out and standard in are not well defined for these types of programs.

- The statement `g.drawString("Hello World!", 5, 25);` writes to the graphical environment. It performs the drawString method in the Graphics class. This method accepts a String input parameter and writes it to the graphical environment. There are additional controls to this method. In our example, we've specified the starting position in the graphical window to place our String. Think of it as analogous to this type of Cobol statement, extended with the ability to position the text anywhere on the screen:

```
DISPLAY "Hello World!" AT COLUMN 5 LINE 25
```

- The statement `import java.awt.Graphics;` at the beginning of the class tells the Java compiler where to find the Graphics class.
- Subsequent calls to drawString write text to the specified place in the graphical window.

To begin with, our examples have worked the same way in both development environments. You are about to enter the world of write once, debug anywhere.

In Microsoft's J++ environment, if the same text is written twice to the same place in the window, the text appears **bold**. In Sun's JDK, this same code rewrites the text exactly in the same position, making it appear as if only one drawString statement was executed.

In Microsoft's J++ environment, changing the 5 to a 6 causes the text to appear slightly out of alignment, making it unreadable. In Sun's JDK, this same code makes the text appear **bold**.

Finally, in both environments, writing once with a 5, 25 and then a second time with 5, 35 causes two lines of text to appear.

MSFT J++

```
g.drawString("Hello Applet World!", 5, 25);
g.drawString("Hello Applet World!", 5, 25);
```

Hello Applet World!

```
g.drawString("Hello Applet World!", 5, 25);
g.drawString("Hello Applet World!", 6, 25);
```

Hello Applet World!

```
g.drawString("Hello Applet World!", 5, 25);
g.drawString("Hello Applet World!", 5, 35);
```

Hello Applet World!
Hello Applet World!

JDK

```
g.drawString("Hello Applet World!", 5, 25);
g.drawString("Hello Applet World!", 5, 25);
```

Hello Applet World!

```
g.drawString("Hello Applet World!", 5, 25);
g.drawString("Hello Applet World!", 6, 25);
```

Hello Applet World!

```
g.drawString("Hello Applet World!", 5, 25);
g.drawString("Hello Applet World!", 5, 35);
```

Hello Applet World!
Hello Applet World!

These examples should work with any development toolset, but they have only been tested with J++ (version 1.1) and Sun's JDK.

CHAPTER

3

Messages and Methods

Let's return to our object-oriented concept discussion. We can extend our Cobol example to explore some other Java concepts.

A subroutine call can be viewed as a message, passed from one object to another.

When we called MYSUB from CALLER, we prepared some information (in TEXT-STRING) and asked MYSUB to evaluate it. In OO terms, this is sometimes referred to as *message passing*. That is, CALLER passed a particular type of message to MYSUB.

In Java, objects can send messages to other objects. In almost all respects, this is similar to a subroutine call. However, objects typically support more than one type of message. Cobol subroutines can do this, too, but it takes a little planning.

In our example so far, MYSUB can only support one message type (i.e., evaluate TEXT-STRING). Suppose we want MYSUB to support multiple functions that are in some way related? We can do this by extending our MYSUB-CONTROL to include an ACTION-SWITCH. This item is used by the calling program to specify the function requested.

MYSUB COBOL

```
IDENTIFICATION DIVISION.
PROGRAM-ID. MYSUB.
DATA DIVISION.
WORKING-STORAGE SECTION.

*************************************************************************
* This routine accepts a text item as a parameter and evaluates the    *
* text. If the text is all spaces, MSG-SIZE will be set to 0. Else,    *
* MSG-SIZE will be set to                                               *
* Only if requested, the text item will also be stored                  *
* in the passed control structure.                                      *
*************************************************************************

LINKAGE SECTION.
01 MYSUB-CONTROL.
    03   MYSUB-ACTION-SWITCH      PIC X.
         88 MYSUB-ACTION-EVALUATE          VALUE "E".
         88 MYSUB-ACTION-SET-AND-EVALUATE  VALUE "S".
    03   MSG-TEXT                 PIC X(20).
    03   MSG-SIZE                 PIC 9(8).

01 TEXT-STRING              PIC X(20).

PROCEDURE DIVISION USING MYSUB-CONTROL, TEXT-STRING.

MYSUB-INITIAL SECTION.
MYSUB-INITIAL-S.
```

*   Perform the subroutine's function.

```
     IF TEXT-STRING = SPACES
          MOVE 0 TO MSG-SIZE
     ELSE
          MOVE 1 TO MSG-SIZE.
```

*   Evaluate if this additional function was requested.
*   If yes, perform it (i.e., save the string in TEXT-STRING).

```
     IF MYSUB-ACTION-SET-AND-EVALUATE
          MOVE TEXT-STRING TO MSG-TEXT.

 EXIT-PROGRAM.
     EXIT PROGRAM.
```

Using this interface definition, the CALLER program can ask MYSUB to store the TEXT-STRING in MSG-TEXT. It can also ask MYSUB to evaluate TEXT-STRING in order to determine whether it contains only spaces. The result is stored in MSG-SIZE.

Alternatively, the CALLER can ask MYSUB to simply perform the evaluation and not store the TEXT-STRING in MSG-TEXT. This would be a slight variation on MYSUB's basic function. CALLER can then request either of these two functions by setting ACTION-SW to the appropriate value. Here is an example:

CALLER COBOL

```
IDENTIFICATION DIVISION.
PROGRAM-ID. CALLER.
DATA DIVISION.
WORKING-STORAGE SECTION.

01 MYSUB-CONTROL.
    03   MYSUB-ACTION-SWITCH          PIC X.
         88 MYSUB-ACTION-EVALUATE             VALUE "E".
         88 MYSUB-ACTION-SET-AND-EVALUATE     VALUE "S".
    03   MSG-TEXT                     PIC X(20).
    03   MSG-SIZE                     PIC 9(8).

01 TEXT-STRING                   PIC X(20).

PROCEDURE DIVISION.
START-PROGRAM SECTION.
START-PROGRAM-S.
```

*   Set ACTION-SWITCH to the function required (set and evaluate)

```
     MOVE "S" TO MYSUB-ACTION-SWITCH.
```

*   Prepare the text parameter to this subroutine

```
     MOVE "ANYTEXT" TO TEXT-STRING.
```

*   Call the subroutine to perform this function

```
     CALL "MYSUB" USING MYSUB-CONTROL, TEXT-STRING.
```

```
    DISPLAY "MSG-TEXT: ", MSG-TEXT,
            "MSG-SIZE: ", MSG-SIZE.

EXIT-PROGRAM.
    EXIT PROGRAM.
    STOP RUN.
```

TECHNICAL NOTE: You may have noticed that we separate MYSUB's parameters into two types: items in the CONTROL-AREA and other parameter items. This is done by design in order to distinguish parameters in the CONTROL-AREA (these are analogous to class data members) and other parameters (these are analogous to parameters passed to a class's methods, or functions). We will expand on this convention as we go.

MESSAGES IN JAVA

Once again, let's compare what we've done in Cobol to the way we would do it in Java.

ERRORMSG CLASS

```
public class ErrorMsg {

     public String msgText;
     public int  msgSize;

     public void setErrorMsg (String inputMsg) {
          ...
 // Some logic
          ...
          ;
     }
}
```

The statement that contains `setErrorMsg` describes a public entry point (i.e., a function or *method*) to the class `ErrorMsg`. These methods can be called by other classes to perform some function in this class.

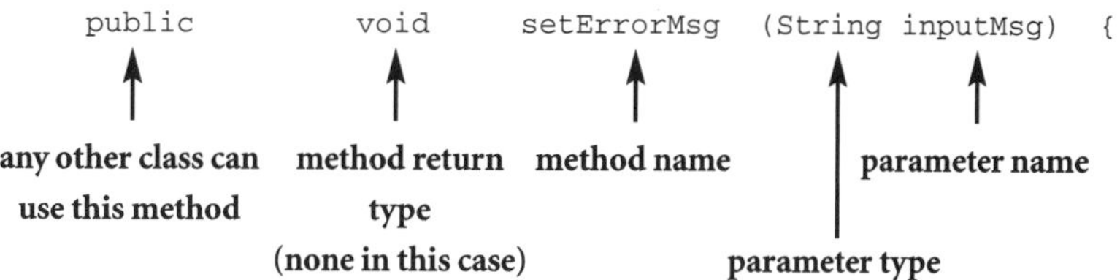

The statement could be read this way; "Define a `public` method for class `ErrorMsg`. This method returns no data (`void`) and its name is `setErrorMsg`. This method accepts one parameter of type `String`; the parameter's name as used by the class is `inputMsg`."

A consumer (calling) class can use this method in the following way:

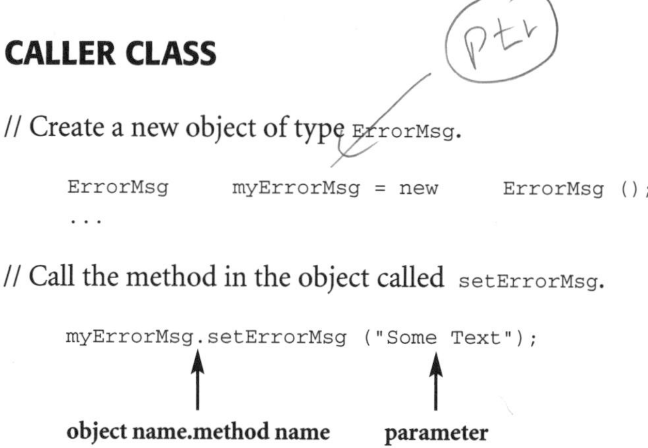

CALLER CLASS

// Create a new object of type `ErrorMsg`.

```
ErrorMsg     myErrorMsg = new     ErrorMsg ();
...
```

// Call the method in the object called `setErrorMsg`.

```
myErrorMsg.setErrorMsg ("Some Text");
```


This statement calls the object's method and requests that it perform a function based on the passed parameter. Sometimes this is a described as sending a *message* to that object.

MULTIPLE MESSAGES

Classes can easily support more than one message definition or even variations on a single message. In fact, it is this easy-to-use message specification that helps distinguish OO languages from their more procedural cousins. Lets look some examples of how a class publishes the types of messages it can receive, using Java's syntax.

CLASS ERRORMSG

```
public class ErrorMsg {

      public String msgText;
      public int  msgSize;

(1)         public void setErrorMsg (String inputMsg) {
                  ...
      // Some logic
                  ...
```

// The method is complete. Return to the caller.

```
                  return;
            }

(2)         public String getErrorMsg () {
                  ...
        // Some logic
                  ...
```

// The method is complete.
// Return a String variable as the result (or return argument) of this method.

```
                  return (returnMsg);
            }

(3)         public String getErrorMsg (int msgCode) {
                  ...
      // Some logic
                  ...
                  return (returnMsg);
            }
      }
```

The new message definition statements (2 and 3) could be read this way; "Define a `public` method for class `ErrorMsg`. This method returns a `String` data item, and the method's name is `getErrorMsg`. One form of this method accepts no parameters (statement 2), and another form accepts one parameter of type int (statement 3)."

The methods getErrorMsg define other functions that ErrorMsg can support. As such, these are additional *interfaces* to ErrorMsg. These methods can access any of ErrorMsg's data items or methods (both public and private ones). Since the methods are themselves public, any class can call these methods.

Notice that the methods named getErrorMsg have different signatures (interface definitions) than the setErrorMsg method. They do not have a String input parameter, but do return a String variable.

Notice also that the method getErrorMsg is defined twice in ErrorMsg. The first method specification accepts no parameters, and the second accepts one parameter of type int. This parameter's name (as used internally by the method) is msgCode.

METHOD OVERLOADING

Having two variations on the same method is an example of *method overloading*. This is another mechanism to request a specific function in the class ErrorMsg. Methods with the same name can be defined to require variable numbers or different types of parameters. Consumer (calling) classes can request any of these public methods. The compiler will examine a method call, including its input parameters and return type, and call the correct public method of the class. After the ErrorMsg class has been properly compiled, a consumer class can use these various methods in the following way:

CALLER CLASS

// Define an instance of the ErrorMsg class.

```
ErrorMsg    myErrorMsg = new    ErrorMsg ();
```

// Define a few local variables.

```
int msgCode;
String myString;
...
```

// Get the error message from myErrorMsg; store the result in myString

```
myString = myErrorMsg.getErrorMsg ();
    ↑            ↑           ↑
```

local variable **object name.method name**

// Get the error message from myErrorMsg based on the integer value in msgCode

METHOD OVERLOADING IN COBOL

There is not direct analogy to method overloading in Cobol, but there is a coding technique that is pretty close. Cobol compilers will generally let you call a subroutine and pass fewer parameters than specified in the USING statement. Suppose you designed a subroutine where some actions performed by the subroutine might require two parameters and other actions might require three. Calling programs can pass in either two or three parameters but would be responsible to pass the correct number of parameters, based on the action requested. It would then be the responsibility of the subroutine to make sure that no missing parameters are accessed by the subroutine during this particular call. Parameters that have been actually passed can be accessed by the subroutine, but the subroutine designer must be careful not to perform any statement that accesses an item defined in LINKAGE SECTION but not passed by the caller. In fact, some compilers support this technique explicitly by providing a mechanism to detect (at runtime) the number of passed parameters. In some systems, you may have to call an Assembler program to detect the number of parameters. Our example below presents the "GET$NARGS" function as provided by the AcuCorp Cobol compiler.

MYSUB COBOL

```
IDENTIFICATION DIVISION.
PROGRAM-ID. MYSUB.

*************************************************************************
* This routine accepts a text item as a parameter and                   *
* evaluates the text. If the text is all spaces,                        *
* MSG-SIZE will be set to 0. Else, MSG-SIZE                             *
* will be set to 1.                                                     *
* If requested, the text item will also be stored in the                *
* passed control structure.                                             *
* If the text item is not passed, then MSG-TEXT                         *
* will be evaluated instead.                                            *
*************************************************************************
```

```
DATA DIVISION.
WORKING-STORAGE SECTION.

01 ARGUMENT-COUNT          PIC 9.
01 LOCAL-TEXT              PIC X(20).

LINKAGE SECTION.
01 MYSUB-CONTROL.
    03   MYSUB-ACTION-SWITCH      PIC X.
         88 MYSUB-ACTION-EVALUATE              VALUE "E".
         88 MYSUB-ACTION-SET-AND-EVALUATE      VALUE "S".
    03   MSG-TEXT                 PIC X(20).
    03   MSG-SIZE                 PIC 9(8).

01 TEXT-STRING              PIC X(20).

PROCEDURE DIVISION USING MYSUB-CONTROL, TEXT-STRING.

MYSUB-INITIAL SECTION.
MYSUB-INITIAL-S.
```

*   Perform some function to detect the number of arguments

```
     PERFORM GET-ARGUMENT-COUNT.
```

*   Determine whether TEXT-STRING or MSG-TEXT should be
*   evaluated. Store the correct item in LOCAL-TEXT.

```
     IF ARGUMENT-COUNT = 2
          MOVE TEXT-STRING TO LOCAL-TEXT
     ELSE
          MOVE MSG-TEXT TO LOCAL-TEXT.
```

*   Now, use LOCAL-TEXT in the subroutine's logic.

```
    IF LOCAL-TEXT = SPACES
          MOVE 0 TO MSG-SIZE
     ELSE
          MOVE 1 TO MSG-SIZE.

     IF MYSUB-ACTION-SET-AND-EVALUATE
          MOVE LOCAL-TEXT TO MSG-TEXT.

 EXIT-PROGRAM.
     EXIT PROGRAM.
```

```
GET-ARGUMENT-COUNT SECTION.
GET-ARGUMENT-COUNT-S.
```

*   Set ARGUMENT-COUNT to the result.

```
    CALL "GET$NARGS" USING ARGUMENT-COUNT.
```

In this example, there are really two interfaces defined for MYSUB, one with a single parameter and another with two parameters. Calling programs can use either interface, depending on their requirements.

CALLER COBOL

```
IDENTIFICATION DIVISION.
PROGRAM-ID. CALLER.
DATA DIVISION.
WORKING-STORAGE SECTION.

01 MYSUB-CONTROL.
    03   MYSUB-ACTION-SWITCH      PIC X.
         88 MYSUB-ACTION-EVALUATE            VALUE "E".
         88 MYSUB-ACTION-SET-AND-EVALUATE    VALUE "S".
    03   MSG-TEXT                 PIC X(20).
    03   MSG-SIZE                 PIC 9(8).

01 TEXT-STRING               PIC X(20).
...
PROCEDURE DIVISION.
START-PROGRAM SECTION.
START-PROGRAM-S.
```

*   Set ACTION-SWITCH to the function required (set and evaluate).

```
     MOVE "S" TO MYSUB-ACTION-SWITCH.
```

*   Clear the two MYSUB control items, to make sure we see the result.

```
     MOVE SPACES TO MYSUB-TEXT.
     MOVE ZEROS TO MYSUB-SIZE.
```

*   Call MYSUB with two parameters.

```
     MOVE "ANYTEXT" TO TEXT-STRING.
     CALL "MYSUB" USING MYSUB-CONTROL, TEXT-STRING.
```

```
    DISPLAY "MSG-TEXT: ", MSG-TEXT,
           " MSG-SIZE: ", MSG-SIZE.

*   Set ACTION-SWITCH to the function required (evaluate only).

    MOVE "E" TO MYSUB-ACTION-SWITCH.

*   Clear the two MYSUB control items, so we make sure to see the
*   result.

    MOVE SPACES TO MYSUB-TEXT.
    MOVE ZEROS TO MYSUB-SIZE.

*   Call MYSUB, passing only one parameter.
*   The stored string in MSG-TEXT will be evaluated.

    CALL "MYSUB" USING MYSUB-CONTROL.

    DISPLAY "MSG-TEXT: ", MSG-TEXT,
           " MSG-SIZE: ", MSG-SIZE.

*   Try it with some text in MSG-TEXT.

    MOVE "Some Text" TO MYSUB-TEXT.
    MOVE ZEROS    TO MYSUB-SIZE.

*   Call MYSUB, passing only one parameter.
*   The stored string in MSG-TEXT will be evaluated.

    CALL "MYSUB" USING MYSUB-CONTROL.

    DISPLAY "MSG-TEXT: ", MSG-TEXT,
           " MSG-SIZE: ", MSG-SIZE.

EXIT-PROGRAM.
    EXIT PROGRAM.
    STOP RUN.
```

We have demonstrated how a developer can support multiple interfaces to a single Cobol subroutine. This avoids the problem of having to write and support two separate yet similar routines; a single routine can perform both roles. However, care must be exercised in both building and using the routine to make sure that the proper interface is being used at the proper time. A calling program can easily cause a runtime error by requesting one type of interface yet not passing the proper number of parameters.

Java's compiler and runtime system support this technique more explicitly and with much more functionality. The developer does not need to worry about which interface will be called and which parameter(s) may or may not be available; instead, the compiler automatically takes care of these details.

TECHNICAL NOTE: Remember the distinctions we have made between MYSUB's CONTROL-AREA and the other parameters passed to MYSUB? In our examples, every call to MYSUB must pass the CONTROL-AREA, regardless of the other parameters passed. Only the other parameters are optional.

This is similar to the way Java distinguishes between member data items and passed parameters. Class member items are always available, regardless of the interface used. For example, one method may require a single integer parameter and return a String data type, whereas another accepts no parameters, and does not return a data type (i.e., its return type is void). However, both of these methods can access any of the class members, both the public and the private ones. The caller, on the other hand, can access only the public class members, either before or after performing the method.

Let's return, for a moment, to our Java example. This call to the method getErrorMsg (by the CALLER) will always perform the method in ErrorMsg that accepts no parameter and returns a String result:

```
    myString = myErrorMsg.getErrorMsg ();↷

(2)                 public String getErrorMsg () {…}
```

On the other hand, this call to `getErrorMsg` will always perform the method that accepts one integer parameter and returns a String result:

```
    myString = myErrorMsg.getErrorMsg (msgCode);↷

(3)                 public String getErrorMsg (int msgCode) {…}
```

The Java compiler will automatically match up the particulars of the method invocation (in CALLER) with the particulars of the method interface (in ErrorMsg), and make sure the proper method is executed.

TERMS TO REVIEW

Let's review some of the object-oriented concepts we've just discussed and how you can understand them from a Java perspective.

Methods: Methods are the functions that a class can perform. Performing a method is similar to calling a function, or sending a message (to an object).

Method signatures: The method signatures of a class are the view it presents to external programs. A class can have many public methods. Each method can be further qualified by its method name, arguments, and return type. This combination of unique method name, argument profile, and return value is sometimes referred to as an interface in OO design terms, although this term is formally reserved for a specific construct in the Java language.

Method Overloading: A class can define a method and then create more than one signature for this method. These unique interfaces are distinguished by their input parameters and return type.

EXERCISES—CLASSES, OBJECTS, AND METHODS

It's to use the keyboard and—as a good piano teacher might say—let your fingers teach your mind. We'll experiment with some of the sample classes presented so far.

USING JAVA 2'S JDK

Create an ErrorMsg class:

1. Using a text editor, create a Java source file named ErrorMsg.java in the java4cobol directory. The source file should contain these statements:

```
public class ErrorMsg {
```

\\ Define some *public* class instance variables.

```
        public  String  msgText = " ";
        public  int     msgSize;
```

\\ Define a *public* method.

```
public void setErrorMsg (String inputMsg) {
```

\\ Modify one of the public variables. Set this variable to the text String that \\ was passed as a parameter.

```
        msgText = inputMsg;
```

\\ Return from this method. Since this method has no return value (i.e., it is \\ declared as *void*), no return statement is necessary.

```
    }
```

\\ Define another *public* method.

```
    public String getErrorMsg () {
        String returnMsg;
```

\\ Set the local variable returnMsg to the data member msgText.

```
        returnMsg = msgText;
```

\\ Return from this method, and return this String variable.

```
        return (returnMsg);
    }

}
```

Remember to save this source as a text file instead of a document file. The file name should be c:\java4cobol\ErrorMsg.java.

2. In the DOS command window, change the current directory to your java4cobol directory:

➢ cd c:\java4cobol

3. Compile your class, using the javac compiler:

➢ javac ErrorMsg.java

Again, your class should compile successfully at this point. If it doesn't, review the suggestions mentioned in the introductory JDK exercises.

4. Using a text editor, modify and compile your HelloWorld.java source file in the java4cobol directory. The source file should contain these statements:

```
public class HelloWorld
{
     public static void main(String args[])
     {
          String tempMsg;
```

// Our original println statement:

```
          System.out.println("Hello World!");
```

// Create a new instance of the ErrorMsg class:

```
          ErrorMsg myErrorMsg = new ErrorMsg ();
```

// Get the value of the text item in ErrorMsg, by calling the getErrorMsg
// method.

```
          tempMsg = myErrorMsg.getErrorMsg ();
```

// Print the contents of the String returned by this method.

```
          System.out.println (tempMsg);
```

// Set the text item in ErrorMsg to some text String, and print its contents.

```
          myErrorMsg.setErrorMsg ("Some Text");
          tempMsg = myErrorMsg.getErrorMsg ();
          System.out.println (tempMsg);
```

// Call the setErrorMsg method again to set ErrorMsg to some other text.

```
          myErrorMsg.setErrorMsg ("Some New Text");
          tempMsg = myErrorMsg.getErrorMsg ();
          System.out.println (tempMsg);

     }

}
```

5. Now run your program, using the Java runtime that comes with the JDK:

➢ java HelloWorld

If you've done everything correctly, then your MS-DOS window should look like this:

```
C:>javac ErrorMsg.java

C:>javac HelloWorld.java

C:>java HelloWorld
Hello World!

Some Text
Some New Text

C:\java4cobol>
```

6. Experiment with this program. Add the following lines to the end of your HelloWorld.java source file (i.e., immediately after the last println statement):

// Create a new instance of the ErrorMsg class.

```
ErrorMsg myErrorMsg2 = new ErrorMsg ();
```

// Set the text item to some text String, and print its contents.

```
myErrorMsg2.setErrorMsg ("Some Text for #2");
tempMsg = myErrorMsg2.getErrorMsg ();
System.out.println (tempMsg);
```

// Print the text item in the original object.

```
tempMsg = myErrorMsg.getErrorMsg ();
System.out.println (tempMsg);
```

7. Save the program again. Compile and execute it by performing these statements in the command window:

➢ javac HelloWorld.java

➢ java HelloWorld

Your DOS window should look like this:

```
C:>javac HelloWorld.java

C:>java HelloWorld
Hello World!

Some Text
Some New Text
Some Text for #2
Some New Text


C:\java4cobol>
```

Our ErrorMsg class has two methods defined for it: setErrorMsg and getErrorMsg. We can define a variation on getErrorMsg. This alternative, or overloaded, method will convert the returned String to all upper case.

1. Using a text editor, edit the Java source file ErrorMsg.java in the java4cobol directory.
2. Add the following lines to the end of your ErrorMsg.java source file (i.e., immediately before the last brace (}) in the class):

// Define a variation on the public method getErrorMsg.

```
public String getErrorMsg (char caseFlag) {
    String returnMsg;
```

// Set the local variable returnMsg to the data member msgText.

```
returnMsg = msgText;
```

// Convert to all upper case, if requested.

```
if (caseFlag == 'U')
     returnMsg = returnMsg.toUpperCase ();
```

// Return from this method, and return the String variable.

```
        return (returnMsg);
    }
```

3. Compile the class again in the DOS command window:

➢ javac ErrorMsg.java

4. Modify HelloWorld to use this new method. Using a text editor, edit the Java source file HelloWorld.java in the java4cobol directory
5. Add the following lines to the end of your HelloWorld.java source file (i.e., immediately after the last println statement):

// Call the new variation of the getErrorMsg method.

// This variation will return an all upper case message.

```
tempMsg = myErrorMsg.getErrorMsg ('U');
System.out.println (tempMsg);
```

6. Compile and execute the program again in the DOS command window:

➢ javac HelloWorld.java

➢ java HelloWorld

Your output window should contain these lines:

```
C:>javac ErrorMsg.java

C:>javac HelloWorld.java

C:>java HelloWorld
Hello World!

Some Text
Some New Text
Some Text for #2
Some New Text
SOME NEW TEXT


C:\java4cobol>
```

We will now modify the applet version of your HelloWorld class, so that it also uses the ErrorMsg class.

1. Using the text editor, edit the HelloWorld.java file in your java4cobol\applet directory.
2. Add the required source text to your HelloWorld applet class, so that it looks like this:

```
import java.applet.Applet;
import java.awt.Graphics;

public class HelloWorld extends Applet
{

     public void paint(Graphics g)
     {
          String tempMsg;

          g.drawString("Hello applet World!", 5, 25);
```

// Create a new instance of the ErrorMsg class.

```
          ErrorMsg myErrorMsg = new ErrorMsg ();
```

// Print the contents of the public data member msgText in our class.

```
          tempMsg = myErrorMsg.getErrorMsg ();
          g.drawString (tempMsg, 5, 35);
```

// Set msgText to some text String, and print its contents.

```
          myErrorMsg.setErrorMsg ("Some Text");
          tempMsg = myErrorMsg.getErrorMsg ();
          g.drawString (tempMsg, 5, 45);
```

// Call the setErrorMsg method to set the text to some other text, and print its // contents.

```
          myErrorMsg.setErrorMsg ("Some New Text");
          tempMsg = myErrorMsg.getErrorMsg ();
          g.drawString (tempMsg, 5, 55);


     }


}
```

3. Save the source file in text format. The file name should be c:\java4cobol\applet\HelloWorld.java.
4. Compile the program after changing to the applet directory in your DOS window.

➢ cd c:\java4cobol\Applet

➢ javac HelloWorld.java

What happens? Did you get an error message that looked like this?

```
C:>cd applet

C:>javac HelloWorld.java
HelloWorld.java:13: Class ErrorMsg not found.
           ErrorMsg myErrorMsg = new ErrorMsg ();
           ^
HelloWorld.java:13: Class ErrorMsg not found.
           ErrorMsg myErrorMsg = new ErrorMsg ();
                                     ^
2 errors

C:\java4cobol\applet>
```

What is the proper solution for this error? Should you create a new class called "'ErrorMsg' as part of this project? Or should you use the ErrorMsg class that we had previously created?

If you choose the first solution, go to the rear of the class. If you choose the second, congratulations! You are well on your way to becoming an object-oriented programmer! The primary objective when you create a class is to have other programs reuse that class. This objective is not met when a class is copied, so make sure to always resist that temptation.

The JDK Java development environment can use a variety of mechanisms to find the proper class files. We will cover them all soon, but the simplest one to use right now is the *classpath* argument. This argument lists directory names the Java compiler should search in order to find any required classes.

5. Tell the Java compiler where the ErrorMsg class is, by adding the *classpath* argument to the java compile statement in your command window:

➢ javac -classpath c:\java4cobol HelloWorld.java

It should compile successfully now.

6. Now run your new HelloWorld applet. You will need to set the *class-path* argument when you run it as follows:

➢ appletviewer -J-classpath -J.;c:/java4cobol HelloWorld.html

---

TECHNICAL NOTE: The syntax for the class path includes an initial '.', followed by a semicolon. This tells the appletviewer to search in the current directory "." and then in the c:\java4cobol directory for all classes.

Experiment with this applet as well. You can make the changes in the text editor, and then recompile the applet in the command window.

7. Add the following lines to the end of your HelloWorld.java source file (i.e. immediately after the last g.drawString statement).

// Create a new instance of the ErrorMsg class.

```
ErrorMsg myErrorMsg2 = new ErrorMsg ();
```

// Set the text item to some text String, and print its contents.

```
myErrorMsg2.setErrorMsg ("Some Text for #2");
tempMsg = myErrorMsg2.getErrorMsg ();
g.drawString (tempMsg, 5, 75);
```

// Print the text item in the original object.

```
tempMsg = myErrorMsg.getErrorMsg ();
g.drawString (tempMsg, 5, 85);
```

8. Save the program again. Compile and execute it by performing these statements in the command window:

➢ javac -classpath c:\java4cobol HelloWorld.java

➢ appletviewer -J-classpath -J.;c:/java4cobol HelloWorld.html

Your applet window should look like this:

```
Hello applet World!

Some Text
Some New Text

Some Text for #2
Some New Text
```

TECHNICAL NOTE: Three of the four execution environments we have been using (applications and applets for J++ and applications and applets for JDK) print null as the way to represent an unintialized String. Only the appletviewer that comes with JDK does not handle this case the same way, and instead generates an exception, or error condition. Therefore, our ErrorMsg class, (as defined for the JDK) initializes its data member named msgText to a single space.

---

9. Now, have the applet use the overloaded version of getErrorMsg. Add the following lines to the end of your HelloWorld.java source file (i.e., immediately after the last "g.drawString" statement):

// Call the new variation of the getErrorMsg method.

// This variation will return an all upper case message.

```
tempMsg = myErrorMsg.getErrorMsg ('U');
g.drawString (tempMsg, 5, 95);
```

10. Save the program again. Compile and execute it by performing these statements in the command window:

➢ javac -classpath c:\java4cobol HelloWorld.java

➢ appletviewer -J-classpath -J.;c:/java4cobol HelloWorld.html

Your applet window should look like this:

```
Hello applet World!

Some Text
Some New Text

Some Text for #2
Some New Text
SOME NEW TEXT
```

USING J++

Create an ErrorMsg class:

1. Start the J++ design environment. Select your previous java4cobol workspace with the following menu path in the J++ tool:

➢ File → Recent Workspaces → ....\java4cobol. (You will probably also see the applet project in this list as well. Do not select the applet version yet.

2. Create a new class using this menu path:

➢ Insert → New Class

- In the dialog box, type in the name of the class (ErrorMsg) and choose the Public modifier type. Leave the other fields as is.
- Click OK.

3. Type the following Java source statements into your new class. Note that the design environment has already created some of these statements for you. When you are done, the class should look exactly as it does below (without the *italics*).

TECHNICAL NOTE: J++ places the initial brace ({) at the beginning of the second line in every class it creates. As a matter of style, the samples in this book start classes and methods with the brace at the end of the declaration line. What does this mean to you? In order to make your code look exactly as it does in this book, you will have to move the initial brace to the end of the previous line.

```
//
//
// ErrorMsg
//
//
public class ErrorMsg {
```

// Define some *public* class instance variables.

```
        public String msgText;
        public int  msgSize;
```

// Define a *public* method.

```
        public void setErrorMsg (String inputMsg) {
```

// Modify one of the public variables. Set this variable to the text String that
// was passed as a parameter.

```
            msgText = inputMsg;
```

// Return from this method. Since this method has no return value (i.e., it is
// declared as *void*), no return statement is necessary.

```
        }
```

// Define another *public* method.

```
        public String getErrorMsg () {
        String returnMsg;
```

// Set the local variable returnMsg to the data member msgText.

```
        returnMsg = msgText;
```

// Return from this method and return this String variable.

```
        return (returnMsg);
    }

}
```

4. Compile the ErrorMsg class, using this menu path:

➢ Build → Compile ErrorMsg.java

If everything has gone okay, then you should see a message similar to this:

```
ErrorMsg.class - 0 error(s), 0 warning(s)
```

Now, we will modify the original HelloWorld class so that it uses this ErrorMsg class.

5. Select the HelloWorld window, either by clicking on it (behind the ErrorMsg window) or using this menu path:

➢ Window → HelloWorld.java

6. Add additional statements to HelloWorld, so that it class looks like this:

```
//
//
// HelloWorld Application
//
//
public class HelloWorld {
    public static void main(String args[])
    {
        String tempMsg;
```

```
// Our original println statement:

         System.out.println("Hello World!");

// Create a new instance of the ErrorMsg class.

         ErrorMsg myErrorMsg = new ErrorMsg ();

// Get the value of the text item in ErrorMsg, by calling the getErrorMsg
// method.

         tempMsg = myErrorMsg.getErrorMsg ();

// Print the contents of the String returned by this method.

         System.out.println (tempMsg);

// Set the text item in ErrorMsg to some text String, and print its contents.

         myErrorMsg.setErrorMsg ("Some Text");
         tempMsg = myErrorMsg.getErrorMsg ();
         System.out.println (tempMsg);

// Call the setErrorMsg method again to set ErrorMsg to some other text.

         myErrorMsg.setErrorMsg ("Some New Text");
         tempMsg = myErrorMsg.getErrorMsg ();
         System.out.println (tempMsg);

    }

}
```

7. Compile the HelloWorld class, using this menu path:

➢ Build → Compile HelloWorld.java

Again, if everything has gone okay, then you should see a message similar to this:

➢ HelloWorld.class - 0 error(s), 0 warning(s)

8. Now it is time to run your modified program. Use the 'Execute HelloWorld' menu entry as follows:

➢ Build → Execute HelloWorld

A DOS window similar to this should appear. As we did in our previous exercises, you can pause the window by placing a debug breakpoint at the end of the HelloWorld class and using the "Run to cursor" command (menu path Build → Start Debug → Run to Cursor) from the design environment. Or you can execute the new HelloWorld program from a DOS window and use the stand-alone Java runtime jview.exe.

```
Hello World!
null
Some Text
Some New Text
```

9. Experiment with this program. Add the following lines to the end of your HelloWorld.java source file (i.e., immediately after the last println statement):

// Create a new instance of the ErrorMsg class.

```
ErrorMsg myErrorMsg2 = new ErrorMsg ();
```

// Set the text item to some text String and print its contents.

```
myErrorMsg2.setErrorMsg ("Some Text for #2");
tempMsg = myErrorMsg2.getErrorMsg ();
System.out.println (tempMsg);
```

// Print the text item in the original object.

```
tempMsg = myErrorMsg.getErrorMsg ();
System.out.println (tempMsg);
```

10. Compile and execute the program again (menupath Build → Compile HelloWorld.java, then Build → Start Debug → Run to Cursor). Your output window should contain these lines:

```
Hello World!
null
Some Text
Some New Text
Some Text for #2
Some New Text
```

Our ErrorMsg class currently has two methods defined for it; setErrorMsg and getErrorMsg. We can define a variation on getErrorMsg. This alternative, or overloaded, method will convert the returned String to all upper case.

1. Select the ErrorMsg window, by either clicking on it (behind the HelloWorld window) or using this menu path:

➢ Window → ErrorMsg.java

2. Add the following lines to the end of your ErrorMsg.java source file (i.e., immediately before the last brace (}) in the class:

// Define a variation on the public method getErrorMsg.

```
public String getErrorMsg (char caseFlag) {
String returnMsg;
```

// Set the local variable returnMsg to the data member msgText.

```
    returnMsg = msgText;
```

// Convert to all upper case, if requested.

```
    if (caseFlag == 'U')
        returnMsg = returnMsg.toUpperCase ();
```

// Return from this method, and return the String variable.

```
    return (returnMsg);
}
```

3. Compile the class again using this menu path:

➢ Build → Compile ErrorMsg.java.

This class should compile successfully.

4. Modify HelloWorld to use this new method. Select the HelloWorld window, by either clicking on it (behind the ErrorMsg window), or using this menu path:

➢ Window → HelloWorld.java

5. Add the following lines to the end of your HelloWorld.java source file (i.e., immediately after the last println statement):

// Call the new variation of the getErrorMsg method.

// This variation will return an all upper case message.

```
tempMsg = myErrorMsg.getErrorMsg ('U');
System.out.println (tempMsg);
```

6. Compile and execute the program again (menupath Build → Compile HelloWorld.java, then Build → Start Debug → Run to Cursor). Your output window should contain these lines:

```
Hello World!
null
Some Text
Some New Text
Some Text for #2
Some New Text
SOME NEW TEXT
```

We will now modify the applet version of your HelloWorld class and have it use the ErrorMsg class.

1. Select the java4cobolapp workspaces, using this menu path:

➢ File → Recent Workspaces → HelloWorldapp.

2. Add the required source text to your HelloWorld applet class so that it looks like this:

```
import java.applet.Applet;
import java.awt.Graphics;
//
//
// HelloWorld
//
//
public class HelloWorld extends Applet {

     public void paint(Graphics g) {
          String tempMsg;

          g.drawString("Hello applet World!", 5, 25);

// Create a new instance of the ErrorMsg class:

          ErrorMsg myErrorMsg = new ErrorMsg ();

// Print the contents of the public data member msgText in our class.

          tempMsg = myErrorMsg.getErrorMsg ();
          g.drawString (tempMsg, 5, 35);

// Set msgText to some text String, and print its contents.

          myErrorMsg.setErrorMsg ("Some Text");
          tempMsg = myErrorMsg.getErrorMsg ();
          g.drawString (tempMsg, 5, 45);

// Call the setErrorMsg method to set the text to some other text, and print its
// contents.

          myErrorMsg.setErrorMsg ("Some New Text");
          tempMsg = myErrorMsg.getErrorMsg ();
          g.drawString (tempMsg, 5, 55);

     }

}
```

3. Try to compile your program. You should get these messages: "Undefined name ErrorMsg" and "Cannot find definition for class ErrorMsg." What is the proper solution for this error? Should you create a new class called "ErrorMsg" as part of this project? Or should you use the ErrorMsg class that we had previously created?

   If you choose the first solution, go to the rear of the class. If you choose the second, congratulations! you are well on your way to becoming an object-oriented programmer! The primary objective when you create a class is to have other programs reuse that class. This objective is not met when a class is copied, so make sure to always resist that temptation.

   Java development environments use a variety of mechanisms to find the proper class files. We will cover them all in a little bit, but the simplest one to use right now is the CLASSPATH variable. This variable lists directory names the Java environment should search in order to find any required classes.

4. Point your CLASSPATH variable to the directory in which the ErrorMsg class has been created by using this menu path:

➢ Project → Settings

   Select the General dialog tab, and enter the directory name where the ErrorMsg class was compiled. If you have followed the directory naming conventions so far, it should be C:\Program Files\DevStudio\MyProjects\java4cobol. Click OK.

5. Compile your program. It should compile successfully now.

6. Execute your applet:

➢ Build → Execute HelloWorld

You should see a window in your browser similar to this:

```
Hello applet
World!

Some Text
Some New Text
```

Notice that the text *null* does not appear in the output window; instead nothing is displayed in that position.

7. Experiment with this applet as well. Add the following lines to the end of your HelloWorld.java source file (i.e., immediately after the last g.drawString statement):

// Create a new instance of the ErrorMsg class.

```
ErrorMsg myErrorMsg2 = new ErrorMsg ();
```

// Set the text item to some text String, and print its contents.

```
myErrorMsg2.setErrorMsg ("Some Text for #2");
tempMsg = myErrorMsg2.getErrorMsg ();
g.drawString (tempMsg, 5, 75);
```

// Print the text item in the original object.

```
tempMsg = myErrorMsg.getErrorMsg ();
g.drawString (tempMsg, 5, 85);
```

8. Compile and execute the program again (Build → Compile HelloWorld.java, then Build → Execute HelloWorld). Your output window should contain these lines:

```
Hello applet
World!

Some Text
Some New Text

Some Text for #2
Some New Text
```

9. Now, have the applet use the overloaded version of getErrorMsg. Add the following lines to the end of your HelloWorld.java source file (i.e., immediately after the last g.drawString statement):

// Call the new variation of the getErrorMsg method.

// This variation will return an all upper case message.

```
tempMsg = myErrorMsg.getErrorMsg ('U');
g.drawString (tempMsg, 5, 95);
```

10. Compile and execute the program again (Build → Compile HelloWorld.java, then Build → Execute HelloWorld). Your output window should contain these lines:

```
Hello applet
World!

Some Text
Some New Text

Some Text for #2
Some New Text
SOME NEW TEXT
```

REVIEWING OUR SAMPLES

Let's review the class we've created (ErrorMsg) and the main program that uses it (HelloWorld). Try to relate the sample source statements to the result (for example, the output) each statement creates. If necessary, rerun the samples or look at the complete source code at the end of this section. Feel free to experiment by yourself.

- ErrorMsg is our first example of a re-usable class. Our first program HelloWorld was a stand-alone *application*. ErrorMsg, on the other hand, is a class that HelloWorld can use. Our original HelloWorld program from the first set of exercises was modified to use this class.

- HelloWorld first creates a new instance of ErrorMsg with this statement:

```
ErrorMsg myErrorMsg = new ErrorMsg ();
```

- To confirm that an instance has been created, HelloWorld prints out the contents of one of ErrorMsgs public data members. The default value for a String data type is *null*. Our ErrorMsg class as defined in the J++ example does not specified any initial data. Therefore, these statements:

```
System.out.println ("HelloWorld!");
tempMsg = myErrorMsg.getErrorMsg ();
System.out.println (tempMsg);
```

produce:

```
Hello World!
null
```

This println statement causes the text *null* to appear in the output window.

- On the other hand, our JDK version of ErrorMsg initialized the msgText data member to " " (one space). Therefore, these statements:

```
System.out.println ("HelloWorld!");
tempMsg = myErrorMsg.getErrorMsg ();
System.out.println (tempMsg);
```

```
Hello World!
```

cause a single space character appear in the output window (which is invisible).

- The HelloWorld application then stores some text in this instance of ErrorMsg. HelloWorld uses the setErrorMsg method to store this text.

```
myErrorMsg.setErrorMsg ("Some Text");
```

- HelloWorld next gets the text item from ErrorMsg, and prints out the contents of this data member. Note that the output for this statement is the text "Some Text."

```
tempMsg = myErrorMsg.getErrorMsg ();
System.out.println (tempMsg);
```

```
Some Text
```

- Next, HelloWorld modifies the data member and prints out its new contents. In this case, the output for this print statement is the text "Some New Text."

```
myErrorMsg.setErrorMsg ("Some New Text");
tempMsg = myErrorMsg.getErrorMsg ();
System.out.println (tempMsg);
```

```
Some New Text
```

- Finally, we modified HelloWorld to create a second instance of ErrorMsg, and stored a reference to this new instance in the variable myErrorMsg2. We then stored the String "Some Text for #2" in its data member, using the setErrorMsg method:

```
ErrorMsg myErrorMsg2 = new ErrorMsg ();
myErrorMsg2.setErrorMsg ("Some Text for #2");
tempMsg = myErrorMsg2.getErrorMsg ();
System.out.println (tempMsg);
```

```
Some New Text for #2
```

- To show that two unique objects of the same type exist in HelloWorld, we printed out the data contained in both objects. The data associated with myErrorMsg2 contained "Some Text for #2," and the data associated with myErrorMsg contained "Some New Text."

```
tempMsg = myErrorMsg2.getErrorMsg ();
System.out.println (tempMsg);
tempMsg = myErrorMsg.getErrorMsg ();
System.out.println (tempMsg);
```

```
Some New Text for #2
Some New Text
```

- Our applet versions of HelloWorld performed much the same as did our application versions. HelloWorld the applet created an instance of ErrorMsg, stored some text in it, and then printed the text. Instead of printing to standard out, we used the Graphics class to print to a graphical window:

```
System.out.println (tempMsg);          » becomes «
g.drawString (tempMsg, 5, 35);
```

```
Hello applet World!
```

In our JDK applet exercise, this drawString statement causes no data to be displayed. In contrast, our J++ application exercise caused the text null to be printed.

- We were able to simply use the existing version of ErrorMsg in our applets. That is, we did not need to create two versions of ErrorMsg, one for the application and one for the applet.
- We did need to instruct the compile environment where to look for the ErrorMsg class when it was not part of the current directory. We used the CLASSPATH argument (or project setting) to inform the compile environment of the directory that contained ErrorMsg.class
- In the case of the JDK, we also needed to inform the execution environment (appletviewer.exe) where it should look for the ErrorMsg class.

- As we did with the application HelloWorld the applet was then extended to contain two instances of ErrorMsg, each with its own data members.

```
ErrorMsg myErrorMsg2 = new ErrorMsg ();
myErrorMsg2.setErrorMsg ("Some Text for #2");
```

- To show that two unique data members with the same name exist in HelloWorld (one for each object of type ErrorMsg), we displayed both data members. The one associated with myErrorMsg2 contained "Some Text for #2," and the one associated with myErrorMsg contained "Some Text".

```
tempMsg = myErrorMsg2.getErrorMsg ();
g.drawString (tempMsg, 5, 75);
tempMsg = myErrorMsg.getErrorMsg ();
g.drawString (tempMsg, 5, 85);
```

- Finally, we showed how ErrorMsg could define two variations on the same method. The new variation accepted one character argument and is the argument that was set to U. Then the new method would convert the return message all upper case.
- // Define a variation on the public method getErrorMsg.

```
public String getErrorMsg (char caseFlag) {
String returnMsg;
```

- // Set the local variable returnMsg to the data member msgText.

```
     returnMsg = msgText;
```

- // Convert to all upper case, if requested.

```
     if (caseFlag == 'U')
          returnMsg = returnMsg.toUpperCase ();
```

- // Return from this method, and return the String variable.

```
     return (returnMsg);
  }
```

This method could have been simplified as follows:

- // Define a variation on the public method getErrorMsg.

```
public String getErrorMsg (char caseFlag) {
```

- // Convert to all upper case, if requested.

```
     if (caseFlag == 'U')
          return (msgText.toUpperCase ());
```

- // Else, simply return from this method, with the String data
  // member.

```
     return (msgText);
  }
```

- HelloWorld can use this new method to request a return message that is all upper case.

```
tempMsg = myErrorMsg.getErrorMsg ('U');
System.out.println (tempMsg);
```

```
Hello applet World!

Some Text
Some New Text

Some Text for #2
Some New Text
SOME NEW TEXT
```

HELLOWORLD—THE APPLICATION

```
public class HelloWorld {
     public static void main(String args[]) {
          String tempMsg;
```

// Our original println statement:

```
          System.out.println("Hello World!");
```

```
// Create a new instance of the ErrorMsg class.

    ErrorMsg myErrorMsg = new ErrorMsg ();

// Get the value of the text item in ErrorMsg by calling the getErrorMsg
// method.

        tempMsg = myErrorMsg.getErrorMsg ();

// Print the contents of the String returned by this method.

        System.out.println (tempMsg);

// Set the text item in ErrorMsg to some text String, and print its contents:

        myErrorMsg.setErrorMsg ("Some Text");
        tempMsg = myErrorMsg.getErrorMsg ();
        System.out.println (tempMsg);

// Call the setErrorMsg method again to setErrorMsg to some other text.

        myErrorMsg.setErrorMsg ("Some New Text");
        tempMsg = myErrorMsg.getErrorMsg ();
        System.out.println (tempMsg);

// Create a new instance of the ErrorMsg class.

        ErrorMsg myErrorMsg2 = new ErrorMsg ();

// Set the text item to some text String, and print its contents.

        myErrorMsg2.setErrorMsg ("Some Text for #2");
        tempMsg = myErrorMsg2.getErrorMsg ();
        System.out.println (tempMsg);

// Print the text item in the original object.

        tempMsg = myErrorMsg.getErrorMsg ();
        System.out.println (tempMsg);

// Call the new variation of the getErrorMsg method.
// This variation will return an all upper case message.

        tempMsg = myErrorMsg.getErrorMsg ('U');
        System.out.println (tempMsg);

    }
}
```

HELLOWORLD—THE APPLET

```
import java.applet.Applet;
import java.awt.Graphics;

public class HelloWorld extends Applet {

     public void paint(Graphics g) {
          String tempMsg;
          g.drawString("Hello applet World!", 5, 25);
```

// Create a new instance of the ErrorMsg class.

```
          ErrorMsg myErrorMsg = new ErrorMsg ();
```

// Print the contents of the public data member msgText in our class.

```
          tempMsg = myErrorMsg.getErrorMsg ();
          g.drawString (tempMsg, 5, 35);
```

// Set msgText to some text String, and print its contents.

```
          myErrorMsg.setErrorMsg ("Some Text");
          tempMsg = myErrorMsg.getErrorMsg ();
          g.drawString (tempMsg, 5, 45);
```

// Call the setErrorMsg method to set the text to some other text, and print its
// contents.

```
          myErrorMsg.setErrorMsg ("Some New Text");
          tempMsg = myErrorMsg.getErrorMsg ();
          g.drawString (tempMsg, 5, 55);
```

// Create a new instance of the ErrorMsg class.

```
          ErrorMsg myErrorMsg2 = new ErrorMsg ();
```

// Set the text item to some text String, and print its contents.

```
          myErrorMsg2.setErrorMsg ("Some Text for #2");
          tempMsg = myErrorMsg2.getErrorMsg ();
          g.drawString (tempMsg, 5, 75);
```

// Print the text item in the original object.

```
        tempMsg = myErrorMsg.getErrorMsg ();
        g.drawString (tempMsg, 5, 85);
```

// Call the new variation of the getErrorMsg method.

// This variation will return an all upper case message.

```
        tempMsg = myErrorMsg.getErrorMsg ('U');
        g.drawString (tempMsg, 5, 95);

    }
}
```

ERRORMSG—THE CLASS

```
public class ErrorMsg {
```

// Define some public class instance variables.

```
        public String msgText = " ";
        public int  msgSize;
```

// Define a public method.

```
        public void setErrorMsg (String inputMsg) {
```

// Modify one of the public variables. Set this variable to the text String that // was passed as a parameter.

```
            msgText = inputMsg;
```

// Return from this method. Since this method has no return value (i.e., it is // declared as *void*), no return statement is necessary.

```
        }
```

// Define another public method.

```
        public String getErrorMsg () {
            String returnMsg;
```

// Set the local variable returnMsg to the data member msgText.

```
            returnMsg = msgText;
```

// Return from this method, and return this String variable.

```
            return (returnMsg);
        }
```

// Define a variation on the public method getErrorMsg.

```
        public String getErrorMsg (char caseFlag) {
            String returnMsg;
```

// Set the local variable returnMsg to the data member msgText.

```
            returnMsg = msgText;
```

// Convert to all upper case, if requested.

```
            if (caseFlag == 'U')
                returnMsg = returnMsg.toUpperCase ();
```

// Return from this method, and return the String variable.

```
            return (returnMsg);
        }

}
```

CHAPTER

4

Class Members

We can continue to extend our examples in order to explore other Java concepts.

The principal of **DATA ENCAPSULATION** is similar to the difference between a subroutine's working storage and its linkage section.

Cobol specifies that items in a subroutine's WORKING STORAGE can only be viewed and modified by the subroutine. Conversely, items in a subroutine's LINKAGE SECTION are constructed by the caller, then passed into the subroutine. Therefore, LINKAGE SECTION items are available to both the subroutine and the caller, and the items in a subroutine's WORKING STORAGE are not.

Suppose we want MYSUB to count the number of times it has been called. In this case, we would define a variable in WORKING STORAGE and increment it each time MYSUB is called.

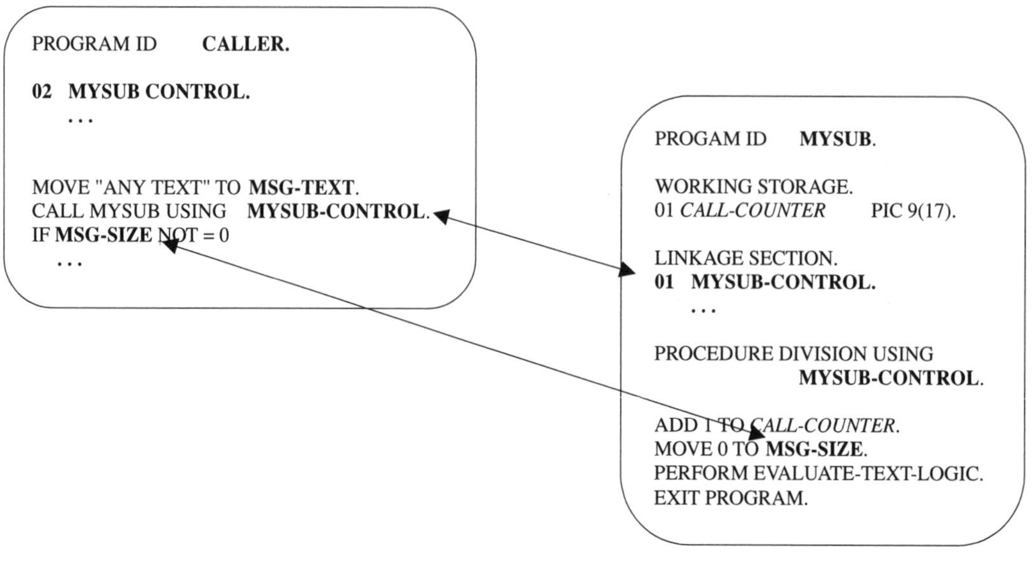

FIGURE 4.1. A subroutine has both LINKAGE AREA and WORKING STORAGE.

Figure 4.1 shows how LINKAGE SECTION items are available to both caller and subroutine, whereas WORKING-STORAGE items in the subroutine are private to the subroutine.

In this way, the subroutine specification defines what is available to external programs and what is private to the subroutine. At the same time, the subroutine is free to define any internal items, based on its own requirements. The calling program is not aware of these details.

MYSUB COBOL

```
PROGRAM-ID. MYSUB.
DATA DIVISION.

WORKING-STORAGE SECTION.
01 CALL-COUNTER                         PIC S9(17) COMP-3 VALUE 0.

LINKAGE SECTION.
01 MYSUB-CONTROL.
    03   MYSUB-ACTION-SWITCH            PIC X.
         88 MYSUB-ACTION-EVALUATE                 VALUE "E".
         88 MYSUB-ACTION-SET-AND-EVALUATE         VALUE "S".
```

```
        03   MSG-TEXT                                PIC X(20).
        03   MSG-SIZE                                PIC 9(8).

    01 TEXT-STRING                        PIC X(20).

    PROCEDURE DIVISION USING MYSUB-CONTROL, TEXT-STRING.

    MYSUB-INITIAL SECTION.
    MYSUB-INITIAL-S.
```

* Increment the counter variable in WORKING-STORAGE
* SECTION.

```
        ADD 1 TO CALL-COUNTER.
```

* Perform some function to detect the number of arguments.

```
        PERFORM GET-ARGUMENT-COUNT.
```

* Determine whether TEXT-STRING or MSG-TEXT should be
* evaluated. Store the correct item in LOCAL-TEXT.

```
        IF ARGUMENT-COUNT = 2
             MOVE TEXT-STRING TO LOCAL-TEXT
        ELSE
             MOVE MSG-TEXT TO LOCAL-TEXT.
```

* Now, use LOCAL-TEXT in the subroutine's logic.

```
        IF LOCAL-TEXT = SPACES
             MOVE 0 TO MSG-SIZE
        ELSE
             MOVE 1 TO MSG-SIZE.

        IF MYSUB-ACTION-SET-AND-EVALUATE
             MOVE LOCAL-TEXT TO MSG-TEXT.

    EXIT-PROGRAM.
        EXIT PROGRAM.

    GET-ARGUMENT-COUNT SECTION.
    GET-ARGUMENT-COUNT-S.
```

* Set ARGUMENT-COUNT to the result.

```
          CALL "GET$NARGS" USING ARGUMENT-COUNT.
```

In this subroutine, CALL-COUNTER is a *private* variable and cannot be directly accessed by a caller. As a result, the number of times MYSUB has been called is not known by calling programs. CALL-COUNTER is available only to MYSUB. Of course, we could define a new ACTION-SWITCH that would allow us to get the current value of CALL-COUNTER as follows.

MYSUB COBOL

```
01 MYSUB-CONTROL.
    03    MYSUB-ACTION-SWITCH                   PIC X.
          88 MYSUB-ACTION-EVALUATE             VALUE "E".
          88 MYSUB-ACTION-SET-AND-EVALUATE VALUE "S".
          88 MYSUB-ACTION-GET-CALL-COUNTER VALUE "G".
    03    MSG-TEXT                              PIC X(20).
    03    MSG-SIZE                              PIC 9(8).
    03    MYSUB-RETURNED-CALL-COUNTER           S9(17) COMP-3.

     ...

 MYSUB-INITIAL SECTION.
 MYSUB-INITIAL-S.

     ...
```

*   If requested, return the value in the counter variable.

```
     IF MYSUB-ACTION-GET-CALL-COUNTER
          MOVE CALL-COUNTER TO MYSUB-RETURNED-CALL-COUNTER.
     ...
```

This type of interface would allow a calling program to ask MYSUB to return the number of times it has been called. An approach such as this one allows the subroutine designer to decide which internal variables to make available, and how a calling program should access them. In support of this design, CALL-COUNTER is managed as a *private* variable, and MYSUB-RETURNED-CALL-COUNTER as a *public* variable.

JAVA MESSAGES

In a similar way, Java variables can be *private* or *public*. Public variables can be directly viewed or modified by other classes, whereas private variables cannot. Java also supports *package* variables, which are somewhere in between (that is, they are available to classes in a defined group of classes called a *package*). Variables that are not declared as private or public will default to package variables.

ERRORMSG CLASS

```
public class ErrorMsg {

    public String msgText;
    public int    msgSize;
    private int   counter = 0;
            char  interfaceInUse;

    public void setErrorMsg (String inputMsg) {
        counter = counter + 1;
        interfaceInUse = 'S';
        ...
// Some logic
        ...
        }
  }
```

We can examine our new member definitions and how they are used:

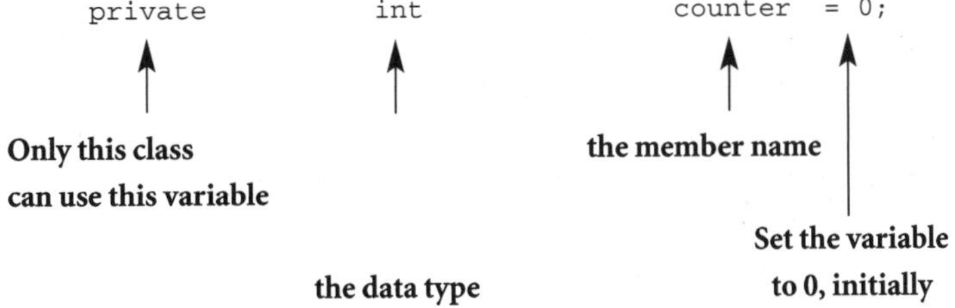

This example also introduces the concept of data variable initialization. Similar to Cobol's syntax, Java variables can be assigned an initial value. Unless a specific value is given, variables are initialized with their default natural values (for example, NULL for character types, and 0 for numeric types). The developer can assign other initial values to variables using the syntax = *value*.

Notice that the variable definition for `interfaceInUse` does not have an explicit *access control*. Therefore, it defaults to *package*:

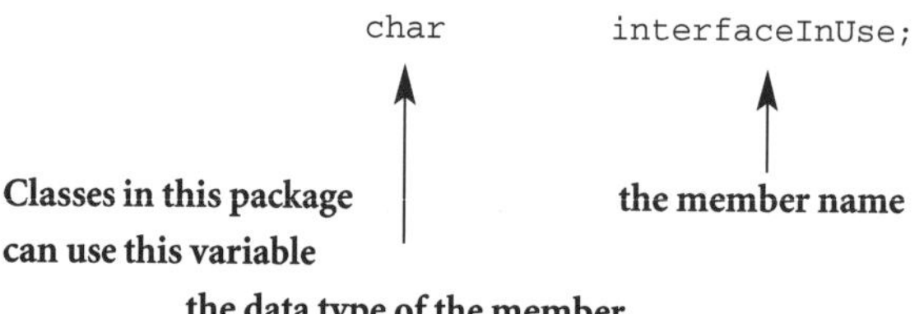

Finally, data members can also be assigned the *static* access control. This control specifies that only one instance of the data member exists, and it is available to all instances of this class in the current run unit. In this sense, these types of data items are like data items in a Cobol subroutine's WORKING STORAGE. That is, only one instance of this variable exists, and every class of this type can access it.

Static class members can be either public or private. If a static data item is private, then only classes of this type can access it (like WORKING STORAGE items in Cobol). If a static data item is public, then every other class can access it as well (like the EXTERNAL access control in Cobol).

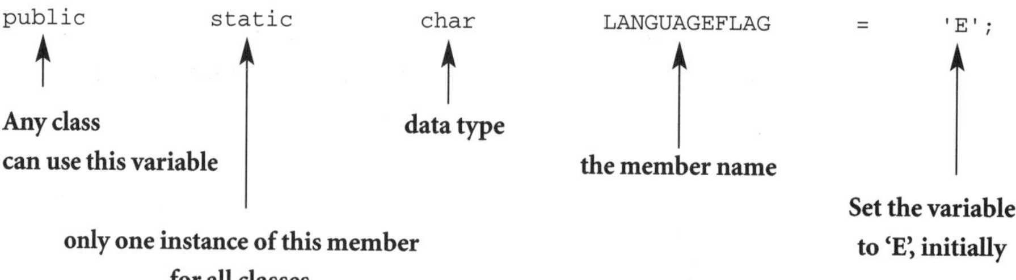

Just like data members, Java methods can also be declared as public, private, package, or static. For example, these statements:

```
public      void setErrorMsg (String inputMsg) () {
private     void countErrorMsg () {
            void checkErrorMsg (String inputMsg) {
public static  void SETLANGUAGE (char languageFlag) {
```

define four methods: one public, one private, one package method, and one that is a static method.

CLASSES, OBJECTS, AND MEMBERS REVIEW

This is a good time review some important concepts.

- A Java *class* is the blueprint, or specification, for all instances of its type.
- A Java *object* is an instance of a class.
- A calling program (a class itself) first creates a *new* object prior to using it.
- In the process, the calling program stores a *reference* to the object in an *object instance variable* (also known as a reference variable). This reference variable is a *handle*, or a pointer, to the object. It contains identifying information about the object, including information such as the object's storage location (in memory).
- The calling program can create many instances of a class and manages each instance by managing the reference variable.
- *Data members* (variables) and *methods* that are defined by this class are automatically members of this object. They are associated with this instance of the object and are accessed using the object instance variable as a prefix.
- A program can use these object instance variables to manage more than one instance of a class. For example:

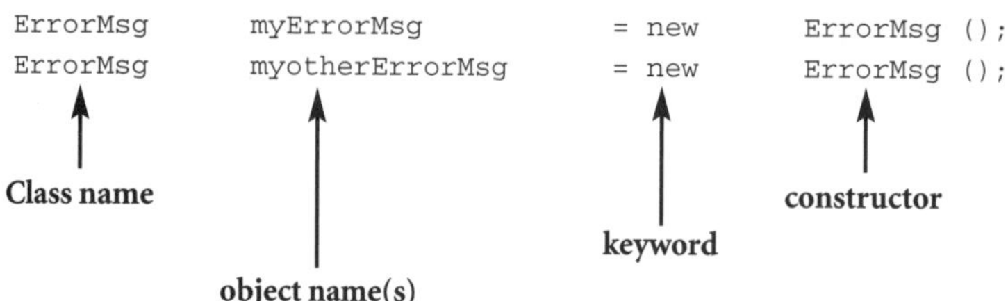

In this example, `myErrorMsg` is one object instance variable, and `myotherErrorMsg` is another. They point to different objects of type `ErrorMsg`.

The object instance variable is used to identify the object that contains the data members or methods:

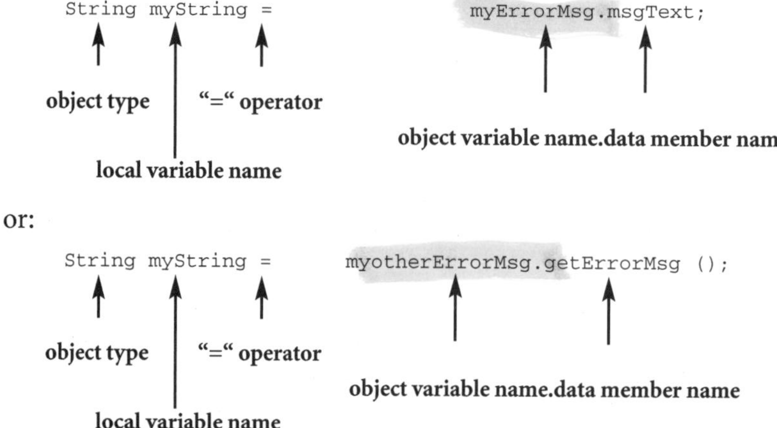

If you understand these terms and followed the descriptions of these concepts, you understand the most important OO concepts (classes, objects, and members). These concepts are the core principals (or building blocks) of any OO language, including Java.

OBJECTS AND COBOL

In our Cobol examples, we simulated the concept of object instance variables by creating unique instances of MYSUB-CONTROL:

```
01 MYSUB1-CONTROL.
     03   MYSUB1-ACTION-SWITCH                PIC X.
     03   MSG-SIZE                            PIC 9(8).
          ...

01 MYSUB2-CONTROL.
     03   MYSUB2-ACTION-SWITCH                PIC X.
     03   MSG-SIZE                            PIC 9(8).
          ...
```

The program that contained both of these definitions and also called MYSUB with each one would now have two unique instances of the variables in MYSUBx-CONTROL, reflecting the result of MYSUB's logic:

```
IF MSG-SIZE OF MYSUB1-CONTROL = 0
     ...
ELSE IF MSG-SIZE OF MYSUB2-CONTROL = 0
     ...
END-IF
```

Of course, any other calling program could use the name MYSUB-CONTROL or MYSUB1-CONTROL. These would refer to a different instance of this CONTROL.

This Cobol coding style represents concepts very similar to the Java concepts of *classes*, *objects*, and *members*. That is, a calling program first defines a unique instance of a class, creating an object that can be referenced by name (MYSUB2-CONTROL). This object variable name is used as a prefix to access the member variables for this particular object.

Although very similar, Java's implementation of these concepts is slightly different. One difference in particular probably causes the most trouble for Cobol programmers. That is, all members of a class, whether private or public, are associated with a *class instance* (or *object*). Members are associated with a particular instance of a class, and not with all instances of that class.

To better understand this from a Cobol perspective, imagine that each time you call a subroutine with a new MYSUB-CONTROL, a unique instance of that subroutine is created for you. Further, imagine that the system automatically calls an initialization section in the subroutine (actually, its *constructor*), so that this instance of the subroutine can perform any initializations required. And finally, suppose that every time a new MYSUB-CONTROL is used as a parameter to the MYSUB subroutine, the system would create your own private copy of the subroutine. Therefore, it would appear as if there were separate copies of all items in WORKING STORAGE (items like CALL-COUNTER), one for each instance of MYSUBx-CONTROL. Actually, it is possible to emulate this behavior quite easily in Cobol.

If your subroutine contains no call-specific WORKING-STORAGE item, and instead only uses items in the LINKAGE SECTION, then it behaves very much like an object. Instead of defining items in WORKING STORAGE, suppose the subroutine defines a slightly different representation of the items in the LINKAGE SECTION which includes items known only to the subroutine. In this case, these items can be considered private, compared to the public items known to the caller. Add an INITIALIZE action switch, and you pretty much have a Cobol object. In fact, this is more or less what every OO compiler does internally, regardless of language.

Let's complete our MYSUB example to present this concept. Up to now, we defined only public items in the LINKAGE SECTION and private items in MYSUB's WORKING-STORAGE SECTION. The items in WORKING-STORAGE will be shared across all instances of MYSUBx-CONTROL. Remember how we used this principal to create the COUNTER variable, which counts the number of times MYSUB is called?

We could create an instance of this COUNTER, one that is specific to each MYSUBx-CONTROL. We do this simply by defining a COUNTER item in MYSUBx-CONTROL. If only MYSUB (the subroutine) is aware of this item, then it could be considered a private variable. Finally, we need to define an INITIALIZE action switch so that we can properly initialize this variable.

```
01 MYSUB-CONTROL.
     03  MYSUB-ACTION-SWITCH                 PIC X.
         88 MYSUB-ACTION-INITIALIZE         VALUE "I".
         88 MYSUB-ACTION-EVALUATE           VALUE "E".
         88 MYSUB-ACTION-SET-AND-EVALUATE   VALUE "S".
         88 MYSUB-ACTION-GET-CALL-COUNTER   VALUE "G".
     03  MSG-TEXT                       PIC X(20).
     03  MSG-SIZE                       PIC 9(8).
     03  MYSUB-RETURNED-CALL-COUNTER         PIC 9(10).
*  The next item contains the private items in MYSUB-CONTROL
     03  MYSUB-PRIVATE-ITEMS                 PIC X(20).
```

Our MYSUB subroutine is expanded as follows:

```
IDENTIFICATION DIVISION.
PROGRAM-ID. MYSUB.
```

```
************************************************************************
* This routine accepts a text item as a parameter and                  *
* evaluates the text. If the text is all spaces,                       *
* MSG-SIZE will be set to 0.                                           *
* If requested, the text item will also be stored in the               *
* passed control structure.                                            *
* If the text item is not passed, then MSG-TEXT                        *
* will be evaluated instead.                                           *
* MYSUB will count the number of times it has been                     *
* with a particular MYSUBx-CONTROL and the number of                   *
* times it has been called using all CONTROLs.                         *
* MYSUB must be called with the INITIALIZE action when                 *
* any new CONTROL is to be used.                                       *
************************************************************************

DATA DIVISION.

WORKING-STORAGE SECTION.
01 CALL-COUNTER                      PIC 9(10) VALUE 0.
01 ARGUMENT-COUNT                    PIC 9.
01 LOCAL-TEXT                        PIC X(20).

LINKAGE SECTION.
```

* Below we have a view of MYSUB-CONTROL that is used by the
* MYSUB subroutine:

```
01 MYSUB-CONTROL.
     03  MYSUB-ACTION-SWITCH               PIC X.
         88 MYSUB-ACTION-INITIALIZE       VALUE "I".
         88 MYSUB-ACTION-EVALUATE         VALUE "E".
         88 MYSUB-ACTION-SET-AND-EVALUATE VALUE "S".
         88 MYSUB-ACTION-GET-CALL-COUNTER VALUE "G".
     03  MSG-TEXT                          PIC X(20).
     03  MSG-SIZE                          PIC 9(8).
     03  MYSUB-RETURNED-CALL-COUNTER       PIC 9(10).
     03  MYSUB-PRIVATE-ITEMS               PIC X(20).
```

* In the subroutine's definition of MYSUB-CONTROL,
* PRIVATE-ITEMS is redefined with items known only to the subroutine.

```
     03   FILLER REDEFINES MYSUB-PRIVATE-ITEMS.
          05   MYSUB-PRIVATE-COUNTER          PIC 9(8).
          05   MYSUB-OTHER-PRIVATE-ITEMS      PIC X(12).

01 TEXT-STRING                                PIC X(20).
```

```
PROCEDURE DIVISION USING MYSUB-CONTROL, TEXT-STRING.

MYSUB-INITIAL SECTION.
MYSUB-INITIAL-S.
```

* Perform some function to detect the number of arguments.

```
     PERFORM GET-ARGUMENT-COUNT.
     IF ARGUMENT-COUNT = 2
          MOVE TEXT-STRING TO LOCAL-TEXT
     ELSE
          MOVE MSG-TEXT TO LOCAL-TEXT.
```

* Increment the Global counter.

```
     ADD 1 TO CALL-COUNTER.
```

* Process the ACTION-SWITCHES.

```
     IF MYSUB-ACTION-INITIALIZE
```

* Initialize the instance counter.

```
          MOVE 0 TO MYSUB-PRIVATE-COUNTER
```

* If requested, return the value in the counter variable.

```
     ELSE IF MYSUB-ACTION-GET-CALL-COUNTER
          MOVE CALL-COUNTER TO MYSUB-RETURNED-CALL-COUNTER
     ELSE IF MYSUB-ACTION-EVALUATE
```

* This is a request to evaluate the text item.

```
          PERFORM EVALUATE-TEXT-ITEM.
```

* Increment the instance counter.

```
     ADD 1 TO MYSUB-PRIVATE-COUNTER.


EXIT-PROGRAM.
     EXIT PROGRAM.

EVALUATE-TEXT-ITEM SECTION.
EVALUATE-TEXT-ITEM-S.
     IF LOCAL-TEXT = SPACES
          MOVE 0 TO MSG-SIZE
     ELSE
```

```
        MOVE 1 TO MSG-SIZE.
    MOVE LOCAL-TEXT TO MSG-TEXT.

GET-ARGUMENT-COUNT SECTION.
GET-ARGUMENT-COUNT-S.
```

* Set ARGUMENT-COUNT to the result.

```
     CALL "C$NARGS" USING ARGUMENT-COUNT.
```

We have just defined a Cobol subroutine that behaves very much like an object! Two characteristics of the way we've used Cobol make this possible. Some data items in MYSUB-CONTROL are *public* (i.e., known to the caller), some are *private* (known only to the subroutine), but *all* data items (in the LINKAGE SECTION) are unique to a given MYSUB-CONTROL. No data associated with a particular MYSUB-CONTROL is stored in the WORKING STORAGE of the subroutine.

USING OBJECTS IN JAVA

Java naturally associates both member variables and methods with a particular instance of a class. This means that you should view class members as being associated with an instance variable (e.g., myErrorMsg.msgText), even though it is defined by the class.

It is this treatment of class members as properties of a particular class, along with the capability of class members to be declared as public or private, that implements the OO principal of *encapsulation*. A class is said to encapsulate some logic or behavior and to publish only those members that are appropriate for other classes to use. Class members are managed as if they were simply attributes of an instance of the class (i.e., an *object*). In many respects, a class is just another data type, one with user-defined attributes, and it includes whatever code is necessary to support those attributes. By extension, then, an object is a variable of type class.

This approach promotes the principal of *reuse*, that is, the practice of writing a class (a piece of code) that will be used by other classes. Consumer classes only have the view(s) of the class that the class designer thinks appropriate. Consumer classes then use these classes as if they were simply another type of variable. As we have demonstrated with our Cobol programs, it is certainly possible to write programs that do this in any programming language, but with Java, it is almost impossible to code in any other way.

Up to this point, we've introduced some OO concepts and described how Java supports these concepts. It's a good time to present a more complete definition of these Java terms and syntax.

JAVA DATA MEMBERS

Data members are variables in the normal understanding of variables in computer languages (for example, data ITEMS in Cobol). They are members of a class in the sense that they are attributes of that class and contain its current state information.

Data members can be qualified with access controls, which define how visible the data members are to other classes. Data members can be either public, private, or package variables. *Public* members are visible outside the class, and they can be set or evaluated by other classes. *Private* members are only visible inside the class; other classes cannot view or modify these variables. *Package* members are visible to all classes in a package (for now, you can think about a package as a sort of directory of related class files). Package is the default access condition.

Java also defines two other data member access controls: *Protected* and *Private Protected*, which are used to support inheritance; we will discuss these controls later, along with inheritance.

All data members are normally associated with an instance of a class (i.e., an object). As we discussed earlier, each new instance of a class contains unique copies of all of its variables, both public and private.

With any rule, there is an exception (Don't you hate it when you think you finally understand something, and then the instructor throws a curve ball?). *Class Variables* are data members that are associated with all instances of a class. These variables persist for the duration of the program and are shared by all instances of this class. In many respects, class variables are similar to items defined in a Cobol subroutine's WORKING-STORAGE, other than the fact that they can be visible to other subroutines. On the other hand, you can think of public class variables as analogous to Cobol EXTERNAL items.

Class member variables can also be qualified with the keyword *Final*, which means that this data member variable cannot be modified by any class. This control is commonly used to declare constants, that is, variables that are only used to set or evaluate other variables. These are very similar to how Level 77 items are used in Cobol.

Here are some examples:

ERRORMSG CLASS

```
public class ErrorMsg {
```

// public instance variables

```
        public String msgText;
        public int  msgSize;
```

// A private instance variable

```
        private int  counter = 0;
```

// A package instance variable

```
          char     interfaceInUse;
```

// A public static variable

```
        public static int     total_counter;
```

// A final (i.e., read only) variable

```
        public final     static int NO_TEXT_FOUND = 0;

        public void setErrorMsg (String inputMsg) {
             interfaceInUse = 'S';
             msgText = inputMsg;
             msgSize = msgText.length ();
             counter = counter + 1;
             total_counter = total_counter + 1;
             ...
             ...
        }
   }
```

Some other class would use these variables as follows:

CALLER CLASS

// Create an instance of ErrorMsg.

```
ErrorMsg        myErrorMsg = new        ErrorMsg ();
```

// Create an instance of a String variable and put some text in it.

```
String inputMsg = "Some input Text";
```

// Call the function setErrorMsg.

```
myErrorMsg.setErrorMsg (inputMsg);
```

// Evaluate the size of this instance of ErrorMsg using the constant
// NO_TEXT_FOUND

```
if (myErrorMsg.msgSize == myErrorMsg.NO_TEXT_FOUND) {
        ...
// Some logic
        ...
}
```

// Evaluate the number of times ErrorMsg has been called.

```
if (myErrorMsg.total_counter == 100) {
        ...
// Some logic
        ...
}
```

// A static class variable can also be identified using only the class name.
// Static variables are not associated with any instance of a class.

```
if (ErrorMsg.total_counter == 100) {
        ...
// Some logic
        ...
}
```

LOCAL VARIABLES

Java supports a concept of local variables, an idea without a good Cobol equivalent. A Java program can define a variable when it is needed, rather than right up front as part of the class definition.

Imagine that Cobol allowed you to insert variable definitions (e.g., "`01 MY-ITEM PIC X`") right in the middle of the PROCEDURE DIVISION. Furthermore, suppose that variables defined this way were only associated with the paragraph in which they were defined. When the paragraph completed, the variable would go away. Finally, suppose that another MY-ITEM variable could be defined in the same program but in a different paragraph. This instance of MY-ITEM would really be a separate variable, having nothing to do with the original MY-ITEM. You might wonder what kind of confused code that could lead to!

Java allows this sort of "as needed" temporary variable definition. You can just define variables as they are needed. There is no need to define them all up front, like Cobol. The language does attempt to tighten up some of the more egregious rules defined by C and C++. (Many C and C++ programmers have struggled to debug a program, only to discover that some instance of a program variable *x* was really a different instance of *x*, even though both instances have the same name.)

Temporary local variables do have some benefits, mostly in the area of efficient memory management. A block of code that temporarily needs a variable does not need to define it as an instance variable for the whole class. Instead, the programmer can define it when necessary, as if it were an executable statement. Then the system will delete the variable when the block of code is completed.

Java restricts the scope of the variable to the block of code in which it is defined. Therefore, a program can define counter variables (*x* appears to be some sort of a standard) as needed, confident that the compiler will detect conflicts in nested blocks of code. Variables that must be shared by multiple blocks of code must be defined as parameters or as class instance variables.

```
if (myErrorMsg.total_counter == 100) {

// Some logic
     ...
```

// Define a local variable.

```
int x;
...
}
```

// It will be deleted after the }.

Finally, values passed as parameters to Java methods are passed *by value.* This means that a copy of the variable is passed and not the actual variable. As a result, any passed values are implicitly local variables. We'll discuss more about variable scope in Chapter 7 when we look at Java's flow control construct.

PRIMITIVE DATA TYPES

As with any language, Java defines some native variable types that can be used to store and represent data. Many languages (especially C) define standard data types, but the implementation details for some types can vary slightly across systems, creating code and data portability problems. Java attempts to deal with these problems by proscribing explicitly these data types and how they are to be defined and implemented across systems.

Type	Description	# of Bits	Range Equivalent	Cobol
boolean	True or false	1	N/A	TRUE, FALSE
char	Unicode character	16	x'0000' to x'FFFF'	N/A
byte	Signed integer	8	-128 to 127	PIC X[1]
short	Signed integer	16	-32768 to 32767	PIC S9(4) BINARY[2]
int	Signed integer	32	-2147483648 to 2147483647	PIC S9(9) BINARY
long	Signed integer	64	-9223372036854775808 to 9223372036854775807	PIC S9(18) COMP-4[3] PIC S9(18) COMP-5
float	IEEE754 number	32	+/-3.40282347E+38 to +/-1.40239846E-45	USAGE IS FLOAT[4]
double	IEEE754 number	64	+/-1.79769313486231570E+308 - +/-4.94065645841246544E-324	USAGE IS DOUBLE[4]

1. Most Cobol compilers handle single byte characters as "unsigned", that is with values between 0 and +255.
2. Some Cobol compilers define BINARY as COMP-4 or COMP-5. Only values with four digits (-9999 thru +9999) are guaranteed to fit in an integer of this size.
3. The range of valid values may be limited on some compilers to those that fit in 18 digits.
4. Supported by some compilers.

These next types are not native types, but are instead standard classes defined by Java. They are often used in the same way that data types are.

String	Sequence of characters	16 (each)	Any set of Unicode characters	PIC X(nnn)[5]
Array	Group of variables	N/A	Any object or data type variable(s)	OCCURS
Big Decimal	Fixed precision number	variable	unlimited	PIC S9(n) COMP-3[6].
Big Integer	Fixed precision Integer	variable	unlimited	PIC S9(n) COMP-3[7].
Object	Object reference variable		An object reference variable for any class type	01 CTL-AREA

Values can be easily converted between the various data types, but in many cases, you have to be explicit. A *type cast* is used to indicate to the compiler that you intend to convert from one type to another; otherwise, the compiler might think you are making a mistake!

```
int     counter = 23;
float   bigNumber = 1.23F;      // 'F' indicates a float constant
double  biggerNumber = 123.45;
```

// Direct assignment from integer to floating point data types is possible.

```
bigNumber = counter;
```

// Direct assignment from floating point to integer data types is not possible.

```
counter = bigNumber; // this is a compile error
```

// Move the floating point number to the integer, using a cast. Of course, some
// precision may be lost, but you've told the compiler you know what you're
// doing.

```
counter = (int) bigNumber;
```

// Direct assignment from floating point to double is fine, but you need a cast
// to go from double to float;

5. Cobol strings are always fixed length 8 bit characters and blank padded to the defined size of the item. Java Strings are variable length Unicode characters and have an imbedded size attribute. We will discuss Strings and arrays in detail later.
6. Sometimes just COMP. Cobol's Packed decimal type.
7. Sometimes just COMP. Cobol's Packed decimal type.

```
biggerNumber = bigNumber;             // OK
bigNumber = biggerNumber;             // an error
bigNumber = (float) biggerNumber;     // OK
```

METHOD MEMBERS

Method members are the functions that a class provides. This concept is similar to our Cobol subroutine which provided multiple functions based on an ACTION-SWITCH. Method members are identified by their names (e.g., setErrorMsg) and their method signatures (that is, the types and number of parameters). Method member references are distinguished from data member references by an argument definition (or ( ), for no arguments).

Remember how class data members could be made visible or invisible to other classes? Class method members can also be qualified with access controls. These controls define whether other classes can access methods directly. Class methods members can be either public, private, or package methods.

Similar to data members, Java also provides a type of method that is not associated with any instance of a class but rather with all instances of a class. These are called *class methods*. Since class methods do not belong to an instance of a class, class methods can access only static variables, not instance variables. Such methods are helpful in managing static variables; for example, to reset a static variable based on some condition.

ERRORMSG CLASS

```
public class ErrorMsg {

     public   String msgText;
     public   int    msgSize;
     private  int    counter = 0;
              char   interfaceInUse;
     public   static int  total_counter;
     public   final   static int   NO_TEXT_FOUND = 0;
```

// A static initializer method with no name and no parameters

```
     static {
          total_counter = 0;
     }
```

// A public method with no parameters

```
public void setErrorMsg () {
}
```

// A public method with the same name and one parameter of type String

// This is actually a different method, or interface definition.

```
public void setErrorMsg (String inputMsg) {
     interfaceInUse = 'S';
     msgText = inputMsg;
     msgSize = msgText.length ();
```

// Call the manageCounters method.

```
     manageCounters ();
}
```

// A package method named manageCounters

// This method is only visible to other classes in this package.

```
void manageCounters () {
     counter = counter + 1;
     total_counter = total_counter + 1;
}

}
```

Classes can also define *Static Initializer* code. Similar to class variables, this is a block of code that will be executed when the first instance of the class is initiated by a runtime. Often this code will perform special initialization logic for the static class variables. In fact, only static class variables can be accessed by the initializer code. There are no member variables available to this code, since class initializer code is performed only once and before any instances of the class have been created.

ERRORMSG CLASS

```
public class ErrorMsg {
```

// public instance variables

```
public String msgText;
public int    msgSize;
```

// A public class variable

```
public static int     TOTAL_COUNTER;
```

// A class initializer code block

```
static void   TOTAL_COUNTER (){
     TOTAL_COUNTER = 1;
}
```

// A regular instance method

```
    public  void  setErrorMsg  (String inputMsg) {
         ...
         ...
    }
}
```

CONSTRUCTORS

We promised to talk about constructors, and this is the time. When an object is first instantiated (with the *new* operator), the compiler will call its *constructor*. This is a special built-in method that performs any initialization logic that may be required by that class. This perform-one-time-only method exists in every object, even if the class designer didn't explicitly define it.

As with any method, a class can have more than one constructor; each one is identified by a unique parameter signature. By default, every class will have at least one constructor, a method that accepts no parameters. This default constructor will be generated by the compiler if the class has no constructors defined for it. Sometimes the default constructor is called the 'no arguments' constructor.

These constructor methods are useful for any number of reasons: for example, to initialize an important member of the object. The programmer defines a constructor by declaring a special method in the class. This method must be the same name *exactly* as the class and have no return type.

```
public class ErrorMsg  {
     public  static  int  total_counter;
```

// A constructor definition for this class. Note that all constructors have the

// same name as the class. This constructor has no parameters

```
ErrorMsg () {
     total_counter = -1;
}
```

// A regular class instance method with no parameters

```
public static void resetErrorMsgCount () {
      total_counter = 0;
}
```

As in regular method definitions, a class can have more than one constructor definition. They are identified by their signature, or number and types of parameters.

```
public class ErrorMsg  {
     public  static  int   total_counter;
```

// A constructor for this class. Note that this constructor has no parameters

```
ErrorMsg () {
     total_counter = -1;
}
```

// A constructor for this class that is passed one parameter.

```
ErrorMsg (String initialMsgText) {
     total_counter = -1;
     msgText = initialMsgText;
}
```

The class consumer does not explicitly *call* the constructor method. Instead, the *new* operation implicitly calls it. The class consumer identifies which constructor to call by adding parameters to the *new* operation.

// Create an instance of ErrorMsg.

// The constructor with no parameters will be called.

```
ErrorMsg      myErrorMsg = new      ErrorMsg ();
```

// Create another instance of ErrorMsg.

// The constructor with one parameters will be called.

```
ErrorMsg myotherErrorMsg = new ErrorMsg ("Some Text");
```

A constructor can call some other constructor in the current class. This is useful if a class has more than one constructor definition but would like to share some code between them. The *this* keyword is used as an object reference variable that points to the current object.

// The standard constructor for a class

// It is passed no parameters.

```
ErrorMsg () {
     total_counter = -1;
}
```

// A constructor for this same class that is passed one parameter

// It will call the standard constructor (to initialize the counter member).

```
ErrorMsg (String initialMsgText) {
     this.ErrorMsg        // Perform the standard constructor
     msgText = initialMsgText;
}
```

EXERCISES: CLASS MEMBERS

Time to revisit our example classes, and try out all these new ideas.

USING JAVA 2'S JDK

1. Using a text editor, edit the Java source file ErrorMsg.java in the java4cobol directory. We will add some additional variables to it and examine how a calling program can access these variables. Add the **bold** lines of code to the beginning of the file so that it looks like this:

```
public class ErrorMsg {
```

```
// Define some public class instance variables.

        public String msgText = " ";
        public int  msgSize;

// Define some private class instance variables.

        private int  counter = 0;
        char interfaceInUse;

// Define a public method.

        public void setErrorMsg (String inputMsg) {

// Modify some of the private variables.

            counter = counter + 1;
            interfaceInUse = 'S';

// Modify one of the public variables. Set this variable to the text String
// parameter.

            msgText = inputMsg;

// Set this variable to the length of the text String.

            msgSize = msgText.length ();

// Return from this method. Since this method has no return value (i.e., it is
// declared as void), no return statement is necessary.

        }

. . .
```

2. Compile the class in the DOS command window:

➢ javac ErrorMsg.java

3. Modify HelloWorld so that it uses these new members. With the text editor, edit the Java source file HelloWorld.java in the java4cobol directory. Add the **bold** lines of code after the third println statement so that it looks like this:

// Set the text item in ErrorMsg to some text String, and print its contents:

```
myErrorMsg.setErrorMsg ("Some Text");
tempMsg = myErrorMsg.getErrorMsg ();
System.out.println (tempMsg);
```

// Print the contents of ErrorMsgs String data member directly.

```
System.out.println (myErrorMsg.msgText);
```

4. Save the file, and then compile and execute the program in the DOS command window:

➢ javac HelloWorld.java

➢ java HelloWorld

Your output window should contain these lines:

```
C:>javac ErrorMsg.java

C:>javac HelloWorld.java

C:>java HelloWorld
Hello World!

Some Text
Some Text
Some New Text
. . .
```

The second “Some Text” line in the output window is the result of your new println statement. This statement printed the text in data member msgText directly from the object myErrorMsg. It can do this because msgText has been defined as a public data member in the class ErrorMsg. For the sake of brevity, the entire output window is not shown here.

5. Now we will try to access ErrorMsg’s other data members from HelloWorld. Add the bold lines of code after your new println statement so that it looks like this:

// Set the text item in ErrorMsg to some text String, and print its contents:

```
myErrorMsg.setErrorMsg ("Some Text");
tempMsg = myErrorMsg.getErrorMsg ();
System.out.println (tempMsg);
```

// Print the contents of ErrorMsg's String data member directly.

```
System.out.println (myErrorMsg.msgText);
```

// Try to access the other data member (s) in ErrorMsg.

```
System.out.println ("msgSize " + myErrorMsg.msgSize);
System.out.println ("counter " + myErrorMsg.counter);
```

6. What happens when you try to compile this class (remember to save the file as a text file)?

➢ javac HelloWorld.java

The compiler knows that private data members cannot be accessed, so don't try it again!

7. Remove the offending statement, and recompile. Now try running the modified program:

➢ javac HelloWorld.java

➢ java HelloWorld

Your output window should look like this:

```
Hello World!

Some Text
Some Text
msgSize 9
Some New Text
Some Text for #2
Some New Text
SOME NEW TEXT
```

The data member msgSize (9) is now printed in the output window.

What is our conclusion? Public members (msgSize and MsgText) can be accessed outside the ErrorMsg class. However, private members (counter) cannot be.

8. Lets build a new method in ErrorMsg that will return counter. We will also adjust ErrorMsg so that counter is incremented for each method. Along the way, we will 'correct' our implementation of one of the setErrorMsg methods to make sure that the overloaded version of this method (the one with one parameter) reuses the original method.

9. Open the ErrorMsg class in the editor. Add the bold lines of code to the first getErrorMsg method, so that it looks like this:

```
public String getErrorMsg () {
   String returnMsg;
```

// Modify some of the private variables.

```
      counter = counter + 1;
      interfaceInUse = 'G';
```

// Set the local variable returnMsg to the data member msgText.

```
      returnMsg = msgText;
```

// Return from this method, and return the String variable.

```
      return (returnMsg);
   }
```

10. Next, adjust the second getErrorMsg method so that it looks like this:

// Define a variation on the public method getErrorMsg.

// Perform the standard getErrorMsg method.

```
public String getErrorMsg (char caseFlag) {
```

// Convert to all upper case, if requested.

```
      if (caseFlag == 'U')
           return (getErrorMsg().toUpperCase ());
      else
```

// Return from this method, without conversion.

```
        return (getErrorMsg());
    }
```

11. Finally, add this new method to `ErrorMsg`:

// Define a method to return counter.

```
    public int getCounter () {
```

// Return from this method with the value of 'counter'.

```
        return (counter);
    }
```

12. Save this class, and then compile it in the command window:

➢ javac ErrorMsg.java

13. Now, we'll adjust HelloWorld so that is uses these new members.

Open the HelloWorld class in the editor. Add the **bold** lines of code after the print of msgSize, so that it looks like this:

// Print the other data members in `ErrorMsg`.

```
    System.out.println ("msgSize " + myErrorMsg.msgSize);
    System.out.println ("interface " + myErrorMsg.interfaceInUse);
    System.out.println ("counter " + myErrorMsg.getCounter ());
```

14. Save the source file, then recompile and run the modified program in the command window:

➢ javac HelloWorld.java

➢ java HelloWorld

Your output window should look like this:

```
Hello World!

Some Text
Some Text
msgSize 9
interface G
counter 3
Some New Text
Some Text for #2
Some New Text
SOME NEW TEXT
```

msgSize, interface, and counter are now printed in the output window.

15. As another experiment, we'll adjust HelloWorld so that it prints out the data members after it calls the overloaded getErrorMsg method (that is, the one that accepts a parameter). Add the **bold** lines of code to the end of the HelloWorld class so that it looks like this:

// Call the new variation on getErrorMsg.

```
tempMsg = myErrorMsg.getErrorMsg ('U');
System.out.println (tempMsg);
```

// Print the public variables after performing this overloaded call.

```
System.out.println ("msgSize " + myErrorMsg.msgSize);
System.out.println ("interface " + myErrorMsg.interfaceInUse);
System.out.println ("counter " + myErrorMsg.getCounter ());
```

16. Save the source file, then recompile and run the modified program in the command window:

➢ javac HelloWorld.java

➢ java HelloWorld

Your output window should look like this:

```
Hello World!

Some Text
Some Text
msgSize 9
interface G
counter 3
Some New Text
Some Text for #
Some New Text
SOME NEW TEXT
msgSize 13
interface G
counter 7
```

17. For our last experiment, we will examine the behavior of local' variables, and observe how they are different from class variables. Add the **bold** lines of code to the setErrorMsg method and the first getErrorMsg method so that they look like this:

// Define a public method.

```
public void setErrorMsg (String inputMsg) {
```

// Define a local variable and increment it.

```
    int localCounter = 0;
    localCounter = localCounter + 1;
```

// Modify some of the private variables.

```
    counter = counter + 1;
    interfaceInUse = 'S';

. . .
```

// Define another public method.

```
public String getErrorMsg () {
    String returnMsg;
```

// Define a local variable and increment it.

```
        int localCounter = 0;
        localCounter = localCounter + 1;
```

// Modify some of the private variables.

```
        counter = counter + 1;
        interfaceInUse = 'G';
    }
```

18. Add the **bold** lines of code to the end of ErrorMsg:

// Define a method to return localCounter.

```
    public int getLocalCounter () {
        int localCounter = 0;
        localCounter = localCounter + 1;
```

// Return from this method with the value of localCounter.

```
        return (localCounter);
    }
```

19. Save this class, and then compile it in the command window:

➢ javac ErrorMsg.java

20. Add the **bold** lines of code to the end of the HelloWorld class so that it looks like this:

// Call the new variation on getErrorMsg.

```
    tempMsg = myErrorMsg.getErrorMsg ('U');
    System.out.println (tempMsg);
```

// Print the public variables after performing this overloaded call.

```
    System.out.println ("msgSize " + myErrorMsg.msgSize);
    System.out.println ("interface " + myErrorMsg.interfaceInUse);
    System.out.println ("counter " + myErrorMsg.getCounter ());
```

// Print the localCounter variable.

```
System.out.println
   ("localCounter " + myErrorMsg.getLocalCounter ());
```

21. Save the source file, then re-compile and run the modified program in the command window:

➢ javac HelloWorld.java

➢ java HelloWorld

```
Hello World!

Some Text
Some Text
msgSize 9
interface G
counter 3
Some New Text
Some Text for #2
Some New Text
SOME NEW TEXT
msgSize 13
interface G
counter 7
localCounter 1
```

Since you are a very clever programmer, try out these adjustments on your own in the HelloWorld applet. For your convenience, the completed applet sample code is on the CD.

USING J++

1. Select your "java4cobol" project from among the recent workspaces using this menu path:

➢ File → Recent Workspaces → java4cobol.

2. Choose the ErrorMsg class. We will add some additional variables to it and examine how a calling program can access these variables. Add the **bold** lines of code to the beginning of the file so that it looks like this:

```
public class ErrorMsg {
```

// Define some public class instance variables.

```
public String msgText = " ";
public int  msgSize;
```

// Define some private class instance variables.

```
private int     counter = 0;
char     interfaceInUse;
```

// Define a public method.

```
public void setErrorMsg (String inputMsg) {
```

// Modify some of the private variables.

```
counter = counter + 1;
interfaceInUse = 'S';
```

// Modify one of the public variables. Set this variable to the text String // parameter.

```
msgText = inputMsg;
```

// Set this variable to the length of the text String.

```
msgSize = msgText.length ();
```

// Return from this method. Since this method has no return value (i.e., it is // declared as void), no return statement is necessary.

```
}
```

3. Compile this class using this menupath:

➢ Build → Compile ErrorMsg.java.

4. Next, select the HelloWorld class from this project. Add the **bold** lines of code after the third println statement so that it looks like this:

// Set the text item in ErrorMsg to some text String, and print its contents:

```
myErrorMsg.setErrorMsg ("Some Text");
tempMsg = myErrorMsg.getErrorMsg ();
System.out.println (tempMsg);
```

// Print the contents of ErrorMsg's String data member directly.

```
System.out.println (myErrorMsg.msgText);
```

5. Compile this class (Build → Compile HelloWorld.java) and then execute it. As we had done in previous examples, you can view the output window by using the Build → Start Debug → Run to Cursor method or by using the stand-alone runtime in a DOS window. Either way, your output window should look like this:

```
Hello World!
null
Some Text
Some Text
Some New Text
. . .
```

The second "Some Text" line in the output window is the result of your new println statement. This statement printed the text in data member "msgText" directly from the object myErrorMsg. It can do this because msgText has been defined as a public data member in the class ErrorMsg. For the sake of brevity, the entire output window is not shown here.

6. Now, we will try to access ErrorMsg's other data members from HelloWorld. Add the **bold** lines of code after your new println statement so that it looks like this:

// Set the text item in ErrorMsg to some text String, and print its contents:

```
myErrorMsg.setErrorMsg ("Some Text");
tempMsg = myErrorMsg.getErrorMsg ();
System.out.println (tempMsg);
```

// Print the contents of ErrorMsg's String data member directly.

```
System.out.println (myErrorMsg.msgText);
```

// Try to access the other data member (s) in ErrorMsg.

```
System.out.println ("msgSize " + myErrorMsg.msgSize);
System.out.println ("counter " + myErrorMsg.counter);
```

7. What happens when you try to compile (Build → Compile HelloWorld.java) this class? The compiler knows that private data members cannot be accessed, so don't try it again! Remove the offending statement, and recompile. Your output window should look like this:

```
Hello World!
null
Some Text
Some Text
msgSize 9
Some New Text
Some Text for
#2. . .
```

The data member `msgSize (9)` is now printed in the output window. The conclusion? Public members (msgSize and MsgText) can be accessed outside the ErrorMsg class. However, private members (counter) cannot be.

8. Let's build a new method in ErrorMsg that will return the value in counter. We will also adjust ErrorMsg, so that counter is incremented for each method. Along the way, we will correct our implementation of one of the setErrorMsg methods to make sure that the overloaded version of this method (the one with one parameter) reuses the original version of this method.

9. Choose the ErrorMsg class in the editor. Add the bold lines of code to the first getErrorMsg method so that it looks like this:

```
public String getErrorMsg () {
     String returnMsg;
```

// Modify some of the private variables.

```
     counter = counter + 1;
     interfaceInUse = 'G';
```

// Set the local variable returnMsg to the data member msgText.

```
     returnMsg = msgText;
```

// Return from this method, and return the String variable.

```
     return (returnMsg);
}
```

10. Next, adjust the second getErrorMsg method so that it looks like this:

// Define a variation on the public method getErrorMsg.

// Perform the standard getErrorMsg method.

```
public String getErrorMsg (char caseFlag) {
```

// Convert to all upper case, if requested.

```
     if (caseFlag == 'U')
          return (getErrorMsg().toUpperCase ());
     else
```

// Return from this method, without conversion.

```
          return (getErrorMsg());
}
```

11. Finally, add this new method to `ErrorMsg`:

// Define a method to return counter.

```
public int getCounter () {
```

// Return from this method, with the value of counter.

```
        return (counter);
    }
```

12. Compile this class using the menupath:

➢ Build → Compile ErrorMsg.java.

13. Now, we'll adjust HelloWorld so that is uses these new members.

    Choose the HelloWorld class in the editor. Add the **bold** lines of code after the print of msgSize, so that it looks like this:

// Print the other data members in ErrorMsg.

```
System.out.println ("msgSize " + myErrorMsg.msgSize);
System.out.println ("interface " + myErrorMsg.interfaceInUse);
System.out.println ("counter " + myErrorMsg.getCounter ());
```

14. Compile this class (Build → StartDebug → Run to Cursor). Your output window should look like this:

```
Hello World!
null
Some Text
Some Text
msgSize 9
interface G
counter 3
Some New Text
Some Text for #2
Some New Text
. . .
```

    msgSize, interface, and counter are now printed in the output window.

15. As another experiment, we'll adjust HelloWorld so that it prints out the data members after calling the overloaded getErrorMsg method (that is, the one that accepts a parameter). Add the bold lines of code to the end of the HelloWorld class, so that it looks like this:

// Call the new variation on getErrorMsg.

```
tempMsg = myErrorMsg.getErrorMsg ('U');
System.out.println (tempMsg);
```

// Print the public variables after performing this overloaded call.

```
System.out.println ("msgSize " + myErrorMsg.msgSize);
System.out.println
        ("interface " + myErrorMsg.interfaceInUse);
System.out.println
        ("counter " + myErrorMsg.getCounter ());
```

16. Compile this class

➢ Build → Start Debug → Run to Cursor

Your output window should look like this:

```
Hello World!
null
Some Text
Some Text
msgSize 9
interface G
counter 3
Some New Text
Some Text for #2
Some New Text
SOME NEW TEXT
msgSize 13
interface G
counter 7
```

17. For our last experiment, we will examine the behavior of local variables, and observe how they are different from class variables. Add the bold lines of code to the setErrorMsg method and the first getErrorMsg method so that they look like this:

// Define a public method.

```
    public void setErrorMsg (String inputMsg) {
```

// Define a local variable and increment it.

```
        int localCounter = 0;
        localCounter = localCounter + 1;
```

// Modify some of the private variables.

```
        counter = counter + 1;
        interfaceInUse = 'S';

    . . .
```

// Define another public method.

```
    public String getErrorMsg () {
        String returnMsg;
```

// Define a local variable and increment it.

```
        int localCounter = 0;
        localCounter = localCounter + 1;
```

// Modify some of the private variables.

```
        counter = counter + 1;
        interfaceInUse = 'G';
    }
```

18. Add the **bold** lines of code to the end of ErrorMsg:

// Define a method to return localCounter.

```
    public int getLocalCounter () {
        int localCounter = 0;
        localCounter = localCounter + 1;
```

// Return from this method, with the value of 'localCounter.

```
        return (localCounter);
    }
```

19. Add the **bold** lines of code to the end of the HelloWorld class so that it looks like this:

// Call the new variation on getErrorMsg.

```
tempMsg = myErrorMsg.getErrorMsg ('U');
System.out.println (tempMsg);
```

// Print the public variables after performing this overloaded call.

```
System.out.println ("msgSize " + myErrorMsg.msgSize);
System.out.println
          ("interface " + myErrorMsg.interfaceInUse);
System.out.println
          ("counter " + myErrorMsg.getCounter ());
```

// Print the localCounter variable.

```
System.out.println
   ("localCounter " + myErrorMsg.getLocalCounter ());
```

20. Compile this class

➢ Build → Start Debug → Run to Cursor

Your output window should look like this:

```
Hello World!
null
Some Text
Some Text
msgSize 9
interface G
counter 3
Some New Text
Some Text for #2
Some New Text
SOME NEW TEXT
msgSize 13
interface G
counter 7
localCounter 1
```

Since you are a very clever programmer, try out these adjustments on your own in the HelloWorld applet. For your convenience, the completed applet sample code is on the CD.

REVIEWING OUR SAMPLES

Let's review the changes we've made to both ErrorMsg and HelloWorld. Try to relate the sample source statements to the result (for example, the output) each statement creates. If necessary, rerun the samples, or look at the complete source code for this exercise on the CD. Feel free to experiment by yourself.

- Our ErrorMsg class was adjusted to include some private and package data members.
- HelloWorld could access the public (msgText, and msgSize) and package (interfaceInUse) data members directly but could not access the private (counter) data members.
- We needed to create a new method (getCounter) in order to access this private data member.
- We changed the second version of the method getErrorMsg (in ErrorMsg) so that it called the first version and then performed its custom logic. Notice that we did not need an object reference variable (like myErrorMsg) for this statement; we can just call the method. In this case, the compiler assumes that we mean this object (that is, the current object).

// Perform the standard getErrorMsg method.

```
returnMsg = getErrorMsg ();
```

// Convert to all upper case, if requested.

```
if (caseFlag == 'U')
    . . .
```

- Local variables are automatically created and then destroyed as needed. They are not shared by various blocks of code, even if these blocks of code are members of the same class. localCount was defined, initialized, and incremented in each method. Each method created its own copy of this temporary variable.

Here are a few more important notes:

- The println statement can accept many parameters. These are all converted into Strings and combined into a single print line. Therefore:

  ```
  System.out.println ("msgSize " + myErrorMsg.msgSize);
  ```

  results in this output window:

  ```
  msgSize 9
  ```

- The result of a method that returns a value (for example, getCounter returns an integer value) can be used as that data type. There is no need to store the result of the method in a temporary variable. Therefore, this statement:

  ```
  System.out.println
            ("counter " + myErrorMsg.getCounter ());
  ```

  results in this output window:

  ```
  counter 3
  ```

CHAPTER

5

Inheritance, Interfaces, and Polymorphism

INHERITANCE AND OBJECT-ORIENTED DESIGN

An important benefit of object-oriented languages such as Java is the ability to use the concept of *Inheritance*. This technique allows a class to be created that *extends* another class in some fashion. The new class might enhance or specialize the capabilities of the original class. This approach is a great alternative to the dreaded suggestion "I'll just copy that program and make a few changes". Before long, the developer will have two versions of the same program to maintain.

When one class inherits from another class, a relationship is defined between the two. The original class is referred to as the *base class* or the *superclass*, and the one that extends it is called the *derived class* or the *subclass*. Subclasses can themselves be inherited by other classes; and these new classes can in turn also be inherited. A typical object-oriented design will present a hierarchy of related base classes and derived classes. As a matter of fact, Java itself is an object-oriented design; everything is inherited from the *Object* base class (see Figure 5.1).

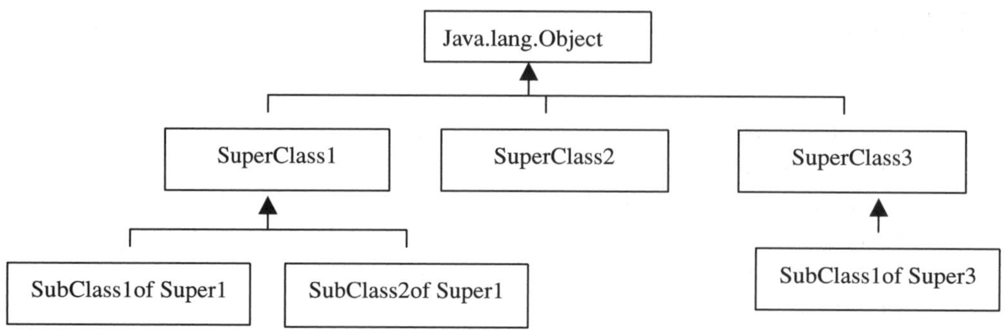

FIGURE 5.1. The subclasses in this diagram inherit from various superclasses. All of these classes ultimately inherit from the Java base class Object (Java.lang.Object).

In order to get the most benefit out of inheritance, a designer should attempt to organize class structures in advance (a "bottom-up" design). To do this, the designer must analyze application requirements and recognize those functions that are similar or are likely to be reused. These must be further examined to *abstract* the common functionality into an organized set of base classes. Then specializations of these classes are designed and constructed to meet the unique application requirements (a "top-down" implementation).

The process of defining the appropriate base classes and the appropriate class hierarchy is one of the most challenging aspects of proper object-oriented design. However, using a well-designed class hierarchy infrastructure is one of the simplest and most efficient processes in object oriented coding.

An object-oriented design uses inheritance for other benefits as well. It can provide for efficient enhancements to a system. Modifications to a system need be made only to the appropriate class in the class hierarchy; all derived classes will automatically benefit from this enhancement.

INHERITANCE AND OBJECTS

From a technical perspective, each subclass, in a sense, *contains* its superclass (i.e., its parent class). Each instance of a subclass automatically creates an instance of its *parent* class. Therefore, an object whose class type is a derived class logically has its own identity, *and* its parent's identity. Both the base object class and the derived object are instantiated (created) when the derived object is instantiated. Afterwards, the derived object can call functions in the base object without first creating the base object.

In the same way, a class (or program) that creates and uses a derived class can directly call methods in the superclass without explicitly creating the superclass. This is because all of the superclass's public methods become public methods of the subclass. The subclass can add its own members or modify the behavior of existing methods, but by default, the subclass contains all of the functions of the parent class.

INHERITING METHODS

Suppose that our ErrorMsg class is derived from a TextMessage class, and TextMessage contains a public method called getTranslation. This method returns a translated version of the message. ErrorMsg defines only one public method named getErrorMsg. Even so, ErrorMsg appears to have two public methods, getErrorMsg, and getTranslation. Figure 5.2 shows this.

A class that uses this type of derived class simply needs to create the ErrorMsg object. The TextMessage object will be automatically created. For example:

CALLER CLASS

// Create an instance of ErrorMsg.

// This will automatically create a new instance of the base class TextMessage.

```
ErrorMsg myErrorMsg = new ErrorMsg ();
```

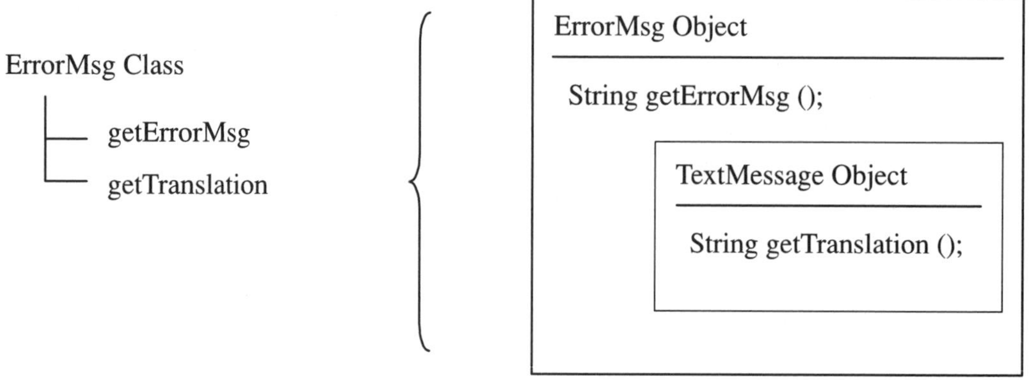

FIGURE 5.2. An object from the ErrorMsg class contains any objects from its superclass(es). Its public interface is the sum of all of the public methods it and its superclass(es) define.

// Call the translate method in the base class TextMessage, using the ErrorMsg
// object reference variable.

```
String FrenchText = myErrorMsg.getTranslation ();
```

Notice that our caller program creates only the subclass (ErrorMsg) and does not need to explicitly create the super class (TextMessage). Yet it still can call the parent class method (getTranslation), using the reference variable (myErrorMsg) of the subclass. Our caller class simply needs to create the subclass; all of the public methods of any inherited base class(es) are instantly available. Likewise, all data members of TextMessage (both public and private data members) are created at the same time. Public data members in TextMessage can be directly accessed by our caller class.

TECHNICAL NOTE: One of the first things that happens in every constructor is the creation of the base class(es) for this object. This is how the compiler makes sure that every class 'contains' its base class. The developer does not have to consciously do this, instead the compiler and runtime system do it automatically.

REDEFINING A METHOD

However, what if the developer of ErrorMsg needs to extend the getTranslation function of TextMessage in some fashion? In this case, the developer could simply define a function with that name in the class definition for ErrorMsg. Now, the getTranslation method in ErrorMsg will be performed by the caller class and not the getTranslation method in TextMessage.

ERRORMSG CLASS

// This class extends the TextMessage class.

// Therefore, TextMessage is the superclass, and ErrorMsg is the subclass.

```
public class ErrorMsg extends TextMessage {

     public void setErrorMsg (String inputMsg) {
          ...
```

// Some logic

```
          ...
     }
}
```

// Define a method named getTranslation. This overrides the method in the // base class (see Figure 5.3).

```
     public String getTranslation () {
          String localString;
          ...
  // Some logic
          ...
          return (localString);
     }
}
```

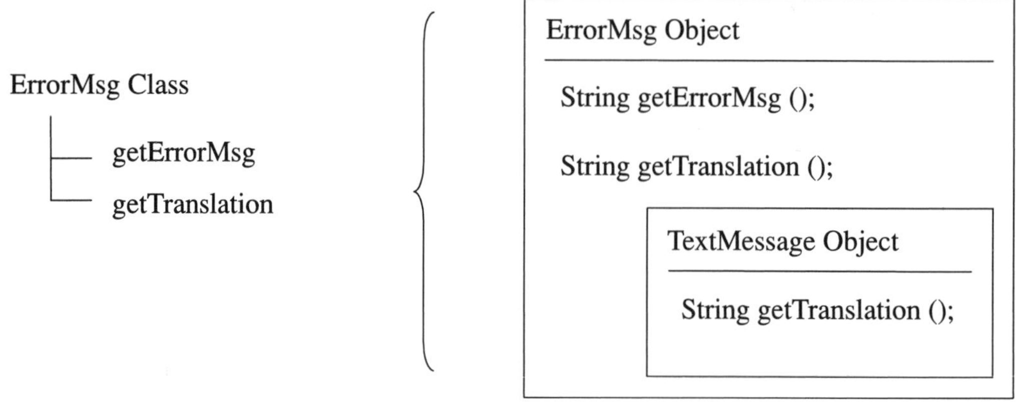

FIGURE 5.3. In this definition of ErrorMsg, the derived class (ErrorMsg) overrides the getTranslation method of its superclass (TextMessage). Yet the public interface to ErrorMsg remains the same.

Notice that the way the consumer class uses ErrorMsg does not change, even though we are performing a new function:

CALLER CLASS

```
ErrorMsg myErrorMsg = new ErrorMsg ();
```

// Call the translate method in the subclass ErrorMsg.

```
String FrenchText = myErrorMsg.getTranslation ();
```

EXTENDING A METHOD

The getTranslation method in the derived class (ErrorMsg) could call the original getTranslation method in the superclass (i.e., TextMessage) if necessary. This is often necessary with derived methods, in order to perform the original method, plus any specific logic in the derived method. The keyword super is the reference variable for the parent object (i.e., the object that was automatically created for this subclass).

ERRORMSG CLASS

```
public class ErrorMsg extends TextMessage {


    public void setErrorMsg (String inputMsg) {
        ...
  // Some logic
        ...
    }
}
```

// Define a method named getTranslation. This method overrides the
// method with the same name in the base class.

```
    public String getTranslation () {
```

// Call the base object's method.

```
        String localString = super.getTranslation ();
```

// Since this is an error message, change it to all upper case.
// Perform the toUpperCase function (this is a method that every String has).

```
        localString = localString.toUpperCase ();
        return (localString);          }
}
```

As before, the way the consumer class uses ErrorMsg does not change, even though we are performing yet a new function (see Figure 5.4).

CALLER CLASS

```
ErrorMsg    myErrorMsg     = new    ErrorMsg ();
```

// Call the translate method in the subclass ErrorMsg.

```
 String FrenchText = myErrorMsg.getTranslation ();
```

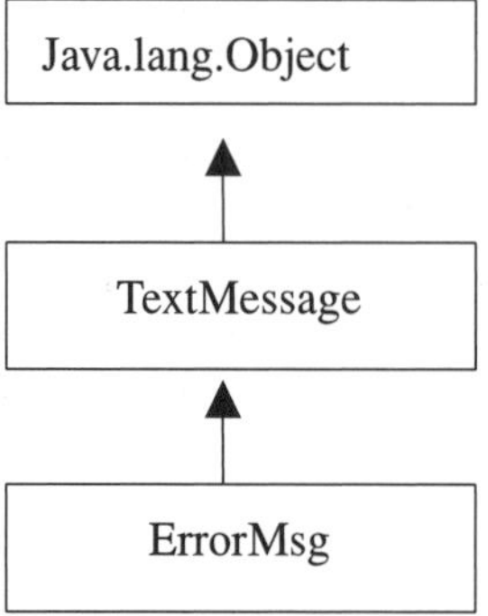

FIGURE 5.4. The class hierarchy for ErrorMsg.

WHY INHERITANCE?

Inheritance is not a concept with a good Cobol equivalent, so you're probably asking "What's the big deal here? Why would anyone want to do this?" The answer is best explained in the context of design patterns[1] a theory that has become an important concept in OO circles. Its basic premise is that application development problems (or more precisely their solutions) are best addressed by breaking down the problem and implementing the most elegant, flexible solution possible.[2] According to design pattern theory, a design pattern-based solution will be cheaper and easier to maintain in the long run. A design pattern analysis attempts to examine a problem using these criteria:

- **What is generic and what is specific about a particular solution?** That is, how can I represent my objects so that the characteristics shared by many objects are isolated from those that are unique to my object?
- **How can I abstract my design so that the things that are likely to change are isolated from those that are constant?** Since maintenance and customization is the most expensive part of any pro-

1. A concept described more fully in *Design Patterns,* by Gamma, Helm, Johnson & Vlissides (Addison-Wesley 1995).
2. "duh" a concept described more fully in Dave Barry in CyberSpace, by Dave Barry (Fawcett 1997).

gramming effort, it is important to concentrate the portions with high activity in one place, separate from those with modest activity.

- **How can I build a solution, so that it can adapt to changes that have not yet been anticipated?** What does it mean to build a structure with flexibility in the right places, without compromising re-use? A rigorous design can often be molded to fit new conditions, without necessarily collapsing the original solution.

When you feel up to it, read the *Design Patterns* book. It will provide unique assistance in breaking down complex problems and give you valuable insights into how you can build elegantly designed solutions.

Inheritance is a basic example of a design pattern. Inheritance allows you to organize elementary functionality into your base classes. This functionality is then extended in derived classes. However, all classes that inherit a super-type *will support some form of the basic functionality.* A consumer class can treat all objects of this super-type as if they are the same. Important design pattern goals are met; the stable and generic portion of your solution is isolated (in the base class) from the more dynamic and specific portion (in the derived class).

At the same time, these boundaries must be fluid. Derived classes may need to enhance, or possibly supplant, functionality in the base classes, without compromising the structural integrity of the system (without making things so complicated, that they become unmanageable). Since derived classes can override base methods, derived classes can always extend existing method behaviors as needed.

INHERITANCE, DESIGN PATTERNS, AND COBOL

The simplest way to understand inheritance from a Cobol perspective is to imagine that a subroutine's interface (that is, the items in its LINKAGE SECTION) can be promoted into a another subroutine's interface. Imagine that a subroutine (NEWSUB, for example) could pick one other subroutine (it must be a subroutine that NEWSUB calls) and that called subroutine's LINKAGE SECTION would automatically become part of NEWSUB's LINKAGE SECTION. If NEWSUB did not have a LINKAGE SECTION defined, then one would be automatically created for it.

Here is a definition for a shell of Cobol program named NEWSUB:

NEWSUB COBOL

```
IDENTIFICATION DIVISION.
PROGRAM-ID. NEWSUB.
DATA DIVISION.
WORKING-STORAGE SECTION.

PROCEDURE DIVISION.
START-PROGRAM SECTION.
START-PROGRAM-S.

         EXIT PROGRAM.
```

Not much there! Now, this is the definition for NEWSUB after NEWSUB *inherits* from MYSUB:

NEWSUB COBOL

```
IDENTIFICATION DIVISION.
PROGRAM-ID. NEWSUB.
DATA DIVISION.
WORKING-STORAGE SECTION.

LINKAGE SECTION.
```

```
01 PASSED-MYSUB-CONTROL.
    03   MYSUB-ACTION-SWITCH     PIC X.
         88 MYSUB-ACTION-EVALUATE        VALUE "E".
         88 MYSUB-ACTION-SET-AND-EVALUATE VALUE "S".
    03   MSG-TEXT                PIC X(20).
    03   MSG-SIZE                PIC 9(8).
01 PASSED-TEXT-STRING            PIC X(20).

PROCEDURE DIVISION USING PASSED-MYSUB-CONTROL,
                         PASSED-TEXT-STRING.
 START-PROGRAM SECTION.
 START-PROGRAM-S.
```

*   Check the passed parameters, and see if we should just call MYSUB.

```
     IF MYSUB-ACTION-EVALUATE OF PASSED-MYSUB-CONTROL OR
        MYSUB-ACTION-SET-AND-EVALUATE OF PASSED-MYSUB-CONTROL
          CALL "MYSUB" USING PASSED-MYSUB-CONTROL,
                             PASSED-TEXT-STRING.

     EXIT PROGRAM.
```

As a result of this change, NEWSUB appears to have some of the same properties of MYSUB. A program (perhaps CALLER) can call either MYSUB or NEWSUB, with the same control structures, and get the same results.

So far little of this makes much sense. Why not just have CALLER call MYSUB directly? But what if you need to enhance MYSUB without affecting other programs that already call MYSUB? In this case, NEWSUB could perform some additional logic and call MYSUB for the old logic.

Suppose we want NEWSUB to always translate the stored text field to all upper case. Programs that needed this feature plus the standard features of MYSUB could call NEWSUB. NEWSUB would now look like this:

NEWSUB COBOL

```
IDENTIFICATION DIVISION.
PROGRAM-ID. NEWSUB.
DATA DIVISION.
WORKING-STORAGE SECTION.
01 TEMP-TEXT-STRING                        PIC X(20).

LINKAGE SECTION.
```

```
01 PASSED-MYSUB-CONTROL.
    03   MYSUB-ACTION-SWITCH      PIC X.
         88 MYSUB-ACTION-EVALUATE            VALUE "E".
         88 MYSUB-ACTION-SET-AND-EVALUATE   VALUE "S".
     03     MSG-TEXT              PIC X(20).
     03     MSG-SIZE              PIC 9(8).
01 PASSED-TEXT-STRING             PIC X(20).

PROCEDURE DIVISION USING PASSED-MYSUB-CONTROL,
                         PASSED-TEXT-STRING.
START-PROGRAM SECTION.
START-PROGRAM-S.
```

*   Check the passed parameters, and see if you should just call MYSUB.

```
     IF MYSUB-ACTION-EVALUATE OF PASSED-MYSUB-CONTROL OR
       MYSUB-ACTION-SET-AND-EVALUATE OF PASSED-MYSUB-CONTROL
          MOVE PASSED-TEXT-STRING TO TEMP-TEXT-STRING
          CALL "MYSUB" USING PASSED-MYSUB-CONTROL,
                             TEMP-TEXT-STRING
```

*   Convert the stored text after calling MYSUB.

```
          INSPECT MSG-TEXT CONVERTING
            "abcdefghijklmnopqrstuvwxyz" TO
            "ABCDEFGHIJKLMNOPQRSTUVWXYZ".

       EXIT PROGRAM.
```

As you can see, this approach can meet some basic design patterns goals. Generic behavior is encapsulated in MYSUB, and more specific behavior is established in NEWSUB.

MORE COBOL DESIGN PATTERNS

There is an even more useful example of inheritance-like behavior in Cobol. As we've seen, a Cobol subroutine is generally a serviceable mechanism to encapsulate some algorithm. Sometimes, however, the restrictions of a Cobol subroutine hinder its use in complex solutions. This is because the subroutine is written as a *black box*, a device with well-defined inputs and equally well-defined outputs.

What happens if your requirements are such that the subroutine fulfills 80 percent or 90 percent of your requirements but not 100 percent? Normally, you'll have to choose among these solutions:

1. Extend the function of the subroutine to meet your requirements.
2. Code the specific requirements in your CALLER.

Any of these scenarios are fine, provided they are technically possible, but each has some potential deficiencies:

1. What if these requirements are too complex or inappropriately unique for inclusion in a subroutine? What if my extensions might break the original design objectives of the subroutine?
2. What if the requirements can only be met by modifying the subroutine's logic and not simply its input parameters? For example, it may be necessary to insert additional processing logic into MYSUB's evaluation function. This may not be possible to do in either NEWSUB or in CALLER.

Faced with these dilemmas, Cobol developers will often make the fateful choice to copy the subroutine's logic into another program and rework it to meet the requirements at hand. This is a classic example of how re-use objectives are overwhelmed by the complexities of a particular requirement. There is, however, a potential third solution to subroutine reuse in a complex environment. This solution requires planning in advance, but it can yield substantial benefits.

Some of the design pattern benefits of inheritance can be achieved if a subroutine returns to its caller, prior to completing a function, so that the caller can extend or complete that function.

If a subroutine allows this type of interaction, the caller can modify the subroutine's functions to meet its unique requirements. With this approach, it would not always be necessary to change the subroutine's functions in order to meet new requirements. Think of this type of subroutine not as a black box, but as a box with gloves that extend into the box. These gloves allow you to safely manipulate the internal workings of the box.

Believe it or not, it is possible to implement a form of inheritance with Cobol, even though the language does not directly support this concept. To do so, our interface will include a set of options switches and "traffic cop" items. The subroutine and the calling program use these to coordinate the program flow. The option switches are set by the calling program to indicate that a particular function is to be extended. The subroutine checks this flag and, if required, returns to the calling program prior to completing the function. The calling program then checks the traffic cop item, to see if a *mid function* return has been requested. If so, the caller can perform some additional code to extend the subroutine's function and then return to the subroutine. The subroutine will check the traffic cop and resume processing the incomplete function.

In Figure 5.5 MYSUB-CONTROL is extended to include the options and traffic cop items. Using these variables, the calling program can request that any of the functions available with ACTION-SWITCH be extended by the caller. MYSUB will return control to the caller *prior to* completing the function. The caller will then perform any additional logic for that function as required and then return to the subroutine.

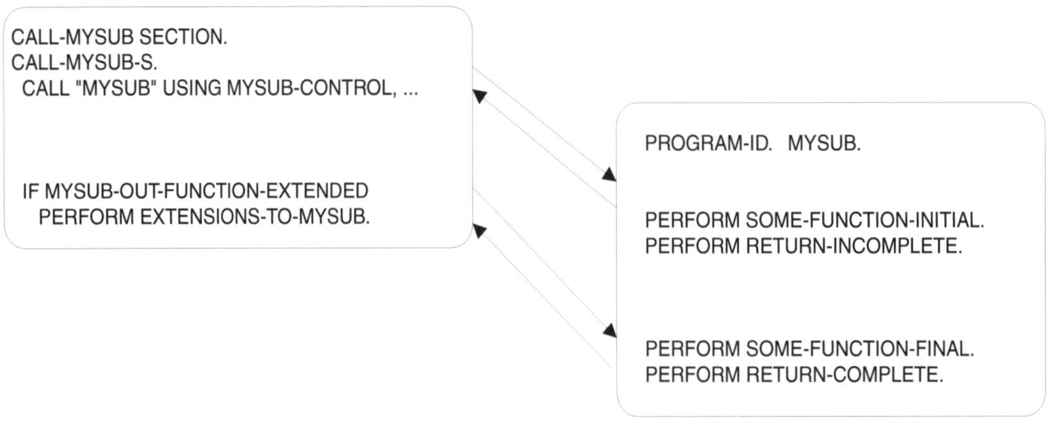

FIGURE 5.5. Extending a Cobol subroutine.

CALLER COBOL

```
 IDENTIFICATION DIVISION.
 PROGRAM-ID. CALLER.
 DATA DIVISION.
 WORKING-STORAGE SECTION.

01 MYSUB-CONTROL.
     03  MYSUB-ACTION-SWITCH                PIC X.
         88 MYSUB-ACTION-INITIALIZE        VALUE "I".
         88 MYSUB-ACTION-EVALUATE          VALUE "E".
         88 MYSUB-ACTION-SET-AND-EVALUATE VALUE "S".
         88 MYSUB-ACTION-GET-CALL-COUNTER VALUE "G".
     03  MYSUB-ACTION-EXTENDED-SWITCH       PIC X VALUE " ".
         88 MYSUB-ACTION-EXTENDED          VALUE "E".
     03  MYSUB-TRAFFIC-COP-IN               PIC X VALUE " ".
         88 MYSUB-IN-FUNCTION-EXTENDED     VALUE "E".
     03  MYSUB-TRAFFIC-COP-OUT              PIC X VALUE " ".
         88 MYSUB-OUT-FUNCTION-EXTENDED    VALUE "E".
     03  MSG-TEXT                           PIC X(20).
     03  MSG-SIZE                           PIC 9(8).
     03  MYSUB-RETURNED-CALL-COUNTER        PIC 9(10).
     03  MYSUB-PRIVATE-ITEMS           PIC X(20).

 01 TEXT-STRING                        PIC X(20).
 01 TEXT-CHANGED-COUNTER                    PIC 99999 VALUE 0.

PROCEDURE DIVISION.
START-PROGRAM SECTION.
START-PROGRAM-S.
```

*   Initialize MYSUB.

```
     SET MYSUB-ACTION-INITIALIZE TO TRUE.
     PERFORM CALL-MYSUB.
```

*   Prepare a text argument for MYSUB.

```
     MOVE "ANYTEXT" TO TEXT-STRING.
     SET MYSUB-ACTION-EVALUATE TO TRUE.
```

*   Request that MYSUB return before completion
*   MYSUB will reset this switch upon completion.

```
     MOVE "E" TO MYSUB-ACTION-EXTENDED-SWITCH.
     PERFORM CALL-MYSUB WITH TEST AFTER UNTIL
```

```
     NOT MYSUB-OUT-FUNCTION-EXTENDED.

     DISPLAY "MSG SIZE ", MSG-SIZE,
            " MSG-TEXT ", MSG-TEXT,
            " MSG TEXT changed ", TEXT-CHANGED-COUNTER,
            " times.".
```

*   Call MYSUB again without changing the TEXT-STRING.

```
     PERFORM CALL-MYSUB WITH TEST AFTER UNTIL
          NOT MYSUB-OUT-FUNCTION-EXTENDED.
```

*   Notice that the changed counter did not increment, but the call
*   counter in MYSUB did.

```
     MOVE "G" TO MYSUB-ACTION-SWITCH.
     MOVE " " TO MYSUB-ACTION-EXTENDED-SWITCH.
     PERFORM CALL-MYSUB.

     DISPLAY "MSG SIZE ", MSG-SIZE,
            " MSG-TEXT ", MSG-TEXT,
            " MYSUB COUNTER ", MYSUB-RETURNED-CALL-COUNTER,
            " MSG TEXT changed ", TEXT-CHANGED-COUNTER,
            " times.".
 EXIT-PROGRAM.
     EXIT PROGRAM.
     STOP RUN.

CALL-MYSUB SECTION.
CALL-MYSUB-S.
     CALL "MYSUB" USING MYSUB-CONTROL, TEXT-STRING.
```

*   If MYSUB returns before completion, perform some extended
*   functions.

```
     IF MYSUB-OUT-FUNCTION-EXTENDED
          PERFORM EXTENSIONS-TO-MYSUB.

 EXTENSIONS-TO-MYSUB SECTION.
 EXTENSIONS-TO-MYSUB-S.
```

*   Count the number of times MYSUB changes MSG-TEXT.
*   If MYSUB is about to change MSG-TEXT, increment a counter.

```
     IF MSG-TEXT NOT = TEXT-STRING
          ADD 1 TO TEXT-CHANGED-COUNTER.
```

MYSUB COBOL

```
IDENTIFICATION DIVISION.
PROGRAM-ID. MYSUB.

*****************************************************************
* This routine accepts a text item as a parameter and           *
* evaluates the text. If the text is all spaces,                *
* MSG-SIZE will be set to 0.                                    *
* If requested, the text item will also be stored in the        *
* passed control structure.                                     *
* If the text item is not passed, then MSG-TEXT                 *
* will be evaluated instead.                                    *
* MYSUB will count the number of times it has been              *
* with a particular MYSUBx-CONTROL and the number of            *
* times it has been called using all CONTROLs.                  *
*                                                               *
* MYSUB must be called with the INITIALIZE action when          *
* any new CONTROL is to be used.                                *
*                                                               *
* MYSUB can return before completing the text evaluation        *
* functions so that the caller can extend this function.        *
*****************************************************************

DATA DIVISION.

WORKING-STORAGE SECTION.
01 CALL-COUNTER          PIC 9(10) VALUE 0.
01 ARGUMENT-COUNT        PIC 9.
01 LOCAL-TEXT            PIC X(20).

LINKAGE SECTION.
```

*   Below we have a view of MYSUB-CONTROL that is used by the
*   MYSUB subroutine:

```
 01 MYSUB-CONTROL.
     03   MYSUB-ACTION-SWITCH                PIC X.
          88 MYSUB-ACTION-INITIALIZE       VALUE "I".
          88 MYSUB-ACTION-EVALUATE         VALUE "E".
          88 MYSUB-ACTION-SET-AND-EVALUATE VALUE "S".
          88 MYSUB-ACTION-GET-CALL-COUNTER VALUE "G".
     03   MYSUB-ACTION-EXTENDED-SWITCH        PIC X.
          88 MYSUB-ACTION-EXTENDED          VALUE "E".
     03   MYSUB-TRAFFIC-COP-IN                PIC X.
          88 MYSUB-IN-FUNCTION-EXTENDED     VALUE "E".
     03   MYSUB-TRAFFIC-COP-OUT               PIC X.
          88 MYSUB-OUT-FUNCTION-EXTENDED    VALUE "E".
```

```
    03   MSG-TEXT                          PIC X(20).
    03   MSG-SIZE                          PIC 9(8).
    03   MYSUB-RETURNED-CALL-COUNTER       PIC 9(10).
    03   MYSUB-PRIVATE-ITEMS               PIC X(20).
```

* In the subroutine's definition of MYSUB-CONTROL,
* PRIVATE-ITEMS is redefined with items known only to the subroutine.

```
    03     FILLER REDEFINES MYSUB-PRIVATE-ITEMS.
           05   MYSUB-PRIVATE-COUNTER           PIC 9(8).
           05   MYSUB-OTHER-PRIVATE-ITEMS       PIC X(12).

01 TEXT-STRING           PIC X(20).

PROCEDURE DIVISION USING MYSUB-CONTROL, TEXT-STRING.

MYSUB-INITIAL SECTION.
MYSUB-INITIAL-S.
```

* Perform the function to detect the number of arguments.

```
    PERFORM GET-ARGUMENT-COUNT.
```

* Perform the INITIALIZE function if requested.

```
    IF MYSUB-ACTION-INITIALIZE
        MOVE 0 TO MYSUB-PRIVATE-COUNTER
    ELSE
```

* Prepare the text argument and increment the counters, but only if
* not "continuing" from an incomplete extended function.

```
    IF NOT MYSUB-IN-FUNCTION-EXTENDED
        IF ARGUMENT-COUNT = 2
            MOVE TEXT-STRING TO LOCAL-TEXT
        ELSE
            MOVE MSG-TEXT TO LOCAL-TEXT
        END-IF
```

* Increment the Global counter.

```
        ADD 1 TO CALL-COUNTER
```

* Increment the Instance counter.

```
        ADD 1 TO MYSUB-PRIVATE-COUNTER.
```

```
*     Process the ACTION-SWITCHES
*     If requested, return the value in the counter variable.

      IF MYSUB-ACTION-GET-CALL-COUNTER
           MOVE CALL-COUNTER TO MYSUB-RETURNED-CALL-COUNTER

      ELSE IF MYSUB-ACTION-EVALUATE

*     This is a request to evaluate the text item.

           PERFORM EVALUATE-TEXT-ITEM.

*     On normal exits, clear the traffic cop switches.

      MOVE " " TO MYSUB-TRAFFIC-COP-OUT.
  MYSUB-TRAFFIC-COP-IN.

  EXIT-PROGRAM.
      EXIT PROGRAM.

 EVALUATE-TEXT-ITEM SECTION.
 EVALUATE-TEXT-ITEM-S.

*     Evaluate the text item, but only if we are not resuming a suspended
*     function.

      IF NOT MYSUB-IN-FUNCTION-EXTENDED
           IF LOCAL-TEXT = SPACES
                MOVE 0 TO MSG-SIZE
           ELSE
                MOVE 1 TO MSG-SIZE
           END-IF

*     If an extended function is requested, return to the caller.

           IF MYSUB-ACTION-EXTENDED
                PERFORM SET-TRAFFIC-COPS-AND-EXIT
           ELSE
*     Else, just move the TEXT in.

                MOVE LOCAL-TEXT TO MSG-TEXT
       ELSE
```

```
*     Else, continue the extended function, and move the TEXT in.

          MOVE LOCAL-TEXT TO MSG-TEXT.

SET-TRAFFIC-COPS-AND-EXIT SECTION.
SET-TRAFFIC-COPS-AND-EXIT-S.
    MOVE "E" TO MYSUB-TRAFFIC-COP-OUT.
MYSUB-TRAFFIC-COP-IN.

SET-TRAFFIC-COPS-AND-EXIT-NOW.
    EXIT PROGRAM.

GET-ARGUMENT-COUNT SECTION.
GET-ARGUMENT-COUNT-S.

*     Set ARGUMENT-COUNT to the result.

      CALL "C$NARGS" USING ARGUMENT-COUNT.
```

This technique can be very useful as a mechanism to define complex subroutines, subroutines whose functions can be extended by calling programs. For example, a set of complex subroutines might serve as a framework for processing multiple items in a list. The items in the list could be rows read in from a database. The list processing frameworks might provide standard list management functions, such as searching and positioning. In this case, the basic control logic necessary to process a list is in the subroutine, and the calling program provides whatever specific processing is required.

With the ability to extend the subroutine built right into the subroutine, it is often possible that these types of routines can be used (reused, actually) to meet new requirements. In order to make this technique useful, it is important that the subroutine be coded so that it returns to the caller at key points, indicating that the function is not complete. The caller can then perform any specialized code required.

A word of caution here: The coding technique necessary to support this mechanism in MYSUB is very ugly and is only recommended to the courageous Cobol programmer. Further, if it is appropriate to create a front-end to MYSUB (like NEWSUB), the ugliness must be promoted into NEWSUB. In that case, NEWSUB must define and manage an interface (i.e., a LINKAGE SECTION) very similar to MYSUB so as to allow the return from the MYSUB subroutine to percolate back through NEWSUB into CALLER.

In summary, the concept of inheritance, while possible to implement in Cobol, can be difficult to implement and requires a very serious commitment to code reuse. In contrast, Java makes these types of designs readily available and directly supported by the language.

INHERITANCE AND JAVA

As we've just noted, Java makes implementation of these concepts much easier, even fundamental. New classes can naturally extended existing classes. Developers need not worry about the program flow and interface specification issues we have discussed, since the compiler handles all of that automatically. Developers are encouraged to reuse existing class definitions to meet new needs—in some cases by modifying the base classes, in others by creating specialized classes that inherit the capabilities of the base classes. In Java, code should never be copied to reproduce or modify an existing class's capabilities.

Java's syntax to define inheritance is the keyword *Extends*. In our previous examples, ErrorMsg extended the class TextMessage. To add an additional level of inheritance, our example now has ErrorMsg extended by the classes PopupErrorMsg and PrintfileErrorMsg. (see Figure 5.6)

ERRORMSG CLASS

```
public class ErrorMsg extends TextMessage {

     ...

     public void setErrorMsg (String inputMsg) {
     ...
     }
}
```

POPUPERRORMSG CLASS

```
public class PopupErrorMsg extends ErrorMsg {
}
```

PRINTFILEERRORMSG CLASS

```
public class PrintfileErrorMsg extends ErrorMsg {
}
```

TECHNICAL NOTE: In other OO languages, a class can simultaneously extend multiple base classes (this is called *multiple inheritance*). In Java, a class can extend only one base class. Any Java class that does not explicitly extend another class is by default an extension of the Java.lang.Object base class. So, all classes ultimately inherit the class *Object*.

As had been previously discussed, any instance variables that belong to the base class are contained in the derived class. Also, public methods of the base class become public methods of the derived class. Of course, the derived class can define additional instance variables as well as new methods.

A Java class that extends another actually has a dual identity: its parent class identity and its own identity. Therefore, *all* members in the derived class (i.e., both new members defined only in this derived class and members derived from the base class) are referenced in the same way by the calling program. Let's extend (gruesome pun intended) our previous class definitions in order to highlight the Java syntax that supports and uses these concepts.

TEXTMESSAGE CLASS

```
public class TextMessage {

     public String msgText;
     public int  msgSize;
     ...

     public void getTranslation () {
     ...
     }
}
```

ERRORMSG CLASS

```
public class ErrorMsg extends TextMessage {

     ...

     public void setErrorMsg (String inputMsg) {
     ...
     }
}
```

POPUPERRORMSG CLASS

```
public class PopupErrorMsg extends ErrorMsg {
     public int windowWidth;
     public int windowHeight;
}
```

PRINTFILEERRORMSG CLASS

```
public class PrintfileErrorMsg extends ErrorMsg {
     public int linesToSkip;
}
```

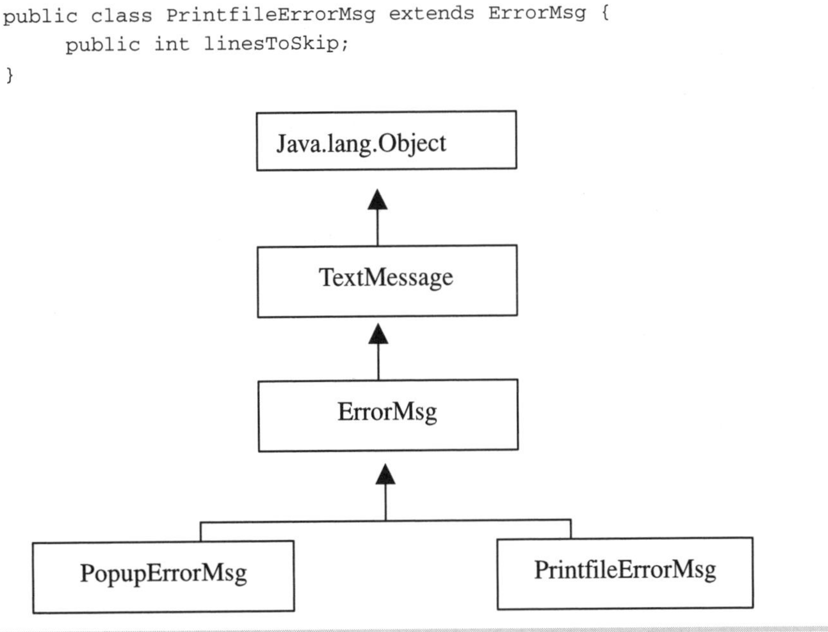

FIGURE 5.6. The class hierarchy for ErrorMsg, Printfile ErrorMsg, and PopupErrorMsg.

A consumer class (are we all members of the consumer class?) can use these derived classes in the following way:

CONSUMER CLASS

// Create new instances of a popup error message and a print file error message.

```
PrintfileErrorMsg myPrintMsg = new PrintfileErrorMsg ();
PopupErrorMsg   myPopupMsg = new PopupErrorMsg ();
...
```

// Capture the length of the pop up message myPopupMsg.
// Note that the public member msgSize is defined in the base class ErrorMsg.
// Even so, the derived class instance myPopupMsg contains it, and the consumer
// class uses it as if it where part of myPopupMsg.

```
int len = myPopupMsg.msgSize;
```

// Now, compare the size of the message to the size of the popup window.
// This public data member is defined in the derived class, not the base class.
// Yet the same ID (myPopupMsg) is used.

```
if (len >= myPopupMsg.windowWidth) {
...
}
```

Classes that are related through inheritance (people actually get inheritance through relations, but no matter) can use the member access control *protected*. The keyword *protected* extends the visibility of a member to any derived classes. Using this keyword, a base class can define members that would be appropriate for a derived class to access but would not be appropriate for a consumer class.

TEXTMESSAGE CLASS

```
public class TextMessage {
```

// This member is available to any class.

```
    public String msgText;
```

// This member is available to any class in this package and to all derived

// classes.

```
        protected int  msgSize;

        ...

    }
```

ERRORMSG CLASS

```
    public class ErrorMsg extends TextMessage {
```

// This member is available only to derived classes and not to other classes in

// the package.

```
        private protected int  counter = 0;
```

// This member is available to classes in this package.

```
                char     msgNumber;
```

// This member is available only to this class.

```
        private char     interfaceInUse;

                ...
    }
```

A class's methods can also be extended by a subclass. That is, a derived class can extend the capabilities of its base class's methods. This is called *overriding* the method. A derived class might override a base class's method to provide some specialized version of this method. A consumer class that creates a derived class can therefore call derived functions in the same way (i.e., with the same name and the same parameters) that the original (or base) function was called. The compiler will figure out which class method to call (in the original class or in the derived class), based on the actual type of the object. Suppose we have a class hierarchy as follows:

ERRORMSG CLASS

```
public class ErrorMsg extends TextMessage {

     ...

     public void setErrorMsg (String inputMsg) {
     ...
     }
}
```

POPUPERRORMSG CLASS

```
public class PopupErrorMsg extends ErrorMsg {
     public int windowWidth;
     public int windowHeight;
}
```

PRINTFILEERRORMSG CLASS

```
public class PrintfileErrorMsg extends ErrorMsg {
     public int linesToSkip;
     ...

     public void setErrorMsg (String inputMsg) {
     ...
     }
}
```

The classes ErrorMsg and PrintfileErrorMsg both define a method called setErrorMsg, whereas PopupErrorMsg does not define this method. However, a consumer class can call setErrorMsg using any of these three object types.

CONSUMER CLASS

// Create three objects of various types.

```
ErrorMsg          myErrorMsg = new ErrorMsg ();
PopupErrorMsg     myPopupMsg = new PopupErrorMsg ();
PrintfileErrorMsg myPrintMsg = new PrintfileErrorMsg ();
```

// Create an object of type PrintfileErrorMsg, even though its nominal type is // ErrorMsg.

```
ErrorMsg     myAnyMsg  = new PrintfileErrorMsg ();
...
```

// Now, call the setErrorMsg function for each of the objects.

```
myErrorMsg.setErrorMsg ("Any Text");
myPopupMsg.setErrorMsg ("Any Text");
myPrintfile.setErrorMsg ("Any Text");
myAnyMsg.setErrorMsg ("Any Text");
```

The first two function calls will perform the method setErrorMsg as defined in the class ErrorMsg. The next two function calls will perform the method as defined in the class PrintfileErrorMsg, since these objects belong to a class that has overridden (i.e., defined new versions of) this method.

You may have noticed that the object type of myAnyMsg appears to be a little ambiguous. Is it of type ErrorMsg or of type PrintfileErrorMsg? There are two answers to this question. Since any derived object always contains its base class(es), one answer is both. In other words, myAnyMsg is of both types, but since myAnyMsg was created using the constructor for the class PrintfileErrorMsg, it is a PrintfileErrorMsg. And since PrintfileErrorMsg contains an override for the method setErrorMsg, the setErrorMsg method for this object type will be called.

Often, a derived class will need to perform the original function in the base class. In this case, the derived class can use the operator *super* to refer to the function in the base class. Note that the base object is not explicitly created with a new statement in the derived class. Instead, it is automatically created at the same time as the derived object.

PRINTFILEERRORMSG CLASS

```
public class PrintfileErrorMsg extends ErrorMsg {
     public int linesToSkip;
     ...

     public void setErrorMsg (String inputMsg) {
```

```
// Call the setErrorMsg function in the base class ErrorMsg.

                super.setErrorMsg (inputMsg);
                if (msgSize != 0) {
                     linesToSkip = 1;
                 }
          }
    }
```

SHARING VARIABLES AND METHODS

When a class derives from another class, it inherits all of the class data members and methods from its base classes. This means that all of the variables and methods defined in the base classes are available in the derived classes. For example, look carefully at the statement in PrintfileErrorMsg that sets linesToSkip:

```
if (msgSize != 0) {
     linesToSkip = 1;
```

Where did the variable msgSize come from? PrintfileErrorMsg did not explicitly define this variable. The only one defined is in TextMessage, which ErrorMsg inherits.

But remember, PrintfileErrorMsg inherits from ErrorMsg (which in turn inherits from TextMessage). Therefore, ErrorMsg, PrintfileErrorMsg, and TextMessage all share the variables defined in TextMessage.

Any of the class instances in this hierarchy can treat msgSize as if it is contained in this class instance. At the same time, if any of these class instances modifies msgSize, then all of the class instances will see this modification. How does this work? When an instance of PrintfileErrorMsg is created, it automatically creates an instance of ErrorMsg, which in turn automatically creates an instance of TextMessage. The variable msgSize is created when TextMessage is created and all of these instances share this single copy of the variable msgSize.

HIDING VARIABLES AND METHODS

A derived class *can* create its own copies of base class variables or methods. To understand this better, let's examine how variable declarations (class data members) are handled.

Variable declaration statements that are at the beginning of a class definition and are named the same as variables in a base class will cause a new variable to be created. These new variables will hide the base class variables from classes that use the derived class (i.e., create an object of this class type) or that derive from it. Identically named variables in the base classes will not be available to consumers of this derived class.

For example, if ErrorMsg declared its own version of msgSize, then PrintfileErrorMsg would only be able to "see" this version of msgSize. The copy of msgSize declared in TextMessage would not be available to PrintfileErrorMsg. Only the class that hides a variable can see both versions of the variable. For example, ErrorMsg can reference both its version of msgSize and the copy of msgSize declared in TextMessage by using the super. reference variable:

```
          if (super.msgSize != 0) {
              msgSize = 1;
}
```

THIS

Sometimes it is a bit unclear which variable, or method, the programmer intends to reference in a class. This ambiguity is especially true of derived classes, which naturally share names.

To clarify which variable to use, the operator *this* can be used. *this* means "the members or methods associated with this instance of the class." The qualifier *this* is a sort of generic reference variable automatically created for each object. Our assignment of msgSize in the ErrorMsg example above could be expressed as:

```
          if (this.msgSize != 0) {
              this.linesToSkip = 1;
}
```

this.linesToSkip specifies the linesToSkip variable that is part of this instance of the PrintfileErrorMsg class (i.e., the object pointed to by myPrintfile). ErrorMsg could use the this. syntax to reference the two different copies of msgSize that it has access to, as follows:

```
          if (super.msgSize != 0) {
              this.msgSize = 1;
}
```

Figure 5.7 depicts these relationships among the classes. The diagram is in the UML (Universal Modeling Language) notation for static class definitions. Each box represents a class. The top section of each box contains the class name. The next section describes the public data member names and their types. The last box describes methods explicitly defined in each class. Finally, the arrows represent the class hierarchy. In this case, PrintfileErrorMsg and PopupErrorMsg inherit from ErrorMsg. ErrorMsg inherits from TextMessage.

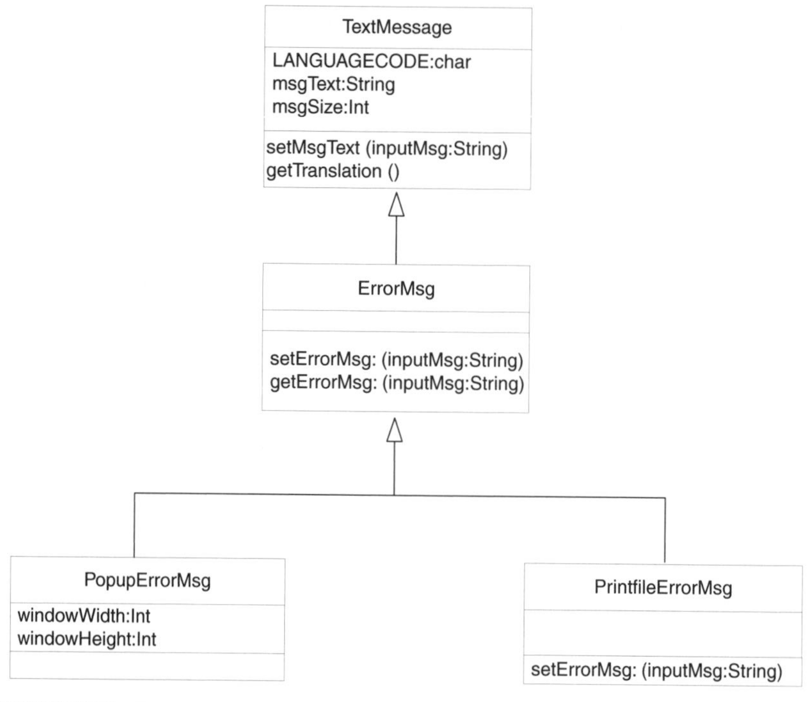

FIGURE 5.7. UML static class notation for ErrorMsg, PrintfileErrorMsg, and PopupErrorMsg.

INTERFACE INHERITANCE

While a Java class cannot extend more than one base class, it can still implement multiple *Interfaces*, or method signatures that have been defined in another source file. This is essentially a simplified version of C++'s *multiple inheritance*, which is the ability of a single class to extend multiple base classes.

Java's designers felt that the multiple inheritance model was too complex and unnecessary for most applications, so they arrived at this compromise. In Java, `super.` refers to only one class (the base class for *this* class). At the same time, *this* class can implement methods modeled on other (unrelated) interface definitions.

A Java *Interface* is like a class but lighter. It does not contain any method logic, and it is not automatically instantiated at runtime. It contains only method signatures (i.e., method names, and method parameter types). Therefore, the class that implements an interface will inherit *no instance variables or method code*. Instead, a class that supports an interface promises to implement the methods described in that interface definition.

You can view an interface as a kind of template, or example, of the types of methods an implementing class might provide. It is up to the implementing class to actually perform the appropriate logic required to support the interface definition, since there is no base class automatically created by Java for interfaces. The signature descriptions in an interface are a means to organize and document the types of messages that similar classes will support.

Java uses the keyword *Implements* to indicate that one class implements the interfaces (method signatures and constants) of an interface definition.

WRITELINE INTERFACE

```
public interface Writeline {
```

// Describe an abstract method (and its signature) that an implementing class
// might need.

```
        public void printLine ();
}
```

PRINTFILEERRORMSG CLASS

```
public class PrintfileErrorMsg extends ErrorMsg
```

// Declare that this class implements the methods from Writeline

// We will mimic the methods described in this interface in our class

// PrintfileErrorMsg.

```
        implements Writeline {

        ...
    }
```

Using this technique, the class PrintfileErrorMsg can now receive a request to print the error message, using the method Writeline. At the same time, PrintfileErrorMsg can also support the methods in the base class ErrorMsg (such as setErrorMsg):

CALLER CLASS

// Create an instance of a PrintfileErrorMsg.

```
PrintfileErrorMsg myPrintMsg = new PrintfileErrorMsg ();
```

// Call the derived method in PrintfileErrorMsg.

```
myPrintMsg.setErrorMsg ("Any Text");
```

// Call the *interface* method in PrintfileErrorMsg.

```
myPrintMsg.printLine();
```

One key difference between these two method implementations is that the class PrintfileErrorMsg *can* override the setErrorMsg method, but if it does not, the method in the base class (ErrorMsg) will be executed. However, in order to receive a request to print its error message (the Writeline method), PrintfileErrorMsg *must* implement this method, since there is no real base class method that can be performed.

USING INTERFACES

Interfaces are often supported by standard classes that perform the basic functions of that interface. In many cases these classes are static classes, although regular instance classes are used as well. These supporting classes provide basic implementations of the defined interface. A class that implements a particular interface can simply use these supporting classes as is or implement additional features in addition to the basic features provided.

This combination of interfaces and supporting classes is often combined within a package called a *framework*. A good example of a framework is the *collections* framework provided with Java 1.2. We will review the collections frameworks in some detail in Chapter 9.

HIDING METHODS AND MEMBERS

Derived classes have to be careful with the use of the *static* keyword when overriding methods in its superclasses. Instance methods (i.e., nonstatic methods) cannot generally override static methods in the superclass, and static methods cannot generally override instance methods in the superclass.

If a derived class declares a method as static, then any static methods with the same signature in the superclass(es) will not be readily available to the derived class. The superclass method can be accessed explicitly by using the *super* keyword *or* an explicit reference to the superclass type (e.g., TextMessage. staticMethod). If a derived class tries to override an instance method with a static method, the compiler will complain. Finally, a static method in a super class cannot be overridden with an instance method in the derived class.

On the other hand, a derived class can hide variables in the superclass, using the *static* keyword. If a derived class declares a variable as static, then any instance variables with the same name in the superclass(es) will not be readily available to the derived class. The superclass variables can be accessed explicitly by using the *super* keyword but *not* with an explicit reference to the superclass type (e.g., TextMessage.staticVariable). However, a derived class can override an instance method with a static method and vice-versa without causing the compiler to complain.

THROWS AND NOT THROWS

Java classes can create error conditions called *exceptions*. A class that inherits from a base class that creates an error condition must either handle the exception or pass the exception along. Exceptions are discussed in more detail in Chapter 10.

POLYMORPHISM

Polymorphism is one of those buzzwords that sounds terrifying at first but, once understood, elicits, "Is that all there is?"

We have already seen that invoking a method in a particular object is often referred to as a *message* in OO parlance. Often, more than one class can handle a particular message. The actual function performed inside any class depends on the algorithm of the class. Therefore, a particular message can be acted on, or interpreted, differently by different classes. Polymorphism is defined as the ability of different classes to support methods and properties of the same name but with different implementations.

A very common example of polymorphism in the real world is the ability of most PC applications to process an open (FileName) message. This message will result in very different actions by various applications, but the message is the same. An originating application (such as the Windows Explorer or an e-mail package) can send this same message to any application, confident that the receiving application will process it correctly.

Classes that are related by inheritance can each accept messages defined in the superclass, and are therefore polymorphic. Take another look at our previous examples where the objects myErrorMsg, myPopupMsg, myPrintfile, and myAnyMsg could all receive the same message (setErrorMsg (Any Text)). Some of the objects were of the same class, so it would be expected that they could handle this message. Others were of different classes, yet they can all receive this message and process it correctly. This is an example of polymorphism.

Unrelated classes can also be polymorphic—that is, two unrelated classes can potentially accept the same message and respond in unique ways to it. Suppose our system had a class called `diagnostic`, and its purpose was to record system events for the purposes of on-site diagnostics. This class may also have a method called setErrorMsg that accepted a text String parameter. An object of this type could receive the same message (setErrorMsg (Any Text)) as our ErrorMsg class did.

Polymorphism delivers a number of advantages to the developer. A program can send a particular message to a whole group of classes without considering the differences between those classes. This has the potential for greatly simplifying code, since distinct objects can be treated in some cases as if they are of the same type. An example might be a component-based system that consisted of many transactional objects of various types (customers, invoices, etc.).

When the system needed each of the objects to commit their data to the database, a single message (commit()) could be sent to all of the objects.

That's all there is to it! Polymorphism is no more than the ability of multiple class types to receive the same message and process it in unique ways.

EXERCISES

It's time to visit our example classes again, and try out all these new ideas.

USING JAVA 2'S JDK

1. Using a text editor, edit a new Java source file, and name it TextMessage.java in the java4cobol directory. Enter this code in the class body. Note that the two member variables are the same name as the member variables in ErrorMsg. We will remove these variables from ErrorMsg in a moment.

```
//
//
// TextMessage
//
//
class TextMessage {

// Define some public class instance variables.

          public String msgText;
          public int  msgSize;
          public static char LANGUAGECODE = 'E';

          public void setMsgText (String inputMsg) {

// Set the msgText and msgSize variables.

               msgText = inputMsg;

// Set this variable to the size of the text String.

               msgSize = msgText.length ();
          }
          public String getTranslation () {
```

// Perform the translation function for this message.

// In a production environment, the translation for this message might

// be accessed from a database.

// In this sample, we will return the original text

// and "French Text" as a generic translation.

```
            if (LANGUAGECODE == 'E')
                return (msgText);
            else
                return (msgText + " -> French Text");
        }
}
```

2. Save this class definition as a text file; then compile the class in the DOS command window:

➢ javac TextMessage.java

3. Edit the ErrorMsg class with the text editor. We will define it as a class that inherits from TextMessage and delete some class variables. Add the **bold** code, and remove the *italicized* code in the beginning of the file, as identified below:

```
public class ErrorMsg extends TextMessage {
```

// Define some public class instance variables.

```
        public String msgText;
        public int  msgSize;
```

// Define some private class instance variables.

```
        private int     counter = 0;
                char    interfaceInUse;
```

// Define a public method.

```
        public void setErrorMsg (String inputMsg) {
```

// Define a local variable and increment it.

```
            int localCounter = 0;
            localCounter = localCounter + 1;
```

```
// Modify some of the private variables.

                    counter = counter + 1;
                    interfaceInUse = 'S';

// Modify one of the public variables. Set this variable to the text String that was
// passed as a parameter.

                    msgText = inputMsg;

// Set this variable to the length of the text String.

                    msgSize = msgText.length ();

                    setMsgText (inputMsg);
               . . .
```

4. Save this class definition as a text file, then compile the class in the DOS command window:

➢ javac ErrorMsg.java

5. Let's simplify the HelloWorld application and add a call to this new method using the text editor. Open the HelloWorld.java source file, and remove the lines after this statement (but remember to leave in the two curly braces at the end of the program):

```
// Print the contents of ErrorMsgs String data member directly.

          System.out.println (myErrorMsg.msgText);
```

Add these lines:

```
// Get the translation for this method.

          tempMsg = myErrorMsg.getTranslation ();
          System.out.println (tempMsg);
```

6. Save, compile, and rerun the HelloWorld application.

➢ javac HelloWorld.java

➢ java HelloWorld

The output should look like this:

```
Hello World!

Some Text
Some Text
Some Text
```

7. Edit the HelloWorld application, and set LANGUAGECODE to F. Add this **bold** line after the statement that creates ErrorMsg:

// Create a new instance of the ErrorMsg class:

```
ErrorMsg myErrorMsg = new ErrorMsg ();
TextMessage.LANGUAGECODE = 'F';
```

8. Save, compile, and rerun the HelloWorld application, and observe the output:

```
Hello World!

Some Text
Some Text
Some Text -> French Text
```

9. Create a new instance of ErrorMsg, and test how it performs translations. Add these **bold** lines to the end of HelloWorld:

// Create a new instance of the ErrorMsg class.

```
ErrorMsg myErrorMsg2 = new ErrorMsg ();
```

// Set the text item to some text String, and print its contents.

```
myErrorMsg2.setErrorMsg ("Some Text for #2");
tempMsg = myErrorMsg2.getErrorMsg ();
System.out.println (tempMsg);
tempMsg = myErrorMsg2.getTranslation ();
System.out.println (tempMsg);
```

10. Save, compile, and rerun the HelloWorld application, and observe the output. Notice how LANGUAGECODE applies to all instances of TextMessage:

```
Hello World!

Some Text
Some Text
Some Text -> French Text
Some Text for #2
Some Text for #2 -> French Text
```

11. Let's create and use the PrintfileErrorMsg class. Create a new java source file in the c:\java4cobol directory named PrintfileErrorMsg.java. Insert these lines of text into the class file definition:

```
//
//
// PrintfileErrorMsg
//
//
class PrintfileErrorMsg extends ErrorMsg {

     private static int outputLineSize = 80;
     public int linesToSkip = 0;
     private int charsToSkip = 0;

// Define a setErrorMsg method that establishes the number of characters to
// output in order to center the text from ErrorMsg.

     public void setErrorMsg (String inputMsg) {
          super.setErrorMsg (inputMsg);
          charsToSkip = (outputLineSize - msgSize) / 2;

// Print out this error message.

          printLine ();
     }
```

// Define a new method that prints this error message to the standard output.
// It will be centered in the output line (based on the size of outputLineSize).
// linesToSkip lines will be skipped first.

```
public void printLine () {
     int i;
```

// Print out some blank lines.

```
     for (i=0; i != linesToSkip; i++)
          System.out.println ();
```

// Print out some blank characters so that the error message text is centered.

```
     for (i=0; i != charsToSkip; i++)
          System.out.print (' ');
```

// Print out the error message.

```
          System.out.println (getErrorMsg ());
     }
}
```

12. Save and then compile this class in the DOS command window:

➢ javac PrintfileErrorMsg.java

13. Edit the HelloWorld application so that is uses this new class. Using the text editor, open the HelloWorld.java source file, and add these lines of code to the bottom of the class:

// Create a new instance of the `PrintfileErrorMsg` class.

```
PrintfileErrorMsg myErrorMsg3 = new PrintfileErrorMsg ();
myErrorMsg3.linesToSkip = 2;
```

// Set the text item to some text String, and print its contents.

```
myErrorMsg3.setErrorMsg ("Some Text for #3");
```

// Print this data member in `PrintfileErrorMsg`.

```
System.out.println ("msgSize for PrintfileErrorMsg = " +
   myErrorMsg3.msgSize);
```

14. Save, compile, and rerun the HelloWorld application. The output should look like this:

```
Hello World!

Some Text
Some Text
SOME TEXT -> FRENCH TEXT
Some Text for #2
SOME TEXT FOR #2 -> FRENCH TEXT


      Some Text for #3
MsgSize for PrintfileErrorMsg = 16
```

15. Let's create a class data member in PrintfileErrorMsg that hides the variable with the same name in MessageText. We will experiment with this variable and see how it affects the classes that use PrintfileErrorMsg. Using the text editor, open the PrintfileErrorMsg.java file, and add these **bold** lines (pay particular attention to the *super.* and *this.* identifiers for msgSize).

```
//
//
// PrintfileErrorMsg
//
//

class PrintfileErrorMsg extends ErrorMsg {


     private static int outputLineSize = 80;
     public int linesToSkip = 0;
     private int charsToSkip = 0;

// Create a version of this variable that hides the one in TextMessage.

     public int  msgSize;
```

// Define a setErrorMsg method that establishes the number of
// chars to output in order to center the error msg.

```
public void setErrorMsg (String inputMsg) {
     super.setErrorMsg (inputMsg);
     charsToSkip = (outputLineSize - super.msgSize) / 2;
     this.msgSize = super.msgSize + charsToSkip;
     . . .
```

At the bottom of the class definition insert the **bold** lines:
// Print out the error message.

```
System.out.println (getErrorMsg ());
```

// Print out the two msgSize variables.

```
System.out.println ("this.msgSize = " + this.msgSize + ",
        super.msgSize = " + super.msgSize);
```

16. Save and compile this class:

➢ javac PrintfileErrorMsg.java

17. Rerun the HelloWorld application. The output should look like this:

```
Hello World!

Some Text
Some Text
SOME TEXT -> FRENCH TEXT
Some Text for #2
SOME TEXT FOR #2 -> FRENCH TEXT


       Some Text for #3
this.msgSize = 48, super.msgSize = 16
MsgSize for PrintfileErrorMsg = 48
```

18. Lets create an example of an Interface definition and a supporting class and have PrintfileErrorMsg use them. Create a new java source file in the c:\java4cobol directory named WriteLineInterface.java. Insert these lines of text into the class file definition:

```
//
//
// WriteLineInterface
//
//
public interface WriteLineInterface {

// Describe an abstract method (and its signature) that an implementing class
// might need.

     public void printLine ();
}
```

19. Compile this class in the DOS command window:

➢ javac WriteLineInterface.java

20. Create a new java source file in the c:\java4cobol directory named WriteLine.java. Insert these lines of text into the class file definition:

```
//
//
// WriteLine
//
//
public class WriteLine {

// Define a STATIC class method that will print out a line.

     public static void printLineWithPosition ( String line,
         int linesToSkip, int charsToSkip) {

         int i;

// Print out some blank lines.

          for (i=0; i != linesToSkip; i++)
                 System.out.println ();
```

// Print out some blank characters.

```
        for (i=0; i != charsToSkip; i++)
             System.out.print (' ');
```

// Print out the error message.

```
        System.out.println (line);

    }
}
```

21. Compile this class in the DOS command window:

➢ javac WriteLine.java

22. Edit the PrintfileErrorMsg class so that is uses this new interface definition and the supporting class. Add these **bold** lines of code to the top and to the bottom of the class, and remove the logic that we've placed in WriteLine. Your PrintfileErrorMsg class should look like this:

//

//

// PrintfileErrorMsg

//

//

```
class PrintfileErrorMsg extends ErrorMsg
    implements WriteLineInterface {

     private static int outputLineSize = 80;
     public int linesToSkip = 0;
     private int charsToSkip = 0;
```

// Create a version of this variable that hides the one in TextMessage.

```
     public int  msgSize;
```

// Define a setErrorMsg method that establishes the number of

// chars to output in order to center the error msg.

```
     public void setErrorMsg (String inputMsg) {
          super.setErrorMsg (inputMsg);
```

```
        charsToSkip = (outputLineSize - super.msgSize) / 2;
        this.msgSize = super.msgSize + charsToSkip;
        printLine ();
    }
```

// Define a new method that prints this error message to the output.
// It will be centered (based on the size of outputLineSize).
// linesToSkip lines will be skipped first.

```
    public void printLine () {
        WriteLine.printLineWithPosition (getErrorMsg (),
            linesToSkip, charsToSkip);
```

// Print out the two msgSize variables.

```
        System.out.println ("this.msgSize = " +
            this.msgSize + ", super.msgSize = " + super.msgSize);

        }
}
```

23. Save and compile this class:

➢ javac PrintfileErrorMsg.java.

24. Now that we've made all of these changes, rerun the HelloWorld application. The output should look the same as it did before:

```
Hello World!
null
Some Text
Some Text
SOME TEXT -> FRENCH TEXT
Some Text for #2
SOME TEXT FOR #2 -> FRENCH TEXT


Some Text for #3
this.msgSize = 48, super.msgSize = 16
MsgSize for PrintfileErrorMsg = 48
```

While the output looks unchanged, our program is in fact very different. We've started to build an infrastructure that will support the ability to print output lines in a standard yet flexible manner. The WriteLineInterface definition, and the supporting WriteLine class, begin to provide the infrastructure necessary to manage report creation properly.

For example, this infrastructure can be extended to support standard pagination functions when every line is printed. These pagination functions might include the ability to print standard heading information as necessary at the beginning of every page, as well as other page management functions.

For our last exercise, we will experiment with the concept of polymorphism. So far, two classes, ErrorMsg and PrintfileErrorMsg contain a method named setErrorMsg. The one defined in PrintfileErrorMsg is an overridden version of the method defined in ErrorMsg. We will create a third version of this method in an unrelated class called Diagnostic. We will then have HelloWorld call each of these methods and examine what happens as a result.

25. Create a new java source file in the c:\java4cobol directory named Diagnostic.java. Insert these lines of text into the class file definition:

```
import java.util.*;
//
// Diagnostic
//
//
public class Diagnostic {

// Define a setErrorMsg method. This method will write an error message to
// the system diagnostic output.

     public static void setErrorMsg (String inputMsg) {
```

// Print a banner.

```
          System.err.println ("====== A serious error has occurred
====== ");
          Date today = new Date();
          System.err.println (today);
          System.err.println ();
```

// Print the message.

```
          System.err.println (inputMsg);
```

// Print a banner end.

```
          System.err.println ();
          System.err.println ();
          Thread.dumpStack();
          System.err.println ();
          System.err.println ("====== End of serious error message
=====");
     }
}
```

26. Save and compile this class:

➢ javac Diagnostic.java

27. Edit the HelloWorld class so that is uses this new class. Using the text editor, open the HelloWorld.java source file, and add these **bold** lines of code to the bottom of the class:

// Print this data member in PrintfileErrorMsg.

```
     System.out.println ("msgSize for PrintfileErrorMsg = " +
          myErrorMsg3.msgSize);
```

// Experiment with polymorphism.

```
     System.out.println ("------ Experiment with polymorphism ------");
```

// Create an error message String, and pass it to each of these setErrorMsg // functions.

```
     tempMsg = "Display this message";

     System.out.println ();
     System.out.println ("~~~~~~~ setErrorMsg in ErrorMsg does this:
~~~~~~~");
     myErrorMsg.setErrorMsg (tempMsg);

     System.out.println ();
     System.out.println ("~~~~~~~ setErrorMsg in PrintfileErrorMsg does
this: ~~~~~~~");
     myErrorMsg3.setErrorMsg (tempMsg);

     System.out.println ();
     System.out.println ("~~~~~~~ setErrorMsg in Diagnostic does this :
~~~~~~~");
     Diagnostic.setErrorMsg (tempMsg);
```

```
. . .
——— Experiment with polymorphism ———

~~~~~~~ setErrorMsg in ErrorMsg does this: ~~~~~~~

~~~~~~~ setErrorMsg in PrintfileErrorMsg does this: ~~~~~~~


               Display this message
this.msgSize = 50, super.msgSize = 20

~~~~~~~ setErrorMsg in Diagnostic does this : ~~~~~~~
====== A serious error has occurred  ======
Fri Apr 16 18:08:50 PDT 1999

Display this message


java.lang.Exception: Stack trace
    at java.lang.Thread.dumpStack(Thread.java:983)
    at Diagnostic.setErrorMsg(Diagnostic.java:27)
    at HelloWorld.main(HelloWorld.java:69)

====== End of serious error message  =====
```

USING J++

1. Select your java4cobol project from among the recent workspaces using this menu path:

➢ File → Recent Workspaces → java4cobol.

2. Add a new class file to your project, using this menupath:

➢ Insert → New Class

In the dialog box, enter the class's name as TextMessage.

3. Enter this code in the class body. Note that the two member variables are the same name as the member variables in ErrorMsg. We will remove these variables from ErrorMsg in a moment.

// Define some public class instance variables.

```
public String msgText;
public int  msgSize;
public static char LANGUAGECODE = 'E';

public void setMsgText (String inputMsg) {
```

// Set the msgText and msgSize variables.

```
     msgText = inputMsg;
```

// Set this variable to the size of the text String.

```
     msgSize = msgText.length ();
}

public String getTranslation () {
```

// Perform the translation function for this message.

// In a production environment, the translation for this message might

// be accessed from a database.

// In this sample, we will return the original text and "French Text" as a generic
// translation.

```
          if (LANGUAGECODE == 'E')
               return (msgText);
          else
               return (msgText + " -> French Text");
     }
```

4. Compile this source using this menupath

➢ Build → Compile TextMessage.java

5. Choose the ErrorMsg class. We will define it as a class that inherits from TextMessage, and delete some class variables. Add the **bold** code, and remove the *italicized* code in the beginning of the file, as identified below:

```
public class ErrorMsg extends TextMessage {
```

// Define some public class instance variables.

```
          public String msgText;
          public int  msgSize;
```

// Define some private class instance variables.

```
          private int  counter = 0;
                  char interfaceInUse;
```

// Define a public method.

```
          public void setErrorMsg (String inputMsg) {
```

// Define a local variable and increment it.

```
               int localCounter = 0;
               localCounter = localCounter + 1;
```

// Modify some of the private variables.

```
               counter = counter + 1;
               interfaceInUse = 'S';
```

// Modify one of the public variables. Set this variable to the text String that
// was passed as a parameter.

```
               msgText = inputMsg;
```

// Set this variable to the length of the text String.

```
        msgSize = msgText.length ();

        setMsgText (inputMsg);
    . . .
```

6. Compile ErrorMsg.java using this menupath

➢ Build → Compile ErrorMsg.java

7. Let's simplify the HelloWorld application and add a call to this new method. Remove the lines after this statement (but remember to leave in the two braces at the end of the program):

// Print the contents of ErrorMsg's String data member directly.

```
System.out.println (myErrorMsg.msgText);
```

Add these lines:

// Get the translation for this method.

```
tempMsg = myErrorMsg.getTranslation ();
System.out.println (tempMsg);
```

8. Rerun the HelloWorld application. The output should look like this:

```
Hello World!
null
Some Text
Some Text
Some Text
```

9. Edit the HelloWorld application, and set LANGUAGECODE to F. Add this **bold** line after the statement that creates ErrorMsg:

// Create a new instance of the ErrorMsg class.

```
ErrorMsg myErrorMsg = new ErrorMsg ();
TextMessage.LANGUAGECODE = 'F';
```

10. Rerun the HelloWorld application, and observe the output:

```
Hello World!
null
Some Text
Some Text
Some Text -> French Text
Some Text
Some Text -> French Text
```

11. Create a new instance of ErrorMsg, and test how it performs translations. Add these **bold** lines to the end of HelloWorld:

// Create a new instance of the ErrorMsg class:

```
ErrorMsg myErrorMsg2 = new ErrorMsg ();
```

// Set the text item to some text String, and print its contents.

```
myErrorMsg2.setErrorMsg ("Some Text for #2");
tempMsg = myErrorMsg2.getErrorMsg ();
System.out.println (tempMsg);
tempMsg = myErrorMsg2.getTranslation ();
System.out.println (tempMsg);
```

12. Rerun the HelloWorld application, and observe the output. Notice how LANGUAGECODE applies to all instances of TextMessage:

```
Hello World!
null
Some Text
Some Text
Some Text -> French Text
Some Text for #2
Some Text for #2 -> French Text
```

13. Choose the ErrorMsg class. We will define a version of the getTranslation function in this class. Add the **bold** statements at the end of the class, as identified below:

```
// Define a method named getTranslation. This method overrides the
// method with the same name in the base class.

    public String getTranslation () {

// Call the base object's method.

        String localString = super.getTranslation ();

// Since this is an error message, change it to all upper case.
// Perform the toUpperCase function (this is a method that every String has).

        localString = localString.toUpperCase ();
        return (localString);
    }
}
```

14. Compile ErrorMsg.java, and rerun the HelloWorld application. Observe the output. Notice how the new version of the getTranslation method defined in ErrorMsg is used by HelloWorld:

```
Hello World!
null
Some Text
Some Text
SOME TEXT -> FRENCH TEXT
Some Text for #2
SOME TEXT FOR #2 -> FRENCH TEXT
```

15. Let's create and use the PrintfileErrorMsg class. Add a new class to your project, using this menu path: Insert → New Class. Enter the class name PrintfileErrorMsg in the dialog and identify this class as one that extends ErrorMsg.

16. Insert these lines of text into the class file definition:

```
//
//
// PrintfileErrorMsg
//
//
class PrintfileErrorMsg extends ErrorMsg {

     private static int outputLineSize = 80;
     public int linesToSkip = 0;
     private int charsToSkip = 0;

// Define a setErrorMsg method, which establishes the number of
// chars to output in order to center the error msg.

     public void setErrorMsg (String inputMsg) {
          super.setErrorMsg (inputMsg);
          charsToSkip = (outputLineSize - msgSize) / 2;

// Print out this error message.

          printLine ();
     }

// Define a new method that prints this error message to the standard output.
// It will be centered in the output line (based on the size of outputLineSize).
// linesToSkip lines will be skipped first.

     public void printLine () {
          int i;

// Print out some blank lines.

          for (i=0; i != linesToSkip; i++)
               System.out.println ();

// Print out some blank characters so that the error message text is centered.

          for (i=0; i != charsToSkip; i++)
               System.out.print (' ');
```

// Print out the error message.

```
        System.out.println (getErrorMsg ());


    }
}
```

17. Compile this class using this menu path

➢ Build → Compile PrintfileErrorMsg.java

18. Edit the HelloWorld application so that is uses this new class. Select the HelloWorld class in the editor, and add these **bold** lines of code to the bottom of the class:

// Create a new instance of the PrintfileErrorMsg class:

```
PrintfileErrorMsg myErrorMsg3 = new PrintfileErrorMsg ();
myErrorMsg3.linesToSkip = 2;
```

// Set the text item to some text String, and print its contents.

```
myErrorMsg3.setErrorMsg ("Some Text for #3");
```

// Print this data member in PrintfileErrorMsg.

```
System.out.println ("msgSize for PrintfileErrorMsg = " +
    myErrorMsg3.msgSize);
```

19. Compile and rerun the HelloWorld application. The output should look like this:

```
Hello World!
null
Some Text
Some Text
SOME TEXT -> FRENCH TEXT
Some Text for #2
SOME TEXT FOR #2 -> FRENCH TEXT


Some Text for #3
MsgSize for PrintfileErrorMsg = 16
```

20. Let's create a class data member in PrintfileErrorMsg that hides the variable with the same name in MessageText. We will experiment with this variable and see how it affects the classes that use PrintfileErrorMsg. Select the PrintfileErrorMsg class in the editor, and add these **bold** lines (pay particular attention to the *super.* and *this.* identifiers for msgSize).

```
class PrintfileErrorMsg extends ErrorMsg {

     private static int outputLineSize = 80;
     public int linesToSkip = 0;
     private int charsToSkip = 0;
```

// Create a version of this variable that hides the one in TextMessage.

```
     public int  msgSize;
```

// Define a setErrorMsg method that establishes the number of
// chars to output in order to center the error msg.

```
     public void setErrorMsg (String inputMsg) {
          super.setErrorMsg (inputMsg);
          charsToSkip = (outputLineSize - super.msgSize) / 2;
          this.msgSize = super.msgSize + charsToSkip;
          . . .
```

At the bottom of the class definition, insert the **bold** lines:
// Print out the error message.

```
          System.out.println (getErrorMsg ());
```

// Print out the two msgSize variables.

```
          System.out.println ("this.msgSize = " + this.msgSize + ",
              super.msgSize = " + super.msgSize);
```

21. Compile this class using this menu path.

➢ Build → Compile PrintfileErrorMsg.java

Run the HelloWorld application. The output should look like this:

```
Hello World!
null
Some Text
Some Text
SOME TEXT -> FRENCH TEXT
Some Text for #2
SOME TEXT FOR #2 -> FRENCH TEXT


Some Text for #3
this.msgSize = 48, super.msgSize = 16
MsgSize for PrintfileErrorMsg = 48
```

22. Lets create an example of an Interface definition and a supporting class and have PrintfileErrorMsg use them. Add a new class to your project, using this menu path

➢ Insert → New Class

Enter the class name WriteLineInterface in the dialog. This class does not extend any other class.

23. Insert these lines of text into the class file definition:

```
//
//
// WriteLineInterface
//
//
public interface WriteLineInterface {

// Describe an abstract method (and its signature) that an implementing class
// might need.

     public void printLine ();
}
```

24. Compile this class, using this menu path.

➢ Build → Compile WriteLineInterface.java

25. Add a new class to your project, using this menu path: Insert → New Class. Enter the class name WriteLine, in the dialog. This class does not extend any other class.
26. Insert these lines of text into the class file definition:

```
//
//
// WriteLine
//
//
public class WriteLine {

// Define a STATIC class method that will print out a line.

    public static void printLineWithPosition ( String line,
        int linesToSkip, int charsToSkip) {

        int i;

// Print out some blank lines.

         for (i=0; i != linesToSkip; i++)
              System.out.println ();

// Print out some blank characters.

         for (i=0; i != charsToSkip; i++)
              System.out.print (' ');

// Print out the error message.

         System.out.println (line);

    }
}
```

27. Compile this class using this menu path:

➢ Build → Compile WriteLine.java

28. Edit the PrintfileErrorMsg class so that is uses this new interface definition and the supporting class. Select the PrintfileErrorMsg class in the editor, and add these **bold** lines of code to the top and to the bottom of the class. Remove the logic that we've placed in WriteLine. Your PrintfileErrorMsg class should look like this:

```
//
//
// PrintfileErrorMsg
//
//
class PrintfileErrorMsg extends ErrorMsg
  implements WriteLineInterface {

     private static int outputLineSize = 80;
     public int linesToSkip = 0;
     private int charsToSkip = 0;

// Create a version of this variable that hides the one in TextMessage.

     public int  msgSize;

// Define a setErrorMsg method that establishes the number of
// chars to output in order to center the error msg.

     public void setErrorMsg (String inputMsg) {
          super.setErrorMsg (inputMsg);
          charsToSkip = (outputLineSize - super.msgSize) / 2;
          this.msgSize = super.msgSize + charsToSkip;
          printLine ();
     }

// Define a new method that prints this error message to the output.
// It will be centered (based on the size of outputLineSize).
```

// linesToSkip lines will be skipped first.

```
public void printLine () {
     WriteLine.printLineWithPosition (getErrorMsg (),
          linesToSkip, charsToSkip);
```

// Print out the two msgSize variables.

```
          System.out.println ("this.msgSize = " +
               this.msgSize + ", super.msgSize = " + super.msgSize);

          }
}
```

29. Compile this class, using this menu path.

➢ Build → Compile PrintfileErrorMsg.java

30. Now that we've made all of these changes, rerun the HelloWorld application. The output should look the same as it did before:

```
Hello World!
null
Some Text
Some Text
SOME TEXT -> FRENCH TEXT
Some Text for #2
SOME TEXT FOR #2 -> FRENCH TEXT


          Some Text for #3
this.msgSize = 48, super.msgSize = 16
MsgSize for PrintfileErrorMsg = 48
```

While the output looks unchanged, our program is now very different. We've started to build an infrastructure that will support the ability to print output lines in a standard yet flexible manner. The WriteLineInterface definition and the supporting WriteLine class begin to provide the infrastructure necessary to manage report creation properly.

For example, this infrastructure can be extended to support standard pagination functions when every line is printed. These pagination functions might include the ability to print standard heading information as necessary at the beginning of every page, as well as other page management functions.

For our last exercise, we will experiment with the concept of polymorphism. So far, two classes (ErrorMsg and PrintfileErrorMsg) contain a method named setErrorMsg. The one defined in PrintfileErrorMsg is an overridden version of the method defined in ErrorMsg. We will create a third version of this method in an unrelated class called Diagnostic. We will then have HelloWorld call each of these methods and examine what happens as a result.

31. Add a new class to your project, using this menu path: Insert → New Class. Enter the class name Diagnostic, in the dialog. This class does not extend any other class, and it is a public class.
32. Insert these lines of text into the class file definition:

```
//
import java.util.*;
//
// Diagnostic
//
//
public class Diagnostic {

// Define a setErrorMsg method. This method will write an error message to
// the system diagnostic output.
     public static void setErrorMsg (String inputMsg) {

// Print a banner.

          System.err.println ("====== A serious error has occurred
====== ");
          Date today = new Date();
          System.err.println (today);
          System.err.println ();
```

// Print the message.

```
          System.err.println (inputMsg);
```

// Print a banner end.

```
        System.err.println ();
        System.err.println ();
        Thread.dumpStack();
        System.err.println ();
        System.err.println ("====== End of serious error message =====");
        }
}
```

33. Compile this class, using this menu path.

➢ Build → Compile Diagnostic.java.

34. Edit the HelloWorld class so that is uses this new class. Add these **bold** lines of code to the bottom of the class:

// Print this data member in PrintfileErrorMsg.

```
     System.out.println ("msgSize for PrintfileErrorMsg = " +
          myErrorMsg3.msgSize);
```

// Experiment with polymorphism.

```
     System.out.println ("—— Experiment with polymorphism ——");
```

// Create an error message String, and pass it to each of these setErrorMsg // functions.

```
     tempMsg = "Display this message";

     System.out.println ();
     System.out.println ("~~~~~~~ setErrorMsg in ErrorMsg does this:
~~~~~~~");
     myErrorMsg.setErrorMsg (tempMsg);

     System.out.println ();
     System.out.println ("~~~~~~~ setErrorMsg in PrintfileErrorMsg does
this: ~~~~~~~");
     myErrorMsg3.setErrorMsg (tempMsg);

     System.out.println ();
```

```
     System.out.println ("~~~~~~~ setErrorMsg in Diagnostic does this :
~~~~~~~");
     Diagnostic.setErrorMsg (tempMsg);
```

```
. . .
—— Experiment with polymorphism ——

~~~~~~~ setErrorMsg in ErrorMsg does this: ~~~~~~~

~~~~~~~ setErrorMsg in PrintfileErrorMsg does this: ~~~~~~~


               Display this message
this.msgSize = 50, super.msgSize = 20

~~~~~~~ setErrorMsg in Diagnostic does this: ~~~~~~~
====== A serious error has occurred  ======
Fri Apr 16 15:33:35 PDT 1999

Display this message


java.lang.Exception: Stack trace
    at java/lang/Thread.dumpStack (Thread.java)
    at Diagnostic.setErrorMsg (Diagnostic.java:30)
    at HelloWorld.main (HelloWorld.java:78)

====== End of serious error message  =====
```

EXPERIMENT A BIT

1. Change the number of lines to skip before printing a message in PrintfileErrorMsg from 2 to 3.
2. Adjust the outputLineSize in PrintfileErrorMsg to 120.

3. Define a class member named msgText in ErrorMsg. What happens? Which classes use this overridden variable, and which ones use the version of this variable defined in TextMessage? Compare your observations to the inheritance hierarchy defined in Figure 5.6.
4. Create a method named getMsgText in TextMessage. In this method, get the current text String in msgText. Change the getErrorMsg method in ErrorMsg so that it uses this new method (getMsgText) to get the value of msgText instead of accessing msgText directly. How does this change the behavior of the overridden variables defined above?
5. Try calling TextMessage with this message: setErrorMsg (tempMsg).

   What happens? Why doesn't this class accept this particular polymorphic message?

REVIEWING OUR SAMPLES

Let's review the changes we've made. Try to relate the sample source statements to the result (for example, the output) each statement creates. If necessary, rerun the samples or look at the complete source code for this exercise on the CD. Feel free to experiment by yourself.

- We first created a new class called TextMessage. We removed some of the data members from ErrorMsg, and placed them in TextMessage.
- Since the data members msgText and msgSize now belong to TextMessage, we defined a setMsgText method in TextMessage in order to set these variables.
- We placed a new method named getTranslation in TextMessage. This method examined the static variable named LANGUAGE-CODE.
- Our ErrorMsg class was adjusted to inherit from this new class. Since ErrorMsg inherits from TextMessage, the public members and methods in TextMessage are automatically available to any class that creates an ErrorMsg class. In our example, HelloWorld creates an instance of ErrorMsg and can access these variables as if they are part of ErrorMsg. ErrorMsg and TextMessage share these variables.

- When we set the static variable LANGUAGECODE to F, all instances of TextMessage simulated a translation into French. Instances of ErrorMsg (which are inherited from TextMessage), also exhibit this behavior.
- We created a new class PrintfileErrorMsg. It inherits from ErrorMsg.
- The statement import java.util at the beginning of the class tells the compiler to introduce the definitions for the java.util classes into the Diagnostic class. We will discuss this topic in more detail in chapter 11.
- We introduced a data member named msgSize in the class PrintfileErrorMsg. This variable hid the similarly named variable in the class TextMessage from HelloWorld. That is, when HelloWorld performed the statement:

// Print this data member in PrintfileErrorMsg.

```
System.out.println ("msgSize for PrintfileErrorMsg = " +
      myErrorMsg3.msgSize);
```

- Before the change, the variable in TextMessage was printed. After the change, the variable in PrintfileErrorMsg, was printed.
- We constructed an Interface definition (WriteLineInterface) and defined a supporting class (WriteLine). We then used this class to simplify the logic in PrintfileErrorMsg. In a real system, any other class could also use the WriteLine infrastructure, in order to centrally manage printing functions.
- We demonstrated how polymorphism can be used. We sent the same message (setErrorMsg (String)) to instances of three different classes (ErrorMsg, PrintfileErrorMsg, and Diagnostic). Each of these classes respond to the message in a unique way:
  - ErrorMsg simply stored the String and did not print any text.
  - PrintfileErrorMsg printed the message after skipping some lines and centering the String in the print line. PrintfileErrorMsg also printed the values in the two msgSize variables.
  - Diagnostic printed the message and then performed a standard Java function to print the current call stack. This function would be very useful in a production system for recording contextual information appropriate for 'postmortem' analysis of application or system failures.

- We used a new object in the System class named *err.* This object is similar to the System.out object we have been using all along, except it is designed to write error messages, instead of standard, or informative messages. Both objects will write to the display device by default.

PART II

Java's Syntax

CHAPTER

6

Java Syntax

Until now, we have concentrated on the object-oriented concepts instead of the Java syntax. We have already introduced some of Java's syntax by way of our examples. This section will present a more complete definition of Java's syntax.

Java's syntax was deliberately based on C++, which was in turn deliberately based on C. Therefore, Cobol programmers sometimes have a harder time understanding Java's syntax than do C and C++ programmers. Harder is not the same as impossible, however, so we expect you to follow along.

COBOL VS. JAVA SYNTAX

Cobol's syntax has the benefit of being very simple and somewhat like English. As a result, Cobol programs tend to be longer than programs written in other languages but are often more readable. Significantly, most Cobol programmers tend to be pretty good typists.

In contrast, Java's syntax is much more concise. For example, a single statement can contain many embedded steps. Another good example of this contrast is the assignment function. In Cobol, the syntax is the wordy (but very clear) MOVE xxx TO yyy. In Java, it is simply yyy = xxx.

Both languages are not, strictly speaking, line oriented. They share the concept of a statement that may span more than one line. Most statements in Cobol can end with a period (.). In Java, all statements *must* end in a semicolon (;).

Cobol uses *verbs* such as IF, ELSE, and END-IF to both test a condition and to group statements that should be performed together as a result of that condition. Java uses the first two verbs (*if* and *else*) to test conditions, but then uses the curly braces ({}) to group conditional statements.

Finally, Java's syntax encourages the liberal use of objects in a program, whereas performing Cobol subroutine calls and using the results properly can be a little confusing. As a result, Java is much better suited to code reuse strategies.

But let's not get ahead of ourselves. Instead, we'll start at the very beginning.

JAVA STATEMENTS

A Java *statement* is the equivalent of a *sentence* in Cobol. A statement is the smallest complete building block in a Java program. A statement can define a variable, perform some logic, or define an interface. Every statement must end in a semicolon.

The simplest statement type is the sort that defines a variable. The syntax for defining a variable is:

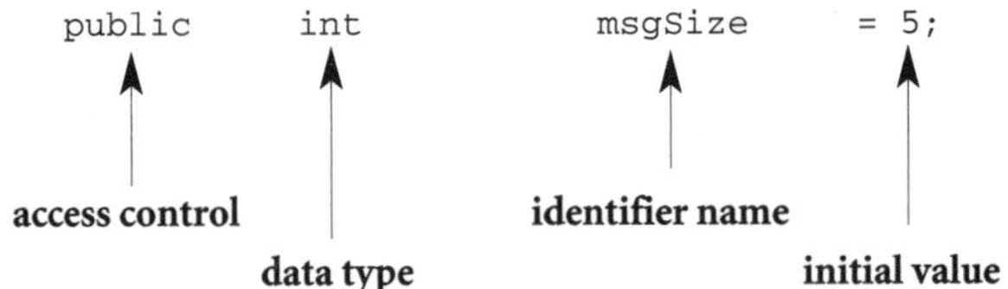

We've already reviewed Java's access control options and the data types that are available. We've also discussed how variables can be assigned initial values when they are first instantiated.

An identifier is any named program component (such as variables, class names, object names, or class members). Similar to a Cobol name, an identifier can be made up from any alphanumeric characters, but must start with an alphabetic character. There are a few differences, some as part of the language definition, some that are simply conventions.

- Java compilers are case sensitive. The identifier MsgSize is not the same as msgSize.
- The dash (-) character is not valid in a variable name in many contexts, and so is never used in a Java identifier name. By convention, the underscore (_) character is sometimes used to separate the parts

of an identifier name, or mixed case can be used for the same purpose.

- By convention, most identifiers are mixed case, and instance identifiers (variables, objects, members, and so on) begin with an initial lowercase. User-defined types such as classes often begin with an initial uppercase. Static class variables and members are normally all uppercase.
- Valid names cannot start with a numeric character.

Here are some examples of valid identifier names, and what they represent, by convention:

```
msgSize                  // an instance identifier
m_ErrorMsg               // an instance identifier, probably an
                         // object identifier
ErrorMsg                 // a user-defined type, such as a class name
NO_TEXT_FOUND            // a static CLASS variable
```

Here are some invalid identifier names:

```
1instanceVariable            // cannot start with nonalpha
another instance variable    // embedded spaces
COBOL-STYLE                  // embedded dashes
public                       // reserved word
```

A Java executable statement performs some part of a class's algorithm (it is similar to a sentence in Cobol's procedure division). These statements can contain multiple *expressions*, all of which will be performed as part of the statement.

This is a simple Java expression that instantiates a String type object:

```
String inputMsg
```

Placing a semicolon at the end makes it a complete Java statement:

```
String inputMsg;
```

This is a Java expression that performs the method getErrorMsg() in the object myErrorMsg and passes no parameters:

```
myErrorMsg.getErrorMsg ()
```

This expression can be combined with an assignment expression, in order to return the result into inputMsg:

```
inputMsg = myErrorMsg.getErrorMsg ()
```

Placing a semicolon at the end makes it a complete Java statement:

```
inputMsg = myErrorMsg.getErrorMsg ();
```

This is a Java statement that compares inputMsg to another String, and performs some logic. Since inputMsg is a String, it has a method called equals(), a method that accepts a String parameter and returns a boolean `true` or `false`. The `if` verb tests the boolean result of this method and performs the statements in the curly braces if the result is true:

```
if (inputMsg.equals ("Any Text")) {
    ...
}
```

Expressions can be combined into more complex Java statements:

```
String inputMsg = myErrorMsg.getErrorMsg ();
```

or this statement:

```
if (myErrorMsg.msgText.equals ("Any Text")) {
    ...
}
```

JAVA COMMENTS

Java programmers are expected to place comments in the code. Imagine that! To support this, Java allows for the following comments styles:

Style	Format	Comments
C comments	`/* . . . */`	Can span multiple lines
C++ comments	`//`	Stops at end of line, avoids some common errors in C
Javadoc comments	`/** . . . */`	Used to autogenerate external documentation

In our examples so far, we have used the C++ style comments, since they are line oriented, similar to Cobol comments:

// This member is available to any class.

```
public String msgText;
```

The C style comments are also sometimes used, especially for multiline comments, but a word of caution: this style can cause code to be inadvertently commented out.

/* This member is available to any class.

Its access modifier is public */

```
public String msgText;
```

/* All these lines are comment lines.

```
public String msgText;
```

Let's hope your editing environment will make this obvious */

Finally, Javadoc comments are marked in this fashion:

/** The purpose of this comment is to help in the automatic generation of documents.

A programmer can insert (well-written) descriptions of classes and members.

These will be extracted and placed into a published document in HTML format.

*/

Javadoc comments are often used to generate HTML documents. Javadoc comments can contain HTML markup tags, such as <TT>, but usually not HTML structural tags (like <H2> or </H2>).

Javadoc comments can also be marked with special markup tags, which provide for additional formatting and cross-reference control for the generated document.

These markup tags are used to document the interface of public methods:

@param

@return

@throws

These markup tags are used to document packages or classes that contain public methods:

@version

@author

It is a good idea to place Javadoc comments (with at least these tags) at the beginning of your classes and methods. Java programmers will expect to see them, and several useful tools are available that will process this type of program comment specification. The output of the Javadoc tool included with the JDK is especially nice looking and useful.

The advantage of in-program documentation is that since the code and the documentation are in the same file, the chances that the documentation will match the code are improved. In addition, the public class interface definitions will always be accurate since the tools automatically generate this information from the Java source code.

One disadvantage is that you still must rely on the programmer to type in the comments and specifications. There is no guarantee that the comments actually *do* match the code. Another problem is that Java editing environments are not WYSIWYG graphical editors. Generating nice looking end-user documentation (even if the end users are developers, and presumably have lower expectations) with Javadoc and HTML markups takes a lot of work.

You can get more details about Javadoc features on Sun's Javadoc home page at www.sun.java.com/products/jdk/javadoc. Documentation about HTML can be obtained at www.w3c.org.

Examples in this book generally use the // style of comments declaration.

JAVA OPERATORS

Java provides for the usual arithmetic assignment operators. Most of these are similar to the operators available in Cobol's COMPUTE statement.

*	Multiplication
/	Division
%	Modulo
+	Addition
-	Subtraction
=	Assignment

As you would expect, there are precedence standards, and parentheses can be used to override or clarify any precedence conventions.

```
x = 2 + 7 * 3;              // x = 23
x = (2 + 7) * 3;            // x = 27
```

The order of precedence is important, but if you have to think about it, you are either writing or reading code that will be hard to maintain. Rather than rely on the order of precedence conventions, always make your intentions explicit by using parentheses.

Unlike Cobol, Java always uses arithmetic symbols instead of words for its math operations. For example, the assignment operator is =, instead of MOVE, or x - y instead of Cobol's SUBTRACT Y FROM X. Math operations in Java always use a syntax similar to Cobol's COMPUTE verb.

BINARY ARITHMETIC OPERATIONS

Binary operations (that is, operations involving two operators) come in several types: arithmetic, conditional, relational, assignment, and bitwise. We will explore the various arithmetic operations here.

Integer operations always create a result type of `int`, unless one of the operands is of type `long`, in which case the result type is `long`. If x in the example preceding had been defined as a short, then we would have had to cast the result into a short in order to avoid a compiler error.

```
short x;
x = (short) (2 + 7 * 3);           // x = 23
```

Likewise, floating point operations always create a result of type `double` unless both operands are of type `float`. Remember that floating point constants by default are of type double. Further, the compiler can automatically convert either an integer or a float into a double, but converting a double into either of these requires a cast. Similarly, integers will automatically convert to floats, but floats won't convert to integers unless you cast them.

```
int i;
float f;
double d;

d = f + 1.2;                 // OK
f = f + 1.2;                 // not good, cast required
f = (float) (f + 1.2);       // OK
f = f + 1.2F;                // also OK
i = (int) f;                 // OK, but possible precision loss
f = (float) (d + 1.2);       // OK, but possible precision loss
d = f + i;                   // OK
```

These conventions for managing numbers are easy to remember if you observe this logic:

- For integer math, the default type is int.
- For floating point math, the default type is double.
- Smaller types can automatically be converted into larger types.
- Larger types must be cast into smaller types. There is the possibility of data loss.
- The size order is double, float, int, short, byte.

Java coders will often use a shortcut (assignment with operator) to perform simple math operations on a single variable:

```
x = x + 7;
x += 7;                      // the same statement
```

This coding style can take a little getting used to since one of the source operands (the second x) that would be expected in an algebraic expression is missing. The additional operator (+, in our example) is normally placed to the left of the = sign in this type of complex assignment expression. Each of the math operators (*, /, +, and -) can be combined with assignment in this fashion (as in: *=, /=, +=, and -=).

Like C and C++, Java provides for increment and decrement operators (++ and --). These provide a convenient mechanism to increment or decrement a variable.

```
x = 7;
x++;                    // x = 8
x--;                    // x = 7
```

These operators come in two types: the postfix (x++) and the prefix (++x). The difference shows up when the auto increment operators are used in an expression. The prefix operator increments or decrements before presenting the value, and the postfix increments or decrements after presenting the value.

```
x = 7;
y = 2 * x++;            // y = 14, and x = 8
x = 7;
y = 2 * ++x;            // y = 16, and x = 8
```

As you can see from the examples, there are subtle differences between postfix and prefix increment operators, especially when used as part of an expression. A number of Java language authorities recommend that these operators not be used as part of an expression, but should be used only as standalone statements in order to avoid confusion on this matter.

```
x = 7;
x++;                    // An increment statement with no ambiguity
y = 2 * x;              // y = 16, and x = 8
```

The following chart lists the operators available in the Java language in the order in which they are evaluated by the compiler:

Operator	Description	Cobol Equivalent
.	Member selection	
[ ]	Array subscript	( )
( )	Expression grouping or function call	( ) as used by expression grouping IF ((A = B) AND (X = Y))
++, - -	Autoincrement/decrement	PERFORM VARYING
*, /, %	Multiply, divide, remainder	COMPUTE or MULTIPLY, DIVIDE GIV-ING
+, -,	Addition, subtraction	COMPUTE or ADD, SUBTRACT GIV-ING
<<, >>, >>>	Bitwise shift operations*	
<=, <, >=, >	Less than or equal to, less than, greater than or equal to, greater than	NOT >, <, NOT <, >
= =, !=	Equality test, inequality test	= , NOT =
&, |, ^, ~	Bitwise AND, OR, XOR, NOT	
&&, ||, !	Logical AND, OR, NOT	AND, OR, NOT
=	Assignment	MOVE
*=, /=, %=, +=, -=, &=	Complex assignment	COMPUTE

The special case of assignment and equality as applied to object reference variables warrants attention. An object reference variable is just like any other variable in many ways. But remember that it contains a reference to the object and does not contain the object's values. Therefore, although two different object reference variables can point to different objects with equal values, they are not the *same* object. The only way that two object reference variables can be equal is if they point to the same object.

Some examples may help clarify this.

Recall that the String data type is not really an intrinsic type, but rather is a class. Therefore, String variable names are actually object reference variables. Consider this example:

```
String s1 = new String ("Some text");
```

* Java includes a number of bitwise operations and makes some important distinction between these operations and boolean logical operations. Since Cobol does not have bitwise operations, and most business applications do not require them, the reader is encouraged to explore this concept in other sources.

The previous declaration is the same as the more commonly used syntax shown here:

```
String s1 = "Some text";
```

Suppose our program also includes this statement:

```
String s2 = "Some other text";
```

Clearly, s1 and s2 are not equivalent, so this test fails, as you would expect.

```
if (s1 == s2) {
    . . .                    // This code would not execute
}
```

In addition, the following test will also fail since s1 and s2 do not contain equivalent text:

```
if (s1.equals (s2)) {
    . . .                    // This code will not execute
}
```

Now, suppose we have two Strings that contain the same text.

```
String s1 = new String ("Some text");
String s2 = new String ("Some Text");

if (s1 == s2) {
                             // This code will not execute
                             // even though the text contained in these
                             // two Strings are equal. s1 and s2 will
                             // point to different String objects
}
```

Yet, the following test always succeeds since the equals() method in the String class compares the value of the String object with the passed String:

```
if (s1.equals (s2)) {
    . . .                    // This code will execute
}
```

What is the bottom line? Always use the equals(), or compareTo() methods when you want to compare two Strings. Never assume that the String reference variables will compare appropriately, based on the text values in the String.

Get ready for the real weirdness. Object reference variables are variables and therefore can be assigned values. Normally, this happened only with the `new` keyword, as in:

```
String s1 = new String ("Some text");
String s2 = new String ("Some other text");
```

But it is perfectly legal to set object reference s2 equal to s1:

```
s2 = s1;
```

Now, both s2 and s1 point to the same object. (As a matter of fact, the object formerly pointed to be s2 is unreferenced and will likely be garbage collected or deleted by the system at some point.) This time, the equality test, when applied to the values of the Strings, will succeed even though the initial object pointed to by s2 was different from s1:

```
if (s1.equals (s2)) {
        . . .              // This code would execute
}
```

As would this test, which compares the object references:

```
if (s1 == s2) {
        . . .              // This code would execute since s1 and s2
        . . .              // point to the same object.
}
```

The only way to modify the text associated with s1 or s2 is to point these reference variables to different String objects. This is normally done by performing some method that returns a String object and assigning the reference variable to that String.

```
String s1 = new String ("Some text");
String s2 = new String ("Some other text");
```

// Assign s2 to a new String object.

// This object is the result of the trim() method, which removes leading and

// trailing spaces.

// String s1 contains no leading or trailing spaces, so the String object returned

// from trim() will contain the same text as String s1.

```
s2 = s1.trim();
```

```
if (s1.equals (s2)) {
                    // This code would execute since s1 and s2 contain
                    // the same text.
}
```

UNDERSTANDING REFERENCE VARIABLES WITH COBOL

It may be useful to revisit our Cobol example to help explain this concept. Recall that our CALLER program defined two instances of MYSUB-CONTROL as follows:

```
01 MYSUB1-CONTROL.
      03    MYSUB1-ACTION-SWITCH              PIC X.
            88 MYSUB1-ACTION-INITIALIZE        VALUE "I".
            88 MYSUB1-ACTION-EVALUATE          VALUE "E".
            88 MYSUB1-ACTION-SET-AND-EVALUATE VALUE "S".
            88 MYSUB1-ACTION-GET-CALL-COUNTER VALUE "G".
      03    MSG-TEXT                          PIC X(20).
      03    MSG-SIZE                          PIC 9(8).
      03    MYSUB1-RETURNED-CALL-COUNTER      PIC 9(10).
      03    MYSUB1-PRIVATE-ITEMS              PIC X(20).

01 MYSUB2-CONTROL.
      03   MYSUB2-ACTION-SWITCH               PIC X.
           88 MYSUB2-ACTION-INITIALIZE         VALUE "I".
           88 MYSUB2-ACTION-EVALUATE           VALUE "E".
           88 MYSUB2-ACTION-SET-AND-EVALUATE  VALUE "S".
           88 MYSUB2-ACTION-GET-CALL-COUNTER  VALUE "G".
      03   MSG-TEXT                           PIC X(20).
      03   MSG-SIZE                           PIC 9(8).
      03   MYSUB2-RETURNED-CALL-COUNTER       PIC 9(10).
      03   MYSUB2-PRIVATE-ITEMS               PIC X(20).
```

Suppose that the MSG-TEXT items in both MYSUBx-CONTROL areas contained the same text ("Some Text," for example). In this case, this Cobol code would display a message:

```
IF MSG-TEXT OF MYSUB1-CONTROL = MSG-TEXT OF MYSUB2-CONTROL
     DISPLAY "MSG-TEXT's are equal".
```

However, this Cobol code may or may not display a message, depending on the value of the other items in the MYSUBx-CONTROL areas:

```
IF MYSUB1-CONTROL = MYSUB2-CONTROL
     DISPLAY "MYSUBx-CONTROL's are equal".
```

When you compare object reference variables (including a String object reference variable) with the == Java operator, it is as if you are comparing two CONTROL areas in Cobol. In order to compare the MSG-TEXT items in the CONTROL areas, you must explicitly compare those items. Likewise, in order to compare text in a Java String, you must use the equals() method.

CHAPTER

7

Flow Control

As with any language, Java defines a set of verbs. The programmer uses these to define the sequence of steps to be performed by the program. In this chapter, we'll examine the way a Java program manages flow control.

Java borrows heavily from C++, which in turn has borrowed heavily from C. Nowhere is this relationship more evident than in Java's syntactic definitions, especially the program flow control operators.

CODE BLOCK

A block of code is a set of Java statements grouped by curly braces {}. Blocks can also have other blocks nested inside them.

```
{this is a statement in a block of code;
 this is another statement in the same block of code;

      {this is a statement in a block nested in the first;
       this is another statement in a nested block;
       }
```

// This is the end of the nested code block.

```
}
```

// This is the end of the first code block.

Cobol organizes statements through the use of verbs such as IF ... ELSE ... END-IF. The end-of-sentence character (period) also defines the end of any conditional group of statements. In Java, multiple statements that are executed as a result of some flow control expression (such as if ... else ...) must be grouped into a code block using the curly braces.

Java also allows a special case of a code block that contains only one statement. This type of code block does not require curly braces. However, the addition of another statement to the code block would require that these two statements be grouped with curly braces. Therefore, it is good practice to place curly braces around single-statement code blocks, especially if they are the result of some conditional expression.

By convention, the statements in a code block are indented to the same column. This helps visually organize the statement groups and improves readability.

In addition, it is good programming practice to build your code blocks (that is, create the *if* and *else* sections, including the braces) before adding the statements inside the code block. This allows you to concentrate on the two steps independently, and therefore reduces the number of compile errors and runtime bugs created by syntax mistakes.

IF

Structure: if (condition) { block }
else {block} ;

This basic conditional statement will evaluate *condition*, and if *true*, the first block of code will execute; if *false*, the second block will be performed. As is the case in Cobol, the second code block (the ELSE condition) is optional.

```
if (inputMsg.equals ("Any Text")) {
     ...
}
else {
     ...
}
```

Condition can be any Java expression that returns a boolean. The result of that expression is evaluated.

```
if (myErrorMsg.msgText.equals ("Any Text")) {
     ...
}
```

Condition must be a *boolean* expression, that is, one that evaluates to either true or false. In our example, the equals() method returns a true or false boolean, so it is a good candidate for inclusion in an *if* statement.

TECHNICAL NOTE: The expression myErrorMsg.msgText.equals contains two member operators (that is, two periods). This implies that two members (a data member and a method member in this case) will be accessed.

Evaluate the expression this way: The data member msgText in the object myErrorMsg is a String variable. As a result, it contains a method named equals(). This method accepts a String parameter, and returns a boolean result of true if the passed String parameter contains the same text as is contained in this String. The boolean result is evaluated by the if operator.

Multiple expressions can be grouped, and the result of such grouping will be evaluated. The logical operators AND (&&), OR(||), and NOT (!) group boolean expressions in the same way their text equivalents do in Cobol. For example, this statement:

```
if (myErrorMsg.msgText.equals ("Any Text")  ||
   (myErrorMsg.msgText.equals ("Some Text")) {
     ...                  // The IF code block
}
```

will perform the code block if myErrorMsg contains either "Any Text" or "Some Text."

This is a syntactically equivalent Cobol statement:

```
IF (MY-ERROR-MSG = "Any Text") OR
   (MY-ERROR-MSG = "Some Text")
...                       // The IF code block
END-IF.
```

Java will "short-circuit" or stop evaluating *condition* as soon as an unambiguous result is available. Therefore, it is possible that some of the expressions in *condition* will not be executed. In our example, if myErrorMsg contains "Any Text," the equals() method will be performed only once.

The order of evaluation of expressions can be controlled using the parentheses (). Just as in Cobol, you should liberally use them to clarify what your intentions are, even if the compiler does figure it out correctly.

```
if (myErrorMsg.msgText.equals ("Any Text") &&
     myErrorMsg.msgSize == 8 ||
     myErrorMsg.msgText.equals ("Some Text") {
```

// This code block will be performed only when the text equals "Any Text" since
// the length of "Some Text" is 9 (that is, it contains 9 characters).

```
        ...
}
```

But the intentions of the developer are unclear, or perhaps there is a bug. The proper code is more likely:

```
if ((myErrorMsg.msgText.equals ("Any Text") &&
      myErrorMsg.msgSize == 8) ||
     myErrorMsg.msgText.equals ("Some Text")) {
```

// This code block will be performed for both "Any Text" and "Some Text."

```
        ...
}
```

This is a good time to talk some more about local variable scope. Local variables are variables that have been defined somewhere in a Java code block:

```
if (inputMsg.equals ("Any Text")) {
    ...
```

// This next statement defines a local variable inputMsgSize and sets it to
// msgSize.

```
    int inputMsgSize = myErrorMsg.msgSize;
    ...
}
else {
    ...
}
```

The variable inputMsgSize is valid only in the code block in which it has been defined. In our example, that would be the first code block, that is, the statements executed if inputMsg is equal to "Any Text." Note that these statements are bounded by the first pair of curly braces.

This variable is also valid in any *inner* code blocks. Therefore, a statement that sets inputMsgSize to -1 in an inner code block is valid:

```
if (inputMsg.equals ("Any Text")) {
    ...
```

// This next statement defines a local variable inputMsgSize and sets it to

// msgSize.

```
        int inputMsgSize = myErrorMsg.msgSize;
        if (inputMsgSize == 0) {
```

// This next statement resets the local variable inputMsgSize.

```
            inputMsgSize = -1;
            ...
    }
        ...
    }
  else {
```

Outside the curly braces for the first code block (for example, in the else condition code block), the variable inputMsg is not valid, and references to it would cause a compile time error:

```
if (inputMsg.equals ("Any Text")) {
...
```

// This next statement defines a local variable inputMsgSize and sets it to

// msgSize.

```
     int inputMsgSize = myErrorMsg.msgSize;
     ...
}
else {
```

// This next statement refers to inputMsgSize outside its code block

// and would be a compile time error.

```
     if (inputMsgSize == 0) {
     }
     ...
}
```

// This next statement refers to inputMsgSize outside the whole *if* statement

// and would be invalid as well.

```
if (inputMsgSize == 0) {
    ...
}
```

Note that local variables cannot be defined *inside* a code block, and subsequently evaluated *outside* it. This sort of result state variable must be defined outside the code block if it is to be used outside the code block. This is, by the way, a departure from C, and C++, where local variable scope generally extends to an entire function or method, regardless of where in the function it was defined.

If an inner code block were to attempt to define a new local variable with the same name as an existing variable (inputMsgSize, in our example), then the Java compiler would detect that as a name collision and report an error.

Finally, a local variable named inputMsgSize could be defined in some other code block and used inside that code block. This often happens with temporary variables and counters, such as the commonly used x. Java's tight scoping rules should allow the compiler to catch most instances of inappropriate use (and reuse) of local variables.

WHILE

Structure: while (*condition*) { block } ;

This basic loop control statement will evaluate *condition* and, if true, will perform the block of code. Let's hope that some statement in the block of code will eventually cause *condition* to not be true, else we would have an endless loop!

// Assume errorMsgs is an array of ErrorMsg objects that has previously been // created

// ARRAY_SIZE is the maximum number of elements allowed in ErrorMsg.

// Examine each ErrorMsg object to find the first with a size equal to 0.

// Define x outside the *while* code block.

```
int x = 0;
while (x < ARRAY_SIZE) {
      int inputMsgSize = errorMsgs[x].msgSize;
      if (inputMsgSize == 0) {
```

// Exit the loop immediately. x will point to this element.

```
                    break;        // The break statement causes the loop to
                                  // exit. The statement after the loop's ending
                                  // brace will be the next statement executed.

            }
            x++;            // Increment the loop variable.
            continue;       // Continue the loop. This statement is not required
                            // but is shown here to show how continue might be
                            // used. The continue statement causes the loop to
                            // proceed with the next iteration.
        }
```

// The loop has completed.

// At this point either we have found an element that contains a 0 size, or we

// have examined all of the objects in ErrorMsgs. Test x to see if we tested all

// of the items in ErrorMsgs (that is, is x equal to ARRAY_SIZE?).

```
        if (x != ARRAY_SIZE) {
```

// We have an ErrorMsg with a 0 size !

```
            ...
        }
        else {
```

// We have none. The array was exhausted

```
            ...
        }
```

As in any programming language, Java loops are often a mechanism to manipulate an array of similar items. We haven't formally introduced arrays yet, but this example is much better with an array than without. We will discuss arrays and collection processing in detail in Chapter 9, but a word about arrays and array processing in Java seems appropriate at this time.

In Cobol, subscripts for arrays (that is, items that OCCUR x TIMES) start with 1. That means that the first item in an array is referenced as ITEM (1), and the last item is referenced as ITEM (x).

For example, the statement:

```
01 MY-ITEMS    PIC X(2) OCCURS 10 TIMES.
```

defines an array called MY-ITEMS. Each item in the array is 2 bytes, and there are 10 items in the array. Any subscript in the range of 1 through 10 is valid:

```
IF (MY-ITEMS(1) = "AA")
    OR (MY-ITEMS(10) = "XX")
```

However, subscripts outside this range are not valid and will generate either a compile error or a runtime error. Both of these statements will generate an error:

```
IF (MY-ITEMS(0) = "AA")
    OR (MY-ITEMS(11) = "XX")
```

In contrast, Java follows the conventions of C and defines the first item in an array as item 0. Therefore, many loops in Java start with a loop variable equal to 0, and end when that variable is equal to the number of items in the array. This means that item[1] is actually the second item in the array, and item[ARRAY_SIZE] is not a valid reference. Instead of the parentheses subscript identifiers that Cobol uses, subscripts in Java are identified with square brackets [ ].

DO .. WHILE

Structure: do { block } while (*condition*) ;

This loop control statement is very similar to the basic *while* statement, except that *block* will always be executed at least once. *Condition* is evaluated after the code block is performed, and if true the code block is reiterated.

// Assume errorMsgs is an array of ErrorMsg objects that has previously been

// created.

// ARRAY_SIZE is the maximum number of elements allowed in ErrorMsg.

// Examine each ErrorMsg object to find the first with a size equal to 0.

// Define x and inputMsgSize outside the *while* code block.

```
int inputMsgSize = 0;
int x = 0;

do {
      inputMsgSize = errorMsgs[x].msgSize;
      if (inputMsgSize == 0) {
```

// Exit the loop immediately. x will point to this element.

```
                break;
            }
            else {
                x++;
            }
        }
        while (x < ARRAY_SIZE);
```

In this example, inputMsgSize will be set at least once. Since it has been defined outside the do .. while loop, it will be valid outside the loop, and will always contain some value as set in the loop.

FOR

Structure: for (expression1; (condition); expression2) { block }

This loop control statement is commonly used to support iteration. The first expression is the counter initialization and is performed only at the start of the loop. The condition is tested to determine if the loop should continue, and if true, the code block is performed. The second expression is the expression that changes the counter. It is performed after the code block is completed, but before the next iteration of the loop. The code block will be performed iteratively as long as condition is true. After every iteration of the code block, and if condition is true, the counter increment expression (expression2) will be performed.

```
for (int x = 0; x < ARRAY_SIZE ; x++) {
      int inputMsgSize = errorMsgs[x].msgSize;
      if (inputMsgSize == 0) {
```

// Exit the loop immediately. x will point to this element.

```
            break;
      }
}
```

Note that our sample is not of much use since both x and inputMsgSize have been defined inside the loop and are therefore not available outside it (x was actually implicitly defined in the *for* statement). If we tried to use either x or inputMsgSize outside the loop, we would create a compiler error.

It would be necessary to define these variables before the loop if we want to use them after it is complete.

// Define x and inputMsgSize outside the *while* code block.

```
int inputMsgSize = 0;
int x = 0;

for (x = 0; x < ARRAY_SIZE ; x++) {
      inputMsgSize = errorMsgs[x].msgSize;
      ...    // as before
}
```

You may have noticed the similarities between the *for* loop and the *while* loop. The *for* loop is a combination of the most common structures used in a *while* loop. For example, this is a common *while* loop structure.

```
initializationExpressionA;
while (testExpressionB) {
     performCode;
     incrementExpressionC;
}
```

This is combined in a *for* loop as follows:

```
for (initializationExpressionA; testExpressionB;
     incrementExpressionC;) {
     performCode;
}
```

SWITCH

```
Structure:   switch (expression) {

   case (statement1):
         code block1 ;
         break;

   case (statement2):
         code block2 ;
         break;

   default:
         code block3 ;
         }
```

This flow control statement is commonly used to perform various functions based on the value in a variable. It is similar to Cobol's EVALUATE verb.

Expression is evaluated and then compared for equality to each of the case statements. If expression is equal to the case statement, the code block for that statement is performed.

```
int inputMsgSize = 0;
int x = 0;

for (x = 0; x < ARRAY_SIZE ; x++) {
      switch ( errorMsgs[x].msgSize)
      {
      case 0:
         errorMsgs[x].setErrorMsg("Default Text");
         break;
     case 1:
     case 2:
     case 3:
        errorMsgs[x].setErrorMsg("Text < 4 chars");
        break;
     default:

     }
}
```

This statement does have a number of limitations. You can evaluate only *char* variables and the integer types. You cannot use ranges of values, as is possible with Level 88s in Cobol. And there are a few surprising little side effects depending on whether the *break* statement is performed.

Normally, each code block is coded with a *break* in order to exit the switch loop. If a break is not defined, then upon completion of the case code block, the evaluation continues with the next case condition. This may or may not be what you intended, so you should always place *breaks* in case statements, and if you want evaluation to continue, make sure that you document it.

BREAK, CONTINUE

We've introduced the statements *break* and *continue* by example, rather than with a formal definition, so let's address these statements. These are verbs that manage flow control in all the loop structures (while, for, switch, and so forth).

Break causes the current loop to exit or complete immediately. *Continue* causes the current loop to be reiterated from its beginning, preserving the current values. Consider the following examples:

```
int x;
int inputMsgSize = 0;
for (x = 0; x < ARRAY_SIZE ; x++) {
      inputMsgSize = errorMsgs[x].msgSize;
      if (inputMsgSize == 0) {
```

// Exit the loop immediately. x will point to this element.

```
          break;
      }
}
```

// Evaluate inputMsgSize after the loop.

```
if (inputMsgSize == 0) {
      ...
}
```

The *break* statement exits the current *for* loop at once. Variables modified by the loop will maintain their current values, and may be available after the break statement is executed depending on how the variables were defined. In our example, inputMsgSize will be set to 0 if the break was performed.

In contrast, consider this example:

```
for (x = 0; x < ARRAY_SIZE ; x++) {
      int inputMsgSize = errorMsgs[x].msgSize;
      if (inputMsgSize == 0) {
```

// Continue with the next item in the loop.

```
          continue;
      }
```

// Translate the error message using the getTranslation method.
// Note that the String parameter passed to the setErrorMsg() method is the
// result of the getTranslation() method.

```
      errorMsgs[x].setErrorMsg ((errorMsgs[x].getTranslation()));
   }
```

The *continue* statement causes the loop to continue with the next iteration. In our example, error messages with sizes equal to 0 will not be translated. But the loop will continue until all the error messages are examined (and translated if they contain text).

Break and *continue* affect only the current loop. If loops are nested, and a *break* is performed, then program flow will continue with the next statement after the current loop. Conversely, *continue* will cause the current loop to be reiterated.

```
for (x = 0; x < ARRAY_SIZE ; x++) {
      int inputMsgSize = errorMsgs[x].msgSize;
      if (inputMsgSize == 0) {
```

// Find the next item with some text. Then move its text into this item's text.

```
            for (y = x + 1; y < ARRAY_SIZE ; y++) {
                inputMsgSize = errorMsgs[y].msgSize;
                if (inputMsgSize != 0) {
                   errorMsgs[x].setErrorMsg
                     (errorMsgs[y].getErrorMsg);
                   break;
                 }
             }
          }
```

// The *break* statement causes this statement to be processed as the next // statement.

// Translate the error message.

```
      errorMsgs[x].setErrorMsg ((errorMsgs[x].getTranslation()));
}
```

In this example, the *break* statement causes the inner *for* loop to be exited. The outer loop will continue.

What happens if no error messages contain text? We would attempt to perform the translate method without any text! Let's hope the method is robust enough to deal with this condition, but suppose it isn't? The best way to code for this situation would be to break out of the outer loop and the inner loop as soon as we discover that there is no text to translate.

Java provides a labeled break statement to help with this requirement. This statement allows the programmer to specify which loop should be exited. It's as close as Java gets to a *goto* statement. *Goto* is not a valid Java word, but it is reserved (that is, it is not valid as a user-defined name).

Without starting any religious arguments, it is fair to say that there are situations where a *goto* is a superior construct than complex and hard-to-maintain *if … break* and *if … continue* statements. This is particularly appropriate as a mechanism to get out of a nested loop. Once the decision is made to exit to a particular point (that is, exit a particular code block), it is better if the code clearly states that intention.

We can extend our example as follows:

// First, define a label at the beginning of your loop.

```
Translate_loop:

     for (x = 0; x < ARRAY_SIZE ; x++) {
           int inputMsgSize = errorMsgs[x].msgSize;
           if (inputMsgSize == 0) {
```

// Find the next item with some text. Then move its text into this item's text.

```
                for (y = x + 1; y < ARRAY_SIZE ; y++) {
                    inputMsgSize = errorMsgs[y].msgSize;
                    if (inputMsgSize != 0) {
                       errorMsgs[x].setErrorMsg
                         (errorMsgs[y].getErrorMsg);
                       break;
                    }
                    else {
                       if (y == (ARRAY_SIZE - 1)) {
```

// We are on the last item, without finding text. Exit the translate loop entirely.

// Do not process any more items.

```
                            break Translate_loop;
                        }
                    }
                }
           }
```

// Translate the error message.

```
          errorMsgs[x].setErrorMsg
                ((errorMsgs[x].getTranslation()));
  }
```

// This statement will be processed as the next statement after
// `break Translate_loop;` is executed.
// It is also perfomed as the next statement after the loop exits normally.

```
    System.out.println ("The loop has completed");
```

The following chart summarizes the Java flow control operators

Construct	Description	Cobol Equivalent
if condition ... else ...	Evaluate condition and perform either the first or the second code block	IF condition .... ELSE ...
for condition ...	Iteratively perform the next code block until condition is not true	PERFORM paragraph VARYING
while condition ...	Perform the next code block until condition is not true	PERFORM paragraph UNTIL
do ... while condition	Perform the next code block evaluate condition, and if true, perform code block again	PERFORM paragraph UNTIL
switch (i) case ... case...	Perform the appropriate code block depending on the value of (i)	EVALUATE
break	Exit the current loop	EXIT
continue	Reiterate the current loop from the beginning	
labeled break	Exit the current loop and go to the statement past the labeled loop	GO TO

EXERCISES: JAVA'S SYNTAX

Time to visit our example classes again and try out all these new ideas.

USING JAVA 2'S JDK

1. Edit the HelloWorld.java source file in your java4cobol directory with a text editor. We'll start by deleting the code that experimented

with inheritance. Remove the lines after this statement (but remember to leave in the two curly braces at the end of the program):

// Print the contents of ErrorMsg's String data member directly.

```
System.out.println (myErrorMsg.msgText);
```

2. Add these Java expressions at the end of the previous statement (before the last two curly braces):

// Experiment with Java statements.

```
String testMsg
myErrorMsg.getErrorMsg ()
```

3. Save these modifications as a text file, and then compile the class in the DOS command window:

➢ javac HelloWorld.java

You should get an error message indicating that a semicolon is missing.

Add a semicolon to the end of each of these expressions. Compile this class again. It should now compile successfully.

4. These two statements simply define a String variable, and execute the getErrorMsg() method in the ErrorMsg class. As written, they are not very useful since we end up with an empty String variable, and the result of this effort is lost. Add this additional **bold** Java code to our statements, making them more useful:

// Experiment with Java statements.

```
String testMsg;
testMsg = myErrorMsg.getErrorMsg ();
```

Compile this class again.

5. Combine these two statements into one as follows:

// Experiment with Java statements.

```
String testMsg = myErrorMsg.getErrorMsg ();
```

Compile this class again.

6. Next, we'll adjust our original statement and make it more complex. Add this additional **bold** Java code:

// Experiment with Java statements.

```
String testMsg = myErrorMsg.getErrorMsg ();
if (myErrorMsg.getErrorMsg ().equals (testMsg)) {
   System.out.println ("testMsg = ErrorMsg text");
}
```

7. Save, compile, and rerun the HelloWorld application.

➢ javac HelloWorld.java

➢ java HelloWorld

The output should look like this:

```
. . .
testMsg = ErrorMsg text
```

8. Next, we'll adjust our *if* code block in order to explore the scope of local variables. Add this additional **bold** Java code:

// Experiment with Java statements.

```
String testMsg = myErrorMsg.getErrorMsg ();
if (myErrorMsg.getErrorMsg ().equals (testMsg)) {
```

// Define a temporary integer variable.

```
   int i = 5;
   System.out.println ("testMsg = ErrorMsg text");
   System.out.println ("i = " + i);
}
```

9. Compile and rerun the HelloWorld application. The output should look like this:

```
. . .
testMsg = ErrorMsg text
i = 5
```

10. So far, pretty simple stuff. Now try to access our temporary variable outside its code block. Add these additional **bold** Java statements:

// Experiment with Java statements.

```
String testMsg = myErrorMsg.getErrorMsg ();
if (myErrorMsg.getErrorMsg ().equals (testMsg)) {
```

// Define a temporary integer variable.

```
  int i = 5;
  System.out.println ("testMsg = text in ErrorMsg");
  System.out.println ("i = " + i);
}
else {
     System.out.println ("i = " + i);
}
System.out.println ("i = " + i);
```

Attempt to compile this class. You should get an error message indicating that the compiler does not know the definition of the variable i. Delete the first println statement, then the other statement. Is either valid? What does this tell you about the scope of local variable i? Can it be accessed outside the code block where it was created (as defined by a pair of matching braces {})? Where would you need to place the definition of i in order to compile the Java statements above? Go ahead and try it.

The code samples presented till now have all used the // style of comment identification. We will experiment with other styles of comment identification.

11. Restore the HelloWorld application to the content described in step 10 above. Now, instead of deleting the incorrect references to the variable "i," comment them out using the multi-line comment identifier:

// Experiment with Java statements.

```
String testMsg = myErrorMsg.getErrorMsg ();
if (myErrorMsg.getErrorMsg ().equals (testMsg)) {
```

// Define a temporary integer variable.

```
     int i = 5;
     System.out.println ("testMsg = text in ErrorMsg");
     System.out.println ("i = " + i);
}
```

/* Comment out the next few lines

```
        else {
             System.out.println ("i = " + i);
        }
        System.out.println ("i = " + i);
```

Comment out the next few lines */

Recompile this program.

12. Next, we'll experiment with javadoc style comments. You will be pleasantly surprised with the result. Edit the ErrorMsg.java source file in your java4cobol directory with a text editor. Add these **bold** javadoc comments to your class. (The code for this class is on the CD, so you don't need to copy it from the book.)

//

//

// ErrorMsg

//

//

/**

*** A class for managing and storing error messages.**

*** This class extends the TextMessage class. As a result, translation**

*** options are also supported.**

@version 1.01 99/01/01

@author John C Byrne

*/

```
public class ErrorMsg extends TextMessage
```

// Define some private class instance variables.

```
         private int  counter = 0;
                  char     interfaceInUse;
```

/**

*** This method sets the text in the ErrorMsg object.**

@param String inputMsg . Contains the text to be stored in this object

*/

// Define a public method.

```
public void setErrorMsg (String inputMsg) {
```

// Define a local variable and increment it.

```
int localCounter = 0;
localCounter = localCounter + 1;
```

// Modify some of the private variables.

```
counter = counter + 1;
interfaceInUse = 'S';
setMsgText (inputMsg);
```

// Return from this method. Since this method has no return value (that is, it is
// declared as void), no return statement is necessary.

```
}
```

/**
*** This method returns the text in the ErrorMsg object.**
@return The current text in this ErrorMsg object
***/**

// Define another public method.

```
public String getErrorMsg () {
     String returnMsg;
```

// Define a local variable and increment it.

```
int localCounter = 0;
localCounter = localCounter + 1;
```

// Modify some of the private variables.

```
counter = counter + 1;
interfaceInUse = 'G';
```

// Set the local variable `returnMsg` to the data member `msgText`.

```
returnMsg = msgText;
```

// Return from this method, and return the string variable.

```
     return (returnMsg);
}
```

```
/**
* This method returns the text in the ErrorMsg object.
@param    char caseFlag. If = "U" then text will be converted
      to all uppercase.
@return    The current text in this ErrorMsg object
*/

// Define a variation on the public method getErrorMsg.

        public String getErrorMsg (char caseFlag) {
            String returnMsg;

// Perform the standard getErrorMsg method.

            returnMsg = getErrorMsg ();

// Convert to all uppercase if requested.

            if (caseFlag == 'U')
                returnMsg = returnMsg.toUpperCase ();

// Return from this method, and return the string variable.

            return (returnMsg);
        }

/**
* This method returns the number of times this ErrorMsg has been called.
@return        The number of times this ErrorMsg object has been called.
*/

// Define a method to return counter.

        public int getCounter () {


// Return from this method, with the value of counter.

            return (counter);
        }

/**
* This method returns the number of times the localCounter has been
incremented.
@return        The number of times localCounter has been incremented.
*/
```

// Define a method to return localCounter.

```
        public int getLocalCounter () {
             int localCounter = 0;
             localCounter = localCounter + 1;
```

// Return from this method with the value of localCounter.

```
             return (localCounter);
        }
```

/**
*** This method returns the translated text for this ErrorMsg object. Since this**
*** is an error message, set the text to all uppercase.**
@return The translated version of this ErrorMsg.
***/**

// Define a method named getTranslation(). This method overrides the
// method with the same name in the base class.

```
        public String getTranslation () {
```

// Call the base object's method.

```
             String localString = super.getTranslation ();
```

// Since this is an error message, change it to all uppercase.
// Perform the toUpperCase() function (this is a method that every String has).

```
             localString = localString.toUpperCase ();
             return (localString);

        }
}
```

13. Save these modifications as a text file, and then compile the class in the DOS command window:

➢ javac ErrorMsg.java

14. Now for the fun part! Create your own professional-looking documentation for the ErrorMsg class using the javadoc tool. Execute this command in the DOS command window:

➢ javadoc ErrorMsg.java

    Several new files should be created in your java4cobol directory. The most interesting one is index.html. Double-click on this file in the Windows Explorer (it is assumed that the file extension .html is associated with an Internet browser). You should be rewarded with a very professional-looking documentation set in HTML format.

    The javadoc output is even more useful when you use it against all the files in a directory (or a package). In this case, the tool will report the association between related files as well as the interfaces to individual files.

15. Next, we'll explore how parentheses can modify the results of a statement. Using a text editor, add these **bold** lines to the end of your HelloWorld.java source file (after the lines that were commented out in step 11):

```
int x, y, z;
x = 3;
y = 4;

z = x + 1 * 2;
System.out.println ("z = " + z);
```

    Compile and rerun the HelloWorld application. The output should look like this:

```
. . .
testMsg = ErrorMsg text
i = 5
z = 5
```

16. Add the parentheses as indicated here.

```
z = (x + 1) * 2;
System.out.println ("z = " + z);
```

Compile and rerun the HelloWorld application. As you would expect, the value of z is different. The output should look like this:

```
. . .
testMsg = ErrorMsg text
i = 5
z = 8
```

17. We'll explore how to use the Java operators to control evaluations. Add these **bold** lines to the end of your HelloWorld java source file:

// Experiment with operators

```
if (((x == y) || (z < x)) &&
  ((z != y) || (x >= 1))) {
     System.out.println ("Condition is true");
}
else {
     System.out.println ("Condition is not true");
}
```

Compile and rerun the HelloWorld application. The output should look like this:

```
. . .
testMsg = ErrorMsg text
i = 5
z = 8
Condition is not true
```

Compare the previous Java statements to this Cobol sentence:

```
IF  (((X = Y) OR (Z < X)) AND
    ((Z NOT = Y) OR (X NOT < 1)))
    DISPLAY "Condition is true"
ELSE
    DISPLAY "Condition is not true".
```

Notice the liberal use of parentheses in the Java example and the use of curly braces around the *if* and *else* code blocks even though these constructs may not be strictly required.

What Java operator can you reverse in order to make the "Condition is true" message appear?

18. We'll experiment a bit with additional data types. Add these **bold** lines to the end of your HelloWorld class:

// Experiment with additional data types.

// These data types are automatically converted to the double data type

// during the comparison.

```
double d = 4;
float f = 4;
short s = 4;
if ((d == y) && (d == f) && (d == s)) {
     System.out.println ("Condition is true");
}
else {
     System.out.println ("Condition is not true");
}
```

Compile and rerun the HelloWorld application. The output should look like this:

```
. . .
testMsg = ErrorMsg text
i = 5
z = 8
Condition is not true
Condition is true
```

19. Try a test involving overflow of integer values. Add these **bold** lines to the end of your HelloWorld class:

// Experiment with overflow.

```
d *= 536870912;
y *= 536870912;
if (d == y) {
     System.out.println ("Condition is true");
}
else {
     System.out.println ("Condition is not true. d = " + d
         + " y = " + y);
}
```

Compile and rerun the HelloWorld application. The output should look like this:

```
. . .
testMsg = ErrorMsg text
i = 5
z = 8
Condition is not true
Condition is true
Condition is not true. d = 2.147483648E9 y = -2147483648
```

Java specifies that integer multiplication will not cause an error condition (exception) even if overflow occurs, so be careful with large integer numbers. Notice the way d is printed. Java double numbers are stored in IEEE 754 format, and this is a String representation of this format.

20. Let's work with one of the more common Java constructs, the *for* loop. As mentioned earlier, this is analogous to the PERFORM Cobol verb. Add these **bold** lines to the end of your HelloWorld class:

// Experiment with for and case.

```
int even = 0, odd = 0, other = 0, total = 0, i;
for (i = 0; i < 9; i++) {

     total++;
     switch (i) {
```

```
        case 1:
        case 3:
        case 5:
        case 7:
            odd ++;
            break;

        case 2:
        case 4:
        case 6:
        case 8:
            even ++;
            break;

        default:
            other ++;
            break;
        }
}
System.out.println ("Odd, Even, Other, and Total = " + odd + ", " +
    even + ", " + other + ", " + total);
```

Compile and rerun the HelloWorld application. The output should look like this:

```
. . .
testMsg = ErrorMsg text
i = 5
z = 8
Condition is not true
Condition is true
Condition is not true. d = 2.147483648E9 y = -2147483648
Odd, Even, Other, and Total = 4, 4, 1, 9
```

Look closely at the *for* loop definition and the output line. How many times did the *for* loop execute? What do you think the range of values for i were as the loop executed?

Remove the *break* statement in each of the case sections. What happens? Why did this happen? Hint: refer to the introductory discussion on the case statement.

21. Let's test how the *continue* statement works in a *for* loop. Add these **bold** lines to your HelloWorld class:

// Experiment with *for* and *case.*

```
int even = 0, odd = 0, other = 0, total = 0, i;
for (i = 0; i < 9; i++) {

    total++;
    if (i > -1 ) {
        continue;
    }
    switch (i) {
```

Compile and rerun the HelloWorld application. The output should look like this:

```
. . .
Odd, Even, Other, and Total = 0, 0, 0, 9
```

Look closely at the for loop definition and the output line. How many times did the for loop execute? Why do you think that no variables except total were incremented?

22. Let's create a *for* loop inside our original one. We will also observe the effect of a *break* statement in a *for* loop. Insert comment markers for the *italicized* lines, and add these **bold** lines to your HelloWorld class:

// Experiment with *for* and *case.*

```
    int even = 0, odd = 0, other = 0, total = 0, i;
    for (i = 0; i < 9; i++) {

        total++;
//      if (i > -1 ) {
//          continue;
//      }
        switch (i) {

        case 1:
        case 3:
        case 5:
        case 7:
            odd ++;
            for (int i2 = 0; i2 < 10; i2++) {
```

```
                    odd++;
                    break;
               }
               break;
          case 2:
          case 4:
          case 6:
          case 8:
               even ++;
               break;
          default:
               other ++;
               break;
          }
     }
     System.out.println ("Odd, Even, Other, and Total = " + odd + ", " +
          even + ", " + other + ", " + total);
```

Compile and rerun the HelloWorld application. The output should look like this:

```
. . .
Odd, Even, Other, and Total = 8, 4, 1, 9
```

Look closely at the *for* loop definition and the output line. How many times did the outer *for* loop execute? Why do you think that the variable named odd was only incremented once for each execution of the inner loop, even though the inner loop definition says it should be performed 10 times?

23. For our last exercise, we'll define a labeled break. This statement allows you to go to the end of a code block from inside the code block. Add these **bold** lines to your HelloWorld class:

// Experiment with *for* and *case*.

```
     int even = 0, odd = 0, other = 0, total = 0, i;
outerloop:
     for (i = 0; i < 9; i++) {

          total++;
          switch (i) {
```

```
            case 1:
            case 3:
            case 5:
            case 7:
                odd ++;
                for (int i2 = 0; i2 < 10; i2++) {
                    odd++;
                    break outerloop;
                }
                break;
            case 2:
            case 4:
            case 6:
            case 8:
                even ++;
                break;

            default:
                other ++;
                break;
            }
        }
        System.out.println ("Odd, Even, Other, and Total = " + odd + ", " +
            even + ", " + other + ", " + total);
```

Compile and rerun the HelloWorld application. The output should look like this:

```
. . .
Odd, Even, Other, and Total = 2, 0, 1, 2
```

Look closely at the labeled *for* loop definition and the output line. How many times did the outer *for* loop execute this time? Why do you think that the variable named even was never incremented in the loop?

EXERCISES: USING J++

1. Select your java4cobol project from among the recent workspaces using this menu path:

➢ File → Recent Workspaces → java4cobol.

2. We'll start by deleting the code that experimented with inheritance. Remove the lines after this statement (but remember to leave in the two curly braces at the end of the program):

// Print the contents of ErrorMsg's String data member directly.

```
System.out.println (myErrorMsg.msgText);
```

3. Add these Java expressions at the end of the previous statement (before the last two curly braces):

// Experiment with Java statements.

```
String testMsg
myErrorMsg.getErrorMsg ()
```

4. Compile this class using this menu path:

➢ Build → Compile HelloWorld.java

You should get several error messages.

Add a semicolon to the end of each of these expressions. Compile this class again. It should now compile successfully.

5. These two statements simply define a String variable and execute the getErrorMsg() method in the ErrorMsg class. As written, they are not very useful since we end up with an empty String variable and the result of this effort is lost. Add this additional **bold** Java code to our statements, making them more useful:

// Experiment with Java statements.

```
String testMsg;
testMsg = myErrorMsg.getErrorMsg ();
```

Compile this class again.

6. Combine these two statements into one as follows:

// Experiment with Java statements.

```
String testMsg = myErrorMsg.getErrorMsg ();
```

Compile this class again.

7. Next, we'll adjust our original statement and make it more complex. Add this additional **bold** Java code:

// Experiment with Java statements.

```
String testMsg = myErrorMsg.getErrorMsg ();
if (myErrorMsg.getErrorMsg ().equals (testMsg)) {
  System.out.println ("testMsg = ErrorMsg text");
}
```

8. Compile and rerun the HelloWorld application. The output should look like this:

```
. . .
testMsg = ErrorMsg text
```

9. Next, we'll adjust our *if* code block in order to explore the scope of local variables. Add this additional **bold** Java code:

// Experiment with Java statements.

```
String testMsg = myErrorMsg.getErrorMsg ();
if (myErrorMsg.getErrorMsg ().equals (testMsg)) {
```

// Define a temporary integer variable.

```
  int i = 5;
  System.out.println ("testMsg = ErrorMsg text");
  System.out.println ("i = " + i);
}
```

10. Compile and rerun the HelloWorld application. The output should look like this:

```
. . .
testMsg = ErrorMsg text
i = 5
```

11. So far, pretty simple stuff. Now try to access our temporary variable outside its code block. Add these additional **bold** Java statements:

// Experiment with Java statements.

```
String testMsg = myErrorMsg.getErrorMsg ();
if (myErrorMsg.getErrorMsg ().equals (testMsg)) {
```

// Define a temporary integer variable.

```
     int i = 5;
     System.out.println ("testMsg = text in ErrorMsg");
     System.out.println ("i = " + i);
}
else {
     System.out.println ("i = " + i);
}
System.out.println ("i = " + i);
```

Attempt to compile this class. You should get an error message indicating that the compiler does not know the definition of the variable i. Delete the first new println statement, then the other. Is either one valid? What does this tell you about the scope of local variable i? Can it be accessed outside the code block where it was created (as defined by a pair of matching braces {})? Where would you need to place the definition of i in order to compile the preceding Java statements? Go ahead and try it.

The code samples presented till now have all used the // style of comment identification. We will experiment with another style of comment identification.

12. Restore the HelloWorld application to the content described in step 11. Now, instead of deleting the incorrect references to the variable i, comment them out using the multiline comment identifier:

// Experiment with Java statements.

```
String testMsg = myErrorMsg.getErrorMsg ();
if (myErrorMsg.getErrorMsg ().equals (testMsg)) {
```

// Define a temporary integer variable.

```
   int i = 5;
   System.out.println ("testMsg = text in ErrorMsg");
   System.out.println ("i = " + i);
}
```

/* Comment out the next few lines

```
else {
     System.out.println ("i = " + i);
 }
 System.out.println ("i = " + I);
```

Comment out the next few lines */

TECHNICAL NOTE: Most graphical IDEs use color to visually identify comment sections. Your commented out code block should appear in a color (green is the default color for comments) distinct from code that will be executed. You can adjust the color used to identify comments (along with other settings) using the Tools options menu path, and then selecting the Format tab.

---

13. Next, we'll explore how parentheses can modify the results of a statement. Add these bold lines to the end of your HelloWorld class:

```
int x, y, z;
x = 3;
y = 4;

z = x + 1 * 2;
System.out.println ("z = " + z);
```

Compile and rerun the HelloWorld application. The output should look like this:

```
. . .
testMsg = ErrorMsg text
i = 5
z = 5
```

14. Add the parentheses as indicated here.

```
z = (x + 1) * 2;
System.out.println ("z = " + z);
```

Compile and rerun the HelloWorld application. As you would expect, the value of z is different. The output should look like this:

```
. . .
testMsg = ErrorMsg text
i = 5
z = 8
```

15. We'll explore how to use the Java operators to control evaluations. Add these **bold** lines to the end of your HelloWorld class:

// Experiment with operators.

```
if (((x == y) || (z < x)) &&
    ((z != y) || (x >= 1))) {
     System.out.println ("Condition is true");
}
else {
     System.out.println ("Condition is not true");
}
```

Compile and rerun the HelloWorld application. The output should look like this:

```
. . .
testMsg = ErrorMsg text
i = 5
z = 8
Condition is not true
```

Compare the previous Java statements to this Cobol sentence:

```
IF (((X = Y) OR (Z < X)) AND
    ((Z NOT = Y) OR (X NOT < 1)))
     DISPLAY "Condition is true"
ELSE
     DISPLAY "Condition is not true".
```

Notice the liberal use of parentheses in the Java example and the use of curly braces around the if and else code blocks even though these constructs may not be strictly required.

What Java operator can you reverse in order to make the "Condition is true" message appear?

16. We'll experiment a bit with additional data types. Add these **bold** lines to the end of your HelloWorld class:

// Experiment with additional data types.

// These data types are automatically converted to the double data type

// during the comparison.

```
double d = 4;
float f = 4;
short s = 4;
if ((d == y) && (d == f) && (d == s)) {
     System.out.println ("Condition is true");
}
else {
     System.out.println ("Condition is not true");
}
```

Compile and rerun the HelloWorld application. The output should look like this:

```
. . .
testMsg = ErrorMsg text
i = 5
z = 8
Condition is not true
Condition is true
```

17. Try a test involving overflow of integer values. Add these **bold** lines to the end of your HelloWorld class:

// Experiment with overflow.

```
d *= 536870912;
y *= 536870912;
if (d == y) {
     System.out.println ("Condition is true");
}
else {
     System.out.println ("Condition is not true. d = " + d
          + " y = " + y);
}
```

Compile and rerun the HelloWorld application. The output should look like this:

```
. . .
testMsg = ErrorMsg text
i = 5
z = 8
Condition is not true
Condition is true
Condition is not true. d = 2.147483648E9 y = -2147483648
```

Java specifies that integer multiplication will not cause an error condition (exception), even if overflow occurs, so be careful with large integer numbers. Notice the way d is printed. Java double numbers are stored in IEEE 754 format, and this is a String representation of this format.

18. Let's work with one of the more common Java constructs, the *for* loop. As mentioned earlier, this is analogous to the PERFORM Cobol verb. Add these **bold** lines to the end of your HelloWorld class:

// Experiment with *for* and *case*.

```
int even = 0, odd = 0, other = 0, total = 0, i;
for (i = 0; i < 9; i++) {

     total++;
     switch (i) {

     case 1:
     case 3:
     case 5:
     case 7:
          odd ++;
          break;

     case 2:
     case 4:
     case 6:
     case 8:
          even ++;
          break;
```

```
        default:
            other ++;
            break;
        }
}
System.out.println ("Odd, Even, Other, and Total = " + odd + ", " +
    even + ", " + other + ", " + total);
```

Compile and rerun the HelloWorld application. The output should look like this:

```
. . .
testMsg = ErrorMsg text
i = 5
z = 8
Condition is not true
Condition is true
Condition is not true. d = 2.147483648E9 y = -2147483648
Odd, Even, Other, and Total = 4, 4, 1, 9
```

Look closely at the *for* loop definition and the output line. How many times did the *for* loop execute? What do you think the range of values for i were as the loop executed?

Remove the break statement in each of the case sections. What happens? Why did this happen? Hint: refer to the introductory discussion on the case statement.

19. Let's test how the continue statement works in a *for* loop. Add these **bold** lines to your HelloWorld class:

// Experiment with *for* and *case*.

```
int even = 0, odd = 0, other = 0, total = 0, i;
for (i = 0; i < 9; i++) {

    total++;
    if (i > -1 ) {
        continue;
    }
    switch (i) {
```

Compile and rerun the HelloWorld application. The output should look like this:

```
. . .
Odd, Even, Other, and Total = 0, 0, 0, 9
```

Look closely at the *for* loop definition and the output line. How many times did the *for* loop execute? Why do you think that no variables except the one named total were incremented?

20. Let's create a *for* loop inside our original one. We will also observe the effect of a break statement in a *for* loop. Insert comment markers for the *italicized* lines, and add these **bold** lines to your HelloWorld class:

// Experiment with for and case.

```
    int even = 0, odd = 0, other = 0, total = 0, i;
    for (i = 0; i < 9; i++) {

        total++;
//      if (i > -1 ) {
//          continue;
//      }
        switch (i) {

        case 1:
        case 3:
        case 5:
        case 7:
            odd ++;
            for (int i2 = 0; i2 < 10; i2++) {
                odd++;
                break;
            }
            break;
        case 2:
        case 4:
        case 6:
        case 8:
            even ++;
            break;

        default:
            other ++;
            break;
        }
    }
```

```
System.out.println ("Odd, Even, Other, and Total = " + odd + ", "
    even + ", " + other + ", " + total);
```

Compile and rerun the HelloWorld application. The output should look like this:

```
. . .
Odd, Even, Other, and Total = 8, 4, 1, 9
```

Look closely at the *for* loop definition and the output line. How many times did the outer *for* loop execute? Why do you think that the variable named odd was incremented only once for each execution of the inner loop even though the inner loop definition says it should be performed it 10 times?

21. For our last exercise, we'll define a labeled break. This statement allows you to go to the end of a code block from inside the code block. Add these **bold** lines to your HelloWorld class:

// Experiment with *for* and *case.*

```
     int even = 0, odd = 0, other = 0, total = 0, i;
outerloop:
     for (i = 0; i < 9; i++) {

          total++;
          switch (i) {

          case 1:
          case 3:
          case 5:
          case 7:
               odd ++;
               for (int i2 = 0; i2 < 10; i2++) {
                    odd++;
                    break outerloop;
               }
               break;
          case 2:
          case 4:
          case 6:
          case 8:
               even ++;
               break;
```

```
        default:
            other ++;
            break;
        }
    }
    System.out.println ("Odd, Even, Other, and Total = " + odd + ", " +
      even + ", " + other + ", " + total);
```

Compile and rerun the HelloWorld application. The output should look like this:

```
. . .
Odd, Even, Other, and Total = 2, 0, 1, 2
```

Look closely at the labeled *for* loop definition and the output line. How many times did the outer *for* loop execute this time? Why do you think that the variable named even was never incremented in the loop?

REVIEWING OUR EXERCISES

Let's review the samples we've created. Try to relate the sample source statements to the result (that is, the output) each statement creates. If necessary, rerun the samples, or look at the complete source code for this exercise on the CD. Feel free to experiment by yourself.

- Java statements must end with a semicolon. A single statement can contain several Java expressions.
- Local variables can be accessed only in the code block that creates them.
- Java uses parentheses to group expressions in much the same way as Cobol. Java's AND, OR, and NOT operators (&&, ||, !) work in much the same way as do their Cobol counterparts.
- Java's for loop is similar to Cobol's PERFORM UNTIL construct. The continue statement causes the current iteration of this loop to terminate and the next iteration to start. The break statement causes the current code block to be exited immediately.

- Finally, we constructed a labeled for loop. After the loop was performed only two times, we exited the labeled loop abruptly, causing the statement after the loop to be executed. In fact, we exited the outer loop from inside an inner loop.

CHAPTER

8

Strings, StringBuffers, Numbers, and BigNumbers

STRINGS

Java provides a String class that developers can use to hold and manipulate character strings (that is, a sequence of chars). The Cobol developer may recognize Strings as the equivalent of the "PIC X(x)" definition, and they are generally similar. However, Java's native String handling functions are much superior to Cobol's notoriously weak character manipulation support. Further, Strings are real objects, and so some differences naturally exist. Java Strings contain 16-bit Unicode characters, which can represent any foreign character, whereas Cobol characters are only 8-bit (typically ASCII or EBCDIC) characters.

The developer can create a String object using the standard Java syntax. You should be familiar with this construct since we have used it several times already.

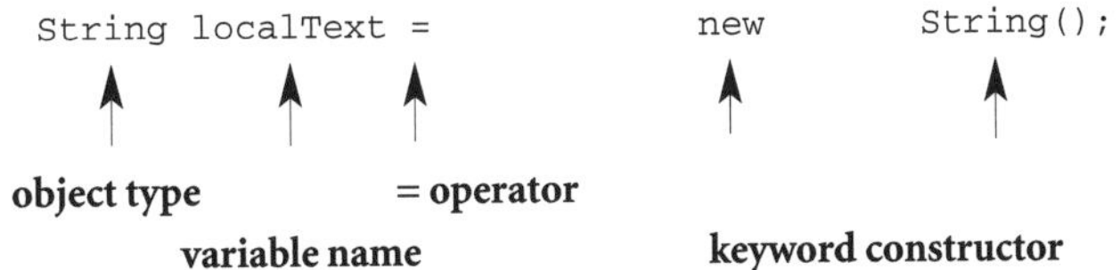

String provides an alternative constructor that accepts a String parameter.

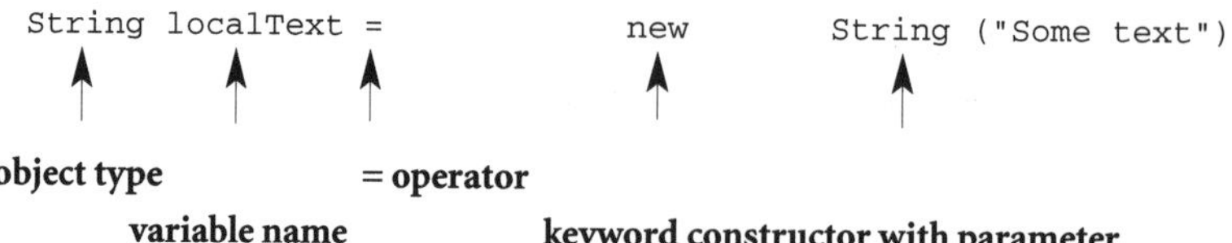

This statement will set the localText String reference equal to a String that contains "Some Text."

This complete syntax is often compressed into the form:

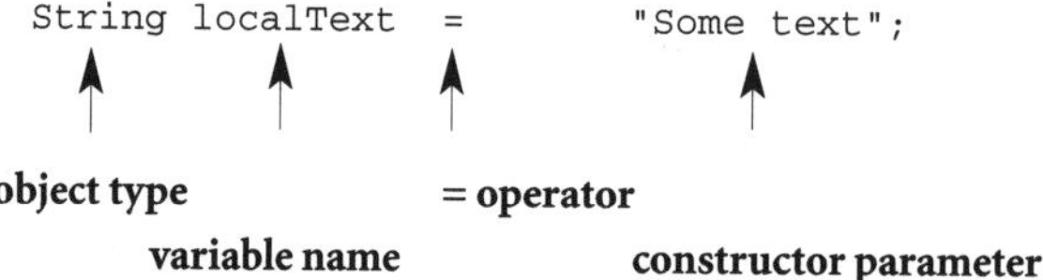

Notice that the compressed syntax is very similar to the syntax used to define primitive data types:

```
int localInt =      1;
```

Despite the similarity in syntax, there is a major difference in our examples. localint is a primitive data type, not an object. In contrast, localtext is an object since all Strings are objects.

Let's review the following statement:

```
String localText =       "Some text";
```

First, a String object containing the text "Some text" was created by the compiler. Then, the object reference variable localText was created and adjusted to reference that object. The compiler handles all this automatically since it treats String variables in a special way. Whenever the compiler sees a double quoted constant, it will automatically create a new String object.

COMPARING STRINGS

The base String class contains many useful manipulation methods. Every String object you create will contain these methods as well. One example is a method called equals() that will compare two Strings for equality:

Return type	Method name	Parameter signature
`boolean`	`equals`	`(String s)`

A Java statement can use this method to compare the text value in a String object (such as localText) to some other String object:

```
if (localText.equals ("Some other text")) {
    . . .
}
```

You may wonder why we didn't use the more familiar equality operator (==) to evaluate localText. This is because Strings are objects and not intrinsic data types. Therefore, the equality operation would compare the object reference variables and not the text contained in those objects.

```
if (localText == "Some other text") {
     . . .
}
```

This is a valid statement and looks natural, but it is really one you will hardly ever use. It can be read the following way: "Compare the object reference variable localText for equality to the (implicit) object reference variable that contains "Some other text." Return true if they are exactly equal."

Since object reference variables contain the memory location of the object, this statement will be true only if both variables point to exactly the same location in memory! This will rarely be true, so the preceding statement will almost always fail. It is clearly not the way to test String variables or any other types of objects for equal text values.

Strings have a number of special characteristics assigned to them by Java. One is the fact that they are considered *immutable*, meaning that they cannot change.

"Wait a minute!" you may be saying. "We saw some examples that changed the value of String variables."

Actually, there were no such examples. In reality, new Strings were created and the String variable was changed to point to the new object. Consider our original String definition statement:

```
String localText =       "Some text";
```

A subsequent statement can cause localText to point to another String:

```
localText =       "Some other text";
```

Follow what really happens when this statement is executed:

1. A new String object containing the text "Some other text" is created automatically by the compiler.
2. The String reference variable is changed to point to this object instead of the original object.
3. The original String object ("Some text") is marked as unused and will eventually be deleted.

WORKING WITH STRINGS

Strings can easily be concatenated using the + operator:

```
String localText =        ("Some text ");
localText += "/ Some other text";
```

After execution of the second statement, localText would point to a (new) String containing "Some text / Some other text."

The + operator will automatically convert any data type into a String if necessary.

```
String localText =        ("Some text ");
int x = 4;
localText += "/ "
localText += x;
```

After execution of the second statement, localText would point to a (new) String containing "Some text / 4."

As a Cobol programmer, one would think that to add a number to a String might be considered a nonsensical operation, yielding unpredictable results. What would happen in Cobol if you said:

```
ADD 4 TO "Some Text".
```

Some sort of compiler error, we hope! But in Java, this type of statement is perfectly legal. The numeric item automatically gets converted into a String.

Java accomplishes this by assigning special processing to the + operator in some cases, such as when the destination is a String variable. In this case, the + operator becomes a *concatenate* operator. If any of the source operands are not Strings, they will automatically be converted into Strings, and then concatenated. In our example, the value 4 was originally created as an integer, and then it was converted into the character String 4. This String was then added to the text in localString, creating a new String object.

TECHNICAL NOTE: This scenario is an example of a concept called *operator overloading.* Some OO languages allow operators such as + to be overloaded, or redefined by the developer. In this way, special processing can be performed based on the class type. Although this is a very powerful tool, it can easily lead to programs that are hard for anyone but the original developer to understand.

For example, a developer might look at the statement x – y, and expect a straight-forward algebraic function. But if the - operator has been overridden when applied to y, then the developer may ask, "What does x - y actually mean in this case, and why is it so different than a - b in the previous statement?"

Java does not allow operators to be overloaded by the developer, although the compiler uses the concept itself in this case.

The conversion of objects and data types into Strings is accomplished by a *toString()* method. Every Java object and data type has a method of this name. The + operator simply calls this method and concatenates the String returned by the method with the current String. (This is actually a good demonstration of the power of polymorphism.)

Java's class definition for Strings includes quite a few very useful methods. Some are described in this chart, along with the (roughly) equivalent Cobol statements:

Method	Description	Cobol Equivalent
char charAt (int index)	Return the character at position *index* in *String*	Reference modification: **STRING1**(3:1)
int compareTo (String string2)	Compare two Strings; return -1, 0, or 1 depending on relative position in Unicode order	IF **STRING1** <,=,> **STRING2**
String concat (String string2)	Return a new String where all *string2's* characters have been appended to *string1's*	STRING **STRING1, STRING2** INTO **STRING3** DELIMITED BY SPACES (or SIZE)
boolean endsWith (String string2)	Test if String ends in *string2*	IF **STRING1**(CTR:SIZE) = **STRING2**
boolean equals (object anyObject)	Test if the text in String equals the text in *object*	IF **STRING1** = **STRING2***
boolean equalsIgnoreCase (String string2)	Test if the text in String equals the text in *string2* regardless of case	MOVE **STRING1 TO NEW-STRING** INSPECT CONVERTING **NEW-STRING**** IF **STRING2** = **NEW-STRING**
int indexOf (String string2)	Test if the text in String contains the text in *string2.* Return its first location or -1	INSPECT **STRING1** TALLYING CTR FOR CHARACTERS BEFORE INITIAL **STRING2**
int lastIndexof (String string2)	Test if the text in String contains the text in *string2.* Return its last location or -1	INSPECT **STRING1** TALLYING **COUNTER** FOR ALL **STRING2**
int lastIndexof (String string2, int fromIndex)	Test if the text in String contains the text in *string2* starting at position *fromIndex*. Return its last location or -1	INSPECT **STRING1**(CTR:SIZE) TALLYING **COUNTER** FOR ALL **STRING2**
int length()	Return the length of *String.*	Items are always fixed length, defined at compile time
String replace (char oldChar, char newChar)	Return a new String where all occurrences of *oldChar* have been replaced with *newChar*	INSPECT **STRING1** REPLACING ALL **OLD-CHAR** BY **NEW-CHAR**
boolean startsWith (String string2)	Test if the text in String begins with the text in *string2*	IF **STRING1**(1:SIZE)=**STRING2**
String substring (int beginIndex)	Return a new String with the characters starting at *beginIndex* to the end of *string*	MOVE **STRING1**(POS:SIZE-REMAINING) TO **STRING2**
String substring (int beginIndex, int endIndex)	Return a new String with the characters starting at *beginIndex* to *endIndex*	MOVE **STRING1**(POS:SIZE) TO **STRING2**
String toLowerCase ()	Return a new String with all the characters in String converted to lowercase	MOVE **STRING1 TO NEW-STRING** INSPECT CONVERTING **NEW-STRING**

* Cobol automatically adds spaces to the end of strings of unequal lengths. Java Strings have an implied length (including all spaces) and will not be equal unless their sizes are also equal.

** Multi-language case conversion is not possible with this approach. Library packages are recommended.

Method	Description	Cobol Equivalent
String toUpperCase ()	Return a new String with all the characters in String converted to uppercase	MOVE **STRING1 TO NEW-STRING** INSPECT CONVERTING **NEW-STRING**
String trim ()	Return a new String with the characters in String, except leading and trailing spaces	STRING **STRING1** INTO **STRING2** DELIMITED BY SPACES
String valueOf (datatype arg)	Return a String representation of *arg.*	MOVE **NUMBER** TO **NUMBER-AS-Z9***

NUMERIC WRAPPER CLASSES

In the same way that numeric items can be converted into Strings, Strings sometimes need to be turned into numbers. However, since primitive data types are not objects, they do not have methods and members. Where can the Java language designers place the necessary methods?

To provide a mechanism to represent primitive types as objects, Java defines special classes that wrap the basic numeric data types into objects. These classes are very useful when objects (rather than intrinsic data types) are required. These classes have familiar names (Integer, Long, Float, Double, Byte), and all are inherited from the parent Number class. All sorts of useful methods are contained in these classes.

One example is the parseInt() method, which the developer can use to convert a String into a numeric item. This method accepts a String input parameter and returns a numeric item of type int.

TECHNICAL NOTE: This method implements the Java construct called exception processing. This means that a program can call the method, but some exception may occur before the method completes. The calling program can use the try and catch code blocks to properly handle possible exceptions. Exceptions are discussed in more detail in Chapter 10.

```
String inputMsg = " 003 ";
int x = 0;
```

* There is no Cobol analogy for a string representation of true or false, but numeric types can be converted into characters.

// Try to convert String to *integer*. Catch any NumberFormat exception errors.

```
try  {
      x = Integer.parseInt (inputMsg.trim());
}
catch (NumberFormatException e) {
     . . .
     x = 0;
}
```

This code sample first removes any trailing or leading spaces from inputMsg (using its trim() method), and then passes that result String to the parseInt() method in the Integer class. (Notice that no Integer object was created before parseInt() was called; this method is a static method, and so can be accessed without first creating an Integer object.) If any nonnumeric characters are discovered in inputMsg, the NumberFormatException exception will be *thrown*. It is best if this code block *catches* the exception and performs any appropriate action (such as setting x to zero).

The Double numeric class wrapper does not have a similar method. Instead, you have to use the doubleValue() method to return a numeric of type double, and then pass the returned String to one of the constructors for the Double class. The (rather gruesome) code looks like this:

```
String inputMsg = " 003 ";
double d = 0;
```

// Try to convert String to a double using the doubleValue() String method.

// Catch any NumberFormat exception errors.

```
try  {
      d = new Double (inputMsg.trim()).doubleValue();
}
catch (NumberFormatException e) {
     . . .
     d = 0;
}
```

Java does provide a slightly more useful and consistent mechanism to convert Strings into numerics: the DecimalFormat class and its parse() method. This method accepts a String parameter and returns an abstract class of type Number (that is, either a Long or a Double object). The Number class, in turn, does implement the doubleValue() method, so you can always get a numeric double value from it if you would like:

```
String inputMsg = "1,003.4";
double d = 0;
```

// Try to convert String to a double. Catch any NumberFormat exception
// errors.

```
try {
     d = new DecimalFormat().parse(inputMsg.trim()).doubleValue();
     }
     catch (NumberFormatException e) {
          . . .
          d = 0;
     }
```

The parse() method for this class will process numeric String input items, even if they contain thousands separator characters (the ,). Still, this is clearly more work than one would expect to simply convert a String to a numeric value! A number of utility class libraries are available from third parties, or as part of your IDE, to make this task quite a bit more manageable.

Primitive data items can be placed into a Double wrapper object quite easily by using the proper constructor:

```
double d = 2.4;
Double dd = new Double (d);
```

And, of course, the Double wrapper class can return a primitive data type as well:

```
Double dd = new Double ("222.3");
double d = dd.doubleValue ();
```

As mentioned earlier, the wrapper classes contain other useful methods, including compareTo(), toString(), and so on. These methods can be used to perform some functions directly on wrapper objects, without having to always convert the objects to primitive data types first.

Method	Description	Cobol Equivalent
int compareTo (double arg)	arg is numerically compared to this double	IF **NUMBER1** = **NUMBER2**
int compareTo (object arg)	arg is compared as an object to this double object	
double doubleValue ()	Returns a primitive numeric data type	
String toString ()	Returns a String representation of this Double	MOVE **NUMBER** TO **NUMBER-AS-Z9**

STRING BUFFERS

Java provides a StringBuffer class, which is a class similar to String, except objects of this class type can be modified. Developers use objects of this type instead of Strings when the text contained in the object needs to be frequently modified. StringBuffers have a size attribute and are automatically increased in size as necessary. The only real downside to StringBuffers is that they are less performant in some cases than Strings, and you cannot use the + operator for concatenation.

StringBuffers can be converted into Strings using the toString() method. Conversely, any data type can be easily added to a StringBuffer using the append() method. In this case, the same operator overloading conventions defined by the String class are used.

Some particularly useful StringBuffer methods are listed below. Unless otherwise noted, the return type is a StringBuffer, and this StringBuffer is modified by the method.

Method	Description	Cobol Equivalent
append (datatype arg)	Arg is converted into a String, and added to the end of StringBuffer	MOVE **NUMBER** TO **NUMBER-AS-Z9** STRING **NUMBER-AS-Z9** TO **STRING1**
char charAt (int index)	Returns the character at position *index* in the StringBuffer	MOVE **STRING2**(POS:1) TO **CHARACTER**
setCharAt (int index, char character)	The character at position *index* is replaced with *character*	MOVE **CHARACTER** TO **STRING2**(POS:1)
insert (int offset, datatype arg)	*Arg* is converted first to a String, and then placed in *StringBuffer* starting at position *offset*	MOVE **NUMBER** TO **NUMBER-AS-Z9** MOVE **STRING1-REDEFINES-NUMBER-AS-Z9** TO **STRING2**(POS:SIZE)
int length ()	Return the length of *StringBuffer*	Items are always fixed length, defined at compile time
replace (int offset, int length, String str)	Replace the characters in *StringBuffer* starting at *offset* for the number of chars in *length* with the characters in *str*	MOVE **STRING1**(POS:LEN) TO **STRING2**
setLength (int length)	Set the length of *StringBuffer* to *length*. Any new character positions will be set to *null*	Items are always fixed length, defined at compile time

Method	Description	Cobol Equivalent
String subString (int offset)	Return a String with all the characters in *stringBuffer* starting at *offset*	MOVE **STRING1** (POS:LEN) TO **STRING2**
String subString (int offset, int length)	Return a String with all the characters in *stringBuffer* starting at *offset* for the number of chars in length.	MOVE **STRING1** (POS:LEN) TO **STRING2**
String toString	Return a String with all of the characters in *StringBuffer**	MOVE **STRING1** TO **STRING2**

Here are examples of how StringBuffers might be used:

// Build an array of Strings.

// This array will contain 6 String objects.

```
String[] inputWords = {"These", "are", "words", "in", "a", "sentence"};
```

// Build a sentence.

```
String sentence = makeSentence (inputWords);
System.out.println (sentence);


public String makeSentence(String[]sentenceWords) {
      StringBuffer sent = new StringBuffer();
      for (int i = 0; i < sentenceWords.length; i++) {
```

// Build up the sentence. Place each word in the StringBuffer followed by a

// space.

// The StringBuffer will be automatically resized for each append.

```
            sent.append(sentenceWords[i]);
            sent.append(" ");
      }
```

// Return the sentence (as a String).

```
return (sent.toString());
```

---

* A new String is not created at first. Instead, the new String simply points to the same place in memory where the text for StringBuffer is stored. If and when Stringbuffer is eventually changed, they will not point to the same place in memory.

BIGNUMBERS

Although Java does not define a primitive data type similar to Cobol's familiar packed decimal, Java 1.1 defines two classes that are similar. These support math functions for numbers of arbitrary (and user-defined) precision. When you use these classes instead of the primitive float and double intrinsic data types, there is no requirement to work around the precision problems of floating point arithmetic. The BigInteger class supports arbitrary precision integer arithmetic, and BigDecimal supports arbitrary precision arithmetic with scale (that is, decimal positions).

Both BigInteger and BigDecimal have constructors with a String as a parameter. This is often how a BigNumber is initialized:

```
BigInteger customerNumber =
     new BigInteger ("123456789012345678901234567890");
BigDecimal currencyValue =
     new BigDecimal ("4.567890123456789012345");
BigDecimal customerOrder =
     new BigDecimal (customerNumber, 10);
```

In our example, currencyValue will have a scale attribute (that is, the number of digits to the right of the decimal) of 11. customerOrder would contain the numeric value in customerNumber, with a scale of 10.

There is also a constructor for BigDecimals that accepts a float or double parameter, but is seldom used since the input fractional numbers are not precise, and precision is the raison d'être for BigNumbers:

```
BigDecimal customerBalance =
     new BigDecimal (12345678901234567834567890.12345);
```

You can also use the static method valueOf() to set a BigNumber to a value:

```
BigInteger currencyValue = BigInteger.valueOf(123);
BigDecimal currencyValue = BigDecimal.valueOf(123, scale);
```

These classes do come with a cost, however. Math functions using these classes are considerably slower than math functions that use the primitive data types. Another inconvenience: you have to use the math functions the classes provide rather than the native Java operators (+, -, *, /, and so forth).

TECHNICAL NOTE: This is another example of where *operator overloading* could make Java applications simpler to read and write. If Java had overloaded the math operators when applied to BigNumbers, this syntax could be used:

```
customerBalanceYen = customerBalance * currencyValue;
```

instead of this syntax:

```
customerBalanceYen = customerBalance.multiply (currencyValue);
```

As it is, the math functions provided with the BigNumber classes are the only way to add, subtract, multiply, and divide BigNumbers.

These are the most commonly used constructors for BigDecimals and BigIntegers:

Constructor	Description	Cobol Equivalent
BigDecimal (BigInteger val)	Converts a BigInteger into a BigDecimal	MOVE **INTEGER1** TO **PACKED-NUM1**
BigDecimal (BigInteger unScaledVal, int scale)	Converts a BigInteger into a BigDecimal with the scale requested	MOVE **INTEGER1** TO **PACKED-NUM1**
BigDecimal (double val)	Converts a double into a BigDecimal	MOVE **DOUBLE-NUM1** TO **PACKED-NUM1***
BigDecimal (String val)	Converts a String representation of a number into a BigDecimal	MOVE WITH CONVERSION **STRING1** TO **PACKED-NUM1**
BigInteger (String val)	Converts the decimal String representation of a number into a BigInteger	MOVE WITH CONVERSION **STRING1** TO **INTEGER-NUM1**
BigInteger (byte[ ] val)	Converts a byte array that contains the 2's complement binary representation of a BigInteger into a BigInteger	MOVE **GROUP-ITEM1** TO **INTEGER-NUM-GROUP-ITEM1**

* Some Cobol compilers do support floating point numerics.

Let's compare some Cobol statements that use packed numbers to their Java equivalents that use BigDecimals.

```
01 DECIMAL-ITEMS USAGE IS COMP-3.
    03 DOLLAR-AMOUNT                 PIC S9(7)V(2)
                                     VALUE "1234567.12".
    03 CURRENCY-RATE                 PIC S9(3)V9(5)
                                     VALUE "123.12345".
     03 EXCHANGE-AMOUNT              PIC S9(10)V9(4).


     MULTIPLY DOLLAR-AMOUNT BY CURRENCY-RATE GIVING
        EXCHANGE-AMOUNT.
```

Note that there is the real possibility that the result of this multiplication may not fit in EXCHANGE-AMOUNT, and the value that is placed in this variable will be an approximation of the actual result. By default, Cobol will truncate the intermediate result to fit the target variable.

The most straightforward way to handle this situation is to define a larger target variable.

```
01 DECIMAL-ITEMS USAGE IS COMP-3.
     03 DOLLAR-AMOUNT                PIC S9(7)V(2)
                                     VALUE "1234567.12".
     03 CURRENCY-RATE                PIC S9(3)V9(5)
                                     VALUE "123.12345".
     03 EXCHANGE-AMOUNT              PIC S9(10)V9(7).

     MULTIPLY DOLLAR-AMOUNT BY CURRENCY-RATE GIVING
     EXCHANGE-AMOUNT.
```

In this example, EXCHANGE-AMOUNT will always be able to contain the result. This is the advantage of fixed decimal arithmetic; the developer can always control the precision of the result by managing the size of the result variable(s).

But at some point you will run into limits. Either the compiler will specify an upper limit on the number of decimal positions available (traditionally 17 digits in Cobol) or a limit is defined in the external representation of the number (for printing or for storage in a database, for example).

In these cases, result values must be *cast* into smaller variables. The Cobol developer can control the precision of the result of this casting by defining the precision of the variables. The developer also has some ability to specify how rounding should be handled.

```
01 DECIMAL-ITEMS USAGE IS COMP-3.
    03 DOLLAR-AMOUNT                  PIC S9(11)V(2)
                                      VALUE "12345678901.12".
    03 CURRENCY-RATE                  PIC S9(3)V9(5)
                                      VALUE "123.12345".
    03 EXCHANGE-AMOUNT                PIC S9(14)V9(3).

    MULTIPLY DOLLAR-AMOUNT BY CURRENCY-RATE GIVING
    EXCHANGE-AMOUNT.


    MULTIPLY DOLLAR-AMOUNT BY CURRENCY-RATE GIVING
    EXCHANGE-AMOUNT ROUNDED.
```

In the first example, any digits beyond the 10^{-3} position will be truncated from the (intermediate) result before being moved into EXCHANGE-AMOUNT. In the second example, the digit in the 10^{-4} position will be evaluated. If greater than 4, the previous digit will be incremented by 1. The remaining digits will be truncated.

Java allows for similar types of fixed precision math functions with its BigDecimal object type and to a lesser extent its BigInteger object type. Both types are examples of arbitrary precision data types. This means they are automatically defined to be the correct size and can, in theory, hold any result. Further, the developer can specify (even at runtime) any number of decimal positions (that is, the scale) in a BigDecimal number. As an added bonus, Java provides eight different rounding options, allowing the developer to have complete control when moving intermediate results into smaller target variables (for external storage or for printing, for example).

```
BigDecimal dollarAmount = new BigDecimal ("12345678901.12");
BigDecimal currencyRate = new BigDecimal ("123.12345");
BigDecimal exchangeAmount = new BigDecimal;


exchangeAmount = dollarAmount.multiply (currencyRate);


exchangeAmount = dollarAmount.multiply (currencyRate,
                              ROUND_HALF_UP);
```

The static integers shown in the following chart values can be passed into some of the math functions of BigDecimals to control their rounding functions:

Mode	Description	Cobol Equivalent
ROUND_CEILING	Round toward positive infinity	
ROUND_DOWN	Round toward zero (and away from 10)	
ROUND_FLOOR	Round toward negative infinity	
ROUND_HALF_DOWN	Round toward "nearest neighbor" (that is toward 0 or 10). If both neighbors are equidistant, round down	
ROUND_HALF_EVEN	Round toward the "nearest neighbor" If both are equidistant, round toward the even neighbor*	
ROUND_HALF_UP	Round toward "nearest neighbor" If both are equidistant, round up	ROUNDED
ROUND_UNNECESSARY	Asserts that the requested operation has an exact result, and no rounding is necessary	
ROUND_UP	Rounds away from zero (toward 10)	

This chart shows the most common math functions involving BigDecimals:

Method	Description	Cobol Equivalent
int compareTo (BigDecimal val)	Compares this BigDecimal with another BigDecimal	IF **PACKED-NUM1** = **PACKED-NUM2**
BigDecimal add (BigDecimal val)	Returns a BigDecimal whose value is (this + val), and whose scale is the greater of this.scale() and val.scale()**	ADD **PACKED-NUM1** TO **PACKED-NUM2** GIVING **PACKED-NUM3**
BigDecimal subtract (BigDecimal val)	Returns a BigDecimal whose value is (this - val), and whose scale is the greater of this.scale() and val.scale()	SUBTRACT **PACKED-NUM1** FROM **PACKED-NUM2** GIVING **PACKED-NUM3**
BigDecimal multiply (BigDecimal val)	Returns a BigDecimal whose value is (this * val), and whose scale is the sum of this.scale() and val.scale()	MULTIPLY **PACKED-NUM1** BY **PACKED-NUM2** GIVING **PACKED-NUM3**
BigDecimal divide (BigDecimal val, int roundingMode)	Returns a BigDecimal whose value is (this / val), and whose scale is the same as this.scale(). Rounding behavior is controlled by the value of roundingMode	DIVIDE **PACKED-NUM1** BY **PACKED-NUM2** GIVING **PACKED-NUM3** ROUNDED
BigDecimal divide (BigDecimal val, int scale, int roundingMode)	Returns a BigDecimal whose value is (this / val), and whose scale is as specified by scale	DIVIDE **PACKED-NUM1,** BY **PACKED-NUM2** GIVING **PACKED-NUM3** ROUNDED

* This mode should, in theory, round up as often as it rounds down in case of equidistant neighbors, thereby reducing one source of rounding error.

** Note that the new decimal created will automatically be sized to hold the results

Method	Description	Cobol Equivalent
int scale (BigDecimal val)	Returns the scale of this BigDecimal	
BigDecimal setScale(int scale, int roundingMode)	Returns a BigDecimal whose scale is as specified. Truncated digits are evaluated based on the roundingMode	MOVE **PACKED-NUM1** INTO **PACKED-NUM2**

EXERCISES: STRINGS, STRINGBUFFERS, NUMBERS, AND BIGNUMBERS

Time to visit our example classes again and try out all these new ideas.

USING JAVA 2'S JDK

1. Edit the HelloWorld.java source file in your java4cobol directory with a text editor. We'll start by deleting the code that experimented with flow control statements. Remove the lines after this statement (but remember to leave in the two curly braces at the end of the program):

// Print the contents of ErrorMsg's String data member directly.

```
System.out.println (myErrorMsg.msgText);
```

2. Add these Java expressions at the end of the previous statement (before the last two curly braces). In this set of examples, a view of the output line is inserted after the println() statement so that the concept explored by the example is easier to follow.

// Experiment with Java Strings.

// Construct a new String and initialize it, using its constructor.

// Point the object reference variable englishCaps to this new String.

```
String englishCaps = " ABCDEFGHIJKLMNOPQRSTUVWXYZ ";
```

// Get the size of the String using the length() method.

```
System.out.println ("length() = " + englishCaps.length ());
```

```
. . .
length() = 28
```

// Remove the leading and trailing spaces from the String.
// Point the reference variable englishCaps to this new String

```
englishCaps = englishCaps.trim ();
```

// Get the new size of the String using the length() method.

```
System.out.println ("length() = " +
      englishCaps.length ());
```

```
. . .
length() = 26
```

// Find the position of the character M.

```
System.out.println ("indexOf(M) = " +
      englishCaps.indexOf("M"));
```

// Get the character at position 12.
// Since all Java indexes start with 0, index 12 is actually the 13th position.
// This method returns a char data type, which is converted
// into a String by the println() method.

```
System.out.println ("charAt(12) = " +
      englishCaps.charAt(12));
```

```
. . .
indexOf(M) = 12
charAt(12) = M
```

// Get the substring at position 12 through 17.

```
System.out.println ("substring(12, 17) = " +
      englishCaps.substring (12, 17));
```

```
. . .
substring(12, 17) = MNOPQ
```

// Make a new String with the lowercase representation of this String.

```
String englishLower = englishCaps.toLowerCase ();
System.out.println ("englishLower = " +
      englishLower);
```

```
. . .
englishLower = abcdefghijklmnopqrstuvwxyz
```

// Compare the two English Strings using two different String methods.

```
System.out.println ("compareTo = " +
      englishCaps.compareTo (englishLower));
System.out.println ("equalsIgnoreCase = " +
      englishCaps.equalsIgnoreCase (englishLower));
```

```
. . .
compareTo = -32
equalsIgnoreCase = true
```

// Create a duplicate of englishCaps.

// Compare it to englishCaps using two String comparison methods.

```
String temp = englishCaps;
System.out.println ("compareTo = " +
      englishCaps.compareTo (temp));
System.out.println ("equals = " +
      englishCaps.equals (temp));
```

```
. . .
compareTo = 0
equals = true
```

// Compare the two String reference variables.

```
System.out.println ("compare reference variables = "
      + (englishCaps == temp));
```

```
. . .
compare reference variables = true
```

// Convert temp to lowercase.

// Compare temp to englishLower using the String method equals().

```
temp = englishCaps.toLowerCase ();
System.out.println ("equals = " +
      englishLower.equals (temp));
```

// Then compare the two String reference variables.

// The result of this comparison is unpredictable, but will normally be false.

```
System.out.println ("compare reference variables = "
   + (englishLower == temp));
```

```
. . .
equals = true
compare reference variables = false
```

3. Save these modifications as a text file, and then compile the class in the DOS command window:

➢ javac HelloWorld.java

```
Hello World!

Some Text
Some Text
length() = 28
length() = 26
indexOf(M) = 12
charAt(12) = M
substring(12, 17) = MNOPQ
englishLower = abcdefghijklmnopqrstuvwxyz
compareTo = -32
equalsIgnoreCase = true
compareTo = 0
equals = true
compare reference variables = true
equals = true
compare reference variables = false
```

Examine the various String methods we've used and the results they have returned. Do they make sense to you? Experiment with some other String methods on your own (perhaps the replace() method).

4. Now we'll experiment with the Numeric wrapper classes. Add this **bold** Java statement to the beginning of your HelloWorld source:

```
import java.text.*;
//
//
// HelloWorld Application
//
//
```

5. Add these Java statements at the end of the previous statement (before the last two curly braces):

```
// Experiment with the numeric wrapper classes.
// Convert from String to several numeric types.
// We will use the static methods in the wrapper classes.

    int i;
    long l;
    double d, d2;
    String inputMsg = "003";
```

// Try to convert String to integer. Catch any NumberFormat exception errors.

```
try     {
        i = Integer.parseInt (inputMsg.trim());
}
catch (NumberFormatException e) {
        i = 0;
}
```

// Try to convert String to a long. Catch any NumberFormat exception errors.

```
try     {
        l = Long.parseLong (inputMsg.trim());
}
catch (NumberFormatException e) {
        l = 0;
}
```

// Try to convert String to a double. Catch any NumberFormat exception
// errors.

```
try     {
        d = new Double (inputMsg.trim()).doubleValue();
}
catch (NumberFormatException e) {
        d = 0;
}
```

// Use the DecimalFormat Static method to convert a complex String to a
// double.

```
try     {
        d2 = new DecimalFormat().parse("3.0").doubleValue();
}
catch (ParseException e) {
        d2 = 0;
}


System.out.println ("Integer value = " + i);
System.out.println ("Long value = " + l);
System.out.println ("Double value = " + d);
System.out.println ("Second Double value = " + d2);
```

6. Compile and run this class. The output should look like this:

```
. . .
compare reference variables = true
equals = true
compare reference variables = false
Integer value = 3
Long value = 3
Double value = 3.0
Second Double value = 3.0
```

7. Let's do some math with the wrapper classes. Add these Java statements to the end of the previous statement (before the last two curly braces):

// Math and the numeric wrapper classes

// Make two objects of type Double.

// Try out both Constructors.

```
Double dd = new Double ("3.0");
Double dd2 = new Double (dd.doubleValue());
```

// Perform an addition function.

// Notice that the wrapper classes do not have any math function themselves.

// You have to convert them to primitive data types (by using the method

// doubleValue()) and then use the result as a constructor parameter to a new

// wrapper class.

```
d = dd.doubleValue ();
d2 = dd2.doubleValue ();
d += d2;
dd = new Double (d);
System.out.println ("dd after addition = " + dd);
```

// Or combine the previous expressions into one statement:

```
dd = new Double (dd.doubleValue () + dd2.doubleValue());
System.out.println ("dd after addition = " + dd);
```

// Compare two Double objects.

// Note that the wrapper classes do have comparison methods (compare(), and

// equals()), so you don't have to extract the value into a primitive data type.

```
if (dd.equals (dd2)) {
      System.out.println ("dd equals dd2");
}
else {
      System.out.println ("dd does not equal dd2");
}
```

8. Compile and run this class. The output should look like this:

```
nd Double value = 3.0
dd after addition = 6.0
dd after addition = 9.0
dd does not equal dd2
```

9. Next we'll experiment with the StringBuffer class. Add these Java statements to the end of the previous statement (before the last two curly braces):

// Experiment with StringBuffers.

// Convert this String array to a StringBuffer.

```
String[] inputWords = {"These", "are", "words", "in", "a",
   "sentence"};
```

// Build a sentence.

```
StringBuffer sent = new StringBuffer();
for (i = 0; i < inputWords.length; i++) {
```

// Build up the sentence. Place each word in the StringBuffer followed by a

// space. The StringBuffer will be automatically resized for each append.

```
          sent.append(inputWords[i]);
          sent.append(" ");
}
System.out.println (sent.toString());
```

10. Compile and run this class The output should look like this:

```
. . .
These are words in a sentence
```

11. Now it's time to experiment with the BigDecimals and the BigInteger classes. Add this **bold** Java statement to the beginning of your HelloWorld source:

```
import java.text.*;
import java.math.*;
```

```
//
//
// HelloWorld Application
//
//
```

12. Add these Java statements to the end of the previous statement (before the last two curly braces):

```
// Experiment with BigNumbers
// Construct some numbers to work with:

     BigDecimal accountBalance1 = new BigDecimal ("12345.678");
     BigDecimal accountBalance2 = new BigDecimal ("876.54321");
     BigDecimal accountBalance3 = new BigDecimal ("1");
     BigDecimal transactionAmount = new BigDecimal ("100.00");

// Add the transaction amount to the account balance.

     accountBalance1 = accountBalance1.add (transactionAmount);
     System.out.println ("accountBalance1 = " +
           accountBalance1);

// Compute the discounted amount of the transaction, and place into a new
// variable with the same scale as the transactionAmount variable

     BigDecimal discountRate = new BigDecimal (".85321");
     BigDecimal discountedTransaction =
          transactionAmount.multiply (discountRate);
     System.out.println ("discountedTransaction = " +
          discountedTransaction);
```

// Subtract the discounted transaction evenly from accounts 2 and 3.

```
BigDecimal discountDistribution =
      discountedTransaction.divide (BigDecimal.valueOf(2),
```

// Make sure the result is the same scale as accountBalance.

```
      accountBalance1.scale(), BigDecimal.ROUND_HALF_EVEN);
System.out.println ("discountDistribution = " +
      discountDistribution);
```

// No need to worry about scale or lost precision here;
// the scale of the result will be the greater of the two BigDecimal operands.

```
accountBalance2 =
     accountBalance2.subtract (discountDistribution);
accountBalance3 =
     accountBalance3.subtract (discountDistribution);
System.out.println ("accountBalance2 = " +
     accountBalance2);
System.out.println ("accountBalance3 = " +
     accountBalance3);
```

// Now you have to set the number's scale so that you can fit it into a print
// column. We want two decimal positions to be printed.

```
BigDecimal printAccountBalance =
      accountBalance1.setScale (2,
      BigDecimal.ROUND_HALF_UP);
System.out.println ("printAccountBalance = " +
      printAccountBalance);
```

13. Compile and run this class. Your output window should look like this:

```
. . .
These are words in a sentence
accountBalance1 = 12445.678
discountedTransaction = 85.3210000
discountDistribution = 42.660
accountBalance2 = 833.88321
accountBalance3 = -41.660
printAccountBalance = 12445.68
```

USING J++

1. Select your java4cobol project from among the recent workspaces using this menu path:

➢ File → Recent Workspaces → java4cobol

2. We'll start by deleting the code that experimented with statements and flow control. Remove the lines after this statement (but remember to leave in the two curly braces at the end of the program):

// Print the contents of ErrorMsg's String data member directly.

```
System.out.println (myErrorMsg.msgText);
```

3. Add these Java statements at the end of the previous statement (before the last two curly braces). In this set of examples, a view of the output line is inserted after the println() statement so that the concept explored by the example is easier to follow.

// Experiment with Java Strings.

// Construct a new String and initialize it, using its constructor.

// Point the object reference variable englishCaps to this new String.

```
String englishCaps = " ABCDEFGHIJKLMNOPQRSTUVWXYZ ";
```

// Get the size of the String using the length() method.

```
System.out.println ("length() = " + englishCaps.length ());
```

```
. . .
length() = 28
```

// Remove the leading and trailing spaces from the String.

// Point the reference variable englishCaps to this new String.

```
englishCaps = englishCaps.trim ();
```

// Get the new size of the String using the length() method.

```
System.out.println ("length() = " +
     englishCaps.length ());
```

```
. . .
length() = 26
```

// Find the position of the character M.

```
System.out.println ("indexOf(M) = " +
  englishCaps.indexOf("M"));
```

// Get the character at position 12.
// Since all Java indexes start with 0, index 12 is actually the 13th position.
// This method actually returns a char data type, which is converted
// into a String by the println() method.

```
System.out.println ("charAt(12) = " +
     englishCaps.charAt(12));
```

```
. . .
indexOf(M) = 12
charAt(12) = M
```

// Get the substring at position 12 through 17.

```
System.out.println ("substring(12, 17) = " +
     englishCaps.substring (12, 17));
```

```
. . .
substring(12, 17) = MNOPQ
```

// Make a new String with the lowercase representation of this String.

```
String englishLower = englishCaps.toLowerCase ();
System.out.println ("englishLower = " +
     englishLower);
```

```
. . .
englishLower = abcdefghijklmnopqrstuvwxyz
```

// Compare the two English Strings using two different String methods.

```
System.out.println ("compareTo = " +
     englishCaps.compareTo (englishLower));
System.out.println ("equalsIgnoreCase = " +
     englishCaps.equalsIgnoreCase (englishLower));
```

```
. . .
compareTo = -32
equalsIgnoreCase = true
```

// Create a duplicate of englishCaps.

// Compare it to englishCaps using two String comparison methods.

```
String temp = englishCaps;
System.out.println ("compareTo = " +
     englishCaps.compareTo (temp));
System.out.println ("equals = " +
     englishCaps.equals (temp));
```

```
. . .
compareTo = 0
equals = true
```

// Compare the two String reference variables.

```
System.out.println ("compare reference variables = "
     + (englishCaps == temp));
```

```
. . .
compare reference variables = true
```

// Convert temp to lowercase.
// Compare temp to the englishLower using the String method equals().

```
temp = englishCaps.toLowerCase ();
System.out.println ("equals = " +
     englishLower.equals (temp));
```

// Then compare the two String reference variables.
// The result of this comparison is unpredictable.

```
System.out.println ("compare reference variables = "
     + (englishLower == temp));
```

```
. . .
equals = true
compare reference variables = false
```

4. Compile this class using this menu path:

➢ Build → Compile HelloWorld.java

Execute this program (Build → Start Debug → Run to Cursor). The output should look like this:

```
. . .
Hello World!
null
Some Text
Some Text
length() = 28
length() = 26
indexOf(M) = 12
charAt(12) = M
substring(12, 17) = MNOPQ
englishLower = abcdefghijklmnopqrstuvwxyz
compareTo = -32
equalsIgnoreCase = true
compareTo = 0
equals = true
compare reference variables = true
equals = true
compare reference variables = false
```

Examine the various String methods we've used and the results they have returned. Do they make sense to you? Experiment with some other String methods on your own (perhaps the replace() method).

5. Now we'll experiment with the Numeric wrapper classes. Add this **bold** Java statement to the beginning of your HelloWorld source:

```
import java.util.*;
import java.text.*;
//
//
// HelloWorld Application
//
//
```

TECHNICAL NOTE: The J++ design environment does not by default include the java.text package in its class path. You can access it, however, by adjusting your project settings to point to the zip file that contains the text package. By default, its location is in the C:\\WINDOWS\JAVA\Packages\ directory, but it may be elsewhere on your system. A reliable way to find this package file is to use the Windows Find utility, and search all files named *.zip in your system directories for the text DecimalFormat. Specify the file found on the ClassPath entry in your Project settings.

6. Add these Java statements to the end of the previous statement (before the last two curly braces):

// Experiment with the numeric wrapper classes.

// Convert from String to several numeric types.

// We will use the static methods in the wrapper classes.

```
int i;
long l;
double d, d2;

String inputMsg = " 003 ";
```

// Try to convert String to integer. Catch any NumberFormat exception errors.

```
try  {
     i = Integer.parseInt (inputMsg.trim());
}
catch (NumberFormatException e) {
     i = 0;
}
```

// Try to convert String to a long. Catch any NumberFormat exception errors.

```
try  {
     l = Long.parseLong (inputMsg.trim());
}
catch (NumberFormatException e) {
     l = 0;
}
```

// Try to convert String to a double. Catch any NumberFormat exception

// errors.

```
try  {
     d = new Double (inputMsg.trim()).doubleValue();
}
catch (NumberFormatException e) {
     d = 0;
}
```

// Use the DecimalFormat Static method to convert a complex String to a

// double.

```
try  {
     d2 = new DecimalFormat().parse("3.0").doubleValue();
}
catch (ParseException e) {
     d2 = 0;
}
System.out.println ("Integer value = " + i);
System.out.println ("Long value = " + l);
System.out.println ("Double value = " + d);
System.out.println ("Second Double value = " + d2);
```

7. Compile and run this class. The output should look like this:

```
. . .
compare reference variables = true
equals = true
compare reference variables =
false
Integer value = 3
Long value = 3
Double value = 3.0
Second Double value = 3.0
```

8. Let's do some math with the wrapper classes. Add these Java statements to the end of the previous statement (before the last two curly braces):

```
// Math and the numeric wrapper classes
// Make two objects of type Double.
// Try out both Constructors.

     Double dd = new Double ("3.0");
     Double dd2 = new Double (dd.doubleValue());

// Perform an addition function.
// Notice that the wrapper classes do not have any math function themselves.
// You have to convert them to primitive data types (by using the method
// doubleValue()) and then use the result as a constructor parameter to a new
// wrapper class.
```

```
d = dd.doubleValue ();
d2 = dd2.doubleValue ();
d += d2;
dd = new Double (d);
System.out.println ("dd after addition = " + dd);
```

// Or combine the previous expressions into one statement.

```
dd = new Double (dd.doubleValue () + dd2.doubleValue());
System.out.println ("dd after addition = " + dd);
```

// Compare two Double objects.

// Note that the wrapper classes do have comparison methods (compare(), and

// equals()), so you don't have to extract the value into a primitive data type.

```
if (dd.equals (dd2)) {
     System.out.println ("dd equals dd2");
}
else {
     System.out.println ("dd does not equal dd2");
}
```

9. Compile and run this class. The output should look like this:

```
. . .
Second Double value = 3.0
dd after addition = 6.0
dd after addition = 9.0
dd does not equal dd2
```

10. Next we'll experiment with the StringBuffer class. Add these Java statements to the end of the previous statement (before the last two curly braces)

// Experiment with StringBuffers.

// Convert this String array to a StringBuffer.

```
String[] inputWords = {"These", "are", "words", "in", "a",
   "sentence"};
```

// Build a sentence.

```
StringBuffer sent = new StringBuffer();
for (i = 0; i < inputWords.length; i++) {
```

// Build up the sentence. Place each word in the StringBuffer followed by a

// space.

// The StringBuffer will be automatically resized for each append.

```
        sent.append(inputWords[i]);
        sent.append(" ");
    }
    System.out.println (sent.toString());
```

11. Compile and run this class. The output should look like this:

```
. . .
These are words in a sentence
```

12. Now it's time to experiment with the BigDecimals and the BigInteger classes. Add this **bold** Java statement to the beginning of your HelloWorld source:

```
import java.util.*;
import java.text.*;
import java.math.*;
```

//
//
// HelloWorld Application
//
//

13. Add these Java statements to the end of the previous statement (before the last two curly braces):

// Experiment with BigNumbers.

// Construct some numbers to work with.

```
BigDecimal accountBalance1 = new BigDecimal ("12345.678");
BigDecimal accountBalance2 = new BigDecimal ("876.54321");
BigDecimal accountBalance3 = new BigDecimal ("1");
BigDecimal transactionAmount = new BigDecimal ("100.00");
```

// Add the transaction amount to the account balance.

```
accountBalance1 = accountBalance1.add (transactionAmount);
System.out.println ("accountBalance1 = " +
      accountBalance1);
```

// Compute the discounted amount of the transaction, and place it into a new
// variable with the same scale as the transactionAmount variable.

```
BigDecimal discountRate = new BigDecimal (".85321");
BigDecimal discountedTransaction =
      transactionAmount.multiply (discountRate);
System.out.println ("discountedTransaction = " +
      discountedTransaction);
```

// Subtract the discounted transaction evenly from accounts 2 and 3.

```
BigDecimal discountDistribution =
      discountedTransaction.divide (BigDecimal.valueOf(2),
```

// Make sure the result is the same scale as accountBalance.

```
accountBalance1.scale(), BigDecimal.ROUND_HALF_EVEN);
System.out.println ("discountDistribution = " +
         discountDistribution);
```

// No need to worry about scale or lost precision here;
// the scale of the result will be the greater of the two BigDecimal operands.

```
accountBalance2 =
      accountBalance2.subtract (discountDistribution);
accountBalance3 =
      accountBalance3.subtract (discountDistribution);
System.out.println ("accountBalance2 = " +
      accountBalance2);
System.out.println ("accountBalance3 = " +
      accountBalance3);
```

// Now you have to set the number's scale so that you can fit it into a print
// column. We want two decimal positions to be printed.

```
BigDecimal printAccountBalance =
      accountBalance1.setScale (2,
        BigDecimal.ROUND_HALF_UP);
System.out.println ("printAccountBalance = " +
        printAccountBalance);
```

14. Compile and run this class. Your output window should look like this:

```
. . .
These are words in a sentence
accountBalance1 = 12445.678
discountedTransaction = 85.3210000
discountDistribution = 42.660
accountBalance2 = 833.88321
accountBalance3 = -41.660
printAccountBalance = 12445.68
```

REVIEWING OUR EXERCISES

Let's review the samples we've created. Try to relate the sample source statements to the result (for example, the output) each statement creates. If necessary, rerun the samples, or look at the complete source code for this exercise on the CD. Feel free to experiment by yourself.

- Java Strings are similar to items defined as PIC X in Cobol. Java Strings contain characters and have an explicit length attribute.
- Java's String class contains many useful methods for manipulating String items. At the same time, Java's compiler sometimes treats String variables similar to intrinsic data types.
- These Java statements:

```
System.out.println ("compareTo = " +
     englishCaps.compareTo (temp));
System.out.println ("equals = " +
     englishCaps.equals (temp));
```

call the compareTo() and then the equals() methods in the object englishCaps. In both cases, the called method is passed a String parameter (temp). The result of this method is printed using the println() method.

- Any Java type (including the primitive types such as integers, and boolean *true* or *false*) can be converted into a String. When the target of a math function (+ in this case) is a String, Java will automatically call the toString() method. These features are why the previous statements cause this output:

```
. . .
compareTo = 0
equals = true
```

Java automatically converted the results of these methods (an integer result in one case, and a boolean result in the other) into Strings suitable for the println() method.

- Java's Numeric wrapper classes can contain numeric data types, such as *double*, and *integer*. These wrapper classes have specific uses (generally when an object data type is required), but are not well suited for use as a general-purpose data store.
- Java's BigNumber classes (BigInteger and BigDecimal) are the appropriate choice when large, fixed precision numbers are required. These classes provide the developer with unlimited precision capabilities and explicit control over scale and rounding. However, since they are less performant than primitive data types, and cannot use the standard Java math operators, developers must determine on a case-by-case basis if these data types should be used, or if the primitive data type should be used.

CHAPTER

9

Arrays, Vectors, and Other Collections

Very often a business process algorithm (a fancy name for a program) must evaluate a group of related items. Arrays, vectors, and collections are Java constructs available to support these types of functions.

ARRAYS

Arrays are very similar in concept to occurrences in Cobol. Arrays are objects that contain a set of other objects or a set of data elements. All the elements in an array must be of the same type. In addition, its size must be defined when it is created, and cannot be dynamically adjusted in size. These are all specifications that should be familiar to the Cobol programmer.

```
01 ERROR-MESSAGE-ITEMS.
     03 ERROR-MESSAGE OCCURS 10 TIMES  PIC X(80).
```

// In Java this would be:

```
ErrorMsg myErrorMsgs[] = new ErrorMsg[10];
```

// or:

```
int errorNumbers[] = new int [10];
```

Note that in the first of our examples, the myErrorMsgs array was created, but the ErrorMsg objects that it will eventually contain were not created. Instead, the object reference variables inside the array are initialized to *null*. In contrast, an array of data items that contains numeric data items are initialized to 0 by default.

The array brackets can be placed by the type name instead of the variable name. This actually is the more common syntax:

```
int[] errorNumbers = new int [10];
```

Interestingly, it is possible to define an array with no more information than the types of elements that it will contain:

```
ErrorMsg[] myErrorMsgs;
```

The array variable myErrorMsgs can be subsequently assigned to some other ErrorMsg array. This feature can be very useful in managing arguments and return values for methods although you should try to use the newer *collection* classes for this purpose, which we will discuss in a moment.

Arrays can be created with initial values assigned to its elements using a syntax similar to C's syntax:

```
int errorNumbers[] = {1, 2, 10, 22, 23};
```

As you might suspect, this array will contain five integer values.

Unlike Cobol, where an array's size is defined only at compile time, a Java array's size can be defined at runtime:

```
int array_size = 10;
ErrorMsg[] myErrorMsgs = new ErrorMsg[array_size];
```

Like Cobol, an array can be multidimensional:

```
int[][] errorNumbers = new int[10][3];
```

Based on the preceding declaration, errorNumbers is an array of ten integer arrays (each of which is three integers in size).

Every array contains a *length* member; this is the number of elements in the array.

```
int[] errorNumbersIO = {1, 2, 10, 22, 23};
for (int x = 0; x < errorNumbersIO.length; x++) {
     if (errorNumbersIO[x] == 30) {
          break;
     }
}
```

This loop will execute five times since there are five elements in errorNumbers and none is equal to 30.

Java checks all array references to prevent "out of bounds" references. Any out of bounds reference will generate an ArrayIndexOutOfBoundsException exception. (Whew! And you thought Cobol was a bit wordy.)

Although we did introduce arrays as a type of object, Java does not treat arrays simply as standard objects. There is enough special syntax in the language for arrays to view them as a special type of reference variable, slightly different from objects.

For example, the assignment and evaluation statements for arrays that contain primitive data types is very similar to the same statements used by the primitive data type. This syntax is valid for arrays: `if (errorNumbersIO[x] == 30)`. It is quite similar to the syntax used by primitive integer types: `if (errorNumber == 30)`. If arrays were simply objects, then this syntax would compare the objects in the arrays, and not the numeric values.

Java also provides a set of useful array-specific methods. In order to copy some part of an array into another, use the arraycopy() function in the Java System class:

```
System.arraycopy (sourceArray, int sourcePosition,
      destinationArray, int destinationPosition, int
      numberOfEntriesToCopy);
```

Suppose you want to copy the IO error numbers array and the logical error numbers array into a single array. You could use the arraycopy() method to do this:

```
int[] errorNumbersIO = {1, 2, 10, 22, 23};
int[] errorNumbersLogical = {101, 102, 108, 122};
int[] errorNumbersAll = new int[errorNumbersIO.length
                        + errorNumbersLogical.length];

System.arraycopy (errorNumbersIO, 0,
                       errorNumbersAll, 0, 5);
System.arraycopy (errorNumbersLogical, 0,
                       errorNumbersAll, 5, 4);
```

// A temporary array can be defined, and then it can be assigned to any of these
// arrays.

```
int[] tempNumbers;
tempNumbers = errorNumbersIO;
tempNumbers = errorNumbersLogical;
tempNumbers = errorNumbersAll;
```

Arrays can be passed into methods, and returned from a method as its return value. This is very useful when a method needs to return a set of values instead of just one.

```
public class ErrorCodes {
```

// Define a static structure that contains all the IO error codes.

```
    static int[] IOCodes = {1, 2, 3, 10, 12, 22, 23, 30};
```

// A method that returns all the error codes for IO functions.

```
    public int[] errorCodesIO {
```

// Create an array to hold the error codes.

```
        int[] results = new int[IOCodes.length];
```

// Copy the array (actually the method System.arraycopy() would be a better
// choice, instead of this loop).

```
        for(int x = 0; x < IOCodes.length; x++) {
           results[x] = IOCodes[x];
        }
```

// Return the array that we have just loaded.

```
        return results;
    }
```

Before we move on to the next topic, let's visit this statement again.

```
ErrorMsg[] myErrorMsgs;
```

What does myErrorMsgs[0] contain after this statement?

Since no values have been placed into the array, it does not contain any ErrorMsg's. However, we did say it *will* contain reference variables of this object type.

After this statement, all the elements in myErrorMsgs will contain empty object reference variables, or *null*. Therefore, this statement:

```
if (myErrorMsgs[0] == null)
```

will always evaluate to *true* until myErrorMsgs[0] is assigned to an actual reference variable.

```
ErrorMsg[] myErrorMsgs;
myErrorMsgs[0] = new ErrorMsg ();
if (myErrorMsgs[0] == null) {
```

// This section will not be executed, since myErrorMsgs[0] has been assigned to
// an object.

```
}
```

ARRAYS AS PARAMETERS

Parameters passed to Java methods are passed by value, and not by reference. In Cobol, parameters are passed by reference to a subroutine although some compilers will support an optional "by value" mechanism.

When arrays are passed to methods as parameters, the method cannot change the array. However, if the array contains objects, then the called method can change the objects contained in the array. Though not exactly the same as a parameter that is passed by reference, this can be a useful mechanism to construct a method that modifies the objects passed to it as an argument.

VECTORS

Vectors are Java constructs that are similar to arrays in many ways, but implement additional capabilities.

1. Vectors are explicitly implemented as a class in the java.util package.
2. Vectors can grow and shrink dynamically as required.
3. Vectors can hold only Objects (that is, vectors cannot contain primitive numeric types).

A program can create a vector using this syntax:

```
Vector errorMsgs = new Vector (10);
```

This vector has ten slots available.

Vectors have two size attributes: *size* and *capacity*. *Size* is the number of elements currently in the vector, and *capacity* is the number of elements that the vector can contain. Our sample vector so far has a *capacity* of ten and a *size* of zero (no elements in the vector). The values of these attributes can be accessed with the size() and capacity() methods.

To add elements to the vector, use the addElement() method. This places a new element in the vector in the next available position and increases the size of the vector by 1.

// Create some objects.

```
ErrorMsg myErrorMsg = new ErrorMsg ();
ErrorMsg myotherErrorMsg = new ErrorMsg ("Some Text");
ErrorMsg mythirdErrorMsg = new ErrorMsg ("Third One");
```

// Place them in the vector.

```
errorMsgs.addElement (myErrorMsg);
errorMsgs.addElement (myotherErrorMsg);
errorMsgs.addElement (mythirdErrorMsg);
```

Now our vector has a size of three. Its capacity is still ten.

A vector will automatically expand when its capacity is exceeded. If we were to add 11 items to our vector, then the vector would resize itself (and probably relocate itself in memory). The default behavior is to double in size whenever the current capacity is exceeded. Defining an increment value when the vector is first created will control how the vector is expanded:

```
Vector errorMsgs = new Vector (10, 20);
```

This vector will have an initial capacity of 10, and will increment by 20 element positions whenever its current capacity is exceeded (that is, first 10, then 30, then 50 elements).

There is a performance penalty incurred when a vector's capacity is exceeded. So it is good practice to properly allocate capacity for a vector, especially one that will hold large numbers of elements (more than 50 or so). The default for a vector is to allocate space for ten elements and to increment by ten.

Actually, using vectors in your program is a little more complex than it should be. This is because you have to use the proper method when you add, change, or retrieve objects from a vector. Furthermore, a vector stores only *Objects*, and not specific class types. Subsequently, any object retrieved from a vector must be cast back into the correct class before it can be properly used.

Let's contrast the statements necessary to access elements in an array with the way you would manage elements in a vector:

// Define an array of five error messages.

```
ErrorMsg[] errorMsgs = new ErrorMsg[5];
```

// Add some elements to the array.

```
errorMsgs[0] = myErrorMsg;
errorMsgs[1] = myotherErrorMsg;
```

// Modify the first element in the array.

```
errorMsgs[0] = mythirdErrorMsg;
```

// Retrieve the first element in the array.

```
myErrorMsg = errorMsgs[0];
```

// Create a potential problem because ErrorMsgs may not be large enough to

// contain all of the error messages in ErrorMsgIO.

```
for (int x = 0; x < errorMsgIO.length; x++) {
     errorMsgs[x] = errorMsgIO[x]
          . . .
}
```

// Retrieve the number of elements in ErrorMsgs.

```
int y = errorMsgs.length;
```

This is how we could code ErrorMsgs as a vector:

// Define a vector for five error messages (or any other type of object).

```
Vector errorMsgs = new Vector (5);
```

// Add some elements to the vector.

```
errorMsgs.addElement (myErrorMsg);
errorMsgs.addElement (myotherErrorMsg);
```

// Modify the first element in the vector.

```
errorMsgs.setElementAt (mythirdErrorMsg, 0);
```

// Retrieve the first element from the array.

// Note that the return from elementAt() is an object and must be cast to the

// correct type.

```
myErrorMsg = (ErrorMsg) errorMsgs.elementAt (0);
```

// This loop will never be a problem because ErrorMsgs will grow as required

// to contain all the error messages in ErrorMsgIO.

```
for (int x = 0; x < errorMsgIO.length; x++) {
    errorMsgs.addElement (errorMsgIO[x]);
            . . .
}
```

// Retrieve the number of elements in errorMsgs.

```
int y = errorMsgs.size();
```

Since vectors can contain only objects, and not primitive data types, numeric items cannot be directly placed into vectors. Instead, numerics must be first cast into their object wrappers before they can be placed into an vector array.

```
Vector myIntegerVector = new Vector (5);
```

// Add an Integer element to the vector.

```
int x = 5;
myInteger = new Integer (x);
myIntegerVector.addElement (myInteger);
```

Another difficulty with Integer objects is that they are immutable, just like String objects. That is, once an Integer object is created, there is no way to change its value. Instead, a new Integer must be created to contain a new value. As a result, most groups of numeric values are managed with arrays (which can contain primitive data types), instead of with vectors.

You can shrink a vector in order to conserve memory. The setSize() method will establish the number of elements in a vector to the passed (integer) value. If the vector contains more elements than the passed value, they will be deleted. If the vector did not already contain this number of elements, then they will be added to the vector as null objects.

The trimToSize() method will truncate the vector's capacity to the current size. You should perform this function only if you are sure the vector will not likely grow since any additions to the vector will immediately cause it to be reallocated.

COLLECTIONS

A new feature of Java 2 is the collection classes. Like the Vector class, these classes help manage groups of other objects. Java collections are organized into a framework, or an extensible assortment of supporting classes, interfaces, and documentation.

In many ways, the collection classes are similar to the Vector class, but with improved characteristics. The collection frameworks are more powerful, often perform better, are better organized, simpler to understand, and easier to extend than the original Vector class. It is hoped that most new generalized APIs will use collections as the preferred parameter type for lists or sets of objects, ultimately replacing the Vector class.

Java defines some collection interfaces (that is, method definitions, without actual code to support them), as well as some general-purpose collection implementations (code to support the basic requirements of some of the interfaces). The idea is that the developer can either use the basic implementation classes as is, or implement collection management classes unique to his or her own requirements. The general-purpose implementation classes are still available to perform basic functions for the custom collection class developer, allowing the developer to focus on the specific requirements of the custom collection class.

One useful way to understand collections is to compare them to traditional Cobol files. Cobol programs can transverse a file in a particular order, looking for specific records, and then modify or perhaps delete those records. In order to examine or modify any particular record, the program must first read it into a record structure. Standard functions exist to read, update, delete, and reorder (sort) the file. Further, the file has a determinate number of records, and the program can detect when it has reached the end of the file.

All Cobol programmers know how to process files. Data stored in files is readily available to a Cobol program. If you need to build a program that processes this file, all you need to know is where the file is stored and its record layout. The Cobol developer can concentrate on the business problem to be solved and efficiently use the syntax appropriate to process a Cobol file.

The above descriptions are (more or less) the characteristics of Java collections. It is also helpful to note that collections have the following differences:

1. Java collections are stored in memory, and not on disk (although you can certainly extend the basic collection class to provide for disk storage).
2. Multiple users (that is, programs) can simultaneously access files, whereas collections are assumed to be contained in a single runtime instance. In fact, the basic collections implementations are not thread-safe (that is, a simple collection cannot be managed properly by two execution threads in the same process). There are interfaces available as part of the frameworks that can upgrade a collection to the thread-safe model.
3. Java collections can be passed as parameters to functions and can be returned as the return item from a method. This would be similar to passing the file selection and file definition to a subroutine, allowing the subroutine to read and update the file. (Actually, some Cobol compilers do allow this!)

Some important constructs that you should be aware of when using collections:

Collection: A set of related objects or elements. One collection may be ordered in some fashion, others may be unordered. A collection type might allow duplicates, whereas another implementation might not.

Core interfaces: These are the basic interfaces that a developer uses to manage collections. They define methods to add, remove, or test an element in the collection, and to check the size of a collection. There is also an interface to create an iterator, or an object that manages the current position in the collection.

The basic collection interface supports a few bulk operations, or methods that can be used to move many elements at one time. As an added bonus, the contents of a collection can be easily moved into arrays and from arrays.

These are some of the interface definitions in Java 2's collection framework:

Set: An interface for a class that supports groups of elements that cannot contain duplicates. Elements in a set are not ordered in any particular fashion.

List: An interface for a class that supports groups of ordered elements. Elements in a list can contain duplicates. Elements in a list are often accessed using an index (or subscript) in a manner very similar to arrays.

Map: An interface for a class that maps key elements to values (i.e., other objects). Roughly analogous to an indexed (ISAM) file in Cobol, where a key is mapped to a record (a file that is contained in memory).

SortedSet: An extension of the set interface. Elements in a SortedSet collection are automatically ordered in some fashion, either through the natural ordering of the elements or because an explicit Comparator object provides for an ordering algorithm.

Implementations: The preceding interfaces are just definitions; it is up to an actual implementation to construct a class that supports these definitions. The Java 2 collections frameworks provide some very useful basic collection implementations. These include some Set collection types, a few List collection types, and two Map collection types. These collection implementations can, in many cases, be used as is by your application.

Sets: HashSet and TreeSet
Lists: ArrayList and LinkedList
Maps: HashMap and TreeMap

Algorithms: The Collections class contains several static methods that provide useful functions on collections, such as sorting and searching. These powerful (and polymorphic) functions demonstrate some of the benefits provided by collections. They are standard mechanisms available to any developer who needs to manage a group of related items. Some examples of the collection algorithms provided with Java 2 are:

sort: Organize a list based on the natural order of the objects in the list, or based on a Comparator (a user-defined ordering method). Sort always orders a list in ascending order.

reverse: The same function as sort(), but the elements are organized in descending order.

fill: Populate a list with copies of the same element. Existing elements in the list will be overwritten, so this method is very useful when you want to reinitialize a list.

copy: Copy n elements from a list into another list. The target list must be large enough to hold all the elements, but if the target list is larger, then the extra elements will not be affected.

binarySearch: Examine a list to find a particular element. If the element is contained in the list, then its index position will be returned. Otherwise, the negative value of the position it can be inserted in is returned.

min and max: Examine a collection to find the element with the lowest or highest value. As with the sort algorithm, the natural ordering of the elements can be used, or a user-defined Comparator can be used to compare one element to another.

Iterator: An iterator is an object that the developer uses to manage the current element in the collection. If a collection can be understood as a type of in memory file, then an iterator can be thought of as an object that contains the current position in the file. The iterator is passed as a parameter to several of the collections methods that "walk," or iterate, through the collection (such as, hasNext() and next()), as well as the remove() method).

When applied to a list-type collection, an iterator can support bidirectional iteration (previous() and next()), insertion and replacement of an element into a particular position, and the ability to get the index number for this element.

Ordering: Elements in a list-type collection are always ordered in some fashion. By default, this is the natural order of the objects. Java 2 has defined an interface (Comparable) that defines how objects of a given class should be compared. Classes that implement this interface use the compareTo() method to compare two elements in a collection. Many of the original Java classes have been retrofitted to support this method.

A specific collection can also define an ordering method unique to that collection type. A user-defined implementation of the Comparator interface, with its compare() and equal() methods, can be passed to the Collection.sort() function. In this case, the user-defined compare function will be used to evaluate elements during any sort operations.

Collections vs. Vectors vs. Arrays: As we mentioned in the beginning of our discussion, collections are meant to replace the use of Vectors in Java programs. Collections will also likely be used instead of arrays in many cases, but there are some situations where collections and arrays will co-exist.

Arrays are a simpler coding construct and support primitive data types directly. In these cases, arrays are a superior (and often faster) language construct. Therefore, the collections frameworks designers have provided for straightforward methods that can convert arrays into collections, and collections into arrays. Similar methods have not been provided for vectors although you could certainly build one if necessary.

Finally, collections are not synchronized (that is, they are not thread-safe) by default. The synchronized*() methods provided in the frameworks can be used to create a new collection from an original or backing collection that is synchronized (one that is thread-safe). If all accesses to the backing collection are done through the synchronized collection, then everything is fine, threadwise.

Some particularly useful collection methods are listed in the following chart. Charts are also provided for each of the basic collection types (set, list, and map). Cobol equivalents are presented from the perspective of standard Cobol file I/O. As such, they present conceptual similarities more than strictly functional similarities.

Method	Description	Cobol Equivalent
boolean add (Object arg)	Adds *arg* to this collection. If this collection does not allow duplicates, and *arg* is already in the collection, *arg* will not be added	WRITE **FILE1**
boolean addAll (Collection col)	Adds all the elements in *col* to this collection	READ **FILE1** IF NOT END OF FILE WRITE **FILE2** (in loop)
clear ()	Clears all the elements from this collection	READ **FILE1** IF NOT END OF FILE DELETE **FILE1** (in loop)
boolean contains (Object arg)	Returns true if this collection contains *arg*	READ **FILE1**
boolean equals (Object arg)	Returns true if this collection is equal to *arg*	IF **FILE1-FILENAME** **= FILE2-FILENAME**

Method	Description	Cobol Equivalent
Iterator iterator ()	Returns an iterator over this collection	START **FILE1**
boolean remove (Object arg)	Removes one instance of *arg* from this collection, if present	
boolean removeAll (Collection arg)	Removes all the elements in collection *arg* from this collection	READ **FILE1** IF NOT END OF FILE DELETE **FILE1** (in loop)
boolean retainAll (Object arg)	Removes all the elements not in collection *arg* from this collection	
int size ()	Returns the number of elements contained in this collection.	FILE1-RECORD-COUNT*
object toArray ()	Returns an array, which contains all of the elements of this collection	READ **FILE1** INTO **RECORD-HOLD** (X)
object toArray (Object[] arg)	Returns an array, which contains all the elements of this collection whose runtime type equals *arg*	READ **FILE1** INTO **RECORD-HOLD** (X)**

Some important methods from the Set collection interface are listed in the chart that follows. This collection type does not allow duplicate elements, meaning that no element in a Set is equal to another element in the same Set (as evaluated by the equals() method for that element). Sequential file processing is a good Cobol analogy for a Java Set.

Elements in the basic Set collection are not in any particular order, whereas elements in a SortedSet are in the order defined by its Comparator.

In Java 2, these methods are implemented in the AbstractSet (a partial implementation) class, the HashSet class, and the TreeSet class. These are essentially the same methods as defined in the Collections interface.

Method	Description	Cobol Equivalent
boolean add (Object arg)	Adds *arg* to this set if it is not already in the set	WRITE **FILE1**
boolean addAll (Collection col)	Adds all the elements in *col* to this set Only elements not already in this set will be added	READ **FILE1** IF NOT END OF FILE WRITE **FILE2** (in loop)
clear ()	Clears all of the elements from this set	READ **FILE1** IF NOT END OF FILE DELETE **FILE1** (in loop)

* This is not, strictly speaking, a Cobol standard, but some compilers do provide a mechanism to access the number of records in a file.

** Some additional logic would be needed to exclude those records not needed in RECORD-HOLD

Method	Description	Cobol Equivalent
boolean contains (Object arg)	Returns true if this set contains *arg*	READ **FILE1**
boolean equals (Object arg)	Returns true if this set is equal to *arg*	IF **FILE1-FILENAME** = **FILE2-FILENAME**
Iterator iterator ()	Returns an iterator over this set	START **FILE1**
boolean remove (Object arg)	Removes one instance of arg from this set if present	
boolean removeAll (Collection arg)	Removes all the elements in collection *arg* from this set	READ **FILE1** IF NOT END OF FILE DELETE **FILE1** (in loop)
boolean retainAll (Object arg)	Removes all the elements not in collection *arg* from this set	
int size ()	Returns the number of elements contained in this set	FILE1-RECORD-COUNT*
object toArray ()	Returns an array, which contains all the elements of this set	READ **FILE1** INTO **RECORD-HOLD** (X)
Object toArray (Object[] arg)	Returns an array, which contains all the elements of this set whose runtime type equals *arg*	READ **FILE1** INTO **RECORD-HOLD** (X)**

The *SortedSet* implementation extends the basic *Set* implementation. Some important methods from the SortedSet collection interface are listed in the following chart. This collection type orders its elements in some fashion but does not allow duplicate elements. The default Comparator is used to compare two elements (and therefore provide ordering), but you can write a specialized Comparator unique to your requirements.

The existence of a Comparator implies that all elements in a SortedSet collection must be comparable with each other. To do this, either the compareTo method of the element (that is, element1.compareTo (element2)) or the compare() method of the Comparator (that is, Comparator.compare()) will be used.

The methods unique to SortedSet are described in the chart. In Java 2, these methods are implemented in the TreeSet class.

* This is not, strictly speaking, a Cobol standard, but some compilers provide a mechanism to access the number of records in a file.

** Some additional logic would be needed to exclude those records not needed in RECORD-HOLD

Method	Description	Cobol Equivalent
Comparator comparator	Returns the Comparator for this collection, or null if this collection does not have a custom Comparator	
Object first ()	Returns the first object in the SortedSet	START **FILE1** WITH LOW-VALUES READ **FILE1**
Object last ()	Returns the last object in the SortedSet	READ **FILE1** UNTIL END OF FILE
SortedSet headSet (Object toElement)	Returns a view of this SortedSet. All the elements less than *toElement* will be in this view.*	READ **FILE1** UNTIL END-OF-FILE OR **RECORD-HOLD** NOT < **TO-ELEMENT**
SortedSet tailSet (Object fromElement)	Returns a view of this SortedSet. All the elements greater than or equal to *fromElement* will be in this view	START **FILE1** WITH FROM-RECORD READ **FILE1** UNTIL END OF FILE
SortedSet subSet (Object fromElement Object toElement)	Returns a view of this SortedSet. This view will contain all the elements greater than or equal to *fromElement* and less than *toElement*	START **FILE1** WITH FROM-RECORD READ **FILE1** UNTIL END-OF-FILE OR **RECORD-HOLD** NOT < **TO-ELEMENT**

Java 2 provides these implementations of the *Set* and *SortedSet* interfaces:

HashSet: A general-purpose yet efficient implementation of the basic set interface. Elements in a HashSet will not be ordered in any particular way, but iteration (that is, sequential access) to these elements will be optimized compared to TreeSets. Performance is also optimized when you allocate the initial capacity of a HashSet properly. This is done using the constructor that accepts an int parameter.

```
Set mySet = new HashSet(200);
```

By default, HashSets will be sized for 101 elements.

TreeSet: A basic implementation of the SortedSet interface. Elements in a TreeSet will be ordered based on its Comparator. The default Comparator orders elements based on their natural order, but you can override this behavior with your own Comparator.

* Elements in a view collection refer to the same elements in the base collection. Therefore changes in the view collection will be reflected in the base collection, and changes in the base collection will be reflected in the view.

A word of caution about the Set collection type. The Set interface defines good semantics that allow a program to add and remove elements from the collection. But there is no reliable way to manage elements that have changed while they are part of a set. This is because the modification is assigned to the element itself, and not the collection (that is, the collection doesn't *see* the modification). The proper sequence in this case is to get the element, remove it from the set, modify it, and then add it into the set. To extend this programming model to our Cobol file processing analogy, we would need to read in the record, modify it, delete the record, and then write the record.

Some important methods from the *list* collection interface are listed in the following chart. This collection type does allow duplicate elements. Elements in a list are often accessed using a positional (integer) index in a manner similar to Java arrays although lists can be sequentially searched for a particular element.

Lists define a special type of iterator (a ListIterator). In addition to the regular functions provided by the Collections Iterator, a ListIterator allows elements to be inserted or replaced, and it supports bidirectional access.

From a Cobol perspective, lists can be viewed as similar to the relative (or random access) file type.

Method	Description	Cobol Equivalent
boolean add (Object arg)	Adds arg to the end of this list	WRITE **FILE1**
add (int index, Object arg)	Inserts arg to this list, in position index	WRITE **FILE1** *
boolean addAll (Collection col)	Adds all the elements in col to the end of this list Elements will be added in the order determined by the collection's iterator	READ **FILE1** IF NOT END OF FILE WRITE **FILE2**
boolean addAll (int index, Collection col)	Adds all the elements in col to this list, starting in position index.	READ **FILE1** IF NOT END OF FILE WRITE **FILE2**
Object get (int index)	Returns the element at position *index*	READ **FILE1**
int indexOf (Object arg)	Returns the index of the first occurrence of *arg*. If *arg* is not in the list, then -1 is returned	READ **FILE1** UNTIL RECORD-HOLD = MY-RECORD
ListIterator listIterator ()	Returns a ListIterator for the elements in the list	START **FILE1**
ListIterator listIterator (int index)	Returns a ListIterator for the elements in the list, starting at position *index*	MOVE **NUMBER** TO **FILE1-RECORD-POS**
Object set (int index, Object arg)	Replaces the element at position *index* with *arg*	START **FILE1** REWRITE **FILE1**
List subList (int fromIndex, int toIndex)	Returns a view of this list, bounded by *fromIndex*, inclusive, and *toIndex*, exclusive.	READ **FILE1** INTO **RECORD-HOLD** (X)

* Actually, this function is more like moving all of the records "down" one position, starting at index, and then writing to position *index*.

Method	Description	Cobol Equivalent
object toArray ()	Returns an array, which contains all the elements of this list. Elements will be placed in the array in the order determined by the collection's iterator	
Object toArray (Object[] arg)	Returns an array, which contains all the elements of this list. The array's runtime type will be the same as *arg*	READ **FILE1** INTO **RECORD-HOLD** (X)*

Java 2 provides these implementations of the *List* interface:

AbstractList: The basic implementation of the list interface. This class is provided in order to simplify the task of a developer who wishes to implement a custom list collection.

AbstractSequentialList: The basic implementation of the list interface, appropriate for sequential access to the members of the list. This class is provided in order to simplify the task of a developer who wishes to implement a custom list collection, one that supports sequential access (for example, a linkedList).

LinkedList: The LinkedList implementation of the list interface. This uses many of the methods provided by the AbstractSequentialList class. It also adds methods to conveniently add, delete, and retrieve elements from the beginning or end of a list.

Vector: The replacement Vector class implementation for Java 2; this class is part of the collections framework. As with the original Vector class, this class supports a growable array of objects that can be accessed with an integer index.

ArrayList: The ArrayList class is very similar to the Vector class, except it is not synchronized. This is probably the most common collection class you will use since it combines flexible features with good overall performance.

Some important methods from the *map* collection interface are listed in the chart that follows. This collection type supports a set of *keys*, which are mapped to *values*. Another way to look at them is to view them as key-value pairs. Three types of map collection views are defined: a set of keys, a collection of values, or a set of key-value pairs.

This collection type does not allow duplicate elements (that is, duplicate keys). Each key can map to only one value. Multiple keys can map to the same value, however.

* Some additional logic would be needed to exclude those records not needed in RECORD-HOLD

The *ordering* of a map is based on the order in which the map's iterator returns elements. The TreeMap (the default implementation of the SortedMap interface) provides a specific order to the keys, whereas keys in a HashMap are in random order.

From a Cobol perspective, maps can be viewed as similar to the indexed file type. The index of the file is analogous to the keys in a map collection, and the record area would be analogous to the values in a map collection. To be more precise, an indexed sequential (ISAM) file type is very similar to the TreeMap collection, and an indexed file accessed via a hashed key is very similar to the HashMap collection.

Method	Description	Cobol Equivalent
Comparator comparator ()	Returns the comparator used to order this SortedMap. If no special comparator exists for this collection, then the keys natural ordering will be used, and null is returned for this call	
boolean containsKey (Object arg)	Returns true if *arg* is a key in this map	READ **FILE1** KEY IS KEY-NAME INVALID KEY . . .
boolean containsValue (Object arg)	Returns true if *arg* is a value in this map (i.e., if one or more keys map to this value)	READ **FILE1** UNTIL RECORD-AREA = MY-RECORD
Set entrySet ()	Returns a (set) view of the key-value mappings in this collection. (i.e., a collection with all of the keys and their values)	
Object firstKey ()	Returns the first (lowest) key in this SortedMap collection	START **FILE1** KEY IS >= LOW-VALUES READ **FILE1**
Object get (Object arg)	Returns the value mapped to *arg* (i.e., use *arg* as a key to this map)	READ **FILE1** KEY IS KEY-NAME INTO RECORD-AREA
SortedMap headMap (Object arg)	Returns a view of this SortedMap whose keys are less than *arg*	START **FILE1** KEY IS < KEY-AREA READ PREVIOUS **FILE1**

Method	Description	Cobol Equivalent
Set keySet ()	Returns a (set) view of all the keys in this map	
Object put (Object key, Object value)	Places the specified *key-value* pair into the collection	WRITE **FILE1**
Object remove (Object arg)	Removes the specified key (*arg*) from the collection.	DELETE **FILE1**
SortedMap subMap (Object arg1, Object arg2)	Returns a view of this SortedMap whose keys are less than or equal to *arg1*, and greater than *arg2*	START **FILE1** KEY IS >= KEY-AREA READ NEXT **FILE1** UNTIL KEY-AREA > END-KEY
SortedMap tailMap (Object arg)	Returns a view of this SortedMap whose keys are greater than or equal to *arg*	START **FILE1** KEY IS >= KEY-AREA
Collection values ()	Returns a (collection) view of all the values in this map	READ NEXT **FILE1**

Java 2 provides these two primary implementations of the *Map* interface (HashMap and TreeMap). They are in many ways analogous to the similarly named implementations of the Set interface (HashSet and SortedSet). So you should decide which map implementation to use based on the same criteria you use for sets: if you need the best implementation for random (unordered) maps, use the HashMap implementation, but if you need access to key-value pairs in some particular order, use the TreeMap implementation.

As with the Set interface, the Map interface must be used with caution when the key elements can be modified. The map interface defines good semantics that allow a program to add and remove key-value pairs from the collection, as well as modifying values in the map. But there is no reliable way to manage key elements that have changed while they are part of a map. This is very similar to the Cobol restriction that primary keys in an indexed file cannot change, but the rest of the record area can be changed. Just like an index file, the proper procedure to change a key is to remove the element from the map, modify it, and then add it into the map.

Iterators: Iterators are objects that support sequential access to the elements in a Collection. Iterators can be conceptually compared to the current position in a Cobol file; that is, the action about to take place is applied to the current logical position in the file.

The methods defined by the Iterator interface are listed in the following chart. Cobol equivalents are presented from the perspective of standard Cobol file I/O. As such, they present conceptual similarities more than strictly functional similarities.

Method	**Description**	**Cobol Equivalent**
boolean hasNext ()	Return *true*, if the collection has more elements past the current position.	
Object next ()	Returns the next element in the collection.	READ **FILE1**
remove ()	Deletes the current item (i.e., the last one returned by *next*()) from the collection.	DELETE **FILE1**

ListIterator is a specialization of Iterator, appropriate for Lists. These allow the list to be traversed in either direction, and allow the elements to be modified during iteration.

The methods unique to ListIterators are listed in the next chart. Cobol equivalents are presented from the perspective of standard Cobol file I/O. As such, they present conceptual similarities more than strictly functional similarities.

Method	**Description**	**Cobol Equivalent**
add (object arg)	Inserts *arg* into the list	WRITE **FILE1**
boolean hasPrevious ()	Returns *true*, if the list has more elements before the current position	
int nextIndex ()	Returns the index of the next element in the list (the one that would be returned by next ())	
Object previous ()	Returns the previous element in the list	READ PREVIOUS **FILE1**
Object previousIndex ()	Returns the index of the previous element in the list	
remove ()	Deletes the current item (i.e., the last one returned by *next* or *previous*) from the list	DELETE **FILE1**
set (Object arg)	Replaces the current item (i.e., the last one returned by *next* or *previous*) in the list	REWRITE **FILE1**

Java 2's collection package includes some complimentary implementations. These are available to simplify common tasks. They are categorized as *wrapper* implementations and *convenience* implementations.

The wrapper implementations are defined here. Replace the interface designation with the actual name of the interface (for example, Collection. unmodifiableMap).

Collection.unmodifiable*Interface*: This method returns a view of the specified collection that does not allow modifications. If a user attempts to modify the collection, then an `UnsupportedOperationException` is thrown. This method is very useful when you want to publish a view of your data (for example, in your API) that cannot be modified by a client application.

Collection.synchronized*Interface*: This method returns a view of the specified collection that is thread-safe. In order to maximize performance, the basic collection implementations are not thread-safe. This method returns a view of the collection that is thread-safe, allowing the developer to control when synchronization is appropriate.

For example, a thread-safe version of a list can be constructed using the synchronizedList method. This is best done when the collection is created so that no unsynchronized references to the list exist.

```
List syncList = Collections.synchronizedList(new ArrayList());
```

Afterwards, the program can synchronize on the synchList object:

```
synchronized(synchList) {
. . .
}
```

The Vector implementation class (intended to replace Java's original Vector class) is an exception to this standard; it is synchronized by default since the original Vector class is synchronized.

The convenience implementations are:

ArrayasList: This allows Java arrays to be viewed as Lists.

EmptySet and **EmptyList:** These constants can be used to test for empty sets and lists, respectively.

singleton: Returns an immutable set that contains only the specified object. Useful as a mechanism to cast an object into a set, for example, when you need to pass a set as a parameter.

nCopies: Creates a list, which contains n copies of the specified object.

EXERCISES: ARRAYS, VECTORS, AND OTHER COLLECTIONS

Time to visit our example classes again, and try out all these new ideas.

USING JAVA 2'S JDK

1. Edit the HelloWorld.java source file in your java4cobol directory with a text editor. We'll start by deleting the code that experimented with Strings. Remove the lines after this statement (but remember to leave in the two curly braces at the end of the program):

// Print the contents of ErrorMsg's String data member directly.

```
System.out.println (myErrorMsg.msgText);
```

2. Add these Java statements to the end of the previous statement. Note that the checkIntArray function is placed between the last two curly braces:

// Create an array of five error codes.

```
int[] errorNumbersIO = {1, 2, 10, 22, 23};
```

// Test if any are equal to 30.

```
checkIntArray (errorNumbersIO);

}
```

// Test if any integers in the passed array are equal to 30.

```
static void checkIntArray (int[] intArray) {
     System.out.println ();
     for (int x = 0; x < intArray.length; x++) {
          if (intArray[x] == 30) {
               System.out.println ("Found '30' at index "
```

```
                        + x);
                      break;
                }
                else {
                      System.out.println ("error Number " +
                            x + " = " + intArray[x]);
                }
          }
     }
}
```

3. Save these modifications as a text file, and then compile the class in the DOS command window. (You may need to add an `import java.util.*;` import statement to the beginning of your HelloWorld class.)

➢ javac HelloWorld.java

Execute this program. The output should look like this:

```
. . .

error Number 0 = 1
error Number 1 = 2
error Number 2 = 10
error Number 3 = 22
error Number 4 = 23
```

4. Add these Java **bold** statements to the end of the HelloWorld class, but before the checkIntArray() function:

// Test if any are equal to 30.

```
checkIntArray (errorNumbersIO);
```

// Set an error code to 30, and call the checkIntArray function again.

```
errorNumbersIO[1] = 30;
checkIntArray (errorNumbersIO);
```

// Reset error code [1].

```
errorNumbersIO[1] = 2;
```

5. Compile and run this class. Your output window should look like this:

```
. . .
error Number 0 = 1
error Number 1 = 2
error Number 2 = 10
error Number 3 = 22
error Number 4 = 23

error Number 0 = 1
Found '30' at index 1
```

6. Next, add these Java statements to the end of the HelloWorld class, but before the checkIntArray() function:

// Create an array of logical error numbers.

```
int[] errorNumbersLogical = {101, 102, 108, 122};
```

// Copy all error numbers into a new array.

```
int[] errorNumbersAll = new int[errorNumbersIO.length
                    + errorNumbersLogical.length];
System.arraycopy (errorNumbersIO, 0, errorNumbersAll, 0, 5);
System.arraycopy (errorNumbersLogical, 0, errorNumbersAll, 5, 4);
```

// Test if any are equal to 30.

```
checkIntArray (errorNumbersAll);
```

7. Compile and run this class. Your output window should look like this:

```
. . .

error Number 0 = 1
error Number 1 = 2
error Number 2 = 10
error Number 3 = 22
error Number 4 = 23

error Number 0 = 1
Found '30' at index 1

error Number 0 = 1
error Number 1 = 2
error Number 2 = 10
error Number 3 = 22
error Number 4 = 23
error Number 5 = 101
error Number 6 = 102
error Number 7 = 108
error Number 8 = 122
```

8. For our last experiment with integer arrays, add these Java statements to the end of the HelloWorld class, but before the checkIntArray() function:

// Create an empty array of integers.

// Set it to the various integer arrays we've created and print them out.

```
int[] tempNumbers;
tempNumbers = errorNumbersIO;
checkIntArray (tempNumbers);

tempNumbers = errorNumbersLogical;
checkIntArray (tempNumbers);

tempNumbers = errorNumbersAll;
checkIntArray (tempNumbers);
```

9. Compile and run this class. Your output window should look like this:

```
. . .

error Number 0 = 1
error Number 1 = 2
error Number 2 = 10
error Number 3 = 22
error Number 4 = 23

error Number 0 = 101
error Number 1 = 102
error Number 2 = 108
error Number 3 = 122

error Number 0 = 1
error Number 1 = 2
error Number 2 = 10
error Number 3 = 22
error Number 4 = 23
error Number 5 = 101
error Number 6 = 102
error Number 7 = 108
error Number 8 = 122
```

10. Next, we'll experiment with arrays of objects. Add these Java statements to the end of the HelloWorld class, but before the checkIntArray() function:

// Create an array of five ErrorMsg's.

```
int ARRAY_SIZE = 5;
ErrorMsg[]  myErrorMsgs =  new ErrorMsg[ARRAY_SIZE];
```

// Create a new ErrorMsg object in each element in the ErrorMsg array,

// and set the msgText member for each object.

```
for (int x = 0; x < myErrorMsgs.length; x++) {
     if (myErrorMsgs[x] == null) {
          myErrorMsgs[x] = new ErrorMsg();
   }
```

// Set msgText to "Text #" for all the elements except the last two.
// Set the msgText member in the last two objects in the array to
// the String "Last two ErrorMsgs."
// Set msgText to "ErrorMsg text #" for the remaining elements.

```
        if (x > (myErrorMsgs.length - 3)) {
              myErrorMsgs[x].setErrorMsg
                    ("Last two ErrorMsgs");
        }
        else {
             myErrorMsgs[x].setErrorMsg
                    ("Text #" + x);
        }
   }
```

// Now, print the msgText Strings.

```
   System.out.println();
   for (int x = 0; x < myErrorMsgs.length; x++) {
        System.out.println (myErrorMsgs[x].getErrorMsg());
   }
```

11. Compile and run this class. Your output window should look like this:

```
. . .
error Number 8 = 122

Text #0
Text #1
Text #2
Last two ErrorMsgs
Last two ErrorMsgs
```

Our next experiments will deal with collections. We'll start with the set collection type and then visit the list and the map type.

12. Add these Java statements to the end of the HelloWorld class, but before the checkIntArray() function.

// First, create a collection.

// Note that we use the interface type (*Set*) in the statement that creates the // collection, and not the implementation (*HashSet*). We will discuss this when // we review our samples.

```
Set errorSet = new HashSet ();
```

// Copy the msgText Strings from the array to the collection.

```
for (int x=0; x < myErrorMsgs.length; x++) {
     errorSet.add(myErrorMsgs[x].getErrorMsg());
}

System.out.println();
System.out.println("There are " + errorSet.size() +
      " Strings in errorSet: " + errorSet);
```

```
. . .
error Number 8 = 122

Text #0
Text #1
Text #2
Last two ErrorMsgs
Last two ErrorMsgs
There are 4 Strings in errorSet: [last two ErrorMsgs, Text #2, Text #1, Text #0]
```

Why do you think only four Strings were inserted into the set even though the add() function was performed five times? Which one is missing?

Sets have a number of bulk operations that modify the current set based on another. These are particularly well suited as mechanisms to perform algebraic operations (subset, union, intersection, and difference) on sets. However, be careful since these operations modify the current set.

13. Add these Java statements to the end of the HelloWorld class, but before the checkIntArray() function. In this set of examples, a view of the output line is inserted after the println() statements so that the concept explored by the example is easier to follow.

// Copy each String from myErrorMsgs into errorSetUnique.

// Record any Strings that are duplicates in errorSetDup.

```
Set errorSetUnique = new HashSet();
Set errorSetDup = new HashSet();
for (int x=0; x < myErrorMsgs.length; x++) {
  if (!errorSetUnique.add(myErrorMsgs[x].getErrorMsg())) {
      errorSetDup.add(myErrorMsgs[x].getErrorMsg());
  }
}
```

// Show the contents of our collections.

```
System.out.println("SetUnique:        " + errorSetUnique);
System.out.println("SetDup:           " + errorSetDup);
```

```
. . .
SetUnique:        [Last two ErrorMsgs, Text #2, Text #1, Text #0]
SetDup:           [Last two ErrorMsgs]
```

// Perform some algebraic functions on the collections.

// Test for subset

```
System.out.println();
System.out.println("Is 'SetDup' a subset of 'SetUnique'? "
      + errorSet.containsAll(errorSetUnique));
System.out.println();
```

```
. . .

Is 'SetDup' a subset of 'SetUnique'? true
```

// Build a collection with the union of Unique and Dup.

```
Set errorSetUnion = new HashSet (errorSetUnique);
errorSetUnion.containsAll(errorSetDup);
System.out.println("SetUnion:        " + errorSetUnion);
```

// Find the difference between Unique and Dup.

```
Set errorSetDifference = new HashSet (errorSetUnique);
errorSetDifference.removeAll(errorSetDup);
System.out.println("SetDifference:   " +
      errorSetDifference);
```

// Find the intersection of Unique and Dup.

```
Set errorSetIntersection = new HashSet (errorSetUnique);
errorSetIntersection.retainAll(errorSetDup);
System.out.println("SetIntersection: " +
      errorSetIntersection);
```

```
. . .
SetUnion:         [Last two ErrorMsgs, Text #2, Text #1, Text #0]
SetDifference:    [Text #2, Text #1, Text #0]
SetIntersection:  [Last two ErrorMsgs]
```

14. Change the implementation class of our errorSet collection(s) from HashSet to TreeSet (as in, replace HashSet with TreeSet in the errorSet declarations). Compile and execute the program again. Why do you think the output has changed? What is the difference between a TreeSet and a HashSet?

USING J++

1. Select your java4cobol project from among the recent workspaces using this menu path:

➢ File → Recent Workspaces → java4cobol

2. We'll start by deleting the code that experimented with inheritance. Remove the lines after this statement (but remember to leave in the two curly braces at the end of the program):

// Print the contents of ErrorMsg's String data member directly.

```
System.out.println (myErrorMsg.msgText);
```

3. Add these Java statements to the end of the previous statement. Note that the checkIntArray() function is placed between the last two curly braces:

// Create an array of five error codes.

```
int[] errorNumbersIO = {1, 2, 10, 22, 23};
```

// Test if any are equal to 30.

```
checkIntArray (errorNumbersIO);

}
```

// Test if any integers in the passed array are equal to .30.

```
static void checkIntArray (int[] intArray) {
     System.out.println ();
     for (int x = 0; x < intArray.length; x++) {
          if (intArray[x] == 30) {
                System.out.println ("Found '30' at index "
                 + x);
                 break;
          }
          else {
               System.out.println ("error Number " +
                    x + " = " + intArray[x]);
          }
     }
     }
}
```

4. Compile this class using the menu path:

➢ Build → Compile HelloWorld.java

Execute this program (Build → Start Debug → Run to Cursor). The output should look like this:

```
. . .

error Number 0 = 1
error Number 1 = 2
error Number 2 = 10
error Number 3 = 22
error Number 4 = 23
```

5. Add these Java **bold** statements to the end of the HelloWorld class, but before the checkIntArray() function:

// Test if any are equal to 30.

```
checkIntArray (errorNumbersIO);
```

// Set an error code to 30, and call the checkIntArray function again

```
errorNumbersIO[1] = 30;
checkIntArray (errorNumbersIO);
```

// Reset error code [1].

```
errorNumbersIO[1] = 2;
```

6. Compile and run this class. Your output window should look like this:

```
. . .
error Number 0 = 1
error Number 1 = 2
error Number 2 = 10
error Number 3 = 22
error Number 4 = 23

error Number 0 = 1
Found '30' at index 1
```

7. Next, add these Java statements to the end of the HelloWorld class, but before the checkIntArray() funtion:

// Create an array of logical error numbers.

```
int[] errorNumbersLogical = {101, 102, 108, 122};
```

// Copy all error numbers into an new array.

```
int[] errorNumbersAll = new int[errorNumbersIO.length
             + errorNumbersLogical.length];
System.arraycopy (errorNumbersIO, 0, errorNumbersAll, 0, 5);
System.arraycopy (errorNumbersLogical, 0, errorNumbersAll, 5, 4);
```

// Test if any are equal to '30'

```
checkIntArray (errorNumbersAll);
```

8. Compile and run this class. Your output window should look like this:

```
. . .

error Number 0 = 1
error Number 1 = 2
error Number 2 = 10
error Number 3 = 22
error Number 4 = 23

error Number 0 = 1
Found '30' at index 1

error Number 0 = 1
error Number 1 = 2
error Number 2 = 10
error Number 3 = 22
error Number 4 = 23
error Number 5 = 101
error Number 6 = 102
error Number 7 = 108
error Number 8 = 122
```

9. For our to last experiment with integer arrays, add these Java statements to the end of the HelloWorld class, but before the checkIntArray() function:

// Create an empty array of integers.

// Set it to the various integer arrays we've created and print them out.

```
int[] tempNumbers;
tempNumbers = errorNumbersIO;
checkIntArray (tempNumbers);

tempNumbers = errorNumbersLogical;
checkIntArray (tempNumbers);

tempNumbers = errorNumbersAll;
checkIntArray (tempNumbers);
```

10. Compile and run this class. Your output window should look like this:

```
. . .
error Number 0 = 1
error Number 1 = 2
error Number 2 = 10
error Number 3 = 22
error Number 4 = 23

error Number 0 = 101
error Number 1 = 102
error Number 2 = 108
error Number 3 = 122

error Number 0 = 1
error Number 1 = 2
error Number 2 = 10
error Number 3 = 22
error Number 4 = 23
error Number 5 = 101
error Number 6 = 102
error Number 7 = 108
error Number 8 = 122
```

11. Next, we'll experiment with arrays of objects. Add these Java statements at the end of the HelloWorld class, but before the checkIntArray() function:

// Create an array of five ErrorMsg's:

```
int ARRAY_SIZE = 5;
ErrorMsg[]  myErrorMsgs =  new ErrorMsg[ARRAY_SIZE];
```

// Create a new ErrorMsg object in each element in the ErrorMsg array,

// and set the msgText member for each object.

```
for (int x = 0; x < myErrorMsgs.length; x++) {
     if (myErrorMsgs[x] == null) {
          myErrorMsgs[x] = new ErrorMsg();
     }
```

// Set msgText to "Text #" for all the elements except the last two.

// Set the msgText member in the last two objects in the array to

// the String "Last two ErrorMsgs"

```
          if (x > (myErrorMsgs.length - 3)) {
               myErrorMsgs[x].setErrorMsg
                     ("Last two ErrorMsgs");
          }
          else {
               myErrorMsgs[x].setErrorMsg
                     ("Text #" + x);
          }
     }
```

// Now, print the msgText Strings.

```
     System.out.println();
     for (int x = 0; x < myErrorMsgs.length; x++) {
          System.out.println (myErrorMsgs[x].getErrorMsg());
     }
```

12. Compile and run this class Your output window should look like this:

```
. . .
error Number 8 = 122

Text #0
Text #1
Text #2
Last two ErrorMsgs
Last two ErrorMsgs
```

REVIEWING OUR EXERCISES

Let's review the samples we've created. Try to relate the sample source statements to the result (for example, the output) each statement creates. If necessary, re-run the samples, or look at the complete source code for this exercise on the CD. Feel free to experiment by yourself.

- First, we created an array of integer numbers. We also created a function (checkIntArray()). This function accepts an array as a parameter and prints out all of the integer values it sees in the array until it finds one equal to 30.

- We used various techniques to create and modify some arrays, and called the checkIntArray() function to examine these arrays in order to see the effect.
- We then moved on to some experiments with arrays of String objects.
- In our JDK exercises, we experimented with Collections (currently, the Microsoft environment does not support Collections). The first collection we created was a Set. We discovered that we cannot place duplicate text objects into a Set.
- Next, we used some of the Set functions (such as containsAll()) to perform standard algebraic functions on the Sets.
- When we changed the collection type of errorSet from HashSet to TreeSet, the order of the items in the collection changed from a random order to a sorted order. All we had to change was the constructor name (from HashSet to TreeSet).

CHAPTER

10

Exceptions, Threads, and Garbage Collectors

Proper error handling is a feature found in every well-designed system. A good system will not only check for and report the obvious errors, but it will also plan for and properly manage the unexpected errors.

The general rules for good error handling in any language might be stated this way:

- Make sure to check for all possible error conditions.
- If your program can handle the error properly (for example, ask the operator for correction, or assume a default processing condition), then do so.
- If your program cannot handle the error, then report the error to the calling program as an error condition as soon as possible.
- Include as much contextual information as is possible (or is practical) in the error. This likely means that the code that detected the error must provide this information.
- Serious processing errors, or unmanaged errors, should be detected as quickly as possible. In general, these types of errors should not allow processing to continue.
- Errors that cause abnormal termination should be logged to a file with complete contextual information for convenient postmortem analysis.

Cobol is very good at managing simple error conditions. For example, most Cobol programs will validate the end user's input and report back any invalid input to the end user. However, processing-type errors (file I/O errors, for example) can be much more cumbersome. If you have been involved with any significant Cobol project, you know already how difficult good error handling can be in some cases. Let us explore the following example.

Suppose your system includes a currency rate calculation subroutine, and your program uses that subroutine to perform currency rate conversions. What should happen if you call the subroutine and that subroutine cannot read the record in the database required for proper currency rate conversion? Clearly, the answer depends on several factors, including whether your application is a batch or an interactive one, and whether or not your application can continue without the rate.

To design and document a currency conversion subroutine interface that supports each of these technical scenarios, in addition to the business interface requirements, is a complex task. The technical interface requirements (batch vs. online mode, calling program error processing capabilities, potential error conditions of the subroutine, error details in message form, and so on.) will likely overwhelm, or at least confuse, the business application interface requirements.

Java has the advantage of being designed more than 30 years after Cobol, and so its architects have come up with a built-in solution for this type of requirement. This solution is, naturally enough, based on the use of objects. Java defines a special object type called Exception. Classes can describe which exception objects they will create, and which ones they can handle. Moreover, the compiler checks class definitions to make sure that your classes contain appropriate logic for any declared exceptions.

One important design objective of Java exceptions is that standard logic should be separated from exception processing logic as much as possible. At the same time, exceptions, when they do happen, should be dealt with as soon as possible and by the class that is closest to the problem.

EXCEPTION CLASS HIERARCHY

The basic class Java provides to assist in error processing is the Exception class. The Java Exception class inherits from the Throwable class. The Throwable class is also the super class for the Error class used by the Java runtime to report serious runtime errors (you should not normally have occasion to use the Error class directly).

The Exception class comes with many prebuilt subclasses. Two subclasses of particular interest are RuntimeException and IOException. As a general rule, RuntimeExceptions are created as a result of logic errors in your program. Most often, effort should be spent in correcting and preventing this type of error instead of handling it. Most Java applications attempt only to manage the IOException class of errors, or some subclass (that is, specialization) of this error type.

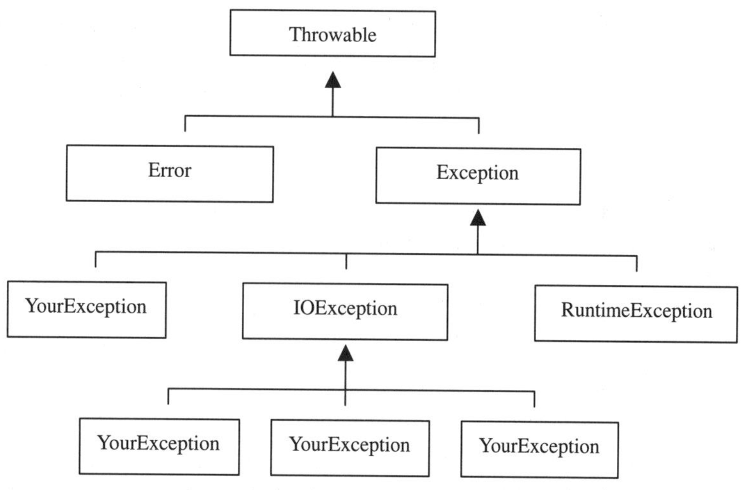

FIGURE 10.1 Exception class hierarchy.

CREATING EXCEPTIONS

A Java class can use any of the predefined Exception objects. These are listed in the JDK1.2 documentation set on the CD, and are also available at www.java.sun.com.

If the standard exception definitions do not meet your requirements, you can create new ones. Simply extend either the Exception or (preferably) the IOException classes.

This exception will be used when no database is available for the application to connect to:

```
class NoDatabaseAvailable extends IOException {
      . . .
}
```

By convention, Exception classes define a constructor that accepts a String parameter. This allows the class that created the exception to place some contextual information in the Exception. In addition, Exception classes normally support a method named getMessage(). This method returns a String that contains the contextual information and perhaps more detailed information about the error condition.

```
class NoDatabaseAvailable extends IOException {

      public NoDatabaseAvailable (String message) {
             super (message);
      }
. . .

      public String getMessage () {
             return "Unable to access the database for" +
             super.getMessage ();
      }

}
```

Your new exception is now ready for use.

You can envision an Exception object as an optional return value from a method. You already know that methods can return values as defined in the method interface. In addition, a method can create an Exception object and return this object, instead of the normal value.

A Java method that may create an exception must publish that property as part of its interface definition. The syntax for this is:

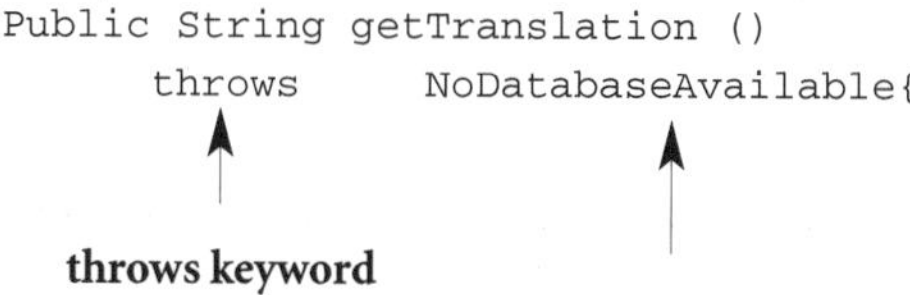

A class defined in this manner may return a NoDatabaseAvailable Exception instead of the standard String return value. Suppose we want our getTranslation() method to return with an Exception if a translation is requested, and no database is available to retrieve the translation. In addition, we would like to return with the current language code and the text of the original message.

Based on these requirements, our conversion class throws an exception with the following syntax:

```
if (database.connect () = null) {
       throw new NoDatabaseAvailable ("LANGUAGECODE = " +
          LANGUAGECODE + " text = " + msgText);
}
```

When the Java runtime processes the throw statement, the method exits immediately to the calling class. Any statements after the *throw* statement are not executed.

This is roughly analogous to the following Cobol syntax. (It is assumed that the required data elements are defined in the subroutine's CONTROL item, and that these items begin with the prefix SUB-.)

```
IF DATABASE-NOT-CONNECTED
        STRING "LANGUAGECODE = ", SUB-LANGUAGE-CODE,
        " text = ", SUB-MESSAGE-TEXT DELIMITED BY SIZE INTO
        SUB-ERROR-MSG
        SET SUB-NO-DATABASE-AVAILABLE TO TRUE
        PERFORM EXIT-PROGRAM.


. . .


 EXIT-PROGRAM.
       EXIT PROGRAM.
```

USING EXCEPTIONS

Now, for the last piece of the puzzle. If a method can throw an exception, then any classes that calls this method must handle the potential exception(s) in some fashion.

A class handles an exception from a method by using the try ... catch construct:

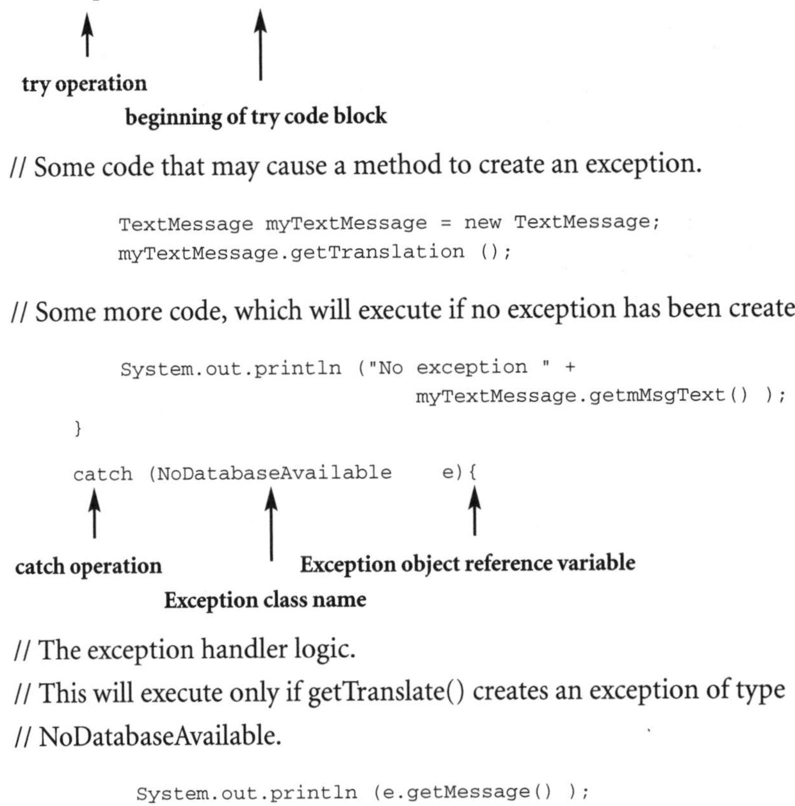


```
try            {
```

// Some code that may cause a method to create an exception.

```
TextMessage myTextMessage = new TextMessage;
myTextMessage.getTranslation ();
```

// Some more code, which will execute if no exception has been created

```
    System.out.println ("No exception " +
                        myTextMessage.getmMsgText() );
}
catch (NoDatabaseAvailable    e){
```

// The exception handler logic.

// This will execute only if getTranslate() creates an exception of type

// NoDatabaseAvailable.

```
    System.out.println (e.getMessage() );
}
```

Statements inside the try code block will stop executing as soon as an exception is created. If no exceptions are created, or if your class has caught and handled the exception, your class will continue with the statement after the try ... catch code block.

Your class can handle multiple exceptions that may be created by statements in the try code block simply by adding an additional catch code block after some other catch code block.

```
try              {
        . . .
}
catch (NoDatabaseAvailable    e){
        . . .
}

catch (IOException    e){
```

// The exception handler logic for all other IO conditions.

```
        System.out.println (e.getMessage() );

}
```

Once in a while, you may need to catch an exception and perform some logic based on the exception, but still not completely manage the primary reason for the exception condition. For example, suppose that our TextMessage really needs to be translated before the application can continue. In this case, we should certainly write the exception message to a file (to the standard output device in our example), but in addition, we may want to inform the end user. To meet these requirements, we can *rethrow* the exception and allow the calling class to complete the error-handling logic.

```
catch (NoDatabaseAvailable    e){
```

// The exception handler logic.

// This will execute only if getTranslate() creates an exception of type

// NoDatabaseAvailable.

```
        System.out.println (e.getMessage() );
```

// Pass the exception to the calling program.

```
        throw e;
}
```

Our last Exception structure is the *finally* operator. This structure provides a mechanism to define statements that should execute even if an exception occurs. Statements in a finally code block will execute after the try block even if an exception is caught. So, you can place logic that is always required in the finally block, and it will always be executed.

```
try             {
      . . .
}
catch (NoDatabaseAvailable    e){
      . . .
}

catch (IOException    e){
      . . .
}

finally {
```

// This statement will always be executed.

```
        System.out.println ("Always printed " +
                                myTextMessage.getmMsgText() );
}
```

This *finally* code block will always be performed. This holds for all the following conditions:

- The try block completes normally
- The try block explicitly throws an exception that is caught in a related catch block.
- The try block explicitly throws an exception that is not caught in a related catch block.
- The try block executes a return statement.
- The try block causes an exception to be thrown in some other class, which is caught in a related catch block.
- The try block causes an exception to be thrown in some other class, which is not caught in a related catch block.

This approach gives the developer complete control over exception processing, yet still provides excellent default exception processing mechanisms. A class can demand that control be returned to it whenever exceptions happen, through the use of the try … catch … finally structure. The runtime will first perform the try function, and then the catch function for matching exceptions. In any event, the *finally* function will be performed. Even if an exception is thrown by the method the runtime will execute the the *finally* code block before it passes control back to any calling class.

A class may not be able to handle the exceptions created by classes that it uses. Or the class may only partially handle the exception. In these cases, the class must pass the exception along to its caller, which must in turn handle it, or pass the exception along as well.

The syntax for defining which exceptions will be passed along is also *throws.* That is, if a class (B) uses a class (C), and C throws an exception, the consumer class (B) does not necessarily need to handle the error. It can simply define that exception in its own exception list. At runtime, the exception created by C will be automatically passed to the caller of B, as if B created that exception. In a sense, B can inherit the exceptions of the classes it creates. (This is another example of where Java comes awfully close to supporting multiple inheritance in order to provide for a specific feature.)

// This class does not handle the NoDatabaseAvailable exception.

// Instead, it is listed as a possible exception in one of its methods.

```
public class TextMessageConsumer
     public void someMethod ()
     throws NoDatabaseAvailable {
     . . .
```

// Some code that may cause a class to create an exception.

// Note that these statements are not in a try … catch code block.

```
TextMessage myTextMessage = new TextMessage;
myTextMessage.getTranslation ();
```

In this example, the TextMessageConsumer class does not explicitly handle the NoDatabaseAvailable exception in a try … catch code block. If this exception were to occur, the caller of TextMessageConsumer.someMethod() would receive the exception, as if the method TextMessageConsumer.someMethod() had created it.

To review, here is the Java specification for exception processing. Suppose that class C throws some exception. Any Java class B that creates an instance of class C must explicitly handle the exception either by catching it or by throwing it to the class that created B. The compiler checks this for you. As a result, you know at compile time that a class you are using may create an error condition, and your class must either handle the error or pass control along to a class that can.

EXCEPTION PROCESSING SUGGESTIONS

Exceptions are a very handy way to describe error conditions and ensure that they are properly managed. As is always true, too much of a good thing is not necessarily a better thing.

For one, exception processing is much more expensive than is simple testing. It is generally better (performancewise) to test for an error condition if you can instead of creating and catching an exception. As a rule, exceptions should be reserved for unusual error conditions and not as a programming technique to test for anticipated conditions.

For another, a class that throws an exception forces its subclasses and its consumer classes to handle the exception. A class designer should define and throw exceptions only when it makes sense for a class consumer to be aware of the error condition. Of course, if you define a class that uses other classes, and these other classes throw exceptions, you may have to throw them in the classes you build if your class cannot handle the exception internally. This situation only highlights the potential problems created by the aggressive use of exceptions.

Another related suggestion: make sure that your base classes that will throw exceptions are defined that way early in the development process. It is extremely frustrating to define a new exception in a low-level class, and then have to edit and recompile all the classes that use this class. You will need to recompile because every class that calls a method that can throw an exception must either handle the exception or throw it.

Make sure that your class is in a proper state if you throw or catch an exception. Since a *throw* statement effectively acts as a go to statement and abruptly interrupts the normal sequence of statements in your class, it is possible that some variable or object in your object will be in an invalid state the next time your object is accessed. If necessary, place appropriate code in the *finally* code block in order to assure that your object is in good shape for the next call.

Finally, group your exception processing into larger try … catch code blocks. For example, don't insert a try … catch block around every statement that may create an exception. If a section of code might create several exceptions, it is very likely that the exception-handling process is the same for each exception. If this is the case, group the statements into a single, larger try … catch code block.

EXCEPTION PROCESSING SUMMARY

As you can see, Java's implementation of exception processing assists complex systems manage error conditions in a standard and predictable manner. The requirements of good error processing (as defined in the beginning of the chapter) are encapsulated in the language definition. Classes can define both their return values and their error conditions. Consumer classes must explicitly define how they wish to handle these error conditions, either with try ... catch code blocks or by rethrowing the exception. The *finally* statement ensures that appropriate state management functions will be executed, even if exceptions occur. Best of all, the compiler understands this definition and checks to make sure you are following the exception processing rules.

THREADS

All modern computer operating systems are multitasking systems. A multitasking system is one that can perform several tasks simultaneously. The operating system task manager will share computer resources (disk, memory, I/O paths, but especially the CPU) between the various jobs running on the system. Robust operating systems are preemptive multitasking systems, meaning that the task manager will make sure that no single task hogs a resource and causes other tasks to wait.

Historically, an operating system manages its jobs at the process level. Operating system processes are self-contained execution units (as defined by the operating system) and share the same address space. The operating system creates, schedules, and provides system resources to processes. Most programming languages (including Cobol and Java) construct a program that will execute as a process in the host operating system.

Inside a traditional process, there is only one thread of execution, that is, only one statement can be performed at any one time. When a statement is complete, the next statement executes. The developer can control the sequence of statements, but there is no way for the developer to have two statements in a program execute at the same time.

In contrast, Java defines a multithreaded execution model. This model allows any number of statements inside a single process to execute simultaneously. That is, your program can have many threads of execution accomplishing work at the same time. A thread is any asynchronous subprocess inside your main program process.

Java threads allow you to construct applications that do not wait for a function to complete before executing another function. Perhaps your program contains an Account object, which reads transactions from a database based on an end-user's request. At the same time that this function is executing, you may need to perform an interrupt() method on a user interface class, which checks to see if the user wants to cancel the request. Without simultaneous threads, you would have to wait for the Account object to complete its work before you could check the user interface class. As a result, the user would not be able to cancel the request until the request was complete!

INHERITING FROM THREAD

Java provides two mechanisms to create new threads. The simplest mechanism is to inherit from the Thread class. This class contains all the logic required to create and execute a new thread. You simply need to define a run() method and place your execution logic in here. The statements in the run() method will execute simultaneously with other statements in your program.

The following statements define a class with a run() method that will print out a message:

```
public class MsgThread extends Thread {
     public MsgThread () {
          super ();
     }

     public void run () {
              for (;;) {                    // Create an infinite loop.
              System.out.println ("Inside a thread");
              }
          }
     }
```

In some other class, we can create several instances of these classes.

```
MsgThread run1 = new MsgThread ();
MsgThread run2 = new MsgThread ();
```

The threads will not execute yet. In order to get the logic in the Thread classes going, we have to call their run() method. We do this (indirectly) by calling its start() method.

```
run1.start();
run2.start();
```

Now, both of these threads will execute simultaneously (and endlessly).

What if you want to stop an executing thread? Simply call the stop() method!

```
run1.stop();
run2.stop();
```

Or you can suspend, and then resume, a thread.

```
run1.suspend();
run2.suspend ();
run1.resume();
run2.resume();
```

Interestingly, any class that has access to the thread object can call the stop, resume, and suspend methods for that thread object. This means that the thread can suspend itself, or the object reference can be passed as an argument to some other method, and the called method can control the thread, even if it didn't actually create the thread.

For example, suppose we've defined a class named ThreadManager that stops a Thread and logs this event.

```
MsgThread run1 = new MsgThread ();
ThreadManager sys1 = new ThreadManager ();

run1.start();
sys1.stopThread(run1);


public class ThreadManager {
     public void stopThread (Thread t1) {
          t1.stop ();
          System.out.println ("Thread cancelled" + t1);
     }
}
```

IMPLEMENTING RUNNABLE

One obvious limitation of the first thread management technique is the fact that your class has to inherit from the Thread class. What if you need to build a threaded class, but it must inherit from some other class? In order to support this requirement, Java provides another mechanism to create in-process threads.

The second approach is to have your class implement the *Runnable* Interface. The class that you want to run as a thread simply needs to define the run() method from this Interface. As a last step, you have to create a new Thread class and pass your object to the Thread constructor.

```
public class MsgThread
     implements Runnable {

   public void run () {
        for (;;) {  // Create an infinite loop.
              System.out.println ("Inside a thread");
          }
     }
}
```

Your class can now create a Thread object based on your non-Thread object as follows:

```
Thread run1 = new Thread (new MsgThread ());
Thread run2 = new Thread (new MsgThread ());

run1.start();
run2.start();
```

SYNCHRONIZATION

Java threads execute inside a single process, and therefore share all the resources normally managed by the operating system. Threads in a process will normally all share the same class instances and address space. Therefore, all object data members are shared between the various threads.

Since Java threads share resources inside the operating system process, the Java program itself has to manage resource utilization conflicts. For example, it would ordinarily be inappropriate for a function to increment a variable while some other function resets that variable to zero.

The solution for this problem is to *synchronize* your methods or objects. When you synchronize a method, it waits for all other currently executing instances of this object's method to complete. When you synchronize on an object, Java makes sure that only one thread at a time modifies that object.

Java's synchronization coordinates access at the object level. This means that two distinct object instances of the same class are not coordinated. Static members can be synchronized, but they do not block access to synchronized object instances.

To protect a critical method against concurrent access, you can use the *synchronized* keyword:

```
public class ErrorMsg {
     public synchronized String getErrorMsg () {
     }
}
```

In this case, only one thread in a process can call the getErrorMsg() method in a particular instance of the ErrorMsg class.

Another way to coordinate activities among threads is to define a synchronization block of code. This is a block of code that has been explicitly marked to synchronize on any object or static class member.

```
public class ErrorMsg {
     DatabaseConnection myDB = new DatabaseConnection ()

     public String getErrorMsg () {
          if (ErrorMsgnotRead) {
               synchronized (myDB.CONNECTION_SYNCH) {
```

// Read the database, and make sure only one instance of DatabaseConnection

// is doing it at a time. The CONNECTION_SYNCH static class member is

// used to synchronize all instances of DatabaseConnection.

```
               . . .
               }
          }
     }
}
```

Of course, it is up to the developer to make sure that all relevant access to this object is also synchronized. Sometimes this technique is referred to as manual synchronization.

BENEFITS AND CAUTIONS

Java's ability to create and execute multiple threads allows the developer to build responsive, powerful applications. In particular, applications that perform significant work, yet still need to respond to user input, are good candidates for a multithreaded design. Another good nominee is an application that needs to respond to end user input from multiple interactive dialogs (the search utility in a word processor, for example).

Other possibilities include applications that contain functions that can be processed in parallel. In today's environment, production systems often have multiple CPUs. Breaking up your task into multiple functions that can run simultaneously allows the system to assign your work to multiple CPUs. The result will likely be more work done in less time.

Some parallel functions are obvious (perhaps you have a data migration application, and it can be structured to extract data from multiple tables simultaneously). Other times the opportunities require a little more thought (how can I break up a single table extract function into multiple steps?). In any event, the effective use of threads can result in more efficient, more responsive applications.

Still, it is important not to treat threads like a shinny new tool that should be used with every project. As with any good thing, it is possible to get carried away with using threads.

- **The use of multiple threads in an application can be a very difficult programming model.** It is up to you (the developer) to anticipate and prevent resource conflicts. In many cases, you even need to manage (schedule, start, stop, and synchronize) threads so that they execute when required. Furthermore, an application that contains a shared resource problem (for example, one thread updates a counter, while another thread decrements it) is a very difficult application to debug. In fact, the debugger will very likely affect the symptoms of the problem you are analyzing, since it runs in a thread of its own.
- **Thread implementations vary significantly across operating systems and virtual machines.** Some VMs use the native operating system thread mechanism, whereas others create their own thread management logic in the VM. In the later case, multithreaded performance is likely to be less than what you would expect.

- **Don't recreate an operating system using threads.** It is unlikely that an average developer can write process management and context-switching logic that is more effective than the process management and context-switching logic built into the operating system. The major advantage of threads is the premise that the developer has more intimate knowledge of the application implementation. Therefore, the developer can identify those portions of the application that can be shared between threads, and those portions that should be isolated into distinct threads. But if your application is actually a collection of individual functions that have little in common, you are probably better off implementing this application in separate processes for each function, and allowing the operating system to manage them for you.
- **Make sure the algorithm behind the application is multi-threaded.** It doesn't do a lot of good to create a thread, and then immediately wait for it to complete. For example, if your application needs to collect all the required transactions from the database before it can analyze them, you should probably not create the transaction collection function as a thread. On the other hand, if you can start to analyze the transactions as they are collected, it might be appropriate to implement the collection function as a separate thread from the analysis function.

GARBAGE COLLECTION

At any construction site, there are not only builders who build the structures, but also garbage collectors. These people (or systems) move around the site and remove any unused materials and equipment. They are important contributors to the efficient and effective operation of the site.

Java's runtime environment works pretty much the same way. Constructors create new objects, and a built-in garbage collection system removes these objects when they are no longer needed. Java determines whether an object is needed using a complex (and ever-improving algorithm), but the most important attribute of an object (at least from the garbage collector's perspective) is whether or not there are any current references to this object. If an object exists in a Java runtime environment, and it is not referenced by any other object, then it will likely be garbage collected, that is, removed from the memory of the currently executing program.

Java's runtime system includes a garbage collector thread. This low-priority system thread runs periodically, and scans the modifiable portion of memory, in order to detect any objects that are not currently referenced. These are marked for deletion (actually they are identified as not referenced by the scanning process). These objects are subsequently deleted by the garbage collection process, and the memory associated with them is made available for other objects.

When an object is deleted, it may be appropriate for that object to first clean up certain resources before it is deleted. For example, an object that contains a database connection should probably close that connection as the last thing it does before it is deleted.

An object that needs to clean up resources as it is deleted can declare a finalize() method (in reality it needs to override the finalize() method in the base java.lang.Object class). The garbage collector will call this method before it deletes the object.

By default, there is no guarantee that the finalize method will be called at all! The Java runtime could exit without first destroying this object. The only guarantee is that if the object is about to be garbage collected, then this method will be called first. There is no guarantee that this object will be garbage collected before the Java runtime exits. In our database connection example, the runtime process may terminate before the object's finalize() method is called and the database connection is properly closed. The database engine will likely detect this event as an application failure and will roll back any incomplete transactions.

Java defines a static method (runFinalizersOnExit() in the System class) that you can use to control this behavior. If you perform this method, with true as the parameter, the Java runtime will call the finalize() method for any objects or classes that have defined them. Calling this method with false as the parameter will return the runtime to its default behavior.

You can also force the garbage collector to run explicitly by calling the System.gc() method. And as a last issue to be aware of, finalize() methods do not automatically call finalize() methods in a class's super class. This is unlike the behavior of constructors, where the super class's constructor is automatically called. Nested finalize() calls must be explicitly coded as shown here:

```
protected void finalize() throws Throwable {
  super.finalize();
}
```

PART III

More Java

CHAPTER

11

Managing Your Java Software

Our discussion on the Java language would be incomplete without a chapter on how to compile, debug, and generally manage your software. You didn't think that object-oriented design meant that you do not have to write and manage lots of code, did you?

Some of the details involved in the actual development process are, by necessity, tied to the development environment that you decide to use. But the major details are defined by Java in a manor that should be fairly consistent, regardless of the integrated development environment (IDE) or the platform you develop on.

CLASSES AND FILENAMES

Java source filenames and public Java class names must all have the same name. The compiler automatically creates a class file with the same name as the source file. Consider our first example class HelloWorld:

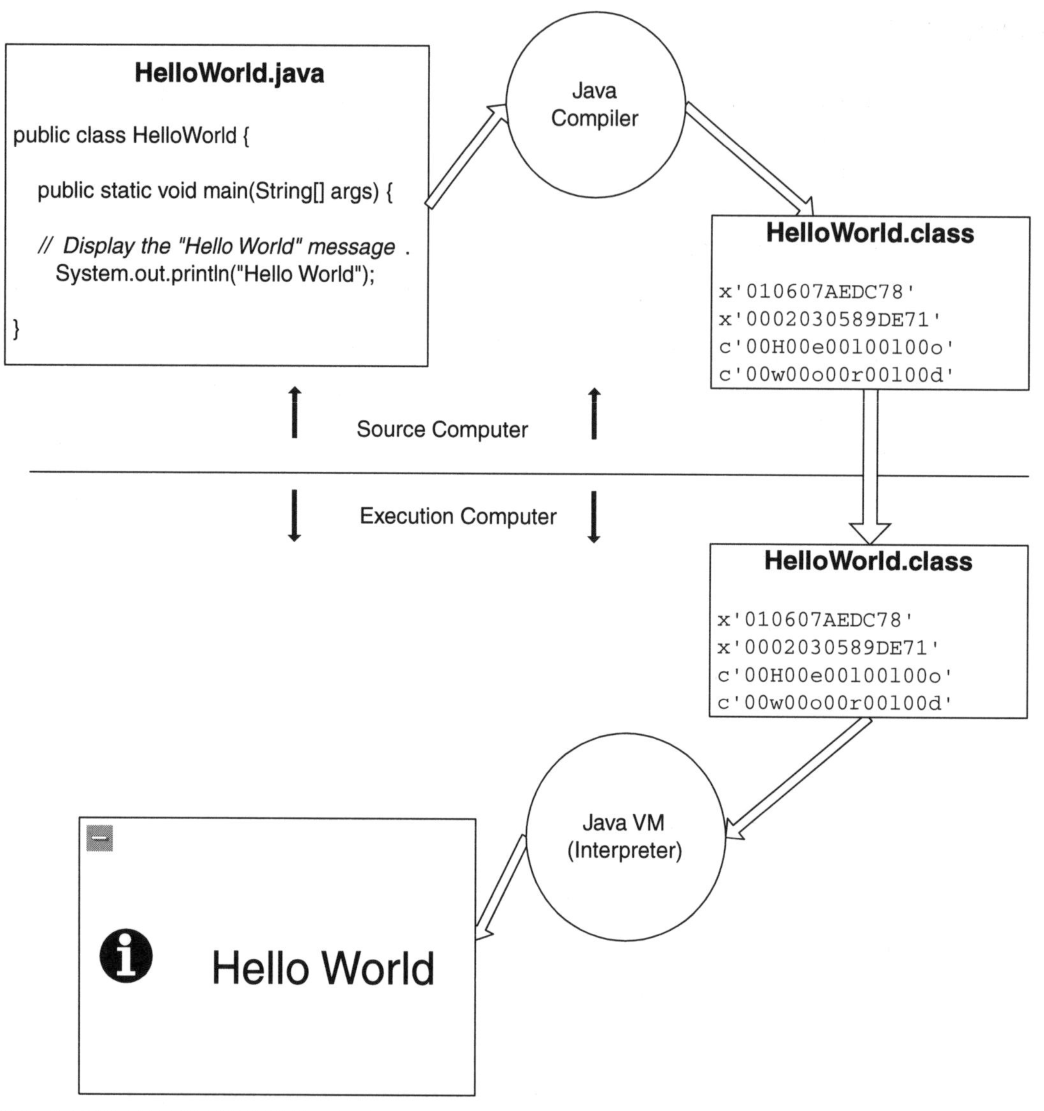

FIGURE 11.1 The Java compiler and execution files.

The name of this class (HelloWorld), its source filename (HelloWorld.java), and its output file (HelloWorld.class) all have the same name. Because of this, the runtime system can easily find the class file for HelloWorld when it is first needed by looking for a file named HelloWorld.class.

CLASSPATH

But where does the runtime system look for the HelloWorld.class? And how does the runtime system find the ErrorMsg class the first time HelloWorld creates an object of this type?

In most cases, this is controlled with the CLASSPATH setting. The CLASSPATH setting details a list of directories on the host operating system that contain classes. The Java runtime will search these directories (in the order they are listed) for class files as they are required. This is similar to the way the PATH variable is used on Windows to find executable program files. The CLASSPATH variable can be set either as an environment variable (that is, a variable defined to the operating system) or as an optional argument to the runtime instance.

For example, the standalone JDK runtime interpreter will search the c:\java4cobol directory for any required classes, given this runtime option:

```
➢ java -cp c:\java4cobol HelloWorld
```

The -cp command argument tells the runtime to search in the c:\java4cobol directory for classes.

The CLASSPATH argument can be a list of directories as well.

```
➢ java -cp c:\windows\java;c:\java4cobol HelloWorld
```

TECHNICAL NOTE: Normally, you will not need to include the standard runtime classes; Java provides a mechanism to find these automatically.

The system environment variable CLASSPATH works in much the same fashion. It can contain a list of directories in which the runtime system can search for classes. Its use is discouraged, however, since this variable applies to all Java runtimes on the system. As a result, coordinating the search requirements of multiple Java applications (especially if they are from various vendors) can be difficult.

On Windows 95/98 and NT, you can set the CLASSPATH environment variable by adding this statement to your autoexec.bat file:

```
set CLASSPATH=c:
```

On Windows NT, you can also use the Settings → System → Environment dialog to set this variable at either the system or the current user level.

Microsoft's standalone runtime (jview.exe) also supports a runtime CLASSPATH argument using this form:

```
➢ jview /cp c:\windows\java;c:\java4cobol HelloWorld
```

Microsoft's J++ development environment provides a way to assign a CLASSPATH variable to a project. We used this technique earlier, when we needed to tell the HelloWorld applet how to find our ErrorMsg class. We used the menu path Project → Settings, and in the General dialog tab, we entered the directory name where the ErrorMsg class was compiled, c:\ProgamFiles\DevStudio\MyProjects\java4cobol. This setting works great for our development project, but we still need to use traditional mechanisms for deployment.

CODEBASE

Instead of the CLASSPATH setting, applets use the CODEBASE reference. This parameter specifies the directory that contains the initial applet, and any supporting classes it requires. This is the syntax:

```
<applet
CODEBASE = codebaseURL
code=HelloWorld
width=200
height=200>
</applet>
```

As you might suspect, CODEBASEs are defined in terms of a URL on the web server. For security reasons, Java applet CODEBASE references must be on the same web server (that is, must have the same domain name) as the HTML page that started the applet.

PACKAGES

A package is a way for the Java developer to group classes that are in some way related. For example, a GeneralLedger package would likely contain an Account class and a Ledger class. These classes might implement the business logic necessary to manage account information or to record a transaction in the Ledger.

These classes can define package variables and methods that would be available only to other classes in this package. In addition, public members are automatically made available to classes in the same package. Consequently, classes in a package do not need to import other classes in the same package.

Java defines a default package for those classes that do not belong to an explicit package. We've already used the default package in our exercises. Until now, its primary benefit has been as a convenient mechanism to access the various example classes. But we could use a Java package to organize our examples.

To do this, we might define a java4cobol package. Simply include the 'package' statement as the first uncommented line in your Java source file:

```
package java4cobol;

     public class ErrorMsg  {

          public String msgText;
          public int    msgSize;
               ...
       // Some logic
               ...
     }
```

Now the ErrorMsg class is part of the java4cobol package. The Fully Qualified Name (FQN) of this class now becomes java4cobol.ErrorMsg.

Packages can be organized into subpackages. For example, we could define a subpackage of java4cobol named message, and place all of our message-related classes into this sub-package:

```
package java4cobol.message;

     public class ErrorMsg  {

          public String msgText;
          public int    msgSize;
               ...
       // Some logic
               ...
     }
```

In this case, the complete name of our ErrorMsg class would be "java4cobol. message.ErrorMsg."

INSIDE A PACKAGE

Since all the classes in a package are related, it follows that they can take advantage of each other. For one, the default access control definition for classes, methods, and variables is package. This means that any of these items that do not have an explicit access control qualifier is visible to all classes in the package.

Another advantage is simpler naming of class names in your code. If a class is part of a package, then other classes in the package can refer to it using only its short name, instead of its fully qualified name. For example, any class in the java4cobol.message package can refer to ErrorMsg as simply ErrorMsg instead of the more precise java4cobol.message.ErrorMsg.

A class from one package can still refer to classes in another package by using the fully qualified name. To continue our examples, an Account class in the general.ledger package could refer to the ErrorMsg class by its package.classname: java4cobol.message.ErrorMsg.

```
package general.ledger;

    public class Accounts  {

        public String accountID;
        public BigDecimal    accountBalance;
            ...
```

// Create a new ErrorMsg object. Use the complete package name and class

// name.

```
         java4cobol.message.ErrorMsg accountNotFound =
                  new java4cobol.message.ErrorMsg ();
         ...
    }
```

However, this is more typing than your average programmer is willing to endure. So, Java has defined a way for you to announce which classes your class will use. This is the *import* statement, which must follow any *package* statements in your program. It tells the compiler that your class might refer to the class identified in the import statement. The full class name is described only once in the import statement; afterwards, the compiler knows to use the full name whenever it sees the short name.

```
package general.ledger;
import java4cobol.message.ErrorMsg;

     public class Accounts  {

          public String accountID;
          public BigDecimal    accountBalance;
               ...
```

// Create a new ErrorMsg object. No need to use the full class name or FQN.

```
          ErrorMsg accountNotFound = new ErrorMsg ();
               ...
     }
```

This type of import statement is officially named a single-type-import declaration statement.

For brevity's sake, a class can identify all of the classes in a package by using the * wildcard instead of listing each class name. This statement will instruct the compiler to import all the classes in java4cobol.message, as they are needed, including ErrorMsg:

```
package general.ledger;
import java4cobol.message.*;
```

This type of import statement is officially named a type-import-on-demand declaration statement.

The import statement looks similar to the Cobol COPY statement. There are similarities, but it is really quite different. No code is actually imported, just the public class definitions. Significantly, the import statement tells the compiler to import the class file (the compiler output) and not the java file (the source file). It is more of an aid to the compiler than it is a technique to copy code from another class.

Now that our Accounts class contains this import statement, it can refer to any class in the java4cobol.message package using only the class name. We do not need to use the full package.classname syntax.

NAME COLLISIONS

When using the wildcard import statement, it is possible for a class to have the same name in two separate packages, or for your program to create a name that collides with a name in an imported package. In this case, the package name can be used to uniquely identify a class in a package:

```
package general.ledger;
import java4cobol.messages.*;

     public class Accounts  {
```

// Create a String object with the same name as the class ErrorMsg.

```
          String ErrorMsg;

          public String accountID;
          public BigDecimal    accountBalance;
                ...
```

// Create a new ErrorMsg object. Specify the full package name.

```
          java4cobol.messages.ErrorMsg accountNotFound =
                new java4cobol.messages.ErrorMsg ();
                ...
```

// Copy the msgText from the ErrorMsg class to the local ErrorMsg String
// variable.

```
          ErrorMsg = java4cobol.messages.ErrorMsg.getErrorMsg();
     }
```

PACKAGES AND FILENAMES

Java packages and the directories on your computer's file system are closely related. As a rule, any package and subpackage name must have a corresponding directory name on the host operating system. This applies to both the development environment and the runtime (deployment) environment.

The name of a package maps to its filename location. In our example, we would expect to find a directory named ..\java4cobol\messages and ..\general\ledger (on Unix systems, the slashes go the other way: ../java4cobol/messages and ../general/ledger). Notice that the periods (.) in the package names (java4cobol.message) are replaced with the correct directory separator character (java4cobol\message or java4cobol/message).

The package name does not normally start at the root directory of the host file system. Instead, Java uses the CLASSPATH variable to point to a list of initial directory names, which are then searched for specific package directory names as well as class names.

In our example, if we set CLASSPATH to c:\windows\java; c:, the compiler will look in both the c:\windows\java directory and the root directory of the c: drive for a directory named java4cobol\messages. In this directory, it will look for a file named ErrorMsg.class.

It is likely that you will use packages from other vendors, or perhaps you will create packages that some other development or deployment environment will use. Since it is not realistic to coordinate class names or package names in advance, a convention is often used to group packages based on the origin of the package. Many package names are prefixed with the Internet address (domain name) of the provider, but in reverse order. Sometimes the .com portion of the domain name is left out.

For example, if an organization's domain name is mycompany.com, then the java4cobol.message packages delivered by this company will likely be in a directory named com.mycompany.java4cobol.message, or mycompany.java4 cobol.message.

Your source files should use the same conventions, but with a different initial directory so that source files and class files are kept separate. In this way, you can ship your class files and not your source files. As applied to our example, the class files would be in classes \mycompany\java4cobol\messages, and the source files (with the .java extension) in source\mycompany\java4cobol\messages.

COMPRESSED PACKAGES

Finally, the Java compiler and the Java runtime system can read compressed (or zipped) files that might contain many classes. Think of these compressed files as the contents of a directory (including perhaps several subdirectories) packaged into a single file. Microsoft's standard for packaging compressed classes is their cab technology; other vendors use the jar file technology for this purpose. This discussion will focus on the jar file convention although many of the benefits and techniques would apply equally to cab files.

Jar files provide several benefits, including these:

- **Related classes can be organized and managed in a single archive.** This simplifies the administration of the classes.
- **A single request (for the jar file) can copy many classes from one system to another.** This is especially important in an Internet browser, where a single HTTP request for the jar file will replace several individual HTTP requests (one for each class in the package). The browser issues HTTP requests to copy files from the web server to the browser. Combining several requests into a single request is a significant performance benefit.
- **The classes in the jar file are compressed (using the zip compression format).** This can improve download performance and reduces disk space requirements.
- **Individual classes can be digitally signed by their author and checked at runtime for authenticity.** Only the single file needs to be checked, instead of each component in the file.

The jar utility program comes with the JDK. It is the tool used to create and manage jar files. Like the rest of the JDK, it must be run from a DOS command window.

The simplest format for using the jar program is:

This command will copy all the classes in the current directory to the jar file named ajarfile. If any sub-directories exist in the current directory, then that directory is processed recursively (that is, any class files in a subdirectory will be included in the jar file, along with the subdirectory name). In addition, a manifest is created and included in the jar file. It describes the contents of the jar file.

This command will update an existing jar file with all the class files in the current directory:

```
➢ jar uf      ajarfile  *.class
```

This command will list the contents of the jar file ajarfile:

```
➢  jar tf      ajarfile
```

or with more details:

```
➢  jar tvf     ajarfile
```

After you've created a jar file, you can use it by treating it like a subdirectory in your CLASSPATH directory. The CLASSPATH variable lists directories where any of these three class container types may exit:

- The directory location of actual class files
- The initial directory for a package (that is, further sub-directories that may contain class files)
- The directory location where a jar file exists (which contain class files, perhaps in subdirectories inside the jar file)

For example, the classes in ajarfile can be included in the CLASSPATH option when running a Java program as follows:

```
➢  java -cp c:\java4cobolm,c:\java4cobol\ajarfile HelloWorld
```

In the case of an applet, a jar file is identified with the *archive*= parameter of the applet tag as follows:

```
<applet
COBASE = codebaseURL
code=HelloWorld
archive="ajarfile"
width=200
height=200>

</applet>
```

As is the case with regular class files, an applet's jar filename is relative to the CODEBASE directory.

CHAPTER

12

Industry Initiatives

Java enjoys the support of a extensive variety of vendors. Many organizations recognize the benefits to be gained from the widespread adoption of Java and related technologies. Companies that produce Java-related products are anxious to participate in the successful adoption of Java as part of a new business application system infrastructure.

Several Java-related initiatives warrant special attention and will be reviewed here. As with all things related to Java, events move very quickly. This review will inevitably at some point seem dated. It is important to keep current and to be aware of where this dynamic technology is heading.

TECHNICAL NOTE: There is a glossary in Appendix C to help with any of the terms that may not be familiar to you.

IDE'S

An integrated development environment (IDE) combines the common functions that developers perform (editing, compiling, debugging, reviewing existing classes and documentation, and so forth.) in an integrated graphical development tool. Because of the phenomenal popularity of the language, several prominent software companies have moved quickly to create IDEs for Java.

There seems to be a very competitive rush to release the latest version, packed with new features, the best design metaphors, and/or support for the most recent language standard.

Here are some criteria to use as you evaluate various IDEs:

- **The platform covered by the IDE (web only, desktop, midrange, mainframe, and so on).** Most IDEs run on Windows NT and Windows 95/98 although some run on other platforms as well. Most will support deployment of your application to other platforms although you may have to tweak the application slightly once it gets there.
- **Not all IDEs can carry the load.** Some IDEs are very focused on the individual developer, whereas others do a better job of supporting a team-based project model.
- **Speed.** Pay attention to the time it takes to compile a project. Rapid compile times help developers concentrate on the problem they are solving. Most IDEs come with a Java runtime, and some require that their runtime be deployed. In this case, test the performance of their runtime against other implementations. Does it perform well enough for your needs?
- **Most modern IDEs come with just in time (JIT) compilers.** These compile some of your Java byte codes at runtime into native code in an effort to improve execution time. Make sure you understand how the JIT works, and whether it will help the performance of your particular project. Other IDEs compile Java applications into native code at compile time. Though this can improve performance dramatically, it can harm portability and ease of deployment.
- **How steep is the learning curve?** This is often overlooked point in your evaluation! If it takes your developers weeks to become proficient in the environment, you may never recover that time.
- **Support for external interfaces.** Graphical user interfaces, database interfaces, access to native operating systems and component based remote services are all important requirements for any large-scale development effort. There are Java-based solutions for all these requirements (AWT/Swing/WFC, JDBC, JNI/JDirect, RMI/EJB/DCOM). How well does an IDE support your most important requirements in these areas?

- **Adherence to standards.** How quickly does your IDE address new standards as they emerge? How serious is the IDE vendor about Java standards? If you want to increase the possibility of deploying your project to platforms not covered by the IDE vendor, or perhaps switching IDE vendors, then adherence to standards should be very important to you.
- **Published reports.** Compare published reviews of your proposed environment in the latest reports. *PCWeek*, *JavaWorld*, and other magazines regularly publish reviews of these products. They compare features, price, performance, and other attributes of the vendor's latest offerings. They will give you a good idea which vendor currently leads the pack at the time you need to make your choice.
- **Published books.** Nothing will bring down that learning curve like a good book. One excellent example if you want to learn about Inprise's Jbuilder is *Teach Yourself Jbuilder 2 in 21 Days*, by Michelle M. Manning and Susan Charlesworth.

It is likely that you will end up using only one IDE. The choice of which package to use might be based on a corporate standard. Or you might have an opportunity to choose a package based on the specifics of the project you are working on. If you are lucky, and have lots of time, you will be able to prototype your application in several IDEs, and choose the one best suited for your requirements. In any event, here is a quick description of the various choices.

IBM: VISUAL AGE FOR JAVA

The latest version of this product has received some very favorable reviews. It is positioned as an enterprise class product that supports both development and deployment on a variety of platforms, with deployment support for more platforms than any other tool. Visual Age has some innovative features. For example, there is no compile menu choice; modified code is automatically compiled when you run the program.

Visual Age for Java supports an intelligent team developer model, and it interfaces with a variety of source control systems. It allows remote debugging, even on platforms like the AS/400 and the mainframe. As you might suspect, IBM's product does the best job of wrapping existing legacy application functions as Java components.

INPRISE CORPORATION: JBUILDER

The latest version of Jbuilder is addressed to both the casual and the enterprise developer. It is said to improve the previous version by cleaning up and polishing both the end-user interfaces created by the tool and the developer interface. It supports the Java 2 platform, but also provides support for previous versions. Jbuilder is very serious about the CORBA remote object management standard and pure Java applications.

It includes more than 300 prepackaged components (including sources) and provides aids to easily access components, build your own components, or connect to a database. It also has a remote debugging feature although there are some reported kinks with this tool.

MICROSOFT: VISUAL J++

Microsoft's offering is part of its Visual Studio developers' suite. Therefore, it shares many of the same features and benefits of Microsoft's world-class development toolset. These include a rich graphical integrated environment, lots of online help (through the MSDN library), seamless debugging (the distinction between editing and debugging is seriously blurred in this environment), and other benefits. Naturally, it is integrated with the Visual Source-Safe Source control system as well.

The difficulties with this product are not technical. Microsoft's future support for the Java language is a very suspect at the moment. It is frequently difficult to build a Java application in this toolset and be confident that it will work in another environment. Support for certain standard Java functions is not available in this tool.

SUN MICROSYSTEMS: JAVA WORKSHOP

Sun's entry in the IDE marketplace has had a checkered history. The early versions were slow and buggy, and Sun's support for the Solaris platform as the primary development environment for this tool has damaged its viability on the Windows platform, where most developers live.

The current version (3.0) is now available in a community edition, a free downloadable version of the IDE toolkit.

SYBASE INC: POWERJ

Sybase's Powersoft division has leveraged some of the benefits in their popular Powersoft graphical development tool in their Java development offering. It sports a DataWindow component that is based on Powerbuilder's popular DataWindow, and other robust controls that are designed to make application construction easier. For example, the JFC swing components in PowerJ are data aware, meaning that they can easily be connected to a database or similar source.

This tool also leverages Sybase's Jaguar component repository, and EAServer Web server products. It also allows you to create an HTML-based user interface and connect these UIs directly into your Java application.

SYMANTEC CORP: VISUAL CAFÉ

Symantec's product has long been a favorite of developers who have been serious about developing pure Java solutions. The latest version incorporates significant improvements in the area of interfaces. These include excellent support for AWT and JFC/Swing classes, database interfaces, JavaBean creation, and a code helper tool that allows you to quickly find out about the objects you are using.

The current product comes in three versions: Standard Edition, Professional Edition, and Database Edition. Each one adds features and capabilities to the other. They all contain an integrated graphical development environment and access to standard components. The more advanced versions include additional features such as server debugging, incremental debugging, integration with source control tools, excellent JDBC support, and support for Swing components.

AWT, JFC/SWING, AND AFC/WFC

The basic graphical user interface functionality for Java is contained in the Abstract Window Toolkit (AWT), released with the earliest versions of Java. AWT is a standard interface that Java applications (or applets) can use to create and interact with graphical UIs. The AWT interfaces talk directly to the underlying graphical operating system interfaces. Since AWT is ported to every Java environment, any Java application that uses AWT can display graphical UIs in any Java environment, although the look and feel of the application may vary.

So far it sounds good, but because of a number of issues, AWT has been regarded by many as the weakest part of the original Java environment. The primary problem is that AWT is too low level for most application developers, and it does not do a good job of hiding all the differences between graphical hosting systems. At the same time, important capabilities required by graphical applications are not available in AWT.

Sun has improved on AWT with the newer Java Foundation Classes (JFC), released as a patch to JDK 1.1. These APIs are grouped in a package named after the code name for the internal development project at Sun (Swing). The Swing package is meant to replace the AWT.

Applications that use Swing have access to more control over the user interface. For example, an application can now manage borders around graphical components, and components do not all need to be rectangular. Swing applications can interact better with native applications. Furthermore, Swing is implemented without native code, and so can be downloaded on demand to any client that has an appropriate VM (at least JDK 1.1 with the Java Plug-in 1.1.1).

With JFC, an application can display either a native look and feel, or a Java look and feel. Currently, the only native look and feel options available are Windows and Motif (Sun workstation).

On the downside, the Swing components are fairly large. A Swing application must download the Swing components to the client if they are not already loaded. Further, since Swing does not work with every VM, or even with every browser, client systems must be managed to some extent.

Microsoft has promoted its own improved graphical presentation toolkit named Application Foundation Classes (AFC) for Java. This collection of supporting classes is based on AWT and provides many ease-of-use features. Microsoft originally intended to support the AFC extensions on other platforms, but that process is now uncertain.

Microsoft also provides another mechanism to define graphical user interfaces called the Windows Foundation Classes (WFC). This is a mechanism that Java application developers can easily use to build applications that take advantage of the native Windows UI controls, or that use dynamic HTML (DHTML) to display a user interface in a browser. Although WFC is not directly available to Java applications, Java developers can use Microsoft's J/Direct technology to access this class library.

JDBC

Most business applications today need to store information in relational databases. Business applications written in Java are no exception. The standard Java database access technology is JDBC. JDBC is essentially a variation on ODBC with some Java bindings. It is designed as a Java API to SQL data.

JDBC is just a specification; it is up to the various database vendors or third parties to create JDBC drivers for a particular database. In some cases, a JDBC to ODBC bridge can be used, but likely not for production purposes.

JDBC provides a fairly complete set of SQL-friendly data access mechanisms, such as scrollable result sets, absolute and relative positioning (in the result set), access to stored procedures, and data type conversions, etc. Most SQL-92 (Entry Level 2) statements are supported in JDBC.

The typical JDBC sequence required to access data is quite involved. The first step is to create a connection to the database. To begin with, you will likely have to load the JDBC driver you intend to use. Then you can create a Connection object provided as a class by the driver and use it to connect to the database. The exact details of this step vary based on the driver and are documented with each driver, so we will not detail it here. But after connecting to the database, you will have created a Connection object, which is used to access the database. In our example, the Connection object is named dbConnection.

Java defines a Statement Interface that you can use to process a variety of SQL statements. You must first create an object of that type, based on your connection object.

```
Statement sqlStmt = dbConnection.createStatement();
```

The next step is to execute an SQL statement and place the results in a ResultSet. A ResultSet object is one that will contain the rows that are returned for your SQL statement. For example, this statement will select posting account IDs and currency IDs from the posting_accounts table, and place the results in the ResultSet object named accounts:

```
ResultSet accounts = sqlStmt.executeQuery(
     "SELECT POSTING_ACCOUNT_ID, CURRENCY_ID FROM POSTING_ACCOUNTS
     WHERE COMPANY_ID = 'CC1'");
```

The ResultSet class contains a next() method. This method positions the *cursor* (the current position in the result set) to the next available row. When the result set is exhausted, next() will return a boolean *false*. This method is similar to the READ NEXT statement in Cobol.

```
while (accounts.next()) {
        . . .
```

However, the next() method does not actually return any data. To get data into your own variables, you will need to call the proper get() method. JDBC is a strongly typed interface, meaning that each get() method is specific to the data type referenced. There is a separate get() method for Strings, and another for Floats.

The statements to retrieve information from the result set might look as follows: (of course, each iteration of the "next" loop as written will overwrite the results of the previous iteration, but we want to keep the example simple.)

```
Integer postingAccountID;
String currencyID;

while (accounts.next()) {
          postingAccountID = acounts.getInteger
                ("POSTING_ACCOUNT_ID");
          currencyID = acounts.getString("CURRENCY_ID");
}
```

JDBC defines other semantics to perform additional SQL functions such as updates, deletes, selections involving many tables (joins), and so forth. The latest version of ODBC also outlines mechanisms that can modify table definitions as well as modify data in the table.

ENTERPRISE JAVA BEANS

Java Beans are Java components, defined in a way that makes them easy to use. In most functional respects, the Java Beans specification is similar to the ActiveX specification, only specific to Java.

Enterprise Java Beans (EJs) bring the benefits of Java-built components to distributed, transaction oriented systems. An EJB can be instantiated (that is, created) on a remote system, and then respond to message requests from an application on a local system. Furthermore, EJBs can contain transaction definitions. EJBs automatically participate in a transactional model as defined by your application. (In a transactional model, either all the work in a transaction will be guaranteed to be intact, or committed to a database, or none of it will be.)

Best of all, EJBs don't have to manage the complex system plumbing that is normally associated with remote component management and transaction integrity control. All these system-level issues (component invocation, lifecycle management, security, transaction semantics, and so on.) are handled by the EJB infrastructure. A major design objective of the EJB spec is to allow developers to focus on writing code that solves the business problem(s) at hand rather than the technical issues surrounding the management of remote distributed component services.

The EJB specification is primarily an effort to standardize remote component management techniques available to Java components. It also attempts to simplify and improve existing techniques such as CORBA and DCOM. EJB is very Java centric; it fits naturally into the Java language. It is only modestly more difficult to build and use EJB components than it is to build and use regular JavaBeans. EJB's are most often built with an EJB creation tool.

EJBs can define the following control options at the class or the method level. By default, the class settings are applied to each method, but an individual method can define its own setting:

- **Security.** What rights are required by the client in order to create this class or perform its methods? EJBs can use the new security model built into Java 2 to define and control access rights.

- **Transaction.** What transaction level is supported or required by this Bean? The possibilities are
  TX_BEAN_MANAGED,
  TX_SUPPORTS,
  TX_NOT_SUPPORTED,
  TX_REQUIRED,
  TX_REQUIRES_NEW, and
  TX_MANDATORY.
  These settings indicate the valid transaction contexts for the Bean. (It may be necessary for the client to first establish a new transaction context in order to meet the transaction requirements of the Bean.)
- **Isolation level.** What JDBC isolation level does the client require when a read is performed? The possibilities are
  TRANSACTION_READ_UNCOMMITTED,
  TRANSACTION_READ_COMMITTED,
  TRANSACTION_REPEATABLE_READ, and
  TRANSACTION_SERIALIZABLE.

EJBs are stored in jar files on an EJB server. When a client requires an EJB, it must first create an EJB container. The container is the construct that manages the transaction context and client/server connection on behalf of the client. The client does not need to be directly involved in details of the transaction semantics, such as begin transaction, commit, or rollback. Instead, the container creates a simplified client view of the EJB for the client, and the client can access the EJB as if it were a simple remote object. If the client needs to, however, it can adjust the default transaction behavior of the Bean.

JAVA APPLICATION SERVERS

The technical infrastructure necessary to properly set up and administer remote Java components can be quite complex. Many operational services are required, such as security services, component name resolution services, load balancing, fail-over services, and others. Significant development effort would be required to build even a partial architecture that addresses these issues.

A number of vendors have developed products that solve some of these issues. Java application server products from BEA, Forte, Sun, Inprise, and others are designed to provide out-of-the-box solutions for these and other problems.

Database vendors have also embraced the concept of Java-on-the-server. All the major database vendors (except Microsoft) currently provide some ability to run Java servlets as extensions to their core database products. For example, Java is becoming the standard language used to write stored procedures in the database. In some cases (particularly, Oracle's 8i, and Sybase's Jaguar), the database support for Java servlets is so robust that the database behaves very much like a Java application server.

JAVA CLONES

Vendors that use Java technology or use the Java label must first acquire a license to these rights from Sun. Microsoft, HP, and other vendors have (for different reasons) reportedly decided to build products that mimic certain Java technology that is not based on a license from Sun.

Companies are allowed to reverse-engineer and reproduce a nonpatented product, provided they can prove that no proprietary or licensed information was used while building the product. Companies meet this standard by building teams that are rigorously isolated from any proprietary information acquired from the company that owns the license. In the cases of HP and Microsoft, they both have licenses to Java technology. Therefore, the teams that may be building unlicensed Java mimic products must be kept away from any information (documentation, source code, and so on.) that is restricted by their license agreements with Sun. They have to operate in sort of a cleanroom.

Microsoft and HP are interested in building their own Java products in order to avoid the restrictions that are part of the license agreements. Microsoft wants to build a Java product that works well on its platforms, but only on its platforms. HP wants to be able to adjust Java technology to meet its own needs (perhaps as a lightweight operating system that will be embedded into products such as household appliances). For a variety of reasons, Java clone vendors do not want either to pay for or to coordinate these initiatives with Sun.

IBM'S SAN FRANCISCO PROJECT

IBM is very committed to endorsing the use of Java as an general-purpose business language. In addition to support for all the leading Java initiatives, IBM has built an entire Java frameworks that can be used to build business applications.

San Francisco is a business systems development toolkit that contains many prebuilt and pretested components. You can use San Francisco components and the San Francisco architecture as the basis for custom-built business systems that meet your specific requirements. San Francisco is the largest, most ambitious server-based Java development project to date. Complete information about IBM's San Francisco project is included on the CD.

UNIFIED MODELING LANGUAGE

The popularity of object-oriented software development has been reflected in the increasing popularity of OO-based software modeling tools and techniques. Software modeling techniques employ rigorous analysis and documentation methodologies to capture a representation of how a system is built and how the system performs its processes. Software modeling is important as a means to communicate system design details to members of a development team and to document system implementation details to external groups.

The unified modeling language (UML) is the result of the merging in the mid-1990s of various software modeling practices. The three primary modeling evangelists, industry leaders Grady Booch, Ivar Jacobson, and Jim Rumbaugh, agreed to work together to create a new modeling language that combines the best features from their previous work. In addition to combining the best ideas from previous modeling techniques, UML is intended to be simpler and more approachable than some of these earlier efforts.

The UML is a rich language that can represent all sorts of system processes, from simple data entry functions to complex real-time distributed systems. Whole systems, or just portions of a system can be defined in the model. UML diagrams can describe how the system is designed, how it works, how people use a system, or even how it is deployed.

The UML can be broken down into these constituent parts:

Use cases. The UML has standardized on use cases as a means to depict how actors (often end users, but possibly other systems) interact with the system that is being modeled. A use case reflects the capabilities of a system as seen by external users of the system.

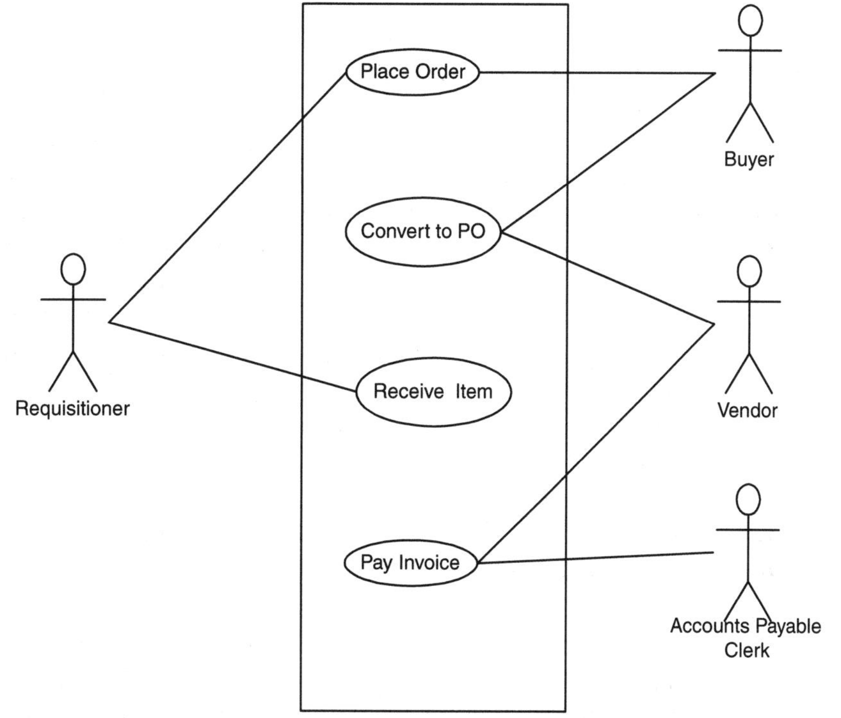

FIGURE 12.1 An example of a use case diagram.

Class diagrams. The basic UML structure that represents classes in an OO system is the class diagram. This diagram type defines the classes that make up the system. Class diagrams show the internal structure of the classes and the relationship between classes. Often, class diagrams reflect implementation classes and are mapped directly into Java or C++ class source modules.

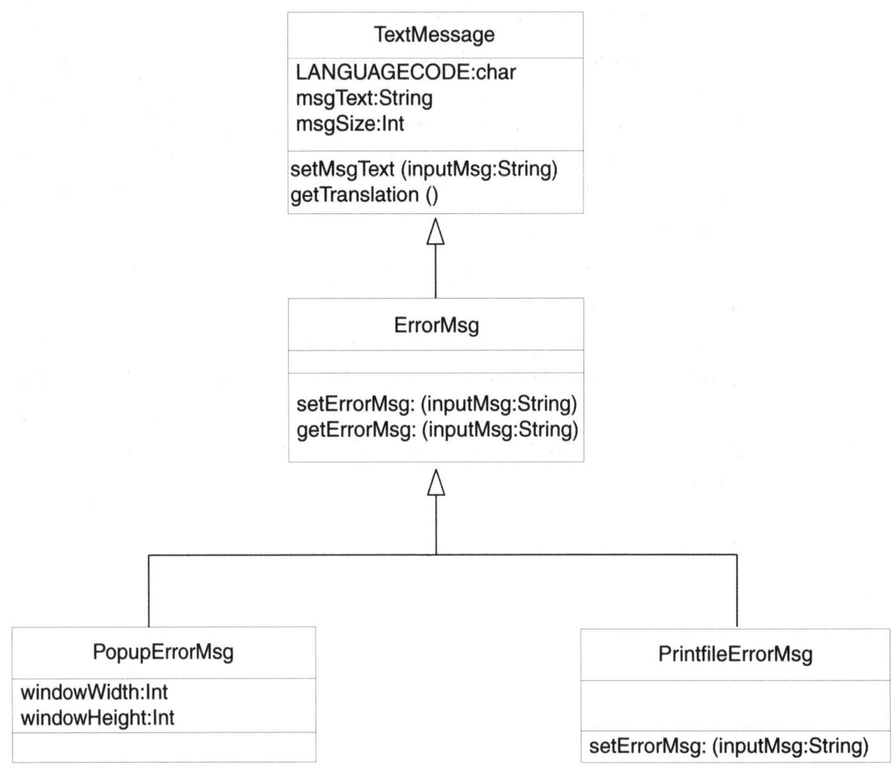

FIGURE 12.2 An example of a class diagram. This diagram reflects the hierarchy of the ErrorMsg class from our samples.

Other diagram types defined by UML include the Statechart, Activity, Sequence, Collaborations, Component, and Deployment diagram types. Another design feature called stereotypes allow for user-defined (that is, customized) diagram features. And finally, the object constraint language (OCL) is a formalized language that designers can use to write any expressions contained within the model.

COBOL/JAVA INTEGRATION TOOLS

A number of vendors have recognized the good business opportunities available in the alliance of Java and Cobol. Some vendors such as Relativity (www.relativity.com), ACM Limited (www.acm.co.uk), Metamorphic (www.metamorphic.com), and Crystal Systems (www.cry-sys.com) have tools that convert existing Cobol code directly to Java.

The JavaMaker product from Intercomp (a division of Crystal Systems) is quite powerful. It scans your Cobol code and creates Java classes that mimic the logic in your Cobol program. The output from this conversion tool is quite intelligible and can easily form the basis for a manageable Java product. The tool is very extensible and allows you to adjust the conversion process based on your unique requirements.

Another vendor, Synkronix (www.synkronix.com), takes a different approach. This company has a product (PerCobol) that attempts to leverage the benefits of Java and existing Cobol applications simultaneously. For example, user interfaces can be defined using a Cobol syntax, and then created as Java user interfaces. Cobol subroutines can be wrapped as Java Beans, and Cobol programs can call Java functions. Information about this product is included in the CD.

CHAPTER

13

Introduction to XML

XML is another example of a new computer language technology that has taken the industry by storm. The only language to match Java's buzz, and to acquire more instant, yet ardent supporters, is this recently introduced language.

Just what is this language, and what does it mean to the business application developer? After reading the latest article extolling the virtues of XML, a developer can easily be left with the impression that XML can be the answer to all of your worries, from uncommunicative business partners to the common cold. But what is the reality? What are the sorts of problems that XML can help the business application developer solve?

THE BASICS

XML is an acronym for extensible markup language. It is simply a language specification for documents that describe and contain data. XML's designers have attempted to combine the simplicity and the ubiquity of HTML (hyper text markup language) with the rich descriptive capabilities of SGML (standard generalized markup language). HTML and XML are, in fact, both SGML document types.

An XML document is a text file that conforms to the XML language specification. It contains data in a structured format and descriptive information about the data. The primary role of an XML document is to present data generated by one application (or system) to another. Consequently, XML documents are well suited as general-purpose data repositories and data transport containers.

XML VS. HTML

XML extends HTML primarily by allowing a document to describe it own tags (similar to a data type, or significantly, a record type). This capability allows a document to organize its data in a structured format. An XML document can also contain enough metadata (information about the data) so that any application can reliably parse the document and extract the data from the document.

In contrast, HTML is designed to describe documents in a format suitable for end user viewing in a graphical browser. HTML documents do not contain information about the meaning of the data, nor are they structured in a way that makes it easy for a program to analyze. Therefore, an application may have a difficult time extracting relevant data from an HTML document.

A relatively simple example makes this point. Here is a portion of an HTML page that might be generated by an Internet book retailer. It informs an Internet browser how to represent the current contents of the shopping cart page to a potential purchaser.

```
<td bgcolor="#FFFFFF" width="51%">
<a href="../81332713233407">
      <em>Debt of Honor</em></a>
<br>
Tom Clancy;
Paperback</b>
<font size=2 face="Verdana, Helvetica, Courier" color=#000000>

<NOBR>Price: <font color=#990>$6.99</font></b></NOBR><br>
</td>

<td bgcolor="#FFFFFF" width="51%">
<a href="../81332713233407">
      <em>The Hunt for Red October</em></a>
<br>
Tom Clancy;
Hardcover</b>
<font size=2 face="Verdana, Helvetica, Courier" color=#000000>

<NOBR>Price: <font color=#990>$18.99</font></b></NOBR><br>
</td>
```

An Internet browser has no trouble understanding how to format and display this information to the end user. While viewing the page in a browser, the end user has no trouble understanding what the data means (the shopping cart contains two books, one for $6.99 and the other for $18.99).

However, what if we want a program to parse this document and to extract the item number and other information, including its price, from the HTML document? In theory, we could use a trial-and-error design approach to build a parser for this particular document. Perhaps we could fine-tune this algorithm so that it can process the shopping cart HTML page and extract the price of the book:

- Look for the string NOBR>Price:.
- Skip past the font declaration (<font ..>).
- The characters before the next font declaration contain the price.
- Ignore the currency symbol in the price character string.
- Convert the price string into a numeric price variable.

However, we would have no guarantee that our parser would work if the vendor made even minor changes to the web site, or that our parser wouldn't be confused by similar pages. More important, we would have no guarantee that our parser would work with another vendor's HTML pages. Furthermore, important contextual information is hard to decipher. For example, what is the identifier (the order ID) for this shopping cart? Is it contained in the href identifier?

An XML document, on the other hand, contains information in a format that can be readily parsed by an application. An XML document would possibly express a shopping cart using this type of syntax:

```
<Order orderNumber="81332713233407">

   <LineItem>

     <Title>Debt of Honor</Title>
     <Author>Tom Clancy</Author>
     <BookType>Paperback</BookType>
     <Price>$6.99</Price>

   </LineItem>

   <LineItem>

     <Title>The Hunt for Red October</Title>
     <Author>Tom Clancy</Author>
     <BookType>Hardcover</BookType>
     <Price>$18.99</Price>

   </LineItem>

</Order>
```

Clearly, this syntax is simpler to parse with a program and will produce more predictable results. An application can process and validate information from this document with confidence.

Notice that XML uses the begin tag . . . end tag construct in a manner similar to HTML. XML data is contained inside user-defined tags. For example, <Title> is the beginning of a tag, and </Title> is the end of the tag. Every XML document must conform to these and other requirements in order to be classified as well-formed, or syntactically correct.

Tags can be nested as data elements inside other tags. Observe how the LineItem tag in our example contains each of these tags: Title, Author, BookType, and Price.

DTDS

An XML document not only contains information in a predictable format, it can also describe the organization of the information it contains. The beginning of an XML document may contain a document type definition (DTD). This section of the XML document defines the structure of the document's contents. It identifies the tags that are allowed in this document, and the relationships between the various tags in the document. An XML parser can use this information to make sure that the document is not only well formed (that is, it conforms to the generic XML syntax rules), but it is also valid (that is, conforms to the layout specified in its DTD).

For example, our XML shopping cart document could possibly contain this partial DTD:

```
<!ELEMENT Order (LineItem)+>
<!ATTLIST Order orderNumber CDATA #REQUIRED>
<!ELEMENT LineItem (Title, Author+, BookType, Price)>
<!ELEMENT Title (#PCDATA)>
<!ELEMENT Author (#PCDATA)>
<!ELEMENT BookType (#PCDATA)>
<!ELEMENT Price (#PCDATA)>
<!ENTITY HARDCOVER "Hardcover">
<!ENTITY PAPERBACK "Paperback">
```

The first statement in this DTD describes an XML element whose name is Order. According to this DTD, an Order consists of one or more LineItem elements (represented by the (LineItem)+ expression in our example). The Order must be further described using the attribute named orderNumber. An orderNumber attribute can contain any valid character sequence (CDATA). It is a required attribute, as specified by the #REQUIRED flag.

A LineItem, in turn, consists of a Title, one or more Authors (as indicated by the command Author+), a BookType, and a Price. These subelements are all user-defined data types, which can contain any character sequence (#PCDATA).

The last section of our DTD declares two variables named HARDCOVER, and PAPERBACK. These variables are assigned the String values "Hardcover" and "Paperback," respectively.

A DTD not only provides the structural information required to properly parse the document, it allows the parser to examine the document for completeness and document integrity. If a DTD specifies that certain elements are required, then these elements must be present in the document. Conversely, only properly identified elements are allowed in an XML document.

An input parser application can quickly scan XML documents to validate that they match their required structure, independent of any data or content validation. An XML document can be independently checked to make sure it is both well-formed (it conforms to proper generic XML syntax) and valid (it conforms to its DTD).

An XML document can either contain its DTD internally (that is, as the initial part of the document) or simply refer to it as an external file. Either a URL or a local file name can be referenced as the DTD repository. External file references work much the same way that COPY statements work in Cobol.

DTD COMPONENTS

A DTD describes these optional XML document components in any combination: elements, attributes, and entities.

ELEMENTS

An element is the basic user-defined tag. An XML document is essentially a collection of elements. An element can contain either text, other elements, or even a combination of the two. The syntax for an element in an XML document is <Name> content </Name>. An element is roughly analogous to a data item in a Cobol program.

These are four of the elements from our XML sample:

```
<Title>Debt of Honor</Title>
<Author>Tom Clancy</Author>
<BookType>&PAPERBACK</BookType>
<Price>$6.99</Price>
```

Our sample also contained a LineItem element, which was comprised solely of other elements:

```
<LineItem>

     <Title>Debt of Honor</Title>
     <Author>Tom Clancy</Author>
     <BookType>&PAPERBACK</BookType>
     <Price>$6.99</Price>

</LineItem>
```

The LineItem element consists of other elements. A group item in a Cobol program is similar, since it consists of other data items.

A document's DTD declares all the elements a document can contain, as well as other characteristics of the element (that is, its attributes). A DTD is roughly equivalent to the WORKING STORAGE area in a Cobol program, except that a DTD can contain much more descriptive information about its elements.

Once an element is defined, the main section of the document can contain one or more instances of this element

In our sample, an element named "Title" is defined in the DTD with the construct:

```
<!ELEMENT Title (#PCDATA)>
```

The Title element can now exist in the body of the sample document as follows:

```
<Title>Debt of Honor</Title>
```

ATTRIBUTES

An element can also be described in more detail with information that varies with each instance of the element in the document. For example, suppose we would like our Order element to contain an attribute named orderNumber. In any particular Order element, this attribute would hold the unique ID that identified this Order.

Attributes are defined and used in much the same manner as elements. The DTD declares which attributes exist for an element. Particular elements in the document body can then be qualified with these attributes

In our sample, an element named "Order" is declared in the DTD. It consists of one or more LineItems. An attribute for Order named "orderNumber" is defined as well. It can contain any valid string and is required for each instance of Order, as specified in this partial DTD:

```
<!ELEMENT Order (LineItem)+>
<!ATTLIST Order orderNumber CDATA #REQUIRED>
```

An Order element can now exist in the body of the sample document as follows:

```
<Order orderNumber="81332713233407">

   <LineItem>

      . . .

   </LineItem>
</Order>
```

Notice that attributes are entered inside the initial element tag

```
(<Order . . >).
```

ENTITIES

An XML document can define its own constants or entities. These are named storage units (portions of valid XML content), defined and used by a document. An entity can contain character strings, markup commands, or even references to external documents. Here are two entities as declared in our sample DTD:

```
<!ENTITY HARDCOVER "Hardcover">
<!ENTITY PAPERBACK "Paperback">
```

After they are declared, entities can be used in any appropriate place in the XML document. In our sample document, we can use the entity (by name, with an ampersand as a prefix, and a semicolon as a suffix) in place of the text represented by the entity. Consequently, both of these constructs are valid:

```
<BookType>&PAPERBACK;</BookType>
<BookType>"Paperback"</BookType>
```

In many ways, entities are similar to Level 88 items in a Cobol program. Entities are often used for XML content that is frequently reproduced in the document, or that varies with each instance of the document type.

DOCUMENT TYPE DECLARATION

An XML document begins by identifying itself as an XML document. The following represents a typical introduction to an XML document:

```
<?xml version="1.0" standalone="yes" encoding="UTF-8"?>
<!DOCTYPE Order [
     . . . <! – DTD specifications –>
]
```

The first expression declares the XML version to which the document conforms. Our document is a version 1.0 document.

Our document is also a standalone XML document, without references to other documents. Since it is a standalone document, it must contain its DTD, if one exists. It is possible for a simple standalone XML document to have no DTD.

Finally, the first line states that the document can contain only 8-bit ASCII characters. An XML document can contain 16-bit characters, similar to Unicode in Java. If this document were a 16-bit document, the required syntax would be encoding= "UTF-16."

The next line in the type declaration identifies the document type as Order. An Order comprises all the elements and attributes specified. These directives will be included inside the braces ([]).

The exclamation point is a tag that represents a comment. The text between <! and the closing > will be ignored by an XML parsing program.

A COMPLETE XML DOCUMENT

The following sample XML document brings all these concepts together. It contains a document type declaration, an internal DTD specification, and then the actual data contents of the document:

```
<?xml version="1.0" standalone="yes" encoding="UTF-8"?>
<!   --      A Book order in XML format    — >
<!DOCTYPE Order [
<!ELEMENT Order (LineItem)+>
<!ATTLIST Order orderNumber CDATA #REQUIRED>
<!ELEMENT LineItem (Title, Author+, BookType, Price)>
<!ELEMENT Title (#PCDATA)>
<!ELEMENT Author (#PCDATA)>
<!ELEMENT BookType (#PCDATA)>
<!ELEMENT Price (#PCDATA)>
<!ENTITY HARDCOVER "Hardcover">
<!ENTITY PAPERBACK "Paperback">
]>


<Order orderNumber="81332713233407">

   <LineItem>

     <Title>Debt of Honor</Title>
     <Author>Tom Clancy</Author>
     <BookType>&PAPERBACK;</BookType>
     <Price>$6.99</Price>

   </LineItem>

   <LineItem>

     <Title>The Hunt for Red October</Title>
     <Author>Tom Clancy</Author>
     <BookType>&HARDCOVER;</BookType>
     <Price>$18.99</Price>

   </LineItem>

</Order>
```

AUTHORING XML DOCUMENTS

In practice, you will not normally need to create XML documents by hand using only a text editor. One possibility is that you will use an XML authoring tool. An even more likely scenario is that you will write an application that generates valid XML documents based on data from an existing system.

As of this writing, interactive XML authoring tools are in their beginning stages. However, there are several editing tools from a variety of sources, and some are freely available. XML Software (www.xmlsoftware.com) contains an excellent list of stand alone XML editors, integrated DTD editors, and other very useful information concerning XML software.

XML AND JAVA

Any programming language can create or process an XML document. Java is no exception. XML is not a specification of a programming language, nor a programming language interface. Rather, it describes how an application can represent data for the benefit of another application. As such, XML is very programming language neutral. For example, there are no predefined XML data types other than quoted character strings.

A number of XML parsers written in Java are available. Some are free, and others are commercial products. IBM, Sun, and a group called OpenXML have been very active in publishing useful XML products and tools. You can incorporate one of these tools into your Java project or write your own parser and XML document generator.

XML AND HTML

Unlike HTML, XML does not define presentation attributes such as </font>. An XML document designer is free to define and use such tags, but they do not currently have a generally understood meaning.

Various initiatives are underway to define a standard for combining XML and HTML in the same document. Industry groups are working on a definition for an HTML DTD (that is, a standard DTD for the most commonly used HTML tags). The more modern browsers have some built-in ability to render XML documents in a suitable manner for end users, with some default formatting conventions.

Microsoft and others have proposed standards for combining HTML and XML in the same document. Two initiatives are the furthest along: cascading style sheets (CSS), a simple syntax that allows style sheets to be associated with elements, and extensible style language (XSL), an XML document type with bits of formatting commands borrowed from HTML and other sources.

WHERE TO USE XML

XML is so important to the business application developer because it finally offers a standard language and syntax suitable for intersystem data transfer. Every business system needs to interact with at least one other system in some fashion. The other system can be an external system at a business partner. Or the other system might be an internal system (perhaps a data warehouse) that needs information from another internal system (for example, the production order entry system).

Till now, the standard technique used to transfer information between two business systems has been to write a set of interface programs. System one would create an interface file with the required information. Or system one might write the information to interface tables in a database. The target system will read that information, validate it, and update the target system database. In rare cases, the source or target system will access the other system's database directly, but this approach requires simultaneous access to both systems and developers who understand both systems.

Interface systems often require serious planning and attention. Carefully predefined and documented interface format specifications are necessary so that each system's developers can understand what is required. The normal process flows in both systems need to be accounted for. Most important, the data transformation requirements are embedded in the interface system logic.

As business requirements and the systems that support these requirements change, interface system requirements may change as well. Implementing these changes will require careful coordination and integrated testing plans, even if only two systems are involved. When multiple target systems or their interfaces need to be adjusted for a single source system, modifications to the existing integration process can become unmanageable. If multiple business partners' systems are involved, one can only hope that their interface specifications are adaptable and up to date and that the original developers are still around.

XML promises to improve this process significantly. As general purpose, self describing data repositories, XML files are readily accessible by multiple systems. Intricate coordination and data mapping designs are not as crucial since the XML files describe themselves. Systems need only to create XML documents based on an agreeable DTD, or to input data from an XML file, based on their own requirements. Modifications to the source or the target system do not need to be so closely coordinated. Often, new data tags (information) in an XML document can be ignored by a processing system if that system has no need for the data. The new data will not, by itself, obscure the data required by the processing system.

EDI

EDI-based processes are prime candidates for improvements with XML. EDI is a standard definition (defined by ANSI or EDIFACT) of acceptable document structures for various types of business transactions. Document structures are defined for purchase orders, acknowledgments, invoices, and other transaction types.

Systems use EDI when they either generate a document in EDI format or receive and subsequently process an EDI document. EDI documents are intended to be transmitted from one business partner to another. In most cases, some data translation and reformatting is necessary so that EDI documents can be properly used by target systems.

Organizations called VANs (value-added networks) provide EDI related services such as secure and reliable document transmission services, business partner connections (that is, electronic access to your business partners), document management (store and forward, translation, logging, and so on). Examples of VANs are GE Information Systems (GEISCO), Sterling Commerce, and Harbinger.

To date, EDI standards have proved useful as well-defined data representation formats. However, their rigid structure (along with other issues such as high implementation and transaction costs) has restricted the acceptance of EDI standards in many situations. Typically, EDI is employed as a data transfer mechanism between business partners only when the number of documents exchanged justifies the effort and the expense, and both organizations have technically savvy IT organizations.

The XML language, combined with widely available Internet technologies, promises to radically change the way business documents are transferred between organizations. Organizations are all interconnected today over the Internet. SSL (secure socket layer), encrypted digital signatures, and other technologies provide adequate transactional security for most situations. These technologies, allied with XML's ability to combine flexible document content with well-understood document structure, enable organizations to confidently, effectively, and efficiently execute electronic business process with a wide variety of business partners.

XML and EDI do not necessarily directly compete as potential solutions. An XML file can contain data that conforms to EDI content specifications, even if it does not conform to EDI's document structure specifications. All that is required is a suitable DTD. In fact, several initiatives are underway to do just that. EDI-based interface systems can easily wrap their documents in XML for external representation to business partners. The business partners can either process the documents directly or first convert the documents into a format suitable for a legacy EDI system.

XML AND OAG

The Open Application Group (OAG) is an organization whose mission is to simplify integration processes between business systems. OAG is frequently addressing integration issues as they apply to enterprise resource planning (ERP), accounting, and human resource packaged application systems.

OAG has defined a set of XML DTDs and is promoting these document definitions as standards for business documents such as purchase orders and invoices. They have also defined intersystem document types such as journal transactions to a general ledger system. Business applications that support these document definitions can reliably integrate with other systems, even when these two systems come from distinct vendors.

For example, an accounts payable system from one vendor can generate an XML document that conforms to OAG's DTD specification for journals. An OAG-compliant general ledger from another system can accept that document as input, and post the transactions in an appropriate manner.

The following is a sample journal DTD from OAG. It has been simplified slightly from its complete representation. The complete OAG DTD specification is included in the CD.

Our sample begins with a pair of base DTDs named domains.dtd, and fields.dtd. These define the basic data type entity (STRDOM) and the field-level entity names that will be used in the OAG documents.

```
<!— String Data: Generic Data Domains —>
<!ENTITY % STRDOM "(#PCDATA)">

<!ELEMENT ACCTPERIOD   %STRDOM;>
<!ELEMENT ACCTTYPE     %STRDOM;>
<!ELEMENT ACCTYEAR     %STRDOM;>
<!ELEMENT BUSNAREA     %STRDOM;>
<!ELEMENT COSTCENTER   %STRDOM;>
<!ELEMENT CURRENCY     %STRDOM;>
<!ELEMENT DRCR         %STRDOM;>
<!ELEMENT DEPARTMENT   %STRDOM;>
<!ELEMENT GLENTITYS    %STRDOM;>
<!ELEMENT GLNOMACCT    %STRDOM;>
<!ELEMENT NUMOFDEC     %STRDOM;>
<!ELEMENT ORIGREF      %STRDOM;>
<!ELEMENT SIGN         %STRDOM;>
<!ELEMENT USERID       %STRDOM;>
<!ELEMENT USERAREA     %STRDOM;>
<!ELEMENT VALUE        %STRDOM;>
<!ELEMENT VALUECLASS   %STRDOM;>
<!ELEMENT VERB         %STRDOM;>
```

Next, our sample contains a higher-level reusable DTD named segments.dtd. Of particular interest in the segment DTD are these elements:

- **AMOUNT.** A general-purpose element that will contain an amount data item. An AMOUNT is a collection of the VALUE, NUMOFDEC, SIGN, CURRENCY, and DRCR elements. It has a required attribute named qualifier. This attribute can contain either of the types defined by the SEG_AMOUNT_QUALIFIERS entity, or the type defined by a generic entity named SEG_AMOUNT_QUALIFIERS_EXTENSION. AMOUNT also has an attribute named type. This attribute can contain either of the values in the SEG_AMOUNT_TYPES entity, or the value defined by a generic entity named SEG_AMOUNT_TYPES_EXTENSION.
- **DATETIME.** A general-purpose element that will contain an amount data item. A DATETIME is a collection of the YEAR, MONTH, DAY, HOUR, MINUTE, SECOND, SUBSECOND, and TIMEZONE elements. It has a required attribute named qualifier.

This attribute can contain either of the types defined by the SEG_DATETIME_QUALIFIERS entity or the type defined by a generic entity named SEG_DATETIME_QUALIFIERS_EXTENSION. DATETIME also has an attribute named type. This attribute can contain either of the values in the SEG_DATETIME_TYPES entity or the value defined by a generic entity named SEG_DATETIME_TYPES_EXTENSION.

```
<!— -From oagis_segments.dtd —>

<!— AMOUNT —>

<!ENTITY % SEG_AMOUNT_QUALIFIERS_EXTENSION "OTHER">
<!ENTITY % SEG_AMOUNT_QUALIFIERS
    "(ACTUAL | APPRVORD | AVAILABLE | BUDGET | COMMISSION |
      DISCNT | DOCUMENT | EXTENDED | ITEM | OPENITEM | ORDER |
       ORDLIMIT | TAX | TAXBASE | TOTLIMIT |
       %SEG_AMOUNT_QUALIFIERS_EXTENSION;)">
<!ENTITY % SEG_AMOUNT_TYPES_EXTENSION "OTHER">
<!ENTITY % SEG_AMOUNT_TYPES
    "(T | F | %SEG_AMOUNT_TYPES_EXTENSION;)">
<!ELEMENT AMOUNT (VALUE, NUMOFDEC, SIGN, CURRENCY, DRCR)>
<!ATTLIST AMOUNT
    qualifier %SEG_AMOUNT_QUALIFIERS; #REQUIRED
    type %SEG_AMOUNT_TYPES; #REQUIRED
     index CDATA #IMPLIED>

<!ENTITY % AMOUNT.ACTUAL.F    "AMOUNT">
<!ENTITY % AMOUNT.ACTUAL.T    "AMOUNT">
<!ENTITY % AMOUNT.DOCUMENT.T  "AMOUNT">



<!— DATETIME —>

<!ENTITY % SEG_DATETIME_QUALIFIERS_EXTENSION "OTHER">
<!ENTITY % SEG_DATETIME_QUALIFIERS
    "(ACCOUNTING | AVAILABLE | CREATION | DELIVACT | DELIVSCHED |
      DISCNT | DOCUMENT | DUE | EFFECTIVE | EXECFINISH | EXECSTART |
       EXPIRATION | FORECASTF | FORECASTS | FROM | INVOICE | LABORFINSH |
       LABORSTART | LASTUSED | LOADING | MATCHING | NEEDDELV | OPFINISH |
```

```
        OPSTART | PAYEND | PROMDELV | PROMSHIP | PYMTTERM | REPORTNGFN |
        REPORTNGST | REQUIRED | RESORCDWNF | RESORCDWNS | SETUPFINSH |
        SETUPSTART | SHIP | TEARDOWNF | TEARDOWNS | TO |
        %SEG_DATETIME_QUALIFIERS_EXTENSION;)">
<!ENTITY % SEG_DATETIME_TYPES_EXTENSION "OTHER">
<!ENTITY % SEG_DATETIME_TYPES
    "(T | F | %SEG_DATETIME_TYPES_EXTENSION;)">
<!ELEMENT DATETIME (YEAR, MONTH, DAY, HOUR, MINUTE, SECOND, SUBSECOND,
    TIMEZONE)>
<!ATTLIST DATETIME
    qualifier %SEG_DATETIME_QUALIFIERS; #REQUIRED
    type %SEG_DATETIME_TYPES; #IMPLIED
     index CDATA #IMPLIED>

<!ENTITY % DATETIME.ACCOUNTING  "DATETIME">
<!ENTITY % DATETIME.DOCUMENT    "DATETIME">
<!ENTITY % DATETIME.PAYEND      "DATETIME">


<!— BSR —>
<!ELEMENT BSR (VERB, NOUN, REVISION)>

<!— SENDER —>
<!ELEMENT SENDER (LOGICALID, COMPONENT, TASK, REFERENCEID, CONFIRMATION,
    LANGUAGE, CODEPAGE, AUTHID)>

<!— CNTROLAREA —>
<!ELEMENT CNTROLAREA (BSR, SENDER, DATETIME)>


<!-- From oagis_segments.dtd —>
```

After the base DTDs, we have a DTD for a specific document type. Our post journal DTD begins by describing the general structure of this document in a comment. According to the comment, a post_journal document consists of JOURNALs, which in turn, consists of one or more sets of JEHEADER and JELINEs.

```
<!-- From 001_post_journal_004.dtd —>

<!—
     Structure Overview

     POST_JOURNAL (JEHEADER, JELINE+)
          JEHEADER ()
          JELINE ()
```

```
    Notes

-->

<!-- ====================================================== -->
```

The following syntax effectively copies the statements in the file named oagis_domains.dtd:

```
<!ENTITY % DOMAINS SYSTEM "oagis_domains.dtd">
%DOMAINS;

<!ENTITY % FIELDS SYSTEM "oagis_fields.dtd">
%FIELDS;

<!ENTITY % SEGMENTS SYSTEM "oagis_segments.dtd">
%SEGMENTS;

<!-- ====================================================== -->
```

Now, the DTD describes the valid content (that is, the elements and attributes) of POST_JOURNAL_004, a sort of container for journals:

```
<!ELEMENT POST_JOURNAL_004 (CNTROLAREA, DATAAREA+)>

    <!ATTLIST VERB value CDATA #FIXED "POST">
    <!ATTLIST NOUN value CDATA #FIXED "JOURNAL">
    <!ATTLIST REVISION value CDATA #FIXED "004">


     <!ELEMENT DATAAREA (POST_JOURNAL)>
```

Next, the DTD describes the valid content (that is, the elements) of POST_JOURNAL (the actual journal information). A POST_JOURNAL consists of a JEHEADER (journal header), and one or more JELINE (journal line) elements:

```
<!ELEMENT POST_JOURNAL (JEHEADER, JELINE+)>
```

This DTD segment describes the valid content (that is, the elements) of JEHEADER (the journal header information). Some of the fields in JEHEADER are optional (as identified by a ?). Elements that are entity names like AMOUNT.DOCUMENT.T are enclosed in parentheses.

```
<!ELEMENT JEHEADER (
(%AMOUNT.DOCUMENT.T;)?,
(%DATETIME.DOCUMENT;)?,
(%DATETIME.PAYEND;)?,
```

```
GLENTITYS, ORIGREF, DESCRIPTN?, DOCTYPE?, JEID?,
LEDGER?, USERID?, USERAREA?)>
```

And finally, the DTD describes the valid content (that is, the elements) of JELINE (the journal line information):

```
<!ELEMENT JELINE (
(%AMOUNT.ACTUAL.T;),
(%AMOUNT.ACTUAL.F;)?,
GLNOMACCT, BUSNAREA?, COSTCENTER?, DEPARTMENT?,
DESCRIPTN?,
. . .

((%DATETIME.ACCOUNTING;) | (ACCTPERIOD, ACCTYEAR)),
USERAREA?)>


<!-- From 001_post_journal_004.dtd ->
```

A sample XML document based on the DTD we've defined would look like this:*

```
<?xml version="1.0" standalone="no"?>

<!-
    $Revision: 6.0.1 $
    $Date: 31 October 1998 $
    Open Applications Group Sample XML Data
    Copyright 1998, All Rights Reserved

    $Name: 001_post_journal_004.xml $


->

<!DOCTYPE POST_JOURNAL_004 SYSTEM "001_post_journal_004.dtd">

<POST_JOURNAL_004>
    <CNTROLAREA>
          <BSR>
               <VERB>POST</VERB>
               <NOUN>JOURNAL</NOUN>
            <REVISION>004</REVISION>
          </BSR>
          <SENDER>
               <LOGICALID>XX141HG09</LOGICALID>
```

*Portions of this XML document Copyright © Open Applications Group. All rights reserved.

```
            <COMPONENT>INVENTORY</COMPONENT>
            <TASK>RECEIPT</TASK>
            <REFERENCEID>95129945823449</REFERENCEID>
            <CONFIRMATION>1</CONFIRMATION>
            <LANGUAGE>EN</LANGUAGE>
         <CODEPAGE>test</CODEPAGE>
            <AUTHID>JOE DOE</AUTHID>
       </SENDER>
     <DATETIME qualifier = "CREATION" >
            <YEAR>1999</YEAR>
            <MONTH>12</MONTH>
            <DAY>31</DAY>
            <HOUR>23</HOUR>
            <MINUTE>59</MINUTE>
            <SECOND>45</SECOND>
            <SUBSECOND>0000</SUBSECOND>
            <TIMEZONE>-0500</TIMEZONE>
       </DATETIME>
</CNTROLAREA>
 <DATAAREA>
       <POST_JOURNAL>
          <JEHEADER>
             <AMOUNT qualifier = "DOCUMENT" type = "T">
                      <VALUE>2340500</VALUE>
                      <NUMOFDEC>2</NUMOFDEC>
                      <SIGN>+</SIGN>
                      <CURRENCY>USD</CURRENCY>
                      <DRCR>D</DRCR>
             </AMOUNT>
             <DATETIME qualifier = "DOCUMENT" type = "T">
                      <YEAR>1995</YEAR>
                      <MONTH>12</MONTH>
                      <DAY>31</DAY>
                      <HOUR>23</HOUR>
                      <MINUTE>59</MINUTE>
                      <SECOND>45</SECOND>
                      <SUBSECOND>0000</SUBSECOND>
                      <TIMEZONE>-0500</TIMEZONE>
                 </DATETIME>
             <DATETIME qualifier = "PAYEND">
                 <YEAR>1998</YEAR>
                 <MONTH>01</MONTH>
                 <DAY>02</DAY>
                 <HOUR>12</HOUR>
                 <MINUTE>00</MINUTE>
                 <SECOND>00</SECOND>
                      <SUBSECOND>0000</SUBSECOND>
```

```
            <TIMEZONE>-0500</TIMEZONE>
        </DATETIME>
        <GLENTITYS>CORPHEADQUARTER</GLENTITYS>
        <ORIGREF>RCPT#12550699</ORIGREF>
        <DESCRIPTN>INVENTORY RECEIVED FROM GLOBAL MANUFAC
        TURING</DESCRIPTN>
        <USERID>KURTC</USERID>
</JEHEADER>
  <JELINE>
        <AMOUNT qualifier = "ACTUAL" type = "T" >
            <VALUE>2340500</VALUE>
            <NUMOFDEC>2</NUMOFDEC>
            <SIGN>+</SIGN>
            <CURRENCY>USD</CURRENCY>
            <DRCR>D</DRCR>
        </AMOUNT>
             <AMOUNT qualifier = "ACTUAL" type = "F" >
                 <VALUE>001001001</VALUE>
            <NUMOFDEC>2</NUMOFDEC>
            <SIGN>+</SIGN>
            <CURRENCY>USD</CURRENCY>
            <DRCR>D</DRCR>
        </AMOUNT>
        <GLNOMACCT>2310</GLNOMACCT>
      <BUSNAREA>INVENTORY</BUSNAREA>
          <COSTCENTER>CC123</COSTCENTER>
          <DEPARTMENT>DEPT001ABC</DEPARTMENT>
        <DESCRIPTN>INVENTORY</DESCRIPTN>
        <DATETIME qualifier = "ACCOUNTING" >
            <YEAR>1996</YEAR>
            <MONTH>01</MONTH>
            <DAY>02</DAY>
            <HOUR>12</HOUR>
            <MINUTE>09</MINUTE>
            <SECOND>45</SECOND>
            <SUBSECOND>0000</SUBSECOND>
            <TIMEZONE>-0500</TIMEZONE>
        </DATETIME>
     </JELINE>
     <JELINE>
             <AMOUNT qualifier = "ACTUAL" type = "T" >
            <VALUE>2340500</VALUE>
            <NUMOFDEC>2</NUMOFDEC>
            <SIGN>-</SIGN>
            <CURRENCY>USD</CURRENCY>
            <DRCR>C</DRCR>
        </AMOUNT>
```

```
                    <GLNOMACCT>6940</GLNOMACCT>
                    <DESCRIPTN>ACCOUNTS PAYABLE</DESCRIPTN>
                    <ACCTPERIOD>03</ACCTPERIOD>
                         <ACCTYEAR>1999</ACCTYEAR>
               </JELINE>
          </POST_JOURNAL>
     </DATAAREA>
</POST_JOURNAL_004>
```

ONLINE XML

The use of XML is not restricted to batch operations. Real-time interfaces to systems necessarily define data structures. Many times, these structures must be self-describing for a variety of reasons.

For example, suppose we have a real-time interface that performs some service on behalf of a client application. This service must support several client applications simultaneously. Suppose further that the interface specification needs to include additional data elements in order to support some new requirement. Not all client systems can be updated simultaneously; in fact, it is likely that at least some older client systems need to be supported for a year or more.

One traditional solution for this requirement is to include a version identifier in the interface structure. The real-time service module can examine the version of a particular message, and respond to either the new or the old type of message. (In this situation, you will be well advised to normalize either message type into some standard internal structure rather than actually leaving the original code as is. Otherwise, there will be two versions of the service module to maintain.)

An XML-based interface specification is a perfect choice for this situation. Each client service request that is based on XML will be self-describing. The service module can extract the data that is actually in a particular message, and perhaps provide defaults for data that is not present in the message. The service module can respond with an XML-based return message, containing either the new or the old data set. A client application can extract the information it requires from the response. An even more sophisticated solution would allow the client application to pass in an initial DTD at runtime. This DTD would define the structure of the request and response method that the client can accept.

These advantages work for the client application as well. Client applications that use XML-based messages when talking to services can talk to new and old services simultaneously. The structure of the messages is not tied to the various versions of the services, only the message content is. This greatly simplifies the coding required to support multiple versions of service modules talking to multiple versions of clients.

XML is an excellent infrastructure for interactive messages between systems as well. For example, an online procurement system might send an XML-based catalog query to a supplier's system. The supplier's system could reply with catalog items described in XML, including prices. The procurement system could simply display the results in a browser, or store the results in a database for later access.

OTHER OPPORTUNITIES

Because XML data is so much more accessible than data stored in proprietary formats, whole new application functions are possible. For example:

- **XML data repositories.** Information publishers can produce information in XML format. XML documents can be stored for later access by a variety of applications, not just the applications that generated the information. Ideally, traditional reports will no longer exist, but will be replaced by XML documents. These documents will be presented to (and manipulated by) end users with XML-capable viewers. These viewers will provide many more analytical capabilities than are available with simple text searching of an ASCII file.
- **Information transfers that have not been cost effective till now.** Custom-built or EDI-based information transfer systems have traditionally been used for high-value or high-volume requirements. Other information transfers have not been addressed although organizations would clearly benefit from the ability to transfer information with a wide variety of business partners.

A classic example is catalog content management. Buyers would like access to the most current catalog information, but the cost and complexity of accepting and processing a variety of suppliers' catalog information is generally too high.

XML-based catalogs are a mechanism by which a supplier can publish a catalog, confident that buyers will be able to process it.

- **Intelligent searching.** XML-based searching guarantees better results. Not only can content be searched (as is the case today), but content can be cross-checked with meaning (structure). An XML search for "mark price" will not return lists of preprinted pricing labels when what you want is information about Mark Price, the basketball player. Not only can data and meaning be searched together, it is possible to search based on meaning only. An XML enabled web site can effectively publish which documents (or web pages) contain information about certain data types.
- **Intelligent agents.** Applications can be built that will browse an environment (the Internet, your local systems, or perhaps just the hard drive on your PC) and detect items of interest. If you are interested in eventually buying at auction a 500 Mz PC when the price drops below $500, then an agent can scan an auction site's XML-based auction status catalog for this information and create an e-mail for you when a system meets your target price.

APPENDIX A

About the CD

In addition to the code samples, source files, and Sun's JDK there are numerous folders on the CD where you will find one or more executable program files that will install various demonstration programs. Descriptions of the contents of each folder and instructions for their use are described below.

ACM

CORECT

ACM, Ltd.

50 Lower Monk Road

Esher, KT10 8HD

ENGLAND

+44 1201 653516

http://www.acm.co.uk

This is another Cobol to Java conversion tool. To install this program, run the program COR0993.exe in the ACM directory.

This installation program contains some sample Cobol applications that have been converted into Java. In addition ACM has included some more complex conversion examples in the directory "Corect_Java_Examples." After installation, run the ACM Corect conversion application from the Windows Start menu. You will be able to select the sample Cobol program to be converted using the Project Directory tree browser (available as the "Proj Dir" icon in the "Projects" menu tab). A word of caution here: only use the Project Directory browser to select files to be processed. Selecting the "Prepare" icon on the Projects menu tab may cause unpredictable results in this demonstration version.

After selecting the Cobol program to process, go to the "Prepare" menu tab, and press the "Analyze" icon. Next, go to the "Processing" menu tab and press the "Start" icon. This will start the Java code generation process. Refer to the ACM documentation for more details.

ADOBE

ADOBE ACROBAT READER 4.0

Adobe Systems Incorporated

345 Park Avenue

San Jose, CA 95110-2704

408-536-6000

http://www.adobe.com

Adobe Acrobat Reader is free, and freely distributable software that lets you view and print PDF files on all major computer platforms. You will need to install Adobe Acrobat Reader in order to view some of the information from the IBMSanFrancisco Folder.

EXERCISES

CODE SAMPLES

The CD contains all the code samples in the book. These are organized by exercise number and development environment. Samples for Sun's Java Developer's Kit and Microsoft's Visual J++ are also included. You can and should use these samples as reference materials as you perform the exercises, but I wouldn't recommend just copying and compiling them. You will get more out of the exercises if you follow the step-by-step instructions in the book. No pain, no gain.

SOURCE FILES

The CD contains the Java source files, the compiled class files, and the HTML files necessary to run the applets in a browser. The Visual J++ directories also contain the required project definition files. All source files are organized by development environment and exercise number.

IBMSANFRANCISCO

INFORMATION ABOUT IBM'S SAN FRANCISCO PROJECT

IBM Corporation

Route 100

Somers, NY 10589

914-766-1235

914-766-8124 FAX

http://www.ibm.com

This business application development environment is the largest commercial Java project to date. Although many of the PDF files are marketing brochure materials, it is a highly informative presentation. Of particular interest is the component organization described in the Common Business Object (filename: sfcbolist.pdf). You will need the Adobe Acrobat Reader (included in the Adobe directory on the CD) to view these files.

The HTML page *IBMSanFranciscoTechnicalSummary.htm* includes a good summary of the project. There is also an interesting discussion of classic design issues, locking, transaction consistency, model view controls, and other topics on the client architecture page. In addition the tools catalog page contains a listing of products that are San Francisco-friendly, and an informative collection of Java related tools that can be used with various other projects. Finally, the bibliography page lists the classic OO literature.

There are a few other directories in the IBMSanFrancisco folder which contain some more detailed information for interested users. Additional HTML files are in the BaseUserGuide directory, the ConceptsAndFacilities directory, and the GLUserGuideExtract directory. Start perusing the information contained in each of these directories by viewing the file "index.html" in a browser.

JDK

JAVA 2

Sun Microsystems, Inc.

901 San Antonio Road

Palo Alto, CA 94303

800-786-7638

http://www.java.sun.com

The Sun JDK is necessary to fully utilize this book. You may either download the JDK from Sun's Web site or install the JDK using this CD. In the folder Jdk run the Program named jdk12-win32.exe to install the JDK. You may place the JDK in any directory. The program named jdk12-doc.zip contains the JDK documentation from Sun, these file is in the "zip" compression format, therefore you will need WinZip (available at *http://www.winzip.com*)to unpack these files.

LEGACYJ

PERCOBOL COMPILER—EDUCATIONAL VERSION

LegacyJ (formerly Synkronix)

4683 Chabot Drive

Suite 211

Pleasanton, CA 94588

925-467-1598

http://www.legacyj.com

This is a demonstration version LegacyJ's (formerly Synkronix) PerCobol Educational Compiler, a Java/Cobol integration product. Using PerCobol, developers can write code in Cobol and deploy in Java. In addition to the PerCobol demo LegacyJ has included both Cobol and Java sample programs for you to review.

To install this program, run the program setup.bat in the LegacyJ directory. Review and answer the license information, then select a directory for loading the software. By default, this will be c:\percobol. Be aware that the installation will adjust your PATH and CLASSPATH variables, and you will have to reboot after installation.

In addition, you should look at the file named \percobol\docs\compl_rts.html, as well as the other HTML files in the document directory for information on how to use this product. PerCobol is intended for use as part of an integrated development environment, particularly the SlickEdit IDE. This educational demonstration version can only be used from the DOS command line; for example you can run the PerCobol conversion program by typing 'percobol' from the DOS command window.

Example: Try converting the hello.cob file in the samples directory using the PerCobol tool.

In the DOS window locate the directory (cd c:\percobol\samples\helloworld).

Convert this program to Java by typing "percobol hello.cob"

This information and demonstration software is updated periodically, you can obtain the most recent versions at *http://www.legacyJ.com/educational/educational.html*

OAGML

XML DOCUMENT DEFINITIONS AND SAMPLES

Open Applications Group, Inc.

http://www.openapplications.org

These DTD's describe XML structures for various types of business documents. This information is updated from time to time and can be obtained at *http://www.openapplicationsgroup.org/xml/loadform.htm.*

RELATIVITY

RESCUEWARE

Relativity Technologies, Inc.

1001 Winstead Drive

Cary, NC 27513

919-678-1500

919-678-1550 FAX

http://www.relativity.com

This tool converts Cobol code into Java code. To view this information, you must first create a directory named "rescue" and then copy the two files in the Relativity directory to the new "rescue" directory.

In order to view the presentation, run the program Rescueware.exe. This installation file will unpack the presentation into the newly created "rescue" directory and run automatically. Click OK on the warning regarding Windows 3.1.

APPENDIX B

Java Information Available Elsewhere

This is a listing of a few of the Java resources available on the net. There are several good introductory tutorials, as well as resources for in depth information. As with any list, this one is surely incomplete, and feedback is welcome.

JAVA RESOURCES

www.java.sun.com. The original source for Java information. Lots of documentation, downloads, tutorials, and other useful information.

www.ibm.com/developer/java. IBM's java site is loaded with information, sample code, FAQ's, training material, etc.

www.zdnet.com/pcweek/filters/java. The latest in Java happenings.

www.progsource.com/java.html. Tools, magazines, FAQ's, employment, and lots of other Java related listings.

www.programmingtutorials.com/javap.html. A good listing of Java tutorials, from the basic to the complex.

JAVA MAGAZINES

www.javareport.com. An informed and informative Java magazine. Absent most of the religious fervor found in some Java publications, it focuses on the current state of the art in Java technologies.

www.javadevelopersjournal.com/java. A Java magazine for developers.

www.java-pro.com. An excellent Java resource, it includes downloads, ask the expert sections, in depth reviews, and other useful material. The online version is quite good.

www.javaworld.com. A complete Java resource, including reviews, code samples, and good writers. A superior on-line presence as well.

JAVA TOOLS

www.tiac.net/users/dchase/javaedit.htm. A free graphical Java IDE, built in Java.

www.chami.com. Java and Web development tools, free downloads, utilities, information.

www.javashareware.com. A complete Java site that contains Java projects of all types, FAQ's, answers to questions from experts, and other great resources. The focus is on promoting Java with free and useful stuff.

COBOL INFORMATION

www.acucobol.com. Acucorp's home page. Cross platform Cobol design and deployment tools.

www.merant.com. The home page for MicroFocus Cobol compiler.

www.software.ibm.com/ad/cobol/cobol.htm. IBM's Cobol site.

www.lib.ox.ac.uk.internet/news/faq/archive/cobol-faq.html. A decent Cobol FAQ site.

www.flexus.com. The home page for Flexus, a Cobol tool vendor. This site also contains a good collection of links to other Cobol sites.

www.infogoal.com/cbd/cbdtol.htm. An exhaustive listing of Cobol tools and information, both on and off-line.

MISCELLANEOUS REVIEWS

www.andromeda.com/people/ddyer/java/Reviews.html
David H. Andrews Group's Consultant Reports.

APPENDIX C

Buzzwords

ACTIVE SERVER PAGES (ASP)

The widespread acceptance of Internet standards and business processes that use the Web have increased the number of deployment environments available to a business developer. One such environment is the web server itself. Normally, a web server simply sends static HTML documents and other file types to a web browser. A business process requires much more dynamic content, as information is collected from business systems and presented to the end user.

The original technique used to extend a web server is common gateway interface (CGI). A browser can request a CGI program instead of a standard HTML page. The web server will execute the CGI program or script at the request of the web browser. The CGI program can in turn reply with HTML data to the web server; this HTML data is passed along to the web browser.

CGI, though widely available and often used, suffers from a number of problems, such as poor performance and incomplete integration. To solve these and other problems, Microsoft has defined a proprietary extensibility model for their web server called active server pages (ASP). ASP allows the developer to program, or script, web server processing in much the same way that a web browser can be scripted. Using ASP, a developer can integrate data from a database with static HTML code and perform program processing logic. The output of an ASP page on the web server is often standard HTML, which is sent to the web browser for display.

The ASP environment combines standard components (see the section on ActiveX) with a choice of scripting languages (VBScript and JavaScript) and an object model that defines the current web page. Using these resources, the developer can control the content, presentation, and sequence of any part of the web page as it is created. The result is a rich, dynamic web page construction environment.

Microsoft has built a good graphical design environment based on ASP called Visual InterDev. This tool provides graphical editors, debuggers, and deployment tools for ASP pages. ASP is also available on other platforms and other web servers via an ASP hosting tool from ChiliSoft.

ACTIVEX

Microsoft's standard for client-side component access is ActiveX (also known as COM). This is a standard architecture that components can use to publish their interfaces (interactively, at design time, or at runtime). Component consumers can access, modify, and call these components. ActiveX components publish the data items they contain as properties, and the functions they support as methods. ActiveX components are language neutral, meaning they can be written in any language, as well as be used by any language. However, ActiveX technology is limited in practice to the Windows platforms.

Microsoft development tools can easily wrap your code in ActiveX components. All Microsoft environments (even environments that are not, strictly speaking, development environments such as Excel) can make use of ActiveX components. ActiveX is optimized for performance on a single PC. Applications can use ActiveX without significant performance penalty as long as both component consumer (the client) and the component are on the same PC.

ActiveX is also a technology that competes with Java applets. Developers can create application functions in any language (VB, for example), wrap them in an ActiveX control, and point to the control with a web page. Microsoft's Internet Explorer (and Netscape's Navigator, if a plug-in has been installed) will automatically download the component and execute the application function on your PC.

AWT

The basic graphical user interface functionality for Java is contained in the abstract window toolkit (AWT), released with the earliest versions of Java. AWT is a standard interface that Java applications (or applets) can use to create and interact with graphical UIs. The AWT interfaces talk directly to the underlying graphical operating system interfaces. Since AWT is ported to every Java environment, any Java application that uses AWT can display graphical UIs in any Java environment.

However, AWT has been generally regarded as the weakest part of the original Java environment. The primary problem is that AWT is too low level for most application developers and does not do a good job of hiding all the differences between graphical hosting systems. At the same time, important capabilities required by graphical applications are not available in AWT. Sun has improved on AWT with the JFC/Swing classes released as a patch to JDK 1.1 and is included in the JDK 1.2.

CLIENT/SERVER

Client/server systems, and the clientserver architecture, have changed the way most new computer systems have been built over the last decade. Client/server systems have effectively replaced the traditional mainframe-hosted model as the most popular environment for new business systems in many organizations.

A client/server system is just that, a system with two primary components: a client (typically, a PC) and a server. The client passes messages to the server, and the server performs the requested function and responds with a result. The simplest client/server architecture is a two-tiered relational database model, with a relational database as the server. The application logic is on the client, and passes SQL requests to the server. The server responds with data from the database. More complex models involve separate application logic layers, which serve as glue to connect the client to the database server.

The server in a client/server system does not need to be a single physical machine or even a single component. Many times, the server actually consists of an application server component and a database component. In high-volume situations, there can be more than one application server and more than one database server.

COMPONENTS

Components are collections of reusable code, organized so that some other application can use them. Components share many of the same characteristics and design goals as objects (code reuse, public interfaces, and so on), but have a different emphasis. The most important thing about a component is not how it is built, but rather how it is to be used.

Components can be created in any language and can publish an interface that has little to do with how it is constructed internally. Components are often collections of objects of various types; as such, they can represent a fairly complex service. One example of a large, commonly used component is a relational database system.

Objects can be represented as components, and a component can consist of one or more objects. However, an object will naturally publish its interface based on its class definition and the definitions of the classes it inherits. In addition, unless your development environment supports multiple inheritance (Java does not), it is difficult to publish an OO interface that reflects the results of a coalition of several objects.

So, building a component and using a component architecture is more than just publishing the interfaces of important objects in your Java system. It involves thinking about how client applications might use these objects (or combinations of these objects) and how you should best publish interfaces. In effect, the component designer is building services to be used by other applications.

COMMON OBJECT REQUEST BROKER ARCHITECTURE (CORBA)

We've discussed how you can create and use objects as part of your program. In some cases, you may need to create and use objects that exists on another system. Objects can be created and accessed on another system by using an object request broker (ORB). An ORB provides services that allow you to create objects on a remote system, and to call that object's public functions.

The OMG has defined a specification for a standard ORB, the common object request broker architecture (CORBA). This detailed specification describes which services a standard ORB should provide and how they should be implemented. A number of vendors (BEA, HP, Inprise, IBM, Sun, and others) have implemented products that conform to the CORBA spec. These products support a wide variety of operating systems and development languages.

CORBA products have been successfully used in a number of large-scale OO projects. They provide good, and efficient, distributed object management services. However, CORBA products have not had wide spread acceptance for a number of reasons:

- **Complexity.** CORBA products and the CORBA interfaces can be difficult to master. Effective use of CORBA requires a serious commitment to learning a complex technology.
- **Language and development environment affinity.** One of CORBA's assets is the fact that it has been designed as a language-neutral and platform-neutral technology. This is also one of its problems. The developer has to step outside the application programming model and address the CORBA model. Only recently have some popular language-specific development environments wrapped CORBA interfaces in a way that feels natural to the application developer.
- **Availability and cost.** As a rule, development projects that do not have special requirements for deployment will be more successful at project rollout time. If your project requires a CORBA product to be installed at each client system, then you will likely have to manage that task as part of your product installation. You may have to charge for it as well.
- **Interoperability.** The CORBA spec does not include a working reference model, so minor differences are likely to exist in any actual implementation. In addition, vendors are free to extend their implementations with specific features. As a result, most CORBA products from different vendors do not work well with each other.

DISTRIBUTED COMPONENT OBJECT MODEL (DCOM)

Microsoft's standard for distributed object services is its distributed component object model (DCOM). This is both a specification and an implementation. Further, it is technology that is embedded in every relevant software Microsoft product, from compilers to transaction servers, to database engines. It is now even part of the Windows operating system.

The good news/bad news about DCOM is that it is very Microsoft specific. Most of the challenges listed in the discussion of CORBA are not problems with DCOM, as long as you use only Microsoft, or Microsoft-centric products. If you need to use non-Microsoft products, or non-Microsoft platforms, then the availability of DCOM on that platform will be questionable.

DCOM has the reputation of being less performant than its competitor, CORBA, although it is hard to find real world studies that confirm this complaint. On the other hand, DCOM is very easy to use. Since DCOM is based on the ActiveX component standard, most Microsoft compilers can easily create DCOM components, and nearly every Microsoft tool can use DCOM components.

ENTERPRISE JAVA BEANS (EJB)

Enterprise Java Beans (EJB) bring the benefits of Java-built components to distributed, transaction-oriented systems. An EJB can be instantiated (created) on a remote system, and then respond to message requests from an application executing on a local system. Best of all, EJBs don't have to manage the complex system plumbing that is normally associated with remote component management and transaction integrity control. All these system-level issues (component invocation, life-cycle management, security, transaction semantics) are handled by the EJB infrastructure. A major design objective of the EJB spec is to allow developers to focus on writing code that solves the business problem(s) at hand rather than the technical issues surrounding the management of remote distributed component services.

The EJB specification is primarily an effort to standardize remote component management techniques available to Java components. It also attempts to simplify and improve existing techniques such as CORBA and DCOM. EJB is very Java centric; it fits naturally into the Java language. It is only modestly more difficult to build and use EJB components than it is to build and use regular objects in Java.

The major problems with EJB are:

- **EJB is a Java-only technology.** If your project requires transaction and remote object management services for other languages, then DCOM and CORBA are the only choices.

- **EJB is a specification although there is a working reference model.** It is possible that some vendors' EJB management products may not work well with each other.
- **EJB is not built into any operating system (although this may change on some Unix platforms).** Therefore, Java-built projects that use EJB may have to distribute the EJB components in addition to the Java components.

FIREWALL

Web servers are designed to be accessible to the public. An Internet mall, or Internet shopping site, wants to place few restrictions on who can visit the site or when they can visit. A "corporate presence" Web site wants to post information about the company for all to see.

Internet systems, because they are so public, are subject to a variety of attacks from hackers. Hackers can be either just curious or malicious "crackers." Recent high profile attacks on government sites have highlighted the potential risks involved in placing important systems in so public a venue.

A firewall system is meant to protect public Web sites from attack. It is placed between the external Internet and the system it is meant to protect. All traffic meant for the protected system is first passed through the firewall where it is inspected, and perhaps rejected. Only approved traffic is allowed to reach the protected web site.

A firewall prevents most of the obvious attacks by restricting traffic to and from a Web server to approved message types. For example, a firewall might allow only HTTP message requests directed to a specific port (a type of input channel) on a particular Web server. Other requests directed to that Web server (for example, requests to copy files or to change passwords) will be rejected.

FILE TRANSFER PROTOCOL (FTP)

The popularity of the Internet is due, in no small part, to the adoption of standard functions by a wide variety of tools. FTP (file transfer protocol) is one of those functions.

FTP is an efficient protocol that can be used to transfer files from one system to another. It includes commands to move both binary and text files, one at a time, or in groups. It also includes commands to list the contents of a directory on either the local system or the remote system. Browsers, Web servers, and other Internet tools all support FTP. Most file downloads performed over the Internet use the FTP protocol.

HYPERTEXT TRANSFER PROTOCOL (HTTP)

HTTP is another important Internet standard. This is a simple mechanism for a client application (a browser, for example) to request a file from a Web server. Typically, Web pages are accessed using the HTTP protocol.

To use HTTP, a browser needs only to access the file using a public address called a URL (universal resource locator). The HTTP request is automatically directed to the Web server identified in the URL, and the required file is transferred by the Web server to the browser. The browser can then read the information contained in the file, and format a user interface based on the commands in the file.

A Web page ordinarily consists of many files. All the graphics files in a Web page are normally stored on the Web server as separate files. A Web browser will actually make many HTTP requests to get all the files necessary to display a Web page. Only after all the files referenced in the Web page have been downloaded and displayed will the entire Web page be complete.

INTEGRATED DEVELOPMENT ENVIRONMENT (IDE)

Java applications are often developed using an integrated development environment (IDE). These tools help the Java developer edit and manage source code, compile applications, and debug problems. Modern IDEs are graphical applications with lots of productivity features, and often include interfaces to source version control systems.

INTERFACE DEFINITION LANGUAGE (IDL)

IDL is both a standard and a technique. IDL files are external descriptions of the interfaces to a component or an object. CORBA includes a standard IDL specification that is used to describe any object that will be managed by an object request broker (ORB). Development tools often use IDL files to store information about the interface to a component in a readily accessible manner. Some tools allow the developer to use a wizard application to quickly create an IDL based on some existing class. Other tools use IDL's as the repository of information about available components.

INTERNET INTER-ORB PROTOCOL (IIOP)

IIOP is a standard mechanism to pass messages between applications (specifically, between an ORB server and the client that uses the ORB) over the Internet. For example, IIOP can also be used as a protocol by which Web servers accept and respond to ORB message requests from Internet clients. An ORB client will typically be a browser, but any Internet client is acceptable, including another Web server. Most of the popular general-purpose web servers support IIOP, as well as some special purpose servers built primarily to service IIOP requests. IIOP is specifically mandated as the Internet message protocol for CORBA.

JAVA BEANS

A Java Bean is a self-contained Java component. It is a self-describing, reusable software unit intended to be used by another application. A Bean is designed so that a development environment can (visually) publish the Bean's interface and allow the developer to easily manipulate the interface. A Java Bean includes special interfaces that allow a development tool to query the component (*introspection*). Developers can adjust how the Bean behaves or looks (*customization*) or set Bean *properties* to control the Bean. Beans support events (pre-defined messages) and can be stored and subsequently reused (*persistence*). The Java Bean standard is roughly equivalent to Microsoft's ActiveX component standard, except that ActiveX is a language-neutral, platform-specific standard, whearas Java Beans are language specific and platform neutral.

JAVASCRIPT

JavaScript is an interpretive programming language developed by Netscape. It is intended as a generic (that is, cross platform) scripting language able to extend the standard functionality of Web servers and Web browsers. It doesn't really have anything to do with Java, per se, other than some syntax similarities and its cross-platform promise.

In many situations, a developer needs a programming language in order to implement certain types of application capabilities. Static HTML pages are not always enough to describe an application with rich functional requirements. JavaScript can be used to create programming logic that extends either the Web server or the HTML pages on the client with application logic. On the server, JavaScript interacts with the data on the Web page and other sources (perhaps data from a database) and generates HTML statements dynamically. Web pages built in this way are interpreted in the standard fashion by a Web browser. On the client, JavaScript interacts with the browser directly and instructs the Web browser to perform functions beyond those available in standard HTML.

JDBC

The standard Java database access technique is JDBC. JDBC is essentially a variation on ODBC with some Java bindings. It is designed as a Java API to SQL data. JDBC is just a specification; it is up to the various database vendors or third parties to create JDBC drivers for a particular database. In some cases, a JDBC to ODBC bridge can be used, but likely not for production purposes.

JDBC provides a fairly complete set of SQL-friendly data access mechanisms, such as scrollable result sets, absolute and relative positioning (in the result set), access to stored procedures, and data type conversions. Most SQL-92 (Entry Level 2) statements are supported in JDBC.

J/DIRECT

Microsoft's standard for access outside the Java VM is J/Direct. This technology allows Java applications to call functions written in other languages, including C and C++. One important benefit of J/Direct is that it makes all the native Windows APIs readily available to a Java application. J/Direct is specific to the Windows platform and the Microsoft provided Java VM.

JNI

The Java native interface (JNI) is the standard mechanism for Java applications to access functions written in other programming languages, including C and C++. Java applications can also use JNI to access features specific to the host operating system. JNI is supported by all the VMs provided by non-Microsoft vendors and on all Java platforms.

JAVA SERVER PAGES (JSP)

Part of the recent Java 2 Enterprise Edition announcements is a technology called Java server pages (JSP). This is a mechanism to extend a Web server with JavaScript and/or components written in Java (servelets). This product is meant to compete directly with Microsoft's active server pages (ASP) technology, as a cross-platform, webserver–neutral development environment for dynamic Web pages.

Using JSP, a developer can build Web pages at run-time based on data from a Java component, static HTML data, or a JavaScript. The result of a JSP page is often standard HTML, which is sent to the client by the Web server.

A number of vendors such as IBM, Bluestone, Netscape and others have already announced JSP development and deployment environments.

MICROSOFT FOUNDATION CLASSES (MFC)

Low-level programming in Microsoft Windows can be a very complex task. Windows comes with hundreds of API interfaces, most of which are designed to display and manage the graphical user interface. Each new release of Windows comes with a new batch of APIs that may or may not be useful to your project, but will certainly clutter up the API reference manual.

Microsoft has attempted to simplify this complexity with their Microsoft Foundation Class (MFC) libraries. The set of libraries is designed to let the C++ programmer easily access the most commonly used UI components, without sacrificing power or flexibility. Furthermore, the MFC programmer can create specializations of the base MFC classes for his or her own purposes. Most sophisticated Windows applications today use MFC classes and the MFC programming environment.

OPEN DATABASE CONNECTIVITY (ODBC)

ODBC is a standard data access technique developed by the SQL Access Group in the early 1990s. This is a specification for a standard call level interface that supports access to data sources. Various vendors, including all the major database vendors, have developed ODBC drivers that can be used to access information stored in their databases. ODBC drivers are now shipped as a standard component of Windows 98 and Windows NT.

Although used primarily with SQL databases, ODBC is sometimes used to access information from other sources, including text files, spreadsheets, and ISAM files. ODBC drivers also are available on other platforms besides Windows, such as Unix and Macintosh.

REMOTE METHOD INVOCATION (RMI)

Sun has defined a standard technique that Java applications can use to create objects on remote systems, and then call their methods. This standard, called remote method invocation (RMI), is similar in principle to traditional RPC function calls (see RPC), only it is tailored for Java. Most Java runtimes (but not all) contain the libraries necessary to support RMI. RMI is an essential building block for EJBs.

REMOTE PROCEDURE CALL (RPC)

Remote procedure call (RPC) is a generic name for a protocol that allows an application on one system to call a function on another system. The best way to understand RPC is to start with a normal procedure call. Suppose that program A calls program B with parameters and then waits for the reply. When program B is complete, it returns to program A, perhaps with return parameters. In an RPC environment, program B can be on another system.

In most RPC implementations, the caller must perform a small amount of specialized logic to initiate the called program on the remote system before calling the remote program. After initialization, an RPC implementation makes the remote program appear as if it were local, except for the performance penalty incurred by remote function calls as compared to a local call.

SECURE SOCKETS LAYER (SSL)

Secure sockets layer (SSL) is a transmission protocol designed by Netscape that employs encryption techniques to provide secure transmissions over the Internet. Other service-based utilities, such as HTTP and FTP, can employ SSL to secure the messages they send over the Internet.

SSL sits between these service utilities and the Internet's basic message passing protocol (TCP/IP). For example, an HTTP server that uses SSL (as in https:/www.domain…) talks to the SSL layer, which encrypts the message and then sends it out over TCP/IP. On the other end of the message pipe, the browser reads the message from the SSL, which gets the encrypted message from TCP/IP, decrypts it, and returns it to the browser. SSL hides the message content sent between partner applications from public scrutiny.

SWING

The basic graphical user interface functionality for Java is contained in the abstract window toolkit (AWT). However, the AWT has been generally regarded as the weakest part of the original Java environment. Sun has improved on AWT with the newer Java Foundation Classes (JFC), released as a patch to JDK 1.1. These APIs are grouped in a package named after the internal development project at Sun (Swing). The Swing package is meant to replace the AWT.

Applications that use Swing have access to more control over the user interface. For example, an application can now manage borders around Swing components, and Swing components do not need to be rectangular. Swing applications can interact better with native applications.

On the downside, the Swing components are fairly large. A Swing application must download the Swing components to the client if they are not already loaded. Further, since Swing does not work with every VM (that is, Microsoft's), or even with every browser, client systems must be managed to some extent.

TCP/IP

The standard transport protocol for the Internet is transmission control protocol/internet protocol, or (TCP/IP). This low-level protocol defines the way messages must be packaged, delivered, and accessed by systems on a network. Other service-based utilities, such as HTTP and FTP, employ TCP/IP as the wire-level protocol to perform their functions.

TCP/IP's most popular feature is the ability to create a virtual *pipe* between a client and a server application. The client and server can use this pipe to send messages to each other, simply by reading and writing to the pipe, as if it were a file. These messages are tagged as belonging to a specific client and server application. Other client applications and other server applications will not see these messages, even if they are on the same machine. Web browsers and Web servers use this capability when they send and process HTTP requests, for example.

By virtue of these and other features, TCP/IP facilitates the transfer of information between applications over a public network, such as the Internet.

UNIFIED MODELING LANGUAGE (UML)

The unified modeling language is a definition of a software modeling language. Software modeling techniques employ rigorous analysis and documentation methodologies to capture a representation of how a system is built and how the system performs its processes. UML combines features from existing software modeling practices. At the same time, UML is intended to be simpler, or more approachable, than some of the previous modeling techniques

The UML is a rich language that can represent all sorts of system processes, from simple data entry functions to complex real-time distributed systems.

UNIVERSAL RESOURCE LOCATOR (URL)

This standard convention identifies a unique location for a file, or other resource, in a manner that is unambiguous. Any application, such as a browser, can use a URL name to locate a file. You are likely familiar with URLs already. The name of your favorite Web site is identified with a URL (www.cnn.com, for example).

The first part of a URL identifies the *domain name* that contains the resource. A domain name is a publicly registered ID of a server on the Internet. Domain names are assigned by government-affiliated organizations to an organization or individual. Domain name servers on the Internet resolve individual domain names to a specific identifier called an IP address. The format of an IP address is nnn.nnn.nnn.nnn, where each n is replaced with a number.

A domain is either a unique physical server or a logical location on a server. It can even be a collection of servers (a server farm), grouped to appear as one.

The remainder of the URL name (that is, the characters after the domain name) point to a file, a directory, or some other resource located on the server.

```
www.cnn.com/TECH/computing.html
```

domain name **resource name**

VBSCRIPT

Microsoft has developed its own web scripting language named VBScript. VBScript is similar in many ways to JavaScript. Like JavaScript, VBScript provides an environment that allows the developer to perform programming logic dynamically (at runtime). VBScript can be executed on either a web client or a web server. As the name suggests, VBScript is similar in syntax to Visual Basic (VB). VBScript and JavaScript can usually be combined on the same web page.

Index

A
Abstract Window Toolkit (AWT), 365–66, 413, 423
AbstractList implementation, 308
AbstractSequentialList implementation, 308
ACM Limited, 375, 401–02
active server pages (ASP), 411–12
ActiveX, 412, 416
Adobe Acrobat Reader, 402
AFC. See Application Foundation Classes (AFC).
AFC/WFC, 365–66
algorithms, 301, 345
amount element, in DTD segment, 390
ANSI, 388
API interfaces, 421
applets
  with J++, 34–41
  with JDK, 27–29
  versus servelets, 22–24
Application Foundation Classes (AFC), 366
ArraysasList implementation, 312
ArrayList implementation, 308
arrays, 291–94
  as parameters, 295
ASP. See Active server pages (ASP).
AWT. See Abstract Window Toolkit (AWT).

B
base classes, 132
BEA, 370, 414
bidirectional iteration, 302
bignumbers, 264–69
binary arithmetic operations, 203–09
binarySearch algorithm, 302
Booch, Grady, 372
bottom-up design, 130
break and continue statements, 221–24
browsers, 358
byte class, 259

C
C++, xvi, 197, 420
caller class, Java message, 12–13, 47, 49–50, 100
caller COBOL, 6–10, 45–46, 52–55, 143–44
calling a subroutine, 4–9
cascading style sheets (CSS), 387
CGI. See Common gateway interface (CGI).
class data members, 10, 14, 46, 85–127
class diagrams, 374
class ErrorMsg, Java message, 48–49
classes and filenames, 13, 349–50
  instances, 9–10
classes and objects, 3–19, 91
  using objects in Java, 97
CLASSPATH
  argument, 62–63
  settings, 73, 351, 357, 359, 405
client/server, 413
COBOL
  design patterns, 140–42
  information, 408
  method overloading, 50
  subroutine, 3–5
  understanding reference variables, 209–10
  versus Java syntax, 197–200
COBOL/Java integration tools, 375
CODEBASE, 352
  directory, 359
code block, 211–19
collection.synchronizedInterface, 312
collection.unmodifiableInterface, 312
collections, 299–312
  versus vectors and arrays, 303–13
Common gateway interface (CGI), 411

Common object request broker architecture (CORBA), 369, 414–15
remote object management, 364
comparators, 302–03, 305–06
comparing strings, 254–56
components, 414
compressed packages, 357–58
concatenate operator, 257
condition statement, 218
constructors, 106–08
context-switching logic, 345
continue statement, 237
copy algorithm, 302
CORBA. See Common object request broker architecture (CORBA).
core interfaces, 300–01
Crystal Systems, 375
CSS. See Cascading style sheets (CSS).

D
databases, 371
data encapsulation, 85
data members, or variables, 91, 98–100
DataWindow, Powerbuilder, 365
datetime, in DTD segment, 390–97
DCOM. See Distributed component object model (DCOM).
debugging Java software, 349–59
design patterns, 137–40
Cobol, 138–39
multithreaded, 344–45
distributed component object model (DCOM), 369, 415–16
document type declaration (DTDs), 380–83, 397
domain name, 425
double class, 259
DTDs. See Document type declaration (DTDs).
dynamic HTML (DHTML), 366

E
EDI, 388–89
EDI-based information transfer systems, 398–99
EDIFACT, 388
EJBs. See Enterprise Java Beans (EJBs).
EmptyList, 312
EmptySet , 312
Enterprise Java Beans (EJBs), 368–70, 416–17
equivalent COBOL statements, 258–61
error handling, 329–30
ErrorMsg class, Java message, 46–47, 89–91
Errormsg, 62–64, 68–72, 75–76, 83–84, 99, 104–06
exceptions, 161
class hierarchy, 331–32
creating, 332–33
processing, 259, 338–39
using, 334–37
extensible style language (XSL), 387

F
file transfer protocol (FTP), 417–18
fill algorithm, 302
finally function, 336–37
firewall, 417
float class, 259
flow control, 211–52
for statement, 219–20
Forte, 370
FTP. See File transfer protocol (FTP).

G
garbage collection, 345–46
GE Information Systems (GEISCO), 388

H
handles, 91
Harbinger, 388
HashSet implementation, 306, 310
HelloWorld, the applet, 82–83, 350
HelloWorld, the application, 80–81, 350
hiding methods and members, 161
hiding variables and methods, 156–57
HTTP. See Hypertext transfer protocol (HTTP).
hypertext markup language (HTML), 201–02, 411, 420
Hypertext transfer protocol (HTTP), 418

I

IBM, 363, 386, 414
  IBMs San Francisco Project, 371–72, 403
IDE. See Integrated development environments (IDEs).
IDL. See Interface definition language (IDL).
IEEE 754 format, 247
IIOP. See Internet inter-orb protocol (IIOP).
implementations, 301
implementing runnable, 341
implements code in Java, 159
import statements, 354–56
indexed sequential (ISAM) file type, 309
inheritance, 129–32, 136–40
inner code blocks, 214–16
Inprise Corporation, 364, 370, 414
instantaneous portability, 20
integer class, 259
integrated development environments (IDEs), 244, 349, 361–64, 418
Intercomp, 375
interface definition language (IDL), 418–19
interface inheritance, 158–60
interface subroutine, 10
Internet inter-orb protocol (IIOP), 419
iterator, 302, 307, 310–11

J

J/Direct, 420–21
J++, 30–33, 65–75
  arrays and vectors, 321–27
  flow control, 240–51
  polymorphism, 177–92
  with strings and bignumbers, 279–89
Jacobson, Ivar, 372
Jaguar, Sybase Inc., 371
jar file technology, 357–59
JAVA 2, 24–27, 108–26, 404
JDK, 55–65, 163–76, 225–40
  applets with JDK, 27–29
  arrays and vectors, 313–21
  with strings and bignumbers, 269–78
JAVA application servers, 370–71
  applications vs. applets vs. servelets, 22–23
  byte codes, 19–20
  clones, 371
  comments, 200–02
  development environment, 19–42
  inheritance, 149–56
  integration tools, 375
  magazines, 408
  messages and methods, 43– 84, 89–90
  operators, 203
  resources, 407
  software management, 349–60
  statements, 198–200
  syntax of, 197–209
  tools, 408
  using objects in, 97
  virtual machines, 19–21, 23
Java compiler and executive files, 350
Java Foundation Classes (JFC), 366
Java native interface (JNI), 421
Java server pages (JSP), 421
Java VM, 420
Java Workshop, Sun Microsystems, 364–65
JavaBeans, 365, 419
JavaMaker, Intercomp, 375
JavaScript, 419–20, 425
Jbuilder, 364
JDBC, 367–68, 420
JDK, 24–27, 41–42, 63–64, 358, 404
JFC. See Java Foundation Classes (JFC).
JFC/Swing, 365–66
JIT compilers. See Just in time (JIT) compilers.
JNI. See Java native interface (JNI).
JSP. See Java server pages (JSP).
just in time (JIT) compilers, 362

L

legacy applications, 363
LegacyJ, 404–05
length member, in arrays, 292
LinkedList implementation, 308
Lisp, 20
list collection interface, 307

list, interface definition, 301
local variables, 101–02
long class, 259

M

manual synchronization, 343
map collection interface, 308–09
map, interface definition, 301
messages in Java, 46–47
Metamorphic, 375
method code, 159
method members, 104–06
method overloading, 49, 55
method signatures, 55
methods
- extending, 134–35
- inheriting, 131–32
- redefining, 133

MFC. See Microsoft foundation classes (MFC).
Microsoft foundation classes (MFC), 421
Microsoft Internet Explorer, 412
Microsoft Visual J++, 364, 402–03
Microsoft's J/direct technology, 366
Microsoft's J++ development environment, 352
min and max algorithm, 302
MSFT J++, 41
multiple messages, 47–48
multiple threads, 344–45
MYSUB COBOL, 5–6, 10, 44–46, 50–54, 86–88, 145–49

N

name collisions, 355–56
nCopies, 313
Netscape Navigator, 412
Newsub Cobol, 138–40
no instance variables. 159
numeric wrapper classes, 259–61, 290

O

OAG. See Open Application Group (OAG).
OAGML, 405
object constraint language (OCL), 374
object instance variable, 91
object request broker (ORB), 414, 418
object-oriented (OO)
- design, xv–xvii, 129–30
- interface, 414
- languages, 257
- software modeling, 372

objects, 3–19, 91
- and Cobol, 91–97
- and Java, 11–12, 97

OCL. See Object constraint language (OCL).
ODBC. See Open database connectivity (ODBC).
online XML, 397–98
OO. See Object-oriented (OO).
Open Application Group (OAG), 389–91, 405
Open database connectivity (ODBC), 420, 422
OpenXML, 386
operator overloading, 2357
operator overloading, 265
Oracle 8I, 371
ORB. See Object request broker (ORB).
ordering, 302–03, 309
out of bounds references, 293

P

packages, 352–57
parent number class, 259
Percobol Compiler, 404–05
polymorphism, 162–63, 175–76, 301
Powerbuilder, 365
PowerJ, Sybase Inc., 365
primitive data types, 102–04
private and public objects, 14
private and public subroutines, 10
private protected access control, 98
programming models, 344–45

R

reference variable, 14
Relativity Technologies, Inc., 375, 406
Remote method invocation (RMI), 422
Remote procedure call (RPC), 422
Rescueware, 406

reverse algorithm, 302
Rimbaugh, Jim, 372
RMI. See Remote method invocation (RMI).
RPC. See Remote procedure call (RPC).
runtime
    environments, 19–22, 38, 345–46
    interpretations, 19–22, 350–51
    systems, 357, 362

S
Secure sockets layer (SSL), 423
set, interface definition, 301
SGML. See Standard generalized markup language (SGML).
sharing variables and methods, 156
singleton, 313
SmallTalk, 20
sort algorithm, 302
SortedSet implementation, 305
sortedSet, 305–06
    interface definition, 301
Sequential Query Language (SQL), 367
SSL. See Secure sockets layer (SSL).
stand-alone application, 38
standard generalized markup language (SGML), 377
Sterling Commerce, 388
stringbuffers, 262–63
strings, 253–90
subroutines, 3–10, 43
Sun Microsystems, 24, 42, 364–65, 370, 386, 414, 423
    Javadoc home page, 202
swing, 423
switch expression, 220–21
switch, 220
Sybase Inc., 365, 371
Symantec Corporation, 365
synchronization, 342–44

T
TCP/IP. See Transmission control protocol/internet protocol (TCP/IP).
this, operator, 157–58
threads, 339–40
    implementing runnable, 341–42
    inheriting from, 340–41
throws and not throws, 161
top-down implementation, 130
transmission control protocol/internet protocol (TCP/IP), 424
TreeSet implementation, 306–07, 310
try and catch code blocks, 259–60

U
UML. See Unified modeling language (UML).
unified modeling language (UML), 372–74, 424
universal resource locator (URL), 424–25
URL. See Universal resource locator (URL).

V
value-added networks (VANs), 388
VANs. See Value-added networks (VANs).
VBScript, 425
vector implementation, 308
vectors, 295–99
    versus arrays, 303–13
virtual machines (VMs), 19–21, 23, 344, 423
Visual Age for Java, 363–64
Visual Café, Symantec Corporation, 365
Visual InterDev, 412
Visual J++, 364
VisualBasic (VB), 412
VMs. See virtual machines(VMs).

W
WFC. See Windows Foundation Classes (WFC).
while code block, 216–18
Windows Foundation Classes (WFC), 366
Windows NT, 352, 362
working storage items, 85–86
writeline interface, 159

X
XML, 377–99

attributes, 382–83
authoring documents in, 386
basics of, 377
data repositories, 398
document type declaration (DTDs), 380–81, 388
document type declaration, 384
DTD components, 381–83
EDI, 388
elements, 381–82
entities, 383–84
intelligent agents, 399
OAG, 389
online, 397–98
parsers, 380, 384, 386
versus HTML, 378–80, 386–87
where to use, 387
XML-based searching, 399
XSL. See Extensible style language (XSL).

Sun Microsystems, Inc.
Binary Code License Agreement

READ THE TERMS OF THIS AGREEMENT AND ANY PROVIDED SUPPLEMENTAL LICENSE TERMS (COLLECTIVELY "AGREEMENT") CAREFULLY BEFORE OPENING THE SOFTWARE MEDIA PACKAGE. BY OPENING THE SOFTWARE MEDIA PACKAGE, YOU AGREE TO THE TERMS OF THIS AGREEMENT. IF YOU ARE ACCESSING THE SOFTWARE ELECTRONICALLY, INDICATE YOUR ACCEPTANCE OF THESE TERMS BY SELECTING THE "ACCEPT" BUTTON AT THE END OF THIS AGREEMENT. IF YOU DO NOT AGREE TO ALL THESE TERMS, PROMPTLY RETURN THE UNUSED SOFTWARE TO YOUR PLACE OF PURCHASE FOR A REFUND OR, IF THE SOFTWARE IS ACCESSED ELECTRONICALLY, SELECT THE "DECLINE" BUTTON AT THE END OF THIS AGREEMENT.

1. LICENSE TO USE. Sun grants you a non-exclusive and non-transferable license for the internal use only of the accompanying software and documentation and any error corrections provided by Sun (collectively "Software"), by the number of users and the class of computer hardware for which the corresponding fee has been paid.

2. RESTRICTIONS. Software is confidential and copyrighted. Title to Software and all associated intellectual property rights is retained by Sun and/or its licensors. Except as specifically authorized in any Supplemental License Terms, you may not make copies of Software, other than a single copy of Software for archival purposes. Unless enforcement is prohibited by applicable law, you maynot modify, decompile, reverse engineer Software. You acknowledge that Software is not designed or licensed for use in on-line control of aircraft, air traffic, aircraft navigation or aircraft communications; or in the design, construction, operation or maintenance of any nuclear facility. Sun disclaims any express or implied warranty of fitness for such uses. No right, title or interest in or to any trademark, service mark, logo or trade name of Sun or its licensors is granted under this Agreement.

3. LIMITED WARRANTY. Sun warrants to you that for a period of ninety (90) days from the date of purchase, as evidenced by a copy of the recei

F MERCHANTABILITY, FITNESS FOR A PARTICULAR PURPOSE, OR NON-INFRINGEMENT, ARE DISCLAIMED, EXCEPT TO THE EXTENT THAT THESE DISCLAIMERS ARE HELD TO BE LEGALLY INVALID.

5. LIMITATION OF LIABILITY. TO THE EXTENT NOT PROHIBITED BY LAW, IN NO EVENT WILL SUN OR ITS LICENSORS BE LIABLE FOR ANY LOST REVENUE, PROFIT OR DATA, OR FOR SPECIAL, INDIRECT, CONSEQUENTIAL, INCIDENTAL OR PUNITIVE DAMAGES, HOWEVER CAUSED REGARDLESS OF THE THEORY OF LIABILITY, ARISING OUT OF OR RELATED TO THE USE OF OR INABILITY TO USE SOFTWARE, EVEN IF SUN HAS BEEN ADVISED OF THE POSSIBILITY OF SUCH DAMAGES. In no event will Sun's liability to you, whether in contract, tort (including negligence), or otherwise, exceed the amount paid by you for Software under this Agreement. The foregoing limitations will apply even if the above stated warranty fails of its essential purpose.

6. Termination. This Agreement is effective until terminated. You may terminate this Agreement at any time by destroying all copies of Software. This Agreement will terminate immediately without notice from Sun if you fail to comply with any provision of this Agreement. Upon Termination, you must destroy all copies of Software.

7. Export Regulations. All Software and technical data delivered under this Agreement are subject to US export control laws and may be subject to export or import regulations in other countries. You agree to comply strictly with all such laws and regulations and acknowledge that you have the responsibility to obtain such licenses to export, re-export, or import as may be required after delivery to you.

8. U.S. Government Rights. If Software is being acquired by or on behalf of the U.S. Government or by a U.S. Government prime contractor or subcontractor (at any tier), then the Government's rights in Software will be only as set forth in this Agreement; this is in accordance with 48 CFR 227.7201 through 227.7202-4 (for Department of Defense (DOD) acquisitions) and with 48 CFR 2.101 and 12.212 (for non-DOD acquisitions).

9. Governing Law. Any action related to this Agreement will be governed by California law and controlling U.S. federal law. No choice of law rules of any jurisdiction will apply.

10. Severability. If any provision of this Agreement is held to be unenforceable, this Agreement will remain in effect with the provision omitted, unless omission would frustrate the intent of the parties, in which case this Agreement will immediately terminate.

11. Integration. This Agreement is the entire agreement between you and Sun relating to its subject matter. It supersedes all prior or contemporaneous oral or written communications, proposals, representations and warranties and prevails over any conflicting or additional terms of any quote, order, acknowledgment, or other communication between the parties relating to its subject matter during the term of this Agreement. No modification of this Agreement will be binding, unless in writing and signed by an authorized representative of each party.

For inquiries please contact: Sun Microsystems, Inc. 901 San Antonio Road, Palo Alto, California 94303

JAVA™ 2 SDK, STANDARD EDITION, V 1.2.1
SUPPLEMENTAL LICENSE TERMS

These supplemental terms ("Supplement") add to the terms of the Binary Code License Agreement (collectively the "Agreement"). Capitalized terms not defined herein shall have the same meanings ascribed to them in the Agreement. The Supplement terms shall supersede any inconsistent or conflicting terms in the Agreement above, or in any license contained within the Software.

1. Limited License Grant. Sun grants to you a non-exclusive, non-transferable limited license to use the Software without fee for evaluation of the Software and for development of Java™ applets and applications provided that you: (i) may not re-distribute the Software in whole or in part, either separately or included with a product; and (ii) may not create, or authorize your licensees to create additional classes, interfaces, or subpackages that are contained in the "java" or "sun" packages or similar as specified by Sun in any class file naming convention. Refer to the Java Runtime Environment Version 1.2.1 binary code license (http://java.sun.com/products/jdk/1.2/jre/index.html) for the availability of runtime code which may be distributed with Java applets and applications.

2. Java Platform Interface. In the event that Licensee creates an additional API(s) which: (i) extends the functionality of a Java Environment; and, (ii) is exposed to third party software developers for the purpose of developing additional software which invokes such additional API, Licensee must promptly publish broadly an accurate specification for such API for free use by all developers.

3. Trademarks and Logos. Licensee acknowledges as between it and Sun that Sun owns the Java trademark and all Java-related trademarks, logos and icons including the Coffee Cup and Duke ("Java Marks") and agrees to comply with the Java Trademark Guidelines at http://www.sun.com/policies/trademarks.

4. Source Code. Software may contain source code that is provided solely for reference purposes pursuant to the terms of this Agreement.